AFGHANISTAN

Realities of War and Rebuilding

2nd edition

AFGHANISTAN
Realities of War and Rebuilding

2nd edition

Bahaudin G. Mujtaba

ILEAD Academy, LLC
Davie, Florida. United States
www.ileadacademy.com

© Bahaudin G. Mujtaba (2007). *Afghanistan: Realities of War and Rebuilding*, 2nd edition.

Published by:
    Dr. Bahaudin G. Mujtaba
    Nova Southeastern University
    3301 College Avenue
    Fort Lauderdale FL 33315-3025
    Phone: (954) 262-5000 Or (800) 672-7223 / (800) 338-4723
    Email: mujtaba@nova.edu

Cover Design: Cagri Tanyar
Back Cover Photo: Ebadullah *waladi* Ezatullah

First edition published in 2006 by Aglob.

ISBN: 978-0-9774211-1-4

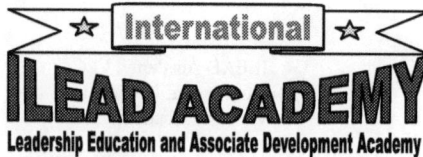

★ International ★
ILEAD ACADEMY
Leadership Education and Associate Development Academy

Book Reviewer Comments

Speaking from a Jamaican perspective, I can say that Dr. Mujtaba has delivered a significant work of literature on the nation, people and culture of Afghanistan through effectively combining the past, present and future outlook of this wonderful country into an interesting and great book: "*Afghanistan: Realities of War and Rebuilding.*" Dr Mujtaba uses personal childhood experiences as a native Afghan to corroborate facts and realities of war and the ongoing "jihads" [struggles to accomplish something] of the Afghan people in their quest for independence, survival, freedom, free will, human rights, and virtuous God-given existence free from artificially induced forces curtailing the progress of their beloved and noble nation.

This book is an extraordinary accomplishment by a gifted academician and scholar whose love for country and humanity are fervently expressed in its vibrant pages with equal thoughts, rigor, and enthusiasm. The intellectual objectivity and mastery with which Dr. Mujtaba communicates the 'realities of war and rebuilding' are excellent as he uses wit and humor, proverbs and essays to give us accurate knowledge. A timely addition to the library of highly needed human knowledge for our growth, progress and survival as a civilization.

Dr. Donovan A. McFarlane, Distinguished Member of the
International Society of Poets, Owing Mills, MD.; Research
Associate of the University of Metaphysics, Ventura, CA.

You will be treated to a masterful presentation of history interwoven with cultural implications today and leadership challenges for tomorrow. Dr. Mujtaba writes with a passion for the reader to understand Afghanistan. If there is to be sustained change in this proud nation it will need to take place at the grassroots level. That means individuals more than it does governments, it means winning hearts more than it means winning battles, and it means developing leaders more than positions of authority.

Dr. Paul Hersey, Chairman
Center for Leadership Studies

I commend Dr. Mujtaba for taking the time to write this book. His praiseworthy efforts demonstrate his passion for his native country. I believe this book would be a very useful tool for anyone going to visit or work in Afghanistan, but especially for the Afghan who has immigrated to another country as a child or was born outside Afghanistan and wants to return. This book will provide a solid reference in which to frame today's evolving Afghan society.

Dr. Yar M. Ebadi, Dean for College of Business
Administration, Kansas State University

In reviewing this book, I found that it discusses the realities of war in today's geopolitical situation in Afghanistan to manage the crisis. The depth and breadth of coverage in the book from factual war related historical information to excellent leadership techniques provides a timely documentation. The book discusses the diversity of the Afghan community, the fact that civil war caused them to be more apart from each other and introduce techniques to bring more unity among the nation.

Professor M. Quasem Kadir, Dean of Information Technology
DeVry University -Southern California

I found it personally rewarding to learn so much about Afghanistan. I must admit many individuals do not realize how much misinformation and misconceptions they are operating under with regard to the issues in Afghanistan.

Dr. Ron Campbell, President
Center for Leadership Studies

Bahaudin Mujtaba has written a timely book during a critical period in Afghanistan's political history. Drawing on his rich academic and corporate background in management, Bahaudin gets to the bottom of state-building challenges in his native homeland and offers lucid and practical lessons to maximize the effectiveness of international aid in rebuilding Afghanistan. The book is a must read for Afghan government leaders, professional Afghans returning home to build institutional capacity in the government, aid community managers and employees, and donor community representatives all of whom share a common objective: to succeed in rebuilding Afghanistan and preventing it from failure again.

M. Ashraf Haidari, Embassy of Afghanistan, Washington, D.C.; Peace Scholar, Georgetown University School of Foreign Services

I admire Dr. Mujtaba's passion and unconditional love toward his homeland of Afghanistan. As a close neighbor in Taiwan, we know so little about what was going on and how people suffered from the wars. This book should attract much needed attention from the world in understanding what needs to be done, and what we can offer. There is too much in Afghan history and richness in this land. As Louis Dupree (1989) said, the people and leaders of Afghanistan would best decide their own future without interference from any outside sources. The race in rebuilding the country demands time, loyalty, sacrifice, and devotion from all "Freedom Fighters" in Afghanistan. The rest of the world should contribute to and respect the reconstruction of the country, and pray for a new glory land of peace and liberty.

Dr. Yaying Mary Chou Yeh, CPA
Yung Ta Institute of Technology, Taiwan, ROC

Dr. Mujtaba's book is a most impressive achievement indeed. The book provides an excellent historical, cultural, and political science foundation for the treatment of the business subject matters. This reader also found the author's reminisces of his own and his family's experiences in Afghanistan to be especially spellbinding. The book will not only make a valuable contribution to the development of the country of Afghanistan, but also will serve a larger purpose of introducing a wider audience to the land, the country, and people of Afghanistan and the challenges that the Afghan people confront in building a just and prosperous society.

Dr. Frank Cavico, J.D., Professor of Ethics and Law
Nova Southeastern University

I found this book to be fascinating. It provides a concise recent history of Afghanistan as well as a fascinating autobiographical account of the author. The book also discusses religion, culture, and even management as applied by Afghans.

Dr. Robert W. McGee, Andreas School of Business,
Barry University

Bahaudin Mujtaba presents a compelling picture of the dynamic rebuilding process currently taking place in Afghanistan. The rich details and personal narratives give the reader an understanding of reality that can energize and guide the rebirth and transformation of a nation.

Dr. Barbara Dastoor, Professor of Human Resources
Nova Southeastern University

Dedication

This book is dedicated to the rebuilding of beautiful and beloved Afghanistan, its "Shaheedawn," and its dedicated people.

TABLE OF CONTENTS

PREFACE

Several decades of war and its subsequent civil turmoil has brought devastating destruction throughout Afghanistan from various sources. Unfortunately, due to the circumstances beyond the control of ordinary citizens, the beautiful country of Afghanistan has endured many long-lasting and painful injuries in the last few decades of the previous millennium; as a result, it is suffering from lack of resources, mismanagement of the workforce, water pollution, air pollution, incomplete learning environment, animosity among people, and perhaps hundreds of other such debilitating elements that threaten and hinder the speedy progress of the country. Furthermore, despite having a semi-democratic environment, some people are still dealing with sporadic violence, animosity, and the consequences of inappropriate war techniques, such as the use of depleted uranium in metal penetrating bombs used in Afghanistan by various friendly and unfriendly forces.

The various chapters in this book highlight the realities of war, atrocities of certain behaviors during the Russian invasion, factional conflicts, human rights violations, and what the current administration is doing with the assistance of officials from the United Nations and other foreign countries such as France, Germany, Canada, the United States, and Turkey (just to name a few) to bring about some relief to the "injured" and "maimed" people of Afghanistan. The book is meant to be non-political...although it praises some of the recent actions taken by officials in the interim government and the current administration to bring about long-term security, peace, and prosperity in the country. The book is written for the general population's awareness of facts as seen by an Afghan-born author, and it is written for discussion material in colleges and universities throughout the world. Some of the international colleges and universities may also adopt this material for cross-cultural discussions, anthropology, understanding developing economies, and workforce skills needed in such labor markets. Official colleges or professors adopting this book or any of its chapters may contact the publisher or the author for receiving the available supplementary facilitator materials. While the content of this book provides an awareness of many unfortunate effects of war, the author's 2007 book about Afghanistan titled: *The Ethics of Management and Leadership in Afghanistan, 2nd edition,* offers the following concepts and skills as a prescription for rebuilding and workforce development:

1. Ethical reasoning and moral decision making.
2. Delivering top value.
3. Managing and adjusting to the changing variables of people and customers.
4. Working synergistically as a team throughout the value chain.
5. Providing a fun work environment for everyone and having a sense of humor.
6. Coaching and mentoring associates to become the best that they can be.
7. Leading situationally to empower all managers toward a decentralized development process.
8. Providing inspirations and successes toward a brighter vision for the future.

Thank you for reading this information on Afghanistan with good intentions, and hopefully you can pass on the relevant material to others who can use it. Please forgive the author for possible misspelling of names and inaccuracies or any information that is not included but should have been researched and documented! As an author, sitting in a nice warm room with a satisfied stomach, I fully understand that I have had more than sufficient time to reflect upon and write this material, while the people involved in the physical war did not have such opportunities as they had to react and make life or death decisions, at times, in matter of seconds. So, I understand that it is easy for me to sit back and "criticize" the actions of others years after the events. However, I want the readers to know that I did "attempt" to be objective, to the extent possible, given that much of this material is subjective and the fact that I too have biases, limitations and emotions due to the nature of the content. I guess that is one limitation I like to acknowledge, which is the challenging task of separating objective material from being influenced by subjective conditioning. Of course, what appears objective to me may not be so in the eyes of others. As such, I extend sincere apologies for statements that appear unjustly too critical of specific individuals, governments or decisions without offering objective justifications since being unfairly critical has not been the goal.

Afghanistan has recently begun to stake out its position on important moral issues, such as terrorism and drug trafficking affecting society. To be successful in this effort, the government officials and the working people of Afghanistan must assess and take seriously their own level of readiness to lead these important agendas. The past cannot be changed by anyone; however, we can change what happens now and in the future. Change must start from within, and each person must take responsibility for his or her own physical, mental, spiritual, and psychological developments. The realities of war point to many losses to all parties involved and such atrocities must be replaced with love, kindness, education, and true "brotherhood" if human beings are to live peacefully. We should all believe in the following statement: "I must be a productive individual and, then, a good leader in order to effectively contribute to the team's goal toward the creation of a peaceful environment for all." Being a peaceful individual, and becoming an effective leader, is a good start for each person in Afghanistan and for those around the world since people have the most control over their own behaviors. May everyone be a productive human being and a good leader in bringing about peace on earth!

Bahaudin

ACKNOWLEDGEMENTS

First and foremost, I thank my colleagues and friends for their guidance, valuable input in the review of this material, and for making the doors of learning open to thousands of individuals throughout the world. My colleagues at Publix Super Markets were extremely respectful and appreciative of cultural differences. The same extends to my friends and colleagues at Fort Myers High School, Edison Community College, University of Central Florida, University of Phoenix, and Nova Southeastern University. In particular, I like to thank Walter Masrshal, Herbert Waschul, Terry Simpson, Robert Manfredo, John Manfredo, Charlie Kiss Kovar, Sing Dang, Patricia Grover, Georgia Dodd, MaryLou DeyArmin, and Ed Davis for energizing me to think of various ways for creating managers and leaders with the requisite skills to effectively compete in the twenty-first century environment. I also would like to thank my other colleagues from human resources and improvement systems departments, including Glenn Eschrich, Jim Rhodes, Joe Carvin, Allison Medelli, Frank Darguzas, David Taylor, Ed Davis, Jack Snow, Anthony Stevens, Annisa Brockington, Max Braddock, Ruth Ferkings, David Richards, and many others whom I think of often. Some of the individuals who served as my academic role models, coaches and mentors include but are not limited to: Mrs. Vanna Crawford, Mr. Wiseman, Dr. Kimble, Dr. Pamela Lewis, Dr. Robert Preziosi, Dr. Timothy McCartney, Dr. Frank Cavico, Dr. Preston Jones, Dr. Randolph Pohlman, Dr. Art Weinstein, Dr. Ronald Fetzer, Dr. Ruth Clarke, Mr. Guy Stone, Dr. Steven Castiglioni, Dr. George Lucas, Dr. Beverly Downing, Dr. Brian Lindquist, Dr. Norma Goonen, Dr. Don Rosenblum, Dr. Ben Mulvey, Dr. Alan Schulman, Dr. Charlie Blackwell, and Dr. Jane Gibson.

Second, I thank my family members (especially my wife, mother, father, brother, sisters, and many "uncles" scattered around the world) for their thoughts, guidance, and caring orientation in the preparation and revisions of this material. Their love, support, patience, encouragement, and wisdom have sustained and inspired me to continue gathering practical material for today's workforce.

Third, I also thank and acknowledge the following friends, colleagues, and family members for generously sharing their thoughts, suggestions, and contributions on Afghanistan and leadership related issues from various perspectives around the world in the preparation and review of this book on Afghanistan:

- Bahawodin Baha, University of Brighton, United Kingdom
- Ron Campbell, Center for Leadership Studies
- Frank Cavico, Nova Southeastern University
- Claudette Chin-Loy, Nova Southeastern University
- Barbara Dastoor, Nova Southeastern University
- Yar M. Ebadi, Kansas State University
- Ashraf Haidari, Georgetown University School of Foreign Services
- Sayed Tayeb Jawad, Embassy of Afghanistan, Washington D.C.
- Quasem Kadir, DeVry University-Southern California
- Donovan McFarlane, Jamaican Research Associate at University of Metaphysics
- Mojkhan Melissa Madani, Nova Southeastern University
- Ghulam Mujtaba, Kabul University
- Mustafa Mujtaba, Florida Gulf Coast University
- Fazil Najafi, University of Florida
- Randi Sims, Nova Southeastern University

Fourth, I thank the thousands of workshop and conference attendees as well as students that have heard my lectures and those who have provided valuable input. Special thanks are extended to colleagues who proof-read the draft versions of this book. Overall, many individuals provided valuable input toward the preparation of this work, and I extend my gratitude and heartfelt appreciations to everyone. Finally, I especially thank you for reading this material on Afghanistan. I wish a life of joy, happiness and peace for you, your family, as well as the country and people of Afghanistan.

Bahaudin

CHAPTER 1

AFGHANISTAN - LAND OF THE AFGHAN

Over a quarter century of war has brought much destruction throughout Afghanistan. Unfortunately, due to the circumstances beyond the control of ordinary Afghans, the country has endured many long-lasting and painful injuries and, as a result, it is suffering from lack of resources, mismanagement of the workforce, water and air pollution, incomplete learning environment, animosity among people, and perhaps hundreds of other such elements that threaten and hinder the speedy progress of the country. Furthermore, some people are still dealing with sporadic violence and the consequences of inappropriate war techniques such as the use of depleted uranium in metal penetrating bombs used in Afghanistan by various friendly and unfriendly forces. The impact and externalities associated with the usage of depleted uranium will unfortunately continue to negatively cause damage to the environment and human life in the near future unless proper interventions are made to reduce or eliminate the impact. There are nearly five million people living in Kabul, the capital of Afghanistan, and its neighboring areas because most of the jobs are centered in these towns. Kabul residents alone, who are near the jobs and factories, need many of the basic services which people around the world take for granted, but for most Afghan citizens, throughout the provinces, such basic services are often insufficient or non-existent. So, while there is a huge need to help Afghans with their physical and economic needs, time is of essence in meeting the educational needs of the growing population which will complement and replace the current workforce in the rebuilding process. Thus, innovative ideas and solutions are needed from all angles to physically rebuild the country and psychologically develop its workforce both mentally and spiritually. As such, relevant literature about management, leadership, and the rebuilding process are in great demand, since the current and prospective generations of Afghan scholars and the workforce are ready to learn, plan, execute, and follow up on the relevant situational variables throughout the country.

There is an old proverb which states: "Sow a thought, and you reap an act; Sow an act, and you reap a habit; Sow a habit, and you reap a character; Sow a character, and you reap a destiny." Many of the Afghan volunteers, elders, and leaders today have sown the seeds of wisdom, and thus created powerful destinies for themselves and other Afghans through their involvement in paving the way toward a better Afghanistan. While having an advanced degree or formal specialization on the part of each official is not a solution for all of Afghanistan's current and prospective challenges, it is great to see that the Constitution has made the credentials of relevant higher education a requirement for selecting ministers, deputy ministers and other such senior leadership officials. Such requirements will certainly encourage learning, creativity, and continuous pursuit of knowledge among all those who want to serve Afghanistan using their mental faculties through peaceful means.

As stated in the preface, the past cannot be changed but we can change what happens now and in the future. Change is most effective when it starts from within, and each person should take personal responsibility for his or her own personal as well as professional growth and development. We must all be productive individuals and good leaders in order to effectively contribute to the team's goal toward the creation of a peaceful environment for all. Of course, being productive individuals, and becoming effective leaders, is a good start for each person in Afghanistan since individuals have the most control over their own behaviors. We can say that improving one's life, knowledge and the community is a personal and professional obligation. Imam Ali said, "Persist in your action with a noble end in mind...Failure to perfect your work while you are sure of the reward is injustice to yourself." A reporter once stated that "It was long ago in my life as a reporter that I decided that facts must never get in the way of truth" (James Cameron, 1911-1985). Many of the children and adults in Afghanistan are currently making great contributions with a noble end in mind...to improve Afghanistan. Christopher Morley had stated that "there are three ingredients in the good life: learning, earning, and yearning." Afghan people have done, and are doing, all three as they yearn for a peaceful and developed Afghanistan. Ursula K. Le Guin has been quoted as saying "it is good to have an end to journey towards; but it is the journey that matters, in the end." Benjamin Franklin said that "all mankind is divided into three classes: those that are immovable, those that are movable, and those that move." Each Afghan has the choice to constantly "move" toward worthwhile and predetermined ethical goals with integrity thereby making his/her life, and that of their family members' and colleagues' more interesting and joyful throughout Afghanistan. Most individuals working for Afghan agencies are doing exactly this as a result of their association with various organizations and their country by progressively moving toward predetermined goals of improving Afghanistan. Afghans and their country have endured much suffering, but they are now selectively, yet slowly, healing and must continue this trend. Most Afghans knew that being injured and defeated is often a temporary condition; however, giving up is what makes it permanent and Afghans cannot afford to give up. Dr. Martin Luther King, Jr. said, "Everyone has the power for greatness, not for fame but for greatness, because greatness is determined by service." Afghans and their country can be great once again so long as they continue to persist in their vision toward peace. The vision of peace and a developed Afghanistan must be followed by the venture. It is not enough to "stare up the steps" as they must "step up the stairs." Dr. G. Rauf Roashan (2005) stated that "The process of development, reconstruction, nation building and reparation of the infrastructure needs manpower, money and materials." He further concluded that the current leaders in Afghanistan must be able to leave a positive mark in Afghan history by increasing the "manpower," "money," and "materials." It is not only the quantity of the three resources that matter, but more so it would be the quality of each.

Rebuilding Afghanistan is basically like a race without a finish line and every Afghan should participate in this rewarding process. It is hoped that you too 'think of the Afghan motherland' and offer best practices that will help the Afghan workforce become better. The author is hopeful that this book has accurately captured the names of many individuals that have contributed to the developing country of Afghanistan...we all know that it takes a village to raise a child. As such, it has required the contributions of many individuals besides the current administration to make a peaceful country available to everyone. Many talented Afghans are doing all they can as they know that they have one life in this world, and they must make the best of it while they have the opportunity to do so because life is short. Afghans know that there is:

"Only one life that soon will pass – Only what is done with love will last."

Instead of being too focused on the past, we need to take actions with good intentions and true love, while being forward-looking and anchored toward the future that we all desire for ourselves and our offspring. Productive individuals and effective leaders are forward-oriented and at challenging times, use professionalism to create synergy with people of diverse backgrounds, ethnicities, religions, and languages. When government officials and corporate leaders do become an integral part of the responsibility involved in leading these major worldly issues, they will realize that diagnosis must come before prescription if Afghans are to bypass or evade much rework and wasted efforts. As such, we can begin by understanding who Afghans are and their desire for "independency." Accordingly, the proceeding chapters deal with the history of turmoil in Afghanistan and focuses on the diagnostic elements. A separate book, entitled *The Ethics of Management and Leadership in Afghanistan* completed by the author in 2007, includes a comprehensive coverage of management and situational leadership tools for developing Afghans, Afghan leaders and their workforce. For ordinary Afghans, and especially their leaders and educators, continuous learning and "adjusting" to the existing needs and demands of local citizens will be the key to simultaneously help Afghanistan become independent and interdependent with the international community. In order for this to happen, Afghans must go beyond complying with the simple definition of literacy and helping more people become functionally literate. Someone once said that the illiterate of the 21st century workplace will not be those who cannot read and write, but those who cannot learn, unlearn, and relearn. So, it is the power of deciding to learn new methods or techniques for individual and workplace success, unlearn what is no longer working or valid, and relearn new knowledge and relevant strategies to make the lives of Afghans a little better each month and each year. Overall, capacity building becomes critical as Afghans who want to make a difference should be capable and flexible enough to learn, unlearn, and relearn as appropriate for the time, location and people they are serving.

AFGHANS AND "INDEPENDENCY"

The word *"Afghan,"* represents all people born in Afghanistan, descendants of Afghans, and those who were official citizens of the country, as agreed upon by the ten-day deliberation of *Loya Jirgah*, the General Assembly, in the 1964 constitution. Symbolically, the term Afghan stands for love, courage, devotion, dignity, commitment, loyalty, and the desire to make sacrifices for one's country and people. It further symbolizes endurance, patriotism, dedication to the Afghan land and flag, and the freedom to soar in the beautiful mountains and deserts which are considered to be their ancestors' gleaned and protected backyards. As one of the Pushtu songs sung by Professor Awwalmir says, "This is my Grandfather's country, this is my father's country, this is so dear to me, it is Afghanistan, the land of the Afghans." Afghans are known to be people of honor, great hospitality, and are committed to being masters of their own destiny. Afghans are also known for their stubbornness (hard-headedness) or animosity to "get even" with those who interfere with them, even if it is other Afghans, a characteristic which has been shown by the civil war. Kurt Lohbeck (1993) wrote that the "honor of these strong and vibrant people is legendary...and their hospitality knows no bounds...now, however, the time had come for the third demand...the Afghan communists and their Soviet comrades would begin to experience Afghan revenge." Afghans have long been committed to being free of outsiders' influence at all costs. A young boy at one of the refugee camps in Pakistan sang a poem with his beautiful and clear voice in Persian: "I would not give a speck of this land for the entire Kremlin - Not even one flower from the land for the city of Washington!" This type of patriotism and conditioning to keep the country independent is weaved into the culture. Afghans need to realize that independency is not the solution to all of the country's challenges and in today's environment all people need to work through "interdependent" relationships with other countries and allies. As a matter of fact, being independent (or isolated from the real world) can mean becoming dependent once again on foreign countries, or donors, which is actually the case now and it has been this way since the invasion of Afghanistan by the former Soviet Union (Russians). So, dependence is not a good stage especially when the nation relies on other countries that are less developed. "Dependence" must be converted to "independence" and simultaneously to "interdependent relationships" with other countries so Afghanistan can benefit from certain comparative advantages which are afforded to it through its natural resources.

Unfortunately, the continuous conditioning on "independence" can also lead to ethnocentricity, as well as xenophobic thinking and paradigm when one is thinking or reflecting only at the "surface level" with regard to receiving international assistance and help from foreigners in the rebuilding process. High illiteracy rates in the country may be causing some individuals to only think at the surface level, since they may not have access to more material for inductive and deductive reasoning for cause and effect analysis. It appears that the current administration (Afghan government), is encouraging capacity building by making literacy a top priority, while building the workforce's capacity for more effective decision making as reinforced by Ambassador Jawad at a luncheon with the Foreign Law Society in Washington, DC during November 17th 2004. Ambassador Jawad stated that "The Afghan government is striving hard to build national institutions, but said that institutional capacity building faced the grave lack of human resources in Afghanistan." According to the Embassy of Afghanistan e-News (EA e-News), Ambassador Jawad encouraged international donors to invest in Afghanistan's education and security sectors through in-country training programs" (EA e-News, December 2004). He singled out the cultivation of poppy and drug trafficking as major obstacles to economic development and political stability throughout

Afghanistan. Fortunately, the current government of Afghanistan has a five-pronged strategy to effectively deal with this challenge. As such, they are willing to:

1. Provide alternative livelihoods and substitute cash crops.
2. Emphasize on counter-narcotic law enforcement and training.
3. Mobilize Islamic institutions to revive religious prohibitions on production, trafficking or use of drugs.
4. Provide long-term economic development.
5. Implement forced eradication of poppy crops.

According to a survey on Afghanistan's opium on 2004, released by the United Nation's Office on Drugs and Crime, the cultivation of opium in Afghanistan has increased by 64% compared to the prior year. Supposedly, Afghanistan produced 42 tons of opium in 2004 making it the world's largest producer of narcotics; this disturbing trend continues today. There are many areas in which the people of Afghanistan should achieve worldly success, but if there is one thing that Afghans should be number one at, it should not be drug cultivation and trafficking. The government of the United States has committed over $780 million to assist Afghan authorities fight the production of illegal drugs or narcotics. The government of United States, as well as the French authorities, further promised to assist on projects initiated in late 2004 toward the reconstruction of poppy farms for cultivation of legal crops. Such assistance from the international community, when effectively delivered and implemented by dedicated Afghan leaders and managers, will produce positive results toward the reduction and elimination of illegal activities in Afghanistan.

Consequently, the government and experts are encouraging Afghan farmers to substitute opium and poppy crops with roses and distil rose oil (a component of perfume), which can be sold for high prices in the open market throughout the world. As such, they can become small entrepreneurs and legally sell products to vendors and retailers around the globe. Such transitions can make the development work better for Afghans, and the world will be a much safer place when people are not intoxicated with various forms of addictive drugs. However, it is clear that encouragement alone is not sufficient to decrease the production of such narcotics. So, the five-pronged strategy must be implemented aggressively in every possible manner to make sure people's energy and lands of Afghanistan are being used for better purposes. High literacy rates, training, and equipping the workforce with the right skills to become industrialized and continuous education are critical elements to Afghanistan's progressive development and growth. Efforts geared toward such personal developments of the workforce generations can speed up the process of economic development and independence of Afghanistan from foreign aid. All such efforts should be accompanied strategically with effective management and strategy. Since no two situations are likely to be similar in all variables, it is best to apply effective leadership skills in order to deal with each challenge. Many Afghan experts tend to agree that one major change in today's corporate and political environment in Kabul might be the transformation and creation of a culture with regard to honest "service" to customers, suppliers, employees, and one's colleagues. Of course, before describing the remedy, leaders need to diagnose the problems, illnesses and pains caused by the thirty years of consecutive war and conflict. As such, this book offers a diagnosis of physical and psychological challenges impacting the people of Afghanistan.

ENVIRONMENTAL AND DEMOGRAPHICAL INFORMATION

Dan Rather of CBS News in 1993 wrote, "To understand why and how Afghanistan became such a pivotal battleground in the Cold War, the first thing to know and ponder is exactly where it is. Look at the map." This mountainous land of Central Asia is bounded on the north by the former Soviet Union countries (Tajikistan, Uzbekistan, Turkmenistan) at the Amu River, on the east and south by Pakistan, in the northeast by the Republic of China, on the west by Iran. Dan Rather further stated that "its geographical location has made Afghanistan a crossroad of history." Many nations in the world thought because of Afghanistan's location in the heart of Asia, some influence or control over them can be used strategically to gain control and/or a competitive edge over many other countries. Afghanistan is a mountainous country with most of it about 4,000 feet above the sea level and only about 20 percent of the land is arable. The Hindu Kush Mountains reach a height of 25,000 feet (about 6,000 meters); Hindu Kush is said to be the second highest mountain in the world. Other mountains include the mountains of Paghman, Salang, Salt, Suleiman, Khwaja Amran, Doshak, Prapamisus or Safed Kuh, and Kuhi Baabah. Afghanistan has four major rivers which are the rivers of Kabul (length 46 kilometers), Helmand (length 1,000 kilometers), Harirud (850 kilometers in length), and the Amu Darya (length of about 800 kilometers), which is at the border of Afghanistan and the former Soviet Union. Afghanistan was known as Ariana during the ancient times, which later became known as Khorasan during the middle-ages. Eventually, the name was changed to Afghanistan. Afghanistan is a small country located in southwest Asia in the northwest of the Indian subcontinent with an area of 253,861 square miles (637,397 square kilometers). The nearest seaport to Afghanistan is in Karachi, Pakistan, about 1,170 kilometers away. Its farthest length from west to east is about 1,240 kilometers, and its extreme width from north to south is about 565 kilometers.

Afghanistan is about the size of the State of Texas in the United States, and with an approximate population of 28,000,000 people (possibly 30,000,000 including those refugees from the 1980s that are still living in Pakistan and Iran). The last official population count was in June 15th to July 4th of 1979 which resulted in a figure of about 15,500,000 people. Some figures were supposedly prognosticated from other records, since there were conflicts in many parts of Afghanistan outside Kabul. In 1972-1974, an unofficial census was completed by the United States Agency for International Development (USAID) along with the Afghan government. This census was also jointly conducted through the State University of New York (SUNY) and The John Hopkins University at Buffalo, New York. Their figures reported a little over 10 million people which did not include nomads. The Nomad population is estimated at two and half million. Some of the reasons for such a low "turnout" might be that many people did not want the female names to be recorded, especially their daughters and wives, which is a cultural influence from centuries ago left by or possibly inherited from the Arabs. Furthermore, some males, especially the freemen, did not want their names recorded because they did not want to be drafted into mandatory military service which was required of all males once they became eighteen years of age. During 1968, the population was recorded as 15,000,000 people by Thomas J. Abercrombie in his National Geographic article about Afghanistan. The ratio of men to women has always been higher, as for every 100 women there has been 106 or higher number of men. However, the Russian-Afghan war, as well as the continued turmoil after their departure, may have changed this figure during the 1980s and 1990s, as more men than women were killed during their service in the war or post-war conflicts. The most populated city has always been Kabul with a pre-invasion population of 750,000 in 1979, over two million in 1983 and over four million in 2007. In 1994, the population of Kabul decreased as more people migrated outside the capital because the civil war operations were severe and mostly in Kabul. During the Russian invasion, as stated in various sources, approximately six to seven million people left Afghanistan and became refugees mainly in Pakistan and Iran, with small percentages of people migrating to Western countries. Since 1978, over two million people have died and another two million individuals have become injured, maimed, orphaned, or widowed. According to The World Almanac and Book of Facts, the life expectancy of males in Afghanistan is around 46 and female life expectancy is about 45 years of age. Infant mortality is estimated to be about 15.3 percent, which is alarmingly high. Literacy rate is about 29 percent, and about 88 percent of Afghans have no formal schooling experience, so some of the literacy has come from Mosque attendance.

There are people of different ethnic backgrounds in Afghanistan and some of the common ethnicities are Pushtuns, Tajiks, Hindus, Baluchis, Nuristanis, Uzbeks, Khirghiz, Hazaras, and Turkmans. As can be seen from the various reports, Pushtuns and Tajiks make up the largest groups of Afghans. There are more than twenty different languages being spoken in Afghanistan, with the main ones being Persian (Dari or Farsi) spoken by at least 60% of Afghans and Pushtu spoken by about 38% of Afghans. An interesting fact is that most Afghans speak two or more languages (such as Dari, Pushtu and Urdu; or Uzbekie, English and Dari). Afghanistan also has about 2.5 million Kuchis (nomads) who travel, sometimes thousands of miles, to different parts of the country as the seasons change. Historically, the nomads used to bring and pass information from one place to another; however, technology has diminished their information transfer role. The dominant religion is Islam, practiced by about 99% of the population, with the other one percent making up the minority religions such as Hindus, Christians and others. Afghanistan is an Islamic country and Lohbeck (1993) said, "It is the Southern California of Islam, not to be compared with the fanaticism of Khomeinie in Iran or the rigidity of Saudi Arabia." The climate of the country varies from place to place ranging from below zero to 120 degrees in deserts.

Afghanistan has always welcomed tourists, investors, entrepreneurs, and other visitors to the country. It was a country of beautiful sceneries and ancient artwork. It was a country of peace, quiet, caring, and friendly neighborhoods. One could hold a conversation with total strangers for half an hour, and at the end they would treat you to lunch or dinner if you were away from home. Abercrombie (1968) states that "I have been spoiled by hosts all over the Middle east, but in the art of hospitality no one excels the Afghans." Lohbeck (1993) wrote that Afghans treat their guests like royalty and he further states it is strange, "but most of the problems I have witnessed between Westerners and Afghans have boiled down to a misunderstanding of the Afghans' attempt to help." Afghanistan is still a beautiful country and, as a natural corollary of stability and peace, more of the visitors will be returning for tourism and entrepreneurship at an increasing rate.

The common foods in the country consist of various forms of rice, tomatoes, potatoes, carrots, stew, chicken, lamb (sheep meat), beef (cow meat), goat, and other agricultural products. Major crops are wheat, corn, rice, cotton, various vegetables, nuts, and other fresh and dry fruits. Agriculture industry is the largest employer, about 60%, of the labor force. Livestock includes approximately 2 million cattle and 14 million sheep. It is cold and snowy during the three months of the winter season, with dry summers in most of the region and warm in a few provinces (i.e. Jalalabad, Qandahar) during the summer. Afghanistan is a mountainous country with about fifty percent of the country over 2,000 meters in elevations. The Hindu Kush Mountain is said to be the second highest mountain in the world. Throughout the history, most major industries have been government owned; however, privatization has been increasing in the last five years. About ten percent of the labor force has been employed for knitting and sewing clothes and carpets. Major industries include natural gas, furniture, cement, textiles, mining, farming, livestock, and fresh dry food processing. Most of the service industry includes trade, transportation, government, and military agencies. The American geographer John F. Shroder, Jr. and other French explorers, have stressed the quality of Afghanistan's mineral wealth through their findings and research, which is one reason the Soviets probably wanted to control this land. Nyrop and Seekins (1986) wrote:

> The natural environment is, in fact, so forbidding that at first glance it seems an unlikely site for invasion by so many hostile armies. The reason lies in the country's location at the crossroads of Central Asia, South Asia, and West Asia. In more recent times Afghanistan has been recognized as a land of unexploited mineral and hydrocarbon wealth as well as a geographical buffer between various political systems, rendering its desirability even greater.

Some of the natural resources are gas, oil, coal, copper, zinc, iron, chrome, barite, lapis lazuli, and others. Other resources include wool, hides, and *qaraqul* pelts. Major exports have been natural gas, dried fruits, carpets, rugs, and animal skins. Major imports have been in the areas of manufacturing, machinery, certain foods, and refined petroleum products.

Kindergarten, if available, starts at age five and elementary school starts at age seven in first grade which continues till eighth grade. Some areas have a middle school for grades seventh through ninth. High school, usually, includes students from ninth or tenth grade through twelfth. Colleges and universities range from two to seven years. At least two years of college education was needed for elementary school teaching and six to seven years for medical students. Almost all of the major universities are located in Kabul, Qandahar , Balkh, and Mazari-e-Sharif.

Many of the villages in Afghanistan still do not have electricity or modernized irrigations systems. The Taliban regime did bring electricity to the people of Qandahar, and this will be Taliban's gift to everyone enjoying its benefits. Perhaps 30 to 50 percent of the people enjoy electricity on regular basis. Most of the power plants and irrigations systems have been destroyed during the war and some will be repaired while others may need new construction. There was only one local television station in the country, which operated on part-time bases; however, now, there are two television stations operating on a regular basis to make certain programs available to people living in various parts of Afghanistan and around the globe. Afghan Radio and cell phones are the main sources of news to people around the country. In the 1980s, there were a total of 18,752 kilometers of roads, of which 20 percent were paved and 80 percent damaged from the war. There are about 41 airfields, and Kabul International Airport (KIA) is the largest and certainly in need of much remodeling and expansion.

GOVERNMENT LEADERS IN AFGHANISTAN

Afghanistan's flag has tended to change with each regime or leadership change, and now it has three distinct colors of black, red, and green. *Black* color represents the occupation of foreigners, the *Red* portion represents the blood of Freedom Fighters, and the *Green* part represents freedom and Islam. It is hoped that these colors will remain as democratic Afghanistan's official flag colors so everyone can take ownership and pride in it. While government officials and leaders can and should (peacefully) change every four to ten years in order to bring new ideas, there is no need for the flag or its colors to change, since it represents Afghanistan to its people and to the rest of the world. Also, consistency is critical for international recognition of any country's flag.

There have been many great leaders and some that were not able to keep peace in Afghanistan in the past three centuries. It is assumed that all leaders intended to create a peaceful Afghanistan, while industrializing it so it could become a powerful force economically, spiritually, physically, and militaristically. However, historically, great leaders are not judged or measured just by what they intended to do, but rather they are judged by what they actually achieved (or caused to be achieved in the coming years) while they were in power. One characteristic of good leaders is to see how they left the government and the country upon their departure. Their goal is, and should be, to leave it better than they found it. Table 1 describes some of Afghanistan's political leaders or heads of state as organized by Afghan-land and other historians.

While there have been many great leaders in Afghanistan, there also have been some that will never be forgotten because of their contributions to either the well-being or the creation of conflict among the people of Afghanistan. The next few sections provide a brief introduction (biography) for some of the recent heads of state in Afghanistan as observed by the author or documented by other sources. While the first communist leader, Noor Mohammad Taraki, took power in 1979 followed by Hafizullah Amin and Babrak Karmal, the last communist leader was Najibullah Ahmadzai. The proceeding biographies start with the last communist leader appointed and supported by the former Soviet Union army and ends with Hamid Karzai, the first democratically elected Afghan President in 2004.

Table 1 – Afghanistan's Political Leaders

Date	Head of State, King, President	Date	Head of State, King, President
1709-1715	Mirwais Khan Hotaki	1879	Yaqoob Khan*
1716-1725	Mahmood Shah Hotaki	1880	Ayub Khan
1725-1729	Ashraf Shah Hotaki	1880-1901	Amir Abdul Rahman Khan
1729-1747	Ahmad Shah Durrani	1901-1919	Amir Habibullah Khan
1747-1773	Mohammad Shah Durrani	1919-1929	King Amanullah Khan
1773-1793	Timur Shah Durrani	1929	Habibullah Kalakani (Bachai Saqao)
1793-1801	Zaman Shah Durrani	1929-1933	King Mohammad Nader Shah
1801-1804	Shah Mahmood Durrani	1933-1973	King Mohammad Zahir Shah
1804-1809	Shah Shuja	1973-1978	Prince Mohammad Daud Khan
1809-1825	Shah Mahmood Durrani	1978-1979	Noor Mohammad Taraki
1826-1839	Dost Mohammad Khan	1979	Hafizullah Amin
1839-1842	Shah Shuja	1979-1986	Babrak Karmal
1843-1846	Mohammad Wazir Akbar Khan	1986-1992	Najibullah Ahmadzai
1846-1863	Dost Mohammad Khan*	1992	Sebghatullah Mojadedi
1863-1866	Amir Shir Ali Khan	1992-1995	Burhanuddin Rabbani
1867	Mohammad Afzal Khan	1995-2001	Mullah Mohammad Omar
1868	Mohammad Azam Khan	2001-2002	Hamid Karzai Interim Leader
1868-1878	Amir Sher Ali Khan	2002-2004	Hamid Karzai Transitional Leader
		2004-2009	President Hamid Karzai

* The name "Khan" is sometimes used as an honorarium for higher authorities. So, it may not be the official name.

NAJIBULLAH AHMADZAI

Dr. Mohammad Najibullah Ahmadzai took over the government from Babrak Karmal in 1986, and was the fourth and last President of Afghanistan during the period of the Communist regime (Democratic Republic of Afghanistan). Najibullah was born in August 1947 to a family linked to the Pushtun Ahmadzai sub-tribe of the Ghilzai. Najibullah was born in Afghanistan's capital city, Kabul. His ancestral village was located between the towns of Said Karam and Gardez, capital of Pakhtia Province (Afghan-land, 2004). His father, Akhtar Mohammad Khan, died in 1983 and he had served during the 1960s as the Afghan trade commissioner and consul in Peshawar, Pakistan. Najibullah was educated at Habibia High School and Kabul University, where he graduated with a degree in Medicine in 1975. He joined the Parcham faction of the communist People's Democratic Party of Afghanistan (PDPA) in 1965. He was jailed twice for his political activities, and he was for equal rights of women and various ethnic minorities.

The PDPA's Khalq faction gained supremacy in 1978, and for a brief period sent Najibullah as ambassador in Tehran. However, Najibullah was soon dismissed from government and went into exile in Europe. He returned to Kabul after the Soviet invasion in 1979. In 1980, he was appointed the head of KHAD, the secret police. KHAD is an abbreviation for Khedamat-e Etelea'at-e Dawlati, the Afghanistan

Marxist regime's secret police, also known as the State Information Agency. Set up in 1980, and controlled by the KGB, this was an agency specifically created for the suppression of the Afghanistan Marxist regime's internal opponents (Afghan-land, 2004).

Najibullah's government survived for three years after the departure of the Russian Army from Afghanistan in 1989. However, his party was divided and many left, including the defection of General Abdul Rashid Dostam that drastically weakened the government's resolve (Afghan-land, 2004). Najibullah had supposedly been working on a compromise settlement to end the civil war with Ahmad Shah Masood, brokered by the United Nations; that did not work and the government fell in 1992. When the Mujahidin forces entered Kabul in 1992, Najibullah tried to escape Kabul, but his departure was blocked; consequently, he sought sanctuary in the United Nation compound in Kabul. Najibullah spent the rest of his days in virtual detention until his death. On September 27th 1996, Taliban entered into the UN compound and dragged Najibullah to the presidential palace, where he was beaten, shot, and hanged.

BURHANUDDIN RABBANI

Burhanuddin Rabbani was born in 1940 in Badakhshan, a province of Afghanistan. After finishing school in his native province, he went to Darul-uloom-e-Sharia (Abu-Hanifa), a religious school in Kabul (Afghan-Land, 2004). Upon graduating from Abu-Hanifa, he attended Kabul University where he studied Islamic Law and Theology. During his four years at Kabul University he became known for his expertise on Islam. Soon after his graduation in 1963, he was hired as a Professor at Kabul University. Rabbani went to Egypt in 1966, and he entered the University of Al-Azhar in Cairo. In two years, he received his Masters degree in Islamic Philosophy. In 1968, Rabbani came back to Afghanistan and the High Council of Jamiat-i-Islami of Afghanistan gave him the duty of organizing the University students. Due to his expertise on Islam, a 15-member council selected him as head of Jamiat-i-Islami of Afghanistan in 1972. In the spring of 1974, the government was attempting to arrest him but he managed to escape to the country side.

In 1992, he became President of the Islamic Council of Afghanistan. Due to the civil war and lack of control, Burhanuddin Rabbani's government eventually lost all authority in Afghanistan. His government was ousted by the Taliban movement, and Kabul was captured by the Taliban in 1996. Rabbani set up headquarters in the northern Afghan town of Faizabad and led, with support from Iran and Russia, one of the five anti-Taliban factions. Stripped of power, he was still recognized as ruler of Afghanistan by the United Nations and most other countries until he formally handed over power to an interim government headed by Hamid Karzai on December 22, 2001.

MULLAH MOHAMMAD OMAR

Mullah Mohammad Omar was born in 1959, and he grew up in the village of Singesar, near Qandahar . He was wounded four times during the 1980s in the fight against the Soviets, leaving him with one usable eye. According to his followers, his strength is his piety and faithfulness or the force of his belief. Omar, known for a pure devotion to Islam, used to be a *mullah* (priest) with a village *madrassah* (religious school for young kids and teenagers) near Qandahar. Supposedly, he disliked the behavior of warlords, who were kidnapping and raping boys and girls, stealing from Afghans at gunpoint on the road, and driving international aid workers out of Qandahar (Afghan-land, 2004). So, Omar and 30 ethnic Pashtun followers initially attempted to eliminate wrongdoings, such as raping, and stealing near Omar's village and later to bring law and order to the entire country.

Mullah Omar and his followers claimed to have had a mission of creating a Muslim state that would practice a strict interpretation of the Quran. One of their objectives was to restore peace to the nation and hand the power to politicians and experienced leaders of Afghanistan. In 1996, Mullah Omar accepted the title of "Amirul Mo'mmineen," or "commander of the faithful," in a meeting in Qandahar. Omar is the first Muslim since the Fourth Caliph, a nephew of Prophet Mohammad, to publicly accept the Amirul title, a ranking in Islam nearly second to the Prophet. By 1997, some Arabs had moved in to top positions with the Taliban government and began to influence Omar's administration. Osama Bin Laden and Pakistani secret service provided majority of their weapons and soldiers (Afghan-land, 2004). In the latter years of their administration, the Taliban's vision and direction of the country were supposedly being headed by Pakistani leaders and members of Bin Laden. On the other side, by the late 1990s, Pakistani government officials seem to have begun to "formally" withdraw or reduce their support for the Taliban regime, perhaps, due to international pressures. Some individuals speculated that by 1998, Al Qaeda was running Afghanistan with Osama Bin Laden as its leader while Mullah Omar serving as a symbolic figure. Supposedly, this movement was still being headed and backed by the Pakistani secret service, since it succeeded beyond anyone's imagination during 1998. While the Taliban and Mullah Omar did initially bring some security and stability in the country, they will also be remembered for destroying the popular and historic statutes in Afghanistan. The idea of blowing up the Buddah of Bamian was presented by a Chechen rebel, and adopted by Al Qaeda (Afghan-land, 2004). Many of Taliban governing officials initially had rejected the idea, and so had Mullah Omar. As known throughout the world, a few months later, the order was carried out and the Buddhas were destroyed and demolished.

On September 9th 2001, two foreign suicide bombers disguised as Arab reporters interviewed Ahmad Shah Masood in the village of Khwaja Bahaudin with a hidden bomb in a video camera and around their waists. Masood was a major opposition leader who was respected by many Afghans throughout the country for his character, intelligence, wisdom, bravery, and faith. The Bomb blast killed Ahmad Shah Masood and a couple of aids. Ahmad Shah Masood died on September 10th 2001. A day later, New York City and Washington D.C. came under attack by nearly 20 hijackers who piloted passenger planes into the World Trade Center buildings and Pentagon. Eventually, Mullah Omar and the Taliban regime lost their power in late 2001 to the Northern Alliance members.

SIBGHATULLAH MOJADDEDI

Sibghatullah Mojaddedi, Head of State during 1992 in Afghanistan, was born in 1925 in Herat province in western Afghanistan. He has been a spiritual leader of the Naqshbandi Sufi order; designated after Bahaudin Naqshband, who died in 1389 (Afghan-land, 2004). Mojaddedi was the leading survivor of this family, which had emigrated from India at the beginning of the 1900s. His family supposedly had played a major role in the revolt against King Amanullah in 1929 and later became affiliated with the conservative dynasty of Nadir Shah and Zahir Shah. Mojaddedi studied theology and Arabic at the Al Uminium-Azhar in Cairo in 1940 and returned in 1950s to study Islamic Law. When he returned to Afghanistan, he began teaching at Habibia High School. He was later appointed professor at the Institute for higher Islamic studies in Kabul. He was arrested in the late 1970s because of his criticism of the pro-Soviet course of the government and spent 3 years in the Kabul prison. Upon release from prison he left Kabul, and in 1979 created "Jabha-e Najat-e Mili Afghanistan," National Liberation Front of Afghanistan to show resistance and fight against the invading Soviet Army.

Sibghatullah Mojaddedi is a conservative Maulawi. In 1992, after the fall of the communist government in Kabul, all seven Mujahidin factions met in Peshawar and decided that a 51-persons body, headed by *Hazrat Sahib* Sibghatullah Mojaddedi, would go inside Afghanistan so that they could take over power from the rulers of Kabul. Mojaddedi completed his short term in office, as agreed upon, and returned to private life until 2004. He was summoned by the United Nations, the interim government officials, and Afghan governing body to head the Loya Jirga in 2004. In late December 2005, Pir Sibghatullah Mojaddedi was voted to be the Leader / Head of the New Parliament. The night after his election as the leader of the new Parliament, the author and his colleagues from the SAE/SAAE Conference were invited for dinner at Pir Mojaddedi's house in Kabul; he was energetic, enthusiastic and totally committed to rebuilding Afghanistan and serving his people. He said the key to Afghanistan's progress and development is education of all Afghans and knowledge dispersion. Pir Sibghatullah Mojaddedi was a keynote speaker at an Islamic Conference in the late 1990s that was held in Orlando, Florida. He used to often visit his family members in Jacksonville, Florida, and where yours truly along with many other Afghans, had benefited from hearing his thoughts and prayers.

HAMID KARZAI

Hamid Karzai, the current President of Afghanistan, comes from the Pashtun tribe and same clan as that of the former King Zahir Shah. Hamid Karzai and his father used to campaign against the Taliban, operating from a base in Quetta, just across the border in Pakistan. In 1999, the Taliban assassinated Karzai's father, Abdul Ahad Karzai, who was once a parliamentary deputy in the Afghan government. Karzai then devoted himself to the campaign against the Taliban, determined to follow his father's wishes that a multi-ethnic, broad-based government rule Afghanistan, starting with the convening of a grand tribal assembly known as a *Loya Jirga* (Afghan-Land, 2004).

Karzai prefers to describe himself as a "politician" and not a "fighter." He was educated partly in India and speaks several languages including Persian, Pushtu, Urdu, and English. Karzai has six brothers and one sister, and some of this brothers own Afghan restaurants in Boston (MA), San Francisco (CA) and Baltimore (MD) in the Unites States. I dined at their San Francisco restaurant in October of 2004, and must say that they offer quality food and great service. All three restaurants are named Helmand, after the province just west of Qandahar.

After the Soviets invaded Afghanistan in 1979, Karzai fled to Pakistan, where he built supply lines between anti-Soviet Afghan guerrillas and American backers. When the Mujahedin took power in 1992, he returned to serve for two years as Deputy Foreign Minister in the government of President Burhanuddin Rabbani. Disillusionment with the infighting of that regime led him to switch over, briefly, to the Taliban, which once tried to make him its U.N. ambassador, a post he declined. But Karzai, an Islamic moderate, soon turned against the Taliban, and returned to Pakistan. Former U.S. Assistant Secretary of State Karl Inderfurth, a friend of Karzai's, said that after the murder of his father, Karzai approached Washington with plans for leading resistance to the Taliban. Having secured the peaceful fall of Qandahar, Karzai headed up to the capital, Kabul. When he formally took charge on Dec. 22nd 2001. Karzai was elected President in October of 2004, and his inauguration took place on December 7th 2004 in Kabul, with nearly 600 foreign diplomats present.

Hamid Karzai stayed in the region, instead of living abroad, and took an active voice in how his province was governed. Karzai was initially appointed the interim leader of Afghanistan for six months after the fall of the Taliban in late 2001. In June 2002, he was elected to a two-year term by the Grand Parliament (Loya Jirga) of Afghanistan. At 46 years of age, Karzai is leading the development toward a peaceful Afghanistan. For years, according to Afghan-land (2004), he remained chief of the Popolzai tribe in southern Afghanistan, and now gets the opportunity to lead the country into peace, prosperity, and development through the assistance of the international community.

PRESIDENTIAL INAUGURATION – (12, 7th 2004)

President Hamid Karzai took the helm on Tuesday December 7th 2004, and began a challenging five-year term to hopefully heal ethnic divisions and develop the war-ravaged nation's decrepit infrastructure. Karzai's promising speech before 600 guests, that included Vice President Dick Cheney and Defense Secretary Donald Rumsfeld of the United States, outlined his agenda to meet Afghans' sky-high expectations.

President Karzai singled out the United States of America, which currently has about 18,000 soldiers in Afghanistan and is providing billions of dollars in aid, for particular thanks, while underlining the continued need for international support (Graham, 2004). He said, "Our fight against terrorism is not yet over and a decisive victory over terrorism requires serious and continuous cooperation at regional and international levels."

Vice President Dick Cheney, the most senior American official to visit Afghanistan since the Taliban regime, which was ousted three years ago, emerged from brief talks with Karzai to laud him as a wise leader and an admired international statesman (Graham, 2004). He continued to say that the establishment of democracy was necessary to Afghanistan's "basic, fundamental transformation." He continued to say that democracies create individuals who "are focused on their own lives and focused on building a free society." Rumsfeld cautioned soldiers that the military mission is not over as "There are still groups, extremists, that would like to take this country back - the Taliban, the al-Qaeda - and use it for a base for terrorist activities around the world as they did on 9/11. But it's not going to happen."

THE PRESIDENT'S SPEECH – (12, 7th 2004)

In the name of Allah, the Merciful, the Compassionate
Praise Be to Allah, the Lord of All Worlds. And Peace and Prayers Be to the Last of God's Prophets.

Dear compatriots,
Distinguished guests,
Ladies and gentlemen,

I am pleased that this grand occasion has brought such a distinguished audience together. I welcome you all here.

On this historical day, many distinguished guests from countries around the world have joined us in Kabul. This is a testament to the sense of solidarity, cooperation and deepening relations between us, Afghans, and the international community. The people of Afghanistan cherish this friendship.

Today, as I take oath as Afghanistan's president, I reflect on the past three years – on ups and downs, on moments of both joy and gloom. During the past three years, I took encouragement and strength from our people – from the meetings I held several times a week with elders and youth, women and men, coming from the provinces; from the strong atmosphere of national unity at the two Loya Jirgas; from the love I found in this nation for progress and prosperity; from the resilience of those fellow Afghans who were determined to leave behind the suffering and oppression they once endured, and move forward to rebuild this great nation. Nothing makes me more hopeful to the future of this country – and my ability to serve it – than the incredible experience of our people's participation in the recent elections. So it is with God's blessing, and our people's support, that I resolve to fulfill this great responsibility that has been put on my shoulders today.

My brothers and sisters,

I have heard, over the past month or so, many extraordinary stories of the Afghan people's participation in the elections. Someone told me the story of an elderly woman in Farah province who arrived at a polling station with two voter's cards. She went up to an election worker and declared that she wanted to vote twice, once for herself, and again for her daughter who, she said, was about to deliver her child and unable to come to the polling station to vote. "We are sorry, but no one can vote for another person, this is the rule", the elderly lady was told. So she voted – for herself – and left the station. Later in the day, the election worker was shocked to see the elderly woman back, this time accompanying her young daughter to the polling station. Her daughter carried her new-born baby, as well as her voting card which she used to cast her vote.

Tens of other stories like this exist that I cannot tell you today. Each of these is remarkable and distinct, but they all tell one truth – the truth of the Afghan people's love for their country and concern for their future.

Every vote that was cast in the elections was a vote for Afghanistan, whether I received it or another candidate. Every voter had Afghanistan's best interests at heart. I thank all the voters who participated in the elections, and I respect their vote. I am confident, and proud, that this nation is determined to rebuild Afghanistan, and rebuild it fast; to live in security, and to stand on its own feet.

I and my colleagues in the new government feel deeply compelled, not only by your votes in the elections but also by your determination, to respect your aspirations and serve your goals. We will stand by the promises which we have made for the good of this nation. We will be steady and unflinching; we will invoke Allah the Almighty for His blessing, and will depend on you for courage and support.

During our election campaign, we presented a manifesto for the future to the people of Afghanistan. Our principal promises are concerning the strengthening of security sector and ensuring lasting stability throughout the country; the elimination of poppy cultivation and the fight against processing and trafficking of drugs; the disarmament and demobilization of former combatants; the eradication of poverty, generation of wealth and the provision of public services especially to the rural areas; the rule of law, and the protection of civil liberties and human rights; the acceleration of administrative reform to strengthen administration, root out corruption, stop the abuse of public funds, and ensure meritocracy; the strengthening of national unity; the rebuilding and building of the country's infrastructure; and of course the strengthening of understanding and cooperation with the international community. We feel obliged to work to deliver on these promises, with the help of God the Almighty, over the next five years.

In addition to the above, a significant challenge facing us over the next few months is conducting parliamentary elections. Again with help of the Almighty, and participation of the people of Afghanistan, this challenge will also be overcome and parliamentary elections will be held on schedule, in a safe and free environment. The election of the legislature will complete the establishment of the third branch of power in our state, paving the way for a law-abiding, progressive and prosperous Afghanistan

I and my colleagues have a duty before the people of Afghanistan to remain steady and persistent as we work to realize their aspirations. We have a duty before our people to deliver, to the best of our ability, an Afghanistan that is free, stable, prosperous and enjoying a dignified place in the family of nations.

Distinguished guests,

I must hasten to say that our fight against terrorism is not yet over, even though we have succeeded to reduce this common enemy of humanity to a lesser threat in this country. The relationship between terrorism and narcotics, and the continued threat of extremism in the region and the world at large, are a source of continued concern. A decisive victory over terrorism requires serious and continued cooperation at regional and international levels.

Three years ago, the firm and productive cooperation of the international cooperation rid Afghanistan from the rule of terrorism. The same cooperation has led to the rebuilding of the Afghan state, and significant progress in restoring peace, stability and security to our country. As a result, we have now left a hard and dark past behind us, and today we are opening a new chapter in our history, in a spirit of friendship with the international community.

May I take this opportunity to thank the United States of America for helping us so generously in so many different ways. I would also like to thank the United Nations, the European Union, Japan, Canada, some of our neighbors and many others. These countries have extended to us a helping hand when we needed it most. The help from the international community has taken us step by step over the past three years to where we are today. I thank them all for their generosity and friendship. And I am joined in this feeling of gratitude by all my fellow Afghans.

With our neighbors, Afghanistan has enjoyed an ever flourishing partnership and cooperation in trade, economic and other fields, over the past three years – thanks to the relative stability in Afghanistan and the region. A peaceful, strong and stable Afghanistan is in the interest of our neighbors and our region – I invite them to take maximum advantage of our trade and investment potential. I pledge that, mindful of our own national interests as well as theirs, we will remain a friend and a partner to all our neighbors.

Ladies and gentlemen,

Last week, during a meeting with the elders of Badghis province, as I went around greeting the guests individually, I saw an elderly man who had tears in his eyes and said to me as I shook his hand: "We want a clean and efficient government from you!" I would like all of you to leave this gathering today having heard one pledge from me: I will do everything it takes to turn that elderly man's tears of hope into the smile of fulfillment.

Once again, my fellow Afghans, I congratulate you on this historical day, on your courage to bring this day about, and on this dawn of a new peaceful and prosperous era for our country.

Oh God, make good the conclusion of our endeavour,
Such that leads to your approval, and to our success.

Source: Received from the Embassy of Afghanistan (in the U.S.A.) on December 7th 2004.

CABINET MEMBERS- (12, 23rd 2004)

President Hamid Karzai's Office on December 23rd 2004 announced a new 25-persons cabinet member. As requested by many Afghans and the international community, President Karzai removed ties with many of the so called major warlords and drug traffickers, while retaining many familiar faces, including many well educated scholars to run the ministries involved in the rehabilitation of Afghanistan's economy. It appears as though at least nine of the originally appointed ministers held doctoral level degrees and significant experience in their areas of authority. Another significant move forward for the first time in Afghanistan's history is that several women have been appointed to the cabinet, including Massouda Jalal who was running against President Karzai in October's presidential elections. He named former presidential candidate Masooda Jalal as Minister for Women's Affairs and Sediqa Balkhi as Minister for Martyrs and Disabled. Dr. Masooda Jalal was a keynote speaker at the University of South Florida, Tampa - Florida, in October 2006 to raise awareness and funds for women issues in Afghanistan and around the globe. President Karzai had pledged to bring in "a clean, efficient, competent cabinet" and such a diversity might very well be the solution to Afghanistan's troubling and complex conflicts. These new diplomats can hopefully tackle Afghanistan's myriad problems such as internal conflicts, mined fields, and the explosion in opium production and drug trafficking.

According to the Office of the Spokesperson to the President of the Islamic Republic of Afghanistan, as announced on December 23, 2004, the following were the initial cabinet members (with the place of birth, when known, following the first and last names):

1. Mr. Hedayat Amin Arsala (Nangarhar); MA in Economic; Minister of Commerce
2. Dr. Abdullah Abdullah (Panjsher); Medical Doctor; Minister of Foreign Affairs
3. Mr. Ali Ahmad Jalali (Ghazni); Minister of Interior
4. General Abdurrahim Wardak (Wardak); Minister of National Defense
5. Dr. Zalmay Rasool (Kabul); National Security Advisor
6. Mr. Noor Mohammad Qarqeen (Jowzjan); Minister of Education
7. Dr. Anwar-ul Haq Ahadi (Nangarha); Ph.D. in political sciences; Minister of Finance
8. Dr. Mohammad Amin Farhang (Kabul); Minister of Economy
9. Dr. Enayatullah Qasemi (Ghazni); Ph.D. in law; Minister of Transport
10. Engineer Amirzai Sangeen (Paktika); Electricity Engineering; Minister of Communication
11. Engineer Mir Mohmamd Sediq; Minister of Mines and Industries
12. General Mohammad Ismael Khan (Herat); Graduate of Military College; Minister of Energy
13. Dr. Suhrab Ali Safari (Wardak); Ph.D. in Engineering and Construction; Minister of Public Works
14. Engineer Yusof Pashtun (Qandahar); Minister of Urban Development
15. Mr. Obaidullah Ramin (Baghlan); BA in Agriculture; Minister of Agriculture and Food
16. Mr. Mohammad Sarwar Danish (Daikondi); MA in Islamic Sharia; Minister of Justice
17. Dr Amir Shah Hasanyar (Bamian); Ph.D. in Agriculture; Minister Higher Education
18. Dr. Sayed Makhdum Rahin (Kabul); Ph.D. in Dari; Minister of Information and Culture
19. Dr. Sayed Mohmmad Amin Fatemi (Nangarhar); Medical Doctor; Minister of Public Health
20. Professor Nematullah Shahrani (Badakhshan); MA in Islamic Science; Minister of Haj and Islamic Affairs
21. Mr. Mohammad Karim Brahoye (Nemrooz); Graduate of Military college; Minister of Borders Affairs
22. *Dr. Masooda Jalal* (Kapisa); Medical Doctor; Minister of Women's Affairs
23. Mr. Sayed Ekramuddin Agha (Takhar); University of Islamabad; Minister of Social Services and Labor
24. Mr. Mohammad Azam Dadfar (Faryab); Medical Doctor; Minister of Refugees
25. *Mrs. Sediqa Balkhi* (Balkh); BA in Sciences; Minister of Martyrs and Disabled
26. Mr. Mohammad Hanif Atmar (Laghman); Minister of Rural Development
27. Engineer Habibullah Qaderi (Zabul); Technical Engineer; Minister of Anti-Narcotics

The President of Afghanistan said that Afghanistan "will be governed by laws and the ministers have been appointed by that standard." Although some ministries are filled by figures that are popular with international donors, President Karzai has selected many new faces to spearhead reform. His selection of the new cabinet members are regarded as critical to getting Afghanistan's economy moving forward while attracting continuing aid from the international community. Karzai has also picked an ethnically-balanced cabinet from various provinces containing at least eight ethnic-majority Pashtuns, nine Tajiks, two Uzbeks, three Hazaras, as well as ministers from the Turkmen and Baluch minorities. President Karzai said, "The Afghan people have elected me and if I do not perform they will kick me out…I have chosen the ministers and if they do not perform I'll ask them to leave." He further mentioned that "The reforms will go on very steadfastly and intensely -- all those things that I have mentioned in my program to the Afghan people."

REFLECTIVE QUESTIONS FOR CRITICAL THINKING

1. Dan Rather of CBS News in 1993 said that "To understand why and how Afghanistan became such a pivotal battleground in the Cold War, the first thing to know and ponder is exactly where it is. Look at the map." Discuss the make up of the countries surrounding Afghanistan and how have these countries impacted Afghanistan,
2. Describe the culture of Afghanistan and how culture impacts the behavior of people within the country. Be specific with the examples.
3. What are the common foods in Afghanistan? Where did they originate from and how have they impacted the eating and dieting habits of people?
4. What are the common natural resources in Afghanistan? How have these natural resources benefited the people of the country? Describe the potential usage of the natural resources to improve Afghanistan's economy.
5. Describe the ethnicities of Afghan people and languages spoken by them.
6. Describe the major contributions of some of the Afghan leaders in the past century.
7. What are some of the common themes and challenges associated with the future of Afghanistan as expressed in the inaugural speech by President Karzai on December 7th 2004?
8. What variables have led to the success of Afghan leaders, and how can they keep this momentum going?
9. What are some specific roles that Afghan women can play better than males given the culture of Afghanistan?
10. How can women assist in the development of education to young and working females in Afghanistan?

CHAPTER 2

AFGHAN GOVERNMENT, COMMUNISM, AND THE CIVIL WAR

Throughout history, many groups of people have passed, and sometimes settled, through the lands of Afghanistan forming a country of various ethnicities. Many armies and governments have come and gone, but always left some type of destruction and chaos in the country. Afghans have several things in common, and two of them are Islam and passion for liberty. Most foreign armies have been defeated because Afghans united based on these two commonalities. Ahmad Shaw Durani, who founded the monarchy in 1774, which lasted until 1973, has been credited for uniting various and sometimes conflicting groups of Afghans into one political power. Maybe Hamid Karzai, and his administration, will be given the same credit in history as they are reuniting everyone towards a speedy development in the country. Afghanistan has been governed by many rulers and emperors of various backgrounds and countries. Its true independence, from the British, came in the twentieth century in 1919 when Amanullah Khan became the King.

GOVERNMENT HISTORY

Many archaeologists have explored Afghanistan and found artifacts that are typical of the Paleolithic, Mesolithic, Neolithic, Bronze, and Iron ages. Afghanistan has been part of, ruled by, or ruled many of its neighboring regions to its west, north, and east. According to past researchers, urban civilization in Afghanistan dawned circa 3,000 to 2,000 B.C. There is not much written information prior to 550-331 B.C. when the Achaemenid Empire ruled under the leadership of Darius the Great (500 B.C.). The Achaemenid Rulers were defeated by Alexander the Great, the Macedonian leader who died in 323 B.C. and his commander, Seleucus, became the nominal leader. During the Alexander and Seleucus Dynasty, the Greek colonist and soldiers came into the Kabul areas. About 30 years after Alexander's death, the Mauryan Empire was developed in the northern region and introduced Indian culture and Buddhism to residents. With the decline of Seleucid nominal control, the Greek-ruled states became known as Bactria. After the fall of the Greek rulers, the Kushan Empire and Hepthalite Empire from the Sassanian Kingdom controlled Kabul and many other regions outside Afghanistan, from 150 B.C. to 700 A.D. The influence of Buddhists cannot be seen in today's Afghanistan with the exception of two sand-stone Buddhas in Bamian Province, which were 35 and 53 meters high. Much of these two statues had been damaged during the Soviet invasion. Parts of the body and the arms had been destroyed because of rockets and bomb explosions. However, the Taliban's forces destroyed what was left of them in April 2001. Prior to the Soviet invasion, researchers had found frescoes (art works), stucco decorations, statuary, and other objects that confirm the existence of ancient civilization from China, Rome, Phoenicia, and others.

After the death of Prophet Muhammad in 632 A.D., in the prospective centuries, the Arab Muslims struggled to conquer what are now Afghanistan and its adjacent regions. While during the next four decades the area was full of fighting and conflicts, it was not until the middle of the tenth century, after the Sammanid Dynasty, the Ghaznavid came in control of Afghanistan and its adjacent regions. All the monuments, buildings, and statues left by the Buddhist (except the two sand-stone Buddhas in Bamian) and other non-Muslims art works or statues were destroyed. Genghis Khan (1155-1227) ruled the area, and left many people killed and cities destroyed, but failed to destroy the strength of Islam in the heart of the Asian countries. A century later, the descendants of Genghis Khan were also Muslims. In 1381, Timur, a Mongol and an ancestor of Genghis Khan, came into power over many central Asian countries. Timur had created an empire that influenced and controlled areas from Samarqand to Turkey and India. By the end of the sixteenth century, the Timurid Empire was defeated and Muhammad Shaybani, also a descendant of Genghis Khan, and his successors succeeded them. In 1738, a fierce leader named Nadir Shah sometimes referred to as "the Napoleon of Persia," became the ruler in Afghanistan and its surrounding regions. He defeated the Mughuls in India killing thousands of people and destroying their cities. The Pukhtuns (Pathans, also referred to as Pushtuns) fought against Nadir Shah and were dispersed into different regions upon their defeat. After the death of Nadir Shaw in 1747, Ahmad Shah "*Baabah*" became the ruler of Afghanistan as well as some of the neighboring regions. "*Baabah"* is a Persian word given to Ahmad Shaw as an honorary, and it means "grandfather" who is the head of the household. Ahmad Shaw Baabah was the first Pukhtun ruler of Afghanistan and its surrounding regions. The regions under Ahmad Shaw Baabah started from the Arabian Sea in Hyderabad to Quetta, Lahore, Srinagar, Balkh, Nishapur, Meshed, and all of the regions known as Afghanistan today. Ahmad Shaw Baabah was also called "*Durr-i-Durran*" which means "pearl of the pearls" or "pearl of the age." Ahmad Shaw Baabah was also a poet and had said in one of his poems, as translated by Afghan writers, that: "*What ever countries I conquer in the world, I would never forget your beautiful gardens. When I remember the summits of your beautiful mountains I forget the greatness of the Delhi throne.*" Ahmad Shah Baabah was also seen as the uniting factor between the various ethnic groups making Afghanistan. He helped the people of Afghanistan become one force most of whom spoke Pushtu. He understood the Afghan people, and continuously sought Pukhtun leader's advice to make decisions. He knew that the people of Afghanistan enjoyed and valued liberty and freedom to make their own decisions; thus, Ahmad Shaw Baabah never attempted to rule the Afghans (Pukhtuns) by force. In 1772, Ahmad Shaw Baabah retired and died in his home in the midst of mountainous Qandahar.

By 1818, most of the regions ruled by Ahmad Shaw Baabah had become independent as Ahmad Shaw Baabah's successors failed to keep the Pukhtuns united. The only areas under the control of Timur Shaw, Ahmad Shaw Baabah's second son and heir, was most of today's Afghanistan. Timur Shaw had a sudden death in 1793 and left 36 legitimate children, 20 of them were boys. All of Timur Shaw's sons wanted to become the ruler as three of them were the governors of Qanadahar, Herat, and Kabul. However, Timur Shaw's fifth son called Zaman became the ruler, and the other brothers were forced to accept his leadership. Zaman Shaw was overthrown in 1800 by rival groups and the violence and bloodshed had begun in Afghanistan. Timur Shaw's other sons, Shaw Shuja and Mahmood Shaw ruled until 1818, and then chaos began without the existence of Afghanistan as a single nation for the next eight years. In 1826, Dost Mohammad "Khan" became the ruler and called himself Amir, and not Shah. "Khan" is a Persian word used as an honorary at the end of people's names. Dost Mohammad Khan was described as a charismatic leader with a charming and shrewd personality. He was able to establish all groups back into one nation, and defeated many leaders in the neighboring regions in Afghanistan. He was involved with the British army and asked for their help in dealing with foreign nations, especially with the Sihks in India and Punjab. However, disagreements over policy and treaties that Dost Mohammad Khan did not sign caused the British army to discontinue their relationship with him, and support his brother Shah Shuja who had gained support in Herat. With the help of British army, Shah Shuja was able to force Dost Mohammad Khan out of Kabul and into Bukhara. The British army wanted to invade Afghanistan, because of the country's geographical location which became very important to their army's strategies. They claimed that the invasion of Afghanistan was not their purpose for coming into the country, but to help Shah Shuja's tiny army to claim his previously held throne in the country of Afghanistan. Of course, both the Russians and the Americans have said the same words as their forces came to Kabul. After Shah Shuja's victory, the British army did not pull out their troops claiming that they had to protect Shah Shuja's government against foreign interference and various other group oppositions. Later in the 19th century, the Russians used this "helping" strategy to invade Afghanistan, as did the British in 1838. Shah Shuja could not rule the country without the presence of the British army, as their garrisons protected much of the areas. In 1841, the tribal leaders were not happy with the current government and were supporting Dost Mohammad's son, Mohammad Akbar Khan, who was in Bamian. The support for Shah Shuja kept decreasing, and the violence against the British army increased each and everyday. Finally, the British leaders wanted to get out peacefully and signed an agreement with some of the tribal leaders to leave safely. However, the army did not wait until all the leaders had agreed and heard of the agreement. They started their journey early, and were attacked by Afghan warriors, who killed all their soldiers with the exception of Dr. Brydon who reached Qandahar's border as an injured man. This was the end of the First Anglo-Afghan War, and the Russians started moving toward Afghanistan by invading Tashkent and Bukhara, which became part of their territory thereafter.

A few months after the British army's defeat, Shah Shuja was killed in the April of 1842 battle. After much violence and chaos in 1843, Mohammad Akbar was able to take control of Kabul, and his father Dost Mohammad Khan came into power once more. By 1863, when Dost Mohammad died, most of what is known today as Afghanistan was under Dost Mohammad Khan's rule and control. Soon after, Shir Ali Khan had established control over much of Afghanistan and died in Mazar-e-Sharif in February of 1879. During this time, as the Russians and the British tried to exert influence and control over Afghanistan, the British army invaded the country and brought Abdul Rahman Khan into power in 1880. Abdul Rahman was able to consolidate the Afghan state by punishing people, forcing people to relocate to other areas with various ethnic groups, and by creating provinces whose governors had much control and influence in local matters. He also established a centralized government and the *Loya Jirgah*, a general assembly. Abdul Rahman was able to modernize Afghanistan by technological advancements, transfer of European machinery, and by creating factories to produce soap and candles. The British were helpful to Abdul Rahman, because they were "concerned with Afghanistan as a buffer between India and the Russians, their greatest interest laid in the definition of the Afghan boundary with Russia" (Nyrop and Seekins, 1986). The British also had total control over the Afghan foreign policy, as agreed with Abdul Rahman. In 1901, Abdul Rahman died and his son, chosen by him to be his successor, named Habibullah became the ruler until 1919. So far, Afghanistan had wars with the British in 1839 and 1878, and both wars ended in tragedy for Afghans as well as the British with the later invasion ending in 1919 leading to Afghanistan's independence. Habibullah had many brothers, but they did not interfere with government decisions as advised by their father. Habibullah was a clever and tactful leader as Nyrop and Seekins (1986) writes:

> During World War I Afghanistan remained neutral, despite pressure to support Turkey when its sultan proclaimed his nation's participation in a holy war. Habibulah did, however, entertain a Turco-German mission in Kabul in 1915. Although, after long procrastination, he won agreement from the Central Powers to a huge payment and provision of arms if he would attack British India, the crafty Afghan ruler clearly viewed the war as an opportunity to play one side off against the other, for he also offered the British to hold off the Central Powers from an attack on India in exchange for an end to British control of Afghan foreign policy (page 40).

Habibullah was assassinated during a hunting trip on February 20th 1919. The throne was assumed by his third son, Amanullah Khan. Amanullah Khan established total independence in Afghanistan by attacking the British and eliminating their influence in Afghanistan. Amanullah Khan was able to establish diplomatic relations with the Soviet Union, Iran, Britain, Turkey, Italy, and France during 1919-1923. He also changed his title from Amir to *Padshah* (King) in 1923. In 1919, Amanullah Khan sent an emissary to Moscow, and Lenin received the envoy with pleasure and sent a Soviet representative to Kabul, while offering aid to his government. Many claim that this was the beginning of the Soviet's political tactics to eventually invade Afghanistan. During May of 1921, the Afghans and the Soviets had signed a Treaty of Friendship, which was Afghanistan's first international agreement since its independence from the British in 1919. The Soviets helped Afghanistan economically, provided 13 airplanes, pilots, and laid telephone and communication lines between Kabul and Mazar-i Sharif. Amanullah was distrustful of the Russians, but wanted their help in terms of technology and for support in protection against possible attacks from the British army. Internally, Amanullah made some drastic changes and wanted many more to happen as advised by Turkish advisers. His minister of war, General Mohammad Nadir Khan, opposed these changes and wanted the King to be more sensitive to the needs of tribal leaders and their people. Nadir Khan did not support the King's internal policy and was sent as an ambassador to France. Amanullah wanted Afghanistan to become Westernized quickly by dressing and schooling similar to them. He wanted to discourage veiling and seclusion of women as well as to end slavery and forced labor. He wanted women to become educated, including nomads and illiterate adults. For that time period, these measures were seen as drastic and impossible in the strong and established culture of Afghanistan. Nadir Khan further established the Afghani unit of currency in 1923 and the Bank-i-Milli (National Bank) in 1928. However, people's dislike of these changes encouraged them to take arms against the King, and he was forced to leave the throne to his brother Inayatullah, who ruled for three days and went into exile in India. Amanullah attempted to recover control but failed and went into exile in Italy. For the next nine months, Bacha-i-Saqqow (son of the Water Carrier), who called himself Habibullah took power. He was a Tajik tribesman from Qala Khan (Khan's village about 30 kilometers north of Kabul), who is usually described as a Tajik bandit. He supposedly used to rob the rich and give to the poor. He did not have much support in Afghanistan and soon after he was captured and executed by Nadir Shah's forces on November 3rd 1929. Soon after in 1929, General Nadir Shah Khan became the new formal king and was referred to as King Mohammad Nadir Shah, who served until 1933. Before his death in 1933, he created an army of 40,000 members. Nadir Shah Khan was killed by a man because of an interfamily feud with the King, and six months later his brother Mohammad Aziz Khan was also killed. The throne was given to Nadir Shah's son, King Mohammad Zahir Shaw at 19 years of age. King Zahir Shaw ruled Afghanistan for 40 years and today resides in Italy. He was heavily supported by his uncles, Mohammad Hashim and Shah Mahmood, who did not seek to take control, but helped their nephew in his kingdom.

During an interview with Thomas J. Abercrombie (1968), King Zahir Shaw implied that he is trying to slowly expand people's interest and participation in the government activities and so on. If that was his only goal, then he succeeded by creating "monsters" of some power-hungry individuals. In the last thirty years, many individuals who have had more than five loyal friends seem to have been trying to become the next leader representing Afghanistan. However, King Zahir Shaw probably just wanted people to be involved in a democratic way to create social equality, and not in the form which it has taken presently. He further stated that:

> One who does not know the Afghan soil could never know the Afghan people. Only recently have the traditional patterns begun to change, as our industries begin to grow, it is not enough just to keep up with the changing times. We must keep ahead of them-to encourage our people to learn and to accept new responsibilities.

During his forty years of service, he was able to keep Afghanistan away from any major catastrophes, and people had the freedom to express their political feeling and thoughts freely to the public as they wished. There were no political or civil wars in any form or shape, and the only dangerous roar was the firing of the *toap-e-chasht,* which was the firing of a cannon every day at noon to represent midday (12 o'clock). During Zahir Shaw's administration, there were some attempts and riots by students to revolutionize the monarchy. In one of these riots, the students supposedly had shaved an Afghan hound's head, which symbolically represented the King, and they were carrying the dog on the streets yelling bad things to affront him and his monarchy. Unfortunately, during one of the student riots three students were killed as supposedly ordered by his son-in-law, General Sardar Abdul Wali. The King was not pleased, since he did not favor violence and people were shocked with these killings, so he appointed Mohammad Hashim Maiwandwal as the new Prime Minister. King Zahir Shaw wanted people to express themselves peacefully. During these riots, people were allowed to express their feelings without any harm coming to them, which was representative of a democratic regime. People wanted such a democracy and "Strangely enough, this is the past that somebody in the future is longing to go back to" (Ashleigh Brilliant).

During the 1960s, the Communist assistance to the country was twice as much as the American assistance. Most of the military and army supplies and equipment were provided by the Soviet Union. Journalist Thomas J. Abercrombie asked General Sardar Abdul Wali - Army Chief of Staff and Zahir Shaw's son-in-law, during the Independence Day celebration, about his concern of Afghan people entrusting so much of its militaristic preparation to its powerful neighbor. He responded by saying "when you ride a good horse, do you care in which country it was born." It appears as though these concerns were not being discussed very seriously during that time. Many believe that they should have been concerned with the intention of the owners who provided those "horses." In the United States, people have a saying: "there is no such thing as a free lunch," which tells us that no country provides anything without expecting something in return and the Afghan people may have underestimated former Soviet Union's (USSR's) power and intention. During 1953, Dauod Khan, son of Muhammad Aziz and King Zahir Shaw's cousin, was appointed as the Prime Minister. Dauod Khan was the first of the Western-educated generation of the royal family, who desired to introduce a more open political system into the country. He encouraged the cabinet members' wives to represent the new unveiled women of Afghanistan and they did. Some of the religious members did not agree with this and Dauod challenged them for showing a verse of the Quran that explicitly stated the culture-based veiling of women. He wanted to take advantage of having a friendly relationship with both the United States and the Soviet Union simultaneously. The fact of the matter was that, at the time, having good relationships with both superpowers were mutually exclusive because of political reasons and the cold war. In Afghanistan, people used to say that "One cannot carry two watermelons in one hand at the same time" which happened to prove true for Dauod Khan, as his friendship became extremely strong with the Soviet Union, which may have served as the catalyst for the success of communist party in Afghanistan. Dauod Khan's relationship with Pakistan leaders grew into animosity over arguments of the

Pushtunistan issue. He wanted Pushtunistan to be part of Afghanistan, so all the Pushtuns could become part of one nation as they were during the first part of the 19th century. All trade treaties between Afghanistan and Pakistan came to a halt as the natural resources could not be exported to India or Pakistan. King Zahir Shah asked Dauod Khan to resign on the basis that Afghanistan was suffering because of his policies with Pakistan. Dauod resigned and Mohammad Yousuf, who was the minister of mines and industries, became the new Prime Minister in 1963. In 1965, the Communist party, called the People's Democratic Party of Afghanistan (PDPA), got started by Nur Mohammad Taraki and Babrak Karmal's leadership. This party split in 1967 into two factions called *Khalq* (Masses), lead by Taraki, and *Parcham* (Banner), lead by Karmal.

Afghanistan's conflicts with the British army in 1839 and 1878 ended in tragedy for the British with the last defeat ending in 1919. Independence Day was celebrated during August 26th by participating in *Jashine Isteqlal* (independence festival). Serving one's country before the Russian invasion was an act of duty, and people proudly volunteered from all parts of Afghanistan to be inducted into the army. In 1929, Afghanistan was established by a unified kingdom by Nadir Shah whose son, Zahir Shaw, was the last of the Kings. He became the nominal King in 1933 after the assassination of his father, King Nadir Shah. Although Mohammad Zahir Shaw was the king, initially most of the major decisions about the political strategies were made by his uncles. He served as the King for about 40 years, until the previous Prime Minister, who was also his cousin and brother-in-law, Dauod Khan, replaced him while he was on a trip to Italy. On July 17th of 1973, Dauod Khan terminated the Kingdom (Monarchy) by a military coup and changed the kingdom into a Republic. There was little resistance and eight people, four soldiers and four policemen died in the process. By 1975, Dauod Khan had established the National Revolutionary Party of Afghanistan (NRPA) under his leadership. It was assumed that Dauod Khan was helped by the communist parties with overcoming resistance in becoming the new ruler. However, he was not concerned about communists very much as Lohbeck (1993) said that Dauod thought communists were not very experienced leaders, and their atheism would not do well with Muslims in Afghanistan. Of course, today we know that his thinking was correct or, as they say in the West, "right on the money." Perhaps Dauod Khan was not aware of how large the communist membership had grown both in military and government agencies. He perhaps thought they were a very small party who could not exert much influence over the people of Afghanistan and did not take them very seriously. Most people in Afghanistan believe that Dauod's presidency was the beginning of Communists' heavy influence and destruction in the country. Dauod received much blame for allowing this Communist influence to take place and eventually destroy the country for the next nearly thirty years. However, many Afghans theorize that Dauod was forced by Leonid Brezhnev and Communist countries to keep a good relationship with them.

Most of the Islamic activists were trying to stop this Communist influence by overthrowing Dauod Khan as a ruler. However, their parties were not large enough and their experience and leadership was limited in government. Islamic leaders Burhanuddin Rabbani, Maulavi Younus Khalis, and Gulbuddin Hekmatyar were supposedly trying to search for strategies to take control of the government. Professor Rabbani wanted to organize a common party that could get enough votes and defeat Dauod's party in a Democratic way by winning the electorates in the Parliament. However, other leaders did not agree and every leader had his own thoughts and feelings about eliminating Dauod's power and exerting Islamic influence over the government. Therefore, Islamic leaders continued to encourage students in starting riots against the government. During one of the riots, Gulbuddin Hetmatyar became badly wounded and Din Mohammad's face was badly burned by communists. Some of the Islamic leaders were arrested, some escaped to Pakistan, while others went into hiding. Islamic parties were very small in numbers, perhaps less than one hundred, and not very well organized at this time. They would attack small government outposts and convoys to get ammunition and supplies. Their strategies were based on a hit-and-run type of actions because they could not resist the army at that time. However, with the passage of time, three to four years later, their financial situation became better as they were receiving help from Pakistani leaders. So, their numbers in the party grew and became much stronger and influential. Their attacks on the government became more organized and damaging. Communist members were also very active in recruiting members for their party. On April 17th of 1978, Mir Akbar Khaibar, an influential Parcham leader, was killed. While no party directly took credit for his death, it was assumed to have been ordered by other communist leaders. At this time President Dauod Khan ordered the arrest of many leaders and started arresting people who were instigating these riots and other political activities. These arrests included communist leaders such as Noor Mohammad Taraki and Hafizullah Amin, who were very active working to overthrow the government by strengthening their party members throughout the government and military. Taraki was put in Pul-i-Charkhi prison and Amin was put under house arrest in his own home with guards watching him 24 hours each day. While in prison, the Communist leaders were able to plan a coup with their contacts inside and outside the jail, and ordered their leaders to follow KGB's plans to take over the government.

THE COMMUNIST COUP D'ETAT OF 1978

In the bloody April 27-28 *coup d'etat* of 1978, President Dauod Khan, along with some of his family members, were killed by the pro-soviet communist party in the Presidential Palace, located in *Arg*. During the three days of this coup d'etat, an estimated two thousand people were killed throughout Afghanistan, most of the resistance and killings happened in Kabul. Noor Mohammad Taraki became the new nominal President and Prime Minister, under the Soviet influence, which in 1979 led to the former Soviet Union's (USSR) invasion. Babrak Karmal was appointed first deputy prime minister, while Hafizullah Amin was appointed deputy prime minister as well as foreign minister. The Communist regime started to take drastic measures like the abolition of usury – a common practice throughout the country, land reforms, and teachings of Lenin and Marxist theories in the schools and government work agencies. These measures were not very popular with the Afghans as the Soviets were attempting to gain the land and support of one more country. Many people in the world thought because of Afghanistan's location, it can be used as a strategic alliance to gain control and/or competitive edge over many other nations. As Dan Rather said,

"Its geographical location has made Afghanistan a crossroad of history." So, the Russians decided to "jump on the bandwagon" without considering the lessons learned during the Afghan-British war in 1919. People say that history repeats itself, and this is most definitely true in Afghanistan. However, in the recent Afghan-Russian war, more than two million Afghans died because advanced technology and chemicals were used that did not exist in 1919. The communist government unintentionally forced many people to support and join the Islamic leaders in their attempts to overthrow them from power.

As a result, the Communist government came into power during the April 27th 1978 coup in Afghanistan and the Soviet Union (USSR) army invaded the country on December 27th of 1979. The communist party leader and the first communist president was Noor Mohammad Taraki- a 61 year old writer, poet and self-declared Marxist, who was born in a farmer's family. He was born in 1917, a son of a farmer, who was a small-time smuggler. He studied in the College of Public Administration in Kabul, and was temporarily placed in Washington as a staff member of the Afghan embassy. Later, he had been hired by the United States Agency as a translator in Kabul. Communist-regime appointed presidents were nominal because the major decisions were made by the Soviet leaders, and this is why people referred to the Afghan communists as the "Russian or Soviet puppets." The beginning of their revolution promised equality between all Afghans, elimination of slavery, benefits and jobs for the farmers, and a people-based government led by the communist party. However, in reality the opposite happened because the farmers became poorer and the rich became richer, as they were able to leave the country and start businesses elsewhere. The activities of different freedom fighting factions became severe and damaging to the government and people of Afghanistan. During 1978, the Communist army with their Russian advisors went to the village of Kerala in the Kunar Province to capture the *Ekhwanies* (which stands for *Ekhwan-ul-Muslimeen* or Muslim brothers), people fighting against the government. The word *Ekhwan* means "brother" and the plural would imply "brothers" of faith who are fighting for a common cause. Since, the communists were not able to find anyone except women, elderly and children, they supposedly slaughtered over 1,000 people and left their bodies to rot in order to show the power of the government. The upper echelons of the Communist party, including Russian advisors, had ordered the killings because these were the people who encouraged, fed and clothed their sons and fathers to fight against the government. The news of this massacre by the communist traveled fast around the country, people became extremely disappointed, and the support for the freedom fighting leaders increased rapidly. Soon after, Islamic parties and Freedom Fighters had grown very large, as thousands and thousands of people became members either directly or indirectly. Some people went to the country villages and rural areas to become full-time Freedom Fighters, while others in military and government were covertly helping the fighters gain access to weapons, food and other political information. A fully grown and supported war had started against the Communist party, because many foreign countries were helping Islamic leaders financially and with needed artilleries. The Freedom Fighters were receiving ammunition from China, United States, Iran, Egypt, Libya, and Pakistan. Financially, the Freedom Fighters received help from Saudi Arabia, Germany, France,

Switzerland, United States, Great Britain, and other countries. According to the media in Peshawar during the early 1980s, the cost of feeding and sheltering the refugees in Pakistan was about one million dollars per day, which was about 12-14 million *ruppees*. Most foreign nations wanted to help so the Afghans could fight the Russians "whole-heartedly" without worrying about their families not having food and shelter. Since the Afghans were fighting the enemy of many nations, other countries were initially very generous in their humanitarian help for the refugees (at least until the cold war was over). The situation in the country was getting worse each and every day. In February 1979, the American ambassador, "Spike" Dubs, was stopped by several armed people in Kabul, then taken to a hotel where he was killed along with all the armed people who took him there. This was blamed on the Freedom Fighters according to the government of Afghanistan, but the truth was that Freedom Fighters did not, and could not, conduct such operations openly in Kabul during that time. It was very dangerous for Freedom Fighters to walk around with guns in the city, because communist soldiers were scattered throughout the city. The truth was unclear, and most of the people assumed it was the work of KGB to destroy the reputation of the Freedom Fighters. People were scared about possible retaliatory actions by the United States. The situation was very scary, but nothing was heard from the Americans; and the position was not filled. A few years later in the mid 1980s, Charles Thornton, a reporter from Arizona Republic, was the first American journalist who died in Afghanistan. His photographer, Peter Schlueter, was alive, but injured, during the explosion of their truck in Qandahar Province of Afghanistan. During 1987, American journalists Lee Shapiro and Jim Lindalos were also killed by Soviets while traveling to cover the war in Afghanistan.

During 1978, Communist leaders formally separated into two factions of *Khalq* (Public) and *Parcham* (Banner). The leading figures from Parchami party were sent to less influential jobs. For example, Babrak Karmal was sent to Czechoslovakia as an ambassador, and Najibullah was appointed the ambassador of Iran. Dr. Anahita Ratebzade, who was one of the first female *Parcham* party members in 1965, was appointed ambassador to Yugoslovia. The situation was bad, and the Russians had sent more and more Soviet advisors to keep communist leaders under control. In 1978, there were approximately 10,000 Soviet advisors and military personnel present in Afghanistan.

HAFIZULLAH AMIN AND BABRAK KARMEL

About eighteen months after becoming president, Taraki was killed on September 14th 1979 by Hafizullah Amin (and his group), who became the next president representing the Communist government. It was rumored that Taraki was going to eliminate Amin from his position because the administration was not doing well; supposedly Amin was the cause of it. Hafizullah Amin was born in 1921 in Paghman and studied mathematics and physics in Kabul University. He was a teacher and principal of a high school before winning a scholarship in 1957 to study in Teachers' College at Columbia University in New York. He came back to New York in 1962 to complete a doctorate program, but became involved in politics and returned to Kabul without finishing the program. He spoke Persian, Pushtu, and English fluently, and his actions had the appearance of wanting to separate

Afghanistan's government from the influence of the Soviet Union. This was later confirmed by President Zia-ul-Haq, former president of Pakistan, who concluded that President Amin wanted to pull away from the Soviets. His conclusion was based on his telephone conversation with Hafizullah Amin. Russians became suspicious of him because he had contacts with Pakistan and possibly with the United States. According to Artyom Borouik (1990), Soviet journalist covering the invasion, since Amin had graduated from Columbia University in New York, Moscow suspected that his intentions were not aligned with their strategy. Yet, before being able to implement his plans, he was killed and replaced by Babrak Karmel, with the help of the "supposedly" invited Russian army. The Time 2006 publication on Middle East summarized the situation as follows:

> So when the Moscow-friendly regime of the U.S.S.R.'s neighbor to the south, Afghanistan, began tilting toward the West in the late 1970s, the Soviet leadership panicked. Late on the night of Dec. 12, 1979, ailing Communist Party chairman Leonid Brezhnev met secretly with his top advisers, who told him Moscow must act fast to keep the U.S. from installing a friendly regime in Kabul. Indeed, it later emerged that the U.S. had been covertly supplying aid to Islamic rebels in Afghanistan earlier that year. The military intervention to put a Moscow-oriented government in place, Brezhnev was told, would be over in three or four weeks. Two weeks later Soviet soldiers…pulled off the coup…President Hafizullah Amin was overthrown and executed. It was the most brutal blow from the Soviet Union's steel fist since the invasion of Czechoslovakia in 1968 (Time Inc., 2006, page 87).

On December 27th 1979, Hafizullah Amin was killed by the Russian KGB led by Colonel Boyarinov and three other men who entered the Presidential Palace (Qasri Amanullah Khan in Darulaman), four miles away from the author's house, and shot him at point blank range. Karmel's prerecorded voice announced the new government from Termez (or Tashkent) located in Russian territory. The transmitter was broadcasting the speech on the same frequency as the Radio Afghanistan in Kabul, however it was much stronger.

Karmel was born in 1929 and his family was closely tied to the royal family because his father, General Mohammad Hussain Khan, was the governor of Paktia. He attended Kabul's *Huquq* (law) University. President Karmel was known for his extemporaneous and motivational speeches as well as his political tactics from previous communist activities in Afghanistan. Karmel was very active in the Parcham (banner) Communist party prior to his presidency, and had served as the deputy prime minister of Afghanistan as well as an ambassador to Czechoslovakia. As the new ruler of the country, he accused Hafizullah Amin of being a traitor and having been in contact with the CIA as an agent. He further claimed that the United States government should hand over the documentations of their contacts otherwise the confidential data might put Afghanistan in a bad position in case they have to defend themselves against foreign attacks.

Karmel's presidency began when the Russians entered Afghanistan and killed Hafizullah Amin along with some of his cabinet members. Karmel announced that the Soviets are helping us defend our country against foreign terrorism instigated by the Chinese and the Americans. Initially, there were only about 10,000 Russian soldiers coming to help the communist government on a temporary basis, but that number kept increasing each day. After a few days the number of Russian soldiers were around 80,000, and within the first year the number had reached around 130,000 soldiers who were scattered throughout the country. According to Russian publications, over 500,000 soldiers had been to Afghanistan during the invasion at one time or another, and were affected psychologically, physically, and emotionally from the trauma of war. However, the real numbers are supposedly around one million soldiers who served in Afghanistan during their ten-year stay. The Russians wanted to establish a stronghold on the country before things got out of control, but they were unable to accomplish this goal. It was because of Moscow's interference in Afghanistan that President Carter of the United States addressed his nation on December 27th of 1979 and announced the cancellation of American wheat sales to Russians, and the withdrawal of United States sport teams from the 1980 Olympic Games, which were held in Moscow.

Based on my experience the situation was very bad as compared to the rest of the time I had lived in Kabul during and prior to the war. Dan Rather (1993) from CBS News said, "When I first walked through the Himalayas into Afghanistan during 1980, I had no idea what I was getting into...There were many harrowing experiences and close calls inside...I was lucky to make it out alive." Rather mentioned other reporters, such as Kim Wimberger of CBS News, who died trying to cover the war in Afghanistan. Unfortunately, war does not care who dies because it cannot see, it cannot hear, and it certainly cannot stop by itself. This is why many innocent children, women, senior citizens, and animals lost their lives during the Afghan war. The majority of the two million people who died by airplane bombings, helicopter gunship, jet aircrafts, artilleries, guns, tortures, and executions were innocent "bystanders" who had nowhere else to go. Many children were left with no one to take care of them as chaos was ubiquitous around the nation. To take better care of the increased number of orphans, Babrak Karmal's wife, Mahboba Karmal, became involved as the president of an organization called *Parwarish-gaahe Watan*, which was an organization that cared for orphans. While this was a great cause and organization, it was speculated that some of these kids were being systematically sent to other socialist nations to be taken care of and trained in military, as they grew. Babrak and Mahboba were both Muslims with communist ideologies and wanted to bring communist regime into Afghanistan, perhaps with good intentions while thinking this would be their way of serving their country. Karmal claimed that he was a devoted Muslim; however, such examples as forgetting to take his shoes off in the Mosque discredited his claims of being a practicing Muslim. In the Mosque (Masjid), everyone is required to take off their shoes before entering, and this requirement does not change according to one's status, since everyone is equal in the eyes of our Creator.

As the destruction in Afghanistan increased, so did the help of the world and surrounding countries. The neighboring countries were trying to protect themselves from the Russians, one of the world superpowers at the time, and the United States of course wanted the Afghans to be successful to avenge the lost American soldiers in Vietnam. The American Congressman Charles Wilson, William Casey, and others were great supporters of the Afghan Freedom Fighters. During a conversation with the author during 1992 in Orlando, Congressman Bill McCollum of Florida said that he was proud of the Afghans who vehemently fought their country's occupants. He mentioned that the United States has always supported the war against the Soviets in Afghanistan by providing help to the Freedom Fighters both financially and in terms of military equipment and supplies.

At the beginning, many of the Russian soldiers could write and speak Persian; so, they were able to communicate effectively with the Afghans. Initially, the soldiers had been told that they were helping their Afghan neighbors fight against the invaders which included the Americans and the Chinese. However, soon after their arrival, the soldiers realized that they were fighting Afghan people (not foreigners) who did not agree with the government and their willingness to continue fighting was weak. The morale in the Russian army was low, so they switched personnel and brought the Red Army soldiers who could not easily communicate with the Afghans. The Russian soldiers were supposedly told that they were helping the people of Afghanistan to fight off the Americans and the Chinese who were terrorizing the country by interfering in the government. During 1983 and 1984, the communist government bombed the Afghan Freedom Fighters in Teri Mangal, a city in Pakistan, killing many immigrant Afghans and local residents. They kept doing this in the years to come, as Lohbeck (1993) writes that three Soviet jet bombers dropped dozens of bombs in Teri Mangal, killing over one hundred people in March 23rd of 1987. These attacks were perhaps the Soviet's way of implicitly telling Pakistan not to help the Freedom Fighters. Of course, as stated by Time Inc. in 2006, "Prodded by republicans in Congress, in 1982 U.S. President Ronald Reagan committed $3.2 billion to Pakistan's President Mohammed Zia ul-Haq," much of which was supposedly funneled to the Freedom Fighters. Furthermore, when the Soviet army helicopters posed the most severe threat to the Freedom Fighters and their families, "the U.S. began supplying the rebels with Stinger surface-to-air missiles, further bedeviling the Soviets" (Time Inc., 2006, p. 87).

Finally, on November 21st of 1985, President Karmel was replaced by president Najibullah, professionally a physician. Najibullah, born in 1946, was the last representative of the Communist government in the presidential position and served until 1992. Karmel went to live in Russia, and finally died of cancer in late November of 1996.

THE LAST COMMUNIST PRESIDENT - NAJIBULLAH

Prior to his presidency, Najibullah was known to have been a "ruthless" security chief and leader of the Communist's secret service called Khad (*Khedamat-e-Atla'at Dowlati*). Under Najbullah's leadership, Khad had become a force of over 25,000 members in and around Afghanistan. Khad members were paid high salaries and were disliked by most Afghans, especially the Freedom Fighters, because usually they were individuals who practiced duplicity and supposedly could live with no moral conscience. I remember a general public protest against the communist regime and government in Darrulamon and other parts of Kabul during 1981, where Najibullah and his Khad (communist party's secret service, KGB) agents were reported to have killed over seventy people, who were unarmed, in order to force everyone else to break the protest. The protesters were not carrying guns as it was a peaceful march where people were showing their dislike of the system. It was very ruthless to order the killings of so many unarmed people quietly protesting in the streets. Similar types of protests and peaceful demonstrations were often initiated throughout the cities and provinces in Afghanistan. However, many of them ended with government officials hurting individuals and killing protestors. In general, most of the Communists' (government and Russian army) attacks on the Freedom Fighters were in forms of bombardments, launching offensive missiles, subversive activities, assassination of influential figures, propaganda, and other such activities. However, the protest in Darrulamon was not initiated by the Freedom Fighters, but rather by the general public who showed their dislike in the form of a protest. It was unfortunate killings like these, in addition to the bombings, that took about two million lives in Afghanistan. This chaos also forced about six million people to become immigrants in Pakistan, Iran, China, and other countries in the Western world.

Finally, during February 15th of 1989, Russian soldiers departed and left Afghanistan because of the closure to the Cold War and their economic, psychological, and political defeat in Afghanistan. Of course, Najibullah has been credited for influencing the departure of Russians from Afghanistan, since he wanted the country to be independent and free of foreign influence. On the other side, extending the "Russian's" ten-year stay in Afghanistan would have meant sending more money and soldiers to deal with the situation, because they were not doing very well protecting the communist government. This departure should have been accompanied by a nascent spirit of hopefulness and enthusiasm among the Afghan people. Instead, the Russian departure exacerbated the war in Afghanistan and this was the beginning of the civil war. At this time, former Freedom Fighters unified alliances and designed their strategy to overthrow the communist government led by President Najibullah and initiate the building of an Islamic led government in Afghanistan. On April 28th of 1992, the Mujahideen forces (otherwise known as Freedom Fighters) achieved power, which ended the 14 year Soviet-backed regimes. Initially, Pir Sibghatullah Mojaddedi was appointed as the Interim Leader and President by the various factional leaders until elections were to take place in a democratic environment. Pir Mojaddedi served for several months and helped with the peaceful transition of the newly elected President. In June 28th 1992, Professor Burhanuddin Rabbani, leader of Jami'at Islami, was selected by the Mujahideen alliance group, as the new President of Islamic Afghanistan. The Islamic Afghanistan continued to function under various group leaders for the next four years, although they still did supposedly have some internal conflicts and war time animosity among various factions.

Eventually, a new faction called Taliban, the insurgent Islamic fundamentalists, controlled parts of Afghanistan in 1995, and in September 27th of 1996 they forced Burhanuddin Rabbani and his forces out of Kabul. Some writers wrote that their extreme style of leadership had brought many negative emotions and consequences and had taken many lives in Afghanistan. Therefore, then, the government in Kabul was being controlled by the Taliban, led by Maulana

Mohammad Omar, a one-eyed former cleric, who was also known as the commander of the faithful.

In late 2001, after the terrorist attacks on the Twin Towers in New York on September 11, the so called Northern Alliance group (made up of all seven freedom fighting factions from the 1980s) with air power assistance from the United States was able to overthrow the Taliban. Professor Rabbani, once again, was the leader until the Interim Government was put in place under the leadership of Hamid Karzai and other leaders from various factions. The first democratic election held in October 2004 was a major success in Afghanistan, as nearly 85% of the registered voters made their voices heard as majority selected Hamid Karzai for President.

THE RUSSIAN INVASION

Alexander the Great once said that "One can occupy Afghanistan, but one cannot vanquish her." In the Hollywood blockbuster movie titled "Alexander," which came out in December of 2004, one actor asks Alexander the Great "why have not the Macedonians ruled Persians since they are an inferior race?" His answer was that it is not that easy and men have gone to those lands and they just disappeared. History has certainly proved that Alexander the Great was right, despite the fact that twenty-first century's war technology has left much destruction in this great land. During the night of the December 24th of 1979, the planes started landing, and the fighting began as the electric power plants throughout Kabul were destroyed and the city went dark. We were not sure of what it was, but we suspected another coup and our suspicions were confirmed the next day, as Babrak Karmel was announced as the new President by the radio. Throughout the night the planes kept landing in Kabul's airport and we were thinking that they were probably making rounds to protect the city. The fact was that the planes were bringing Russian soldiers and troops to Kabul. The invasion was news to many people in Afghanistan, including the military personnel. The author's uncle, Ghulam Yahia, who was a Colonel in Jalalabad Province during the invasion, said that their troops were ready to move into Kabul and fight the invaders once they heard that the Russian soldiers had come in. He said that top officials debated their trip for over two days, and were eventually told that the Russians had been invited by the government as a sign of strengthening their friendship between the two countries, and that they would be here only temporarily. In the mean time, the Parchamis, Karmel's party members, had arrested many of the top officials. After a few months my uncle retired from the military at the young age of 37, because he did not like the regime and where they were headed.

When the Russians invaded Afghanistan in 1979, I (the author) was in seventh grade, and for most people it was a period that did not promise future growth, development and freedom. There were others that thought the Russians were going to help Afghanistan become better than it had ever been by introducing new technology, jobs, and industry. One of my teachers, Mr. Iqball Khan, said that the Russians will give Afghanistan the credit it deserves in the world by building it and helping it to be one of the industrialized countries in the world. The Parcham members told us that there will be better schools, universities, and equal opportunities for all people regardless of ethnicity and financial status. It all sounded good, but nothing good really happened, and many people lost their lives thinking that making Afghanistan better through communism was practical and the true goal of the former Soviet Union. Soviets had many Muslim and Persian-speaking soldiers in Afghanistan at the beginning. These soldiers could communicate and understand the Afghani culture to some extent. I had met many individuals from Dushanbe of Tadjikistan which was located only about one-hundred miles north of Afghanistan. Many of them had been conscripted into the army and had no other choices but to obey orders. According to Jan Goodwin (1985), two of the soldiers who had defected and went with the Freedom Fighters were Nikolai Balabanov and Garek Dzhanalberkov. During an interview with Jan Goodwin in 1985, they mentioned some of their horrible experiences during their service in Afghanistan. They had defected because they were not happy with what they were seeing and how they got treated by their superiors. They were living in bad conditions and their canned food at times had been ten years out of date. They said that they had seen two captured Afghan Freedom Fighters as their testicles had been cut off by the top officers, and then were tied to dynamite and blown up. During a visit to the city of Rabatak, their officers had ordered them to run over the houses that were built from mud with the tanks and get inside the village. They said, that we rolled over them and buried people alive as they were screaming. Then, they had caught thirteen people who "appeared" to be Freedom Fighters, and one of them was blown up with dynamite as the rest watched. The other twelve people were tied and forced to lie down as they drove a tank over them. They witnessed this horrible situation and could not stand it, so they defected.

Soon after, the situation in Kabul became even worse, and my father (Ghulam Mujtaba) left for Pakistan with five other University Professors and friends during 1980. They stayed in Pakistan to assist the Freedom Fighters in the refugee camps. They helped educate refugees and the international community through appropriate publications, on behalf of the Freedom Fighters, to receive more global assistance. That year was an appropriate time for these University professors to leave, because everyday there would be fighting going on in the city of Kabul where I was attending Allowdin Elementary School and then Habibia High School. The high school was one of the largest and best schools in the world, and I had always looked forward to studying there. However, the education quality was below standard at this time because most days the students were on strike and there was no education. Furthermore, teachers either did not care or they were told not to fail anyone. I remember one day when we were on strike, and the army came and the students were being pushed into a corner of the hallway while getting hit by machine guns and knives. The doors and windows were all locked, and one of the students tried to break the thick wall-size glass window by running into it. He broke it, and the glass fell on him and few others, blood was everywhere, and several students' hands got caught under some big pieces of glass. Others tried to help these injured students and got them out, however nobody was able to escape the school boundaries because the army was everywhere. Everyone was forced back into class, and some students ended up in jail, and got beat up for being against the government, being on strike, and participating in the demonstrations. Many students from colleges, high schools, and even elementary schools used to leave their classes and "march" on the streets to voice their discontent with the government and the Russian invasion. One time, there were over twenty-thousand students marching in the streets of Kabul when the

Communists brought their tanks and started shooting at everyone. Thousands of students were arrested and dozens got killed during the walkouts. There were many moments like that during my ninth, tenth, and eleventh year of high school, and that is why the teachers were not really failing anyone, even if they did really bad on their exams. The teachers were also ordered by the government not to fail anyone because the government needed soldiers, and these students were all going to have to go to the army after graduating from high school. Students could not go to college and their only option was to go to the army first. The army duty was originally one year for all high school graduates, but because of the shortage of soldiers it became unlimited during that time; however, after one year of service, if they were still alive, the soldiers got high salaries but did not have the option to leave the army. The government policies and rules kept changing as fast as the need for more soldiers kept rising and often it seemed to be amorphous. It seemed like everything was working against the growing population of students, and the world was ignoring their needs since many countries were focused on bringing the cold war to a closure by defeating the former Soviet Union in Afghanistan. As they say, "In a fight between you and the world, bet on the world" (Franz Kafka). The world won the "cold war" using this beautiful country as their "playground" or battleground and not, to mention, at a huge expense to the people of Afghanistan. Consequently, one can say that the world owes Afghans much assistance in the rebuilding process.

All students received identification cards (IDs), and had to carry their student cards for the first time in the history of Afghanistan. These IDs had the students' pictures, and if you did not have it with you and the soldiers stopped you, then they would take you to the army. The informal rule was that if you appeared to be between the age of fifteen and about forty five years, then the soldiers would stop you and ask for your identification card (if you did not have it with you, you would have to go to the army at that moment). Those who had recently served their duties were able to do whatever they chose, but they still needed their IDs which stated they were free of their duties. One morning someone was knocking on our door of the house in Darulaman, Kabul, and when I opened the door, there were soldiers and the whole area around the house was surrounded. There were three jeeps and two military trucks parked at the front of our house. The soldiers marched into the house claiming that they wanted to search for weapons and so on. I thought it was a general search of the whole neighborhood, but later found that it was not and our house was specifically targeted. They searched each room, and they dug the floors under the carpets in search of finding *shaab-naumas* ("night letters" often secretly used for propaganda against the government), weapons, bombs, documents, and names of Freedom Fighters fighting against the ruling government. They searched through all papers and books in the house. They broke different parts of the floor in different rooms and opened several pillows hoping to find antigovernment material. They took our knife and hunting gun with them, but did not find anything they were expecting. While they were leaving, the soldier called me to the Jeep where my uncle, Faqir, who was 20 years of age at that time, gave me his books and said he will be back. They had picked him up from the college as soon as he got there at 7:30 a.m. and they were at our house (with my uncle being in the back of their car) at about 8:30 a.m. We started panicking trying to find out why they had him handcuffed and where they were taking him. But, nobody was telling us anything and my uncle said he was going to be back pretty soon and not to worry about him right now. My youngest uncle, Farooq, volunteered to go with him but Faqir insisted that he would be back and there is no need for anyone to go with him. My oldest uncle who had retired from the military came home and found out what had happened. Then we started looking for Faqir in all the city jails and other places where he might have been held for interrogation. Yet we had no luck and we concluded that they were holding him because my Dad had escaped to Pakistan, which nobody was supposed to know. We had told everyone that my Dad said he was going to another province for a temporary assignment and has not returned yet, and we have not heard from him. According to the perception of our neighbors and friends, my Dad was lost and nobody knew where he was. This story was not uncommon, since many people were lost because they were either executed or imprisoned by the government, or killed by the Freedom Fighters.

About two weeks later, we were told by the government officials that Faqir was being held in an undisclosed location because he was caught with many documents that proved his activities against the government. Unofficially, we were told that he was being held by the secret police at KHAD headquarters in Sadarat, located in Kabul. About forty days later, we were told that he was being held in the Pull-e-Cherkhee jail, which was about an hour driving distance away from our home. Pull-e-Cherkhee was built during Dauod's presidency to house about five thousand prisoners. At this time in 1981, it supposedly held between 40,000 to 80,000 individuals. According to Faqir, a small cell that was made for 12 people was full of 50 to 60 prisoners. They did not have room to even walk around freely. We were allowed to take some change of clothes for him in the jail, but were not allowed to see him or talk with him. Every other Friday morning we would get to the jail about four o'clock in the morning, and two hours later I would see over six thousand people trying to exchange clothes, or trying to find out if their lost friends and relatives were in jail or at least alive. The situation was bad, and many people were lost, but their friends and family had hope for them to be alive. During the first two years of the communist regime, there were unofficial reports that about 30 thousand people had been executed in Pull-e-Cherkhee. Credible individuals like Haji Shir John, currently living in Florida, confirms some of these atrocities as he was there in Pull-e-Cherkhee and heard or observed some of the steps and actions leading to such events. There were many rumors of "carpet killings" where individuals had been thrown into a large ditch alive while the tractors buried them under soil. Most of these people were highly intelligent and well-educated Afghan scholars that were a threat to the government because of their personal power and influence among the people. One of these individuals was Saed Mir Ahmad Shah (Khan), and was given the title of *Firqa Meshir,* meaning chief of the army or general. We were neighbors, and Saed Mir Ahmad Shaw Khan's sons were named Mustafa, Muzafar, Saed Hasan, and Saed Rasul. Saed Hasan and I were classmates and best friends. I have not seen nor heard from them since 1983, but from what I understand Saed Hasan and some members of his family are living in Germany, but I have not been able to locate them yet. His father (*Firqa Meshir* Ahmad Shah) was one of the two highest ranking military personnel in Afghanistan, and he supposedly had the kind of influence equal to that of General Norman Schwarzkopf's from the United States during Desert Storm.

Firqa Meshir Ahmad Shah, imprisoned during Dauod's presidency, perished just about when the Communist government came in power, and he was put in Pull-e-Cherkhee, where nobody ever heard or saw him again. Another of his colleagues who disappeared was named *Firqa Meshir* Shawpoor Ahmadzai, who was from Surkhaab of Logar Province. They were both well respected individuals who had earned high ranks in the army and with the people of Afghanistan. According to some of the political prisoners, the Communists had executed both of them during the beginning of their regime. Since I personally knew *Firqa Meshir* Ahmad Shah, I can certainly say that he was a very intelligent, kind, influential, and an exemplary person. His wife, who was equally kind and intelligent, Saieda Jaan, was a teacher in Allowdin Elementary school, who taught many of our classes during second and third grades.

Finally, after registration with the prison guards and waiting in line for about four hours in Pull-e-Charkhie, our turn came, and the soldiers took the four pairs of clothes and some fruits, which were allowed to be sent to the prisoners. Then, we waited for the soldiers to return. About three o'clock in the afternoon, the soldiers who took the clothes came back and brought a receipt from my uncle that stated "I am fine and I received the clothes...Say hello to...all family members." So, for about forty days, my uncle Faqir lived on one pair of clothes which he was wearing to school. He had been beaten, electrocuted, confined into dark and wet rooms for long periods of time, and aggravated both physically and psychologically. Some prisoners had their clothes taken away from them leaving them naked and embarrassed (perhaps very similar to what prisoners experienced in Guantanamo Bay and what the Iraqi prisoners experienced at the Abu Graib and other areas in the last four years). Faqir said some prisoners had these permanent scars because they had been forced to stand in some type of water that burned their feet. There have been many individuals who have personally confirmed such abuses and atrocities including my uncle and Haji Shir John who currently lives in Fort Lauderdale, Florida. Haji Shir John was also jailed for several years and he says that he was one of the lucky ones as he too was scheduled to have been executed. Many of these eye-witnesses say that some prisoners had received electric shock treatments in their tongues, necks, legs, hands, and in some cases even their genitals. There were many prisoners who could not even control their bodily functions because of the electric shock treatments to their private parts and their back muscles. There were prisoners who could not talk because their tongues had been connected to electricity during interrogations. Sometimes there had been parts of other prisoners' bodies and blood in the interrogation rooms to scare people. According to Faqir, you could not help but to get chills after seeing the horrible conditions and treatment of the prisoners. Some people had suffered heart arrhythmia during these electric shocks, while others died and were never heard from again. People could not watch television, listen to the radio, or even exercise because there was no room. He said some of the rooms were designed for about twenty people, but sometimes there were about 150 people forced to live there. Faqir said one time the United Nations' representatives came to visit and all political prisoners were carried to one side of the building away from the criminal prisoners. These representatives were shown the cells which had been cleaned and arranged neatly for their visit. These cells belonged to the criminal prisoners and few of the top

Communist prisoners of other factions who could not survive with the anti-Communist prisoners in the same cells.

Five months later, after much punishment and beatings, Faqir was sentenced to two years in jail because "supposedly" his name had turned up on a list of Freedom Fighters. Prisoners could not have lawyers representing them, so everything was decided by the communist leaders, Khad members and military personnel who interrogated the victims. The decisions were not made public so people had to live with sentences they were given. Faqir had argued that it was not his name and it could be some other person named Faqir, or someone else must have been using his name. About one year later, we were able to visit with him in jail for about thirty minutes while a soldier was sitting around the table monitoring our talks. During the beginning of the Communist government, many influential Islamic activists and leaders were captured and executed. However, some people with connection to the top officials in government, and those who had money to payoff specific officials were able to track their prisoners and get them out alive through bribery, hostages, and/or pure pressure. Lohbeck (1993) writes about how Abdul Haq, a charismatic leader, and Din Mohammad's brother, had been ordered to be executed; however, his family members were able to arrange his release by bribing government officials with large amounts of money. Eventually, Abdul Haq was executed in late 2001 by Taliban soldiers as he was supposedly attempting to peacefully negotiate or make a deal with them to handover Osama Bin Laden to the United States, since Al-Qaida members were suspected of having been involved in the 2001 bombing of the Twin Towers in New York. According to Faqir and many other political prisoners such as Haji Shir John, whom I have visited and spoken with several times this year, many brave Freedom Fighters were executed by the Communist government and did not have the opportunity to even see their family members. So, unfortunately torturing and killing seem to be prevalent on all sides when one is involved in a war, and, of course, many innocent individuals pay the price.

While Faqir was serving his time in jail, I was attending school, and every other Friday I took him clothes in jail and got a receipt which was proof that he was still alive. At this time I was in tenth grade and during the winter vacation, I went to my cousins' and grandparent's house in Khoshie, which is about a three hour drive, to visit with everyone. I was a little scared because many bombings had happened near there in the past. A few days prior to one of my visits to Khoshie, the Russian army had come to the village, and the Freedom Fighters had to run away into the mountains, because there were only seven of them and over 1,000 Russian soldiers equipped with tanks, trucks, bombs, and helicopters. I can still picture my two young cousins, eighteen and twenty years of age, as they were supposedly running with no preparation in the cold snow toward the mountain because they would not want to cause a war within the village and/or get caught and killed by the Russians. Furthermore, I remember hearing that everyone was running away from the house into the gardens where people were escaping from their homes into the fields so the bombing of the houses did not trap them underneath walls. Six hours later, the fighting and bombing were over as the Russians left and people started going back to their homes. My grandparents had patched our dog's injured leg, because the Russians shot him three times in his back left leg since he was barking. He too was scared of hearing the bullets being fired, bombs dropping, and the Russian soldiers entering houses unannounced to search for weapons and Freedom Fighters. Again, imagine how scary it is for the dog and the kind of life he was going to lead with only three legs. After patching the dog's leg and putting a bandage around it, my grandfather said that many men had left trying to look for the seven Freedom Fighters who did not return home from the mountains after the Russian's departure from the village. Everyone knew which part of the mountain they were headed for, because the war (bombing and bullet exchanges) lasted several hours between the Freedom Fighters and the Russians near the top portion of the mountain.

The Freedom Fighters could not be caught or easily hurt at the top of the mountain. Even the bombing could not have affected them because they were in a safe part of the mountain as they were firing back at the enemy. It was reported that over 87 Russian soldiers had died, and many more were injured, and they carried the bodies back with them. The villagers finally got to the top of the mountain and supposedly discovered four bodies with no gun wounds or physical harm. However, they were all dead. The bodies of the four Freedom Fighters, including my cousin, were discovered on top of the mountain holding their guns at a firing position as they were supposedly killed by some form of a chemical gas. It appeared as though their bodies had been frozen in time. Several animals and hunting dogs were found dead in the area as well. As the reality and thought of the destruction, which is possible by using chemical gas, hit me in my head and heart, I really became annoyed and scared of these man-made destroyers that cannot be confronted in any human way. I asked myself why the four Freedom Fighters did not stop fighting and run away to Pakistan like the other three people did, but later I found that they were not able to because they were quickly surrounded by the Russian army. I guess the Russian army suffered badly, and decided to use the inhumane way of fighting by using chemical gas as a last resort. I remember after the funeral when people commented that at least they departed this world with bravery and a good fight with the enemy, killing many Russian and communist soldiers who were helping the government. They were considered to be the winners of a war that should not have happened in the first place. Of course, since it was my vacation, I was planning to spend quality time with all my relatives which never happened. At that time, I was wondering about the winners of the war where so many people died, houses were destroyed, many people were injured, animals were killed, and many people experienced unnecessary discomfort that was much worse than most natural disasters. The idea of winning and lying dead did not make much sense to me; however, my general conclusion was that there are no winners as both sides lost, and "lost big." The value of human life cannot be compared with other lives or the destruction and elimination of other physical goods such as tanks, airplanes, and so on. Even though I was as "healthy as a horse" and alive, I still considered myself a loser because I lost the opportunity of spending time with the people I knew as a young boy. While this story was true and took place every day in some part of Afghanistan during the invasion, the people of Sudan, Chechnya, Palestine, Israel, and Iraq have been experiencing similar devastations and violence in the past several years, because human beings are not able to settle their differences through peaceful dialogue and communication. For example, on November 8, 2006, the Israeli soldiers "terrorized" a village of innocent Palestinians in the Gaza Strip as their artilleries hit several homes instantly killing twenty people, fourteen of them were from the same family and eight were children. Of course, many more innocent people were injured as well. One must understand that it is the Israeli soldiers' (as well as other state-sponsored armed forces') formal duty, responsibility and obligation to protect their citizens from being harmed, and in this process of protecting their people, some of their actions are causing more damage and destruction in the long-term than the benefits. Israeli soldiers are not the only groups of state-sponsored forces that have been accused of harming innocent people as armies from Pakistan, Russia and the United States, among others, have also been accused of such accidental and deliberate actions in Afghanistan, Iraq, and other places around the globe. Whether such events or "terrorizing" of innocent individuals are deliberate, state-sponsored strategies or mistakes taking place through the actions of incompetent soldiers and leaders, the "impact" will be the same; consequently, they lead to animosity, hatred, extremism, and more retaliatory conflicts. For another example, let us take a look at the suicide bombing (on November 08, 2006) which killed 40 Pakistani soldiers in a town near Peshawar when their soldiers were involved in a regular training exercise. Once again, of course, many more innocent individuals were injured and scarred for life. Supposedly, this suicide bombing was a planned retaliation for the government's actions toward a group of civilians that were accused of being involved with insurgents and their village was unexpectedly attacked and partially destroyed by the Pakistani army, killing 80 males and females as well as both young and old villagers, while inuring many more.

Is violence really the best solution to settling differences and conflicts in today's diverse world? According to some military leaders' actions, be they state-designated or insurgents, from around the globe, using force and destroying innocent people's lives as collateral damage seem to be the most convenient way they know to settle differences. If this is actually their best means of settling differences and conflicts, then the world needs to get new leaders and military officers as violence tends to further legitimize and breed more of such activities and destructive thoughts for humanity. One can only guess that the leaders of the world are not open to learning from previous experiences, and they do not seem to have learned that violence and destruction are not the best ways to resolve differences. The examples of innocent individuals being "terrorized" are a sample of a few activities that are psychologically and physically harming and intimidating people around the globe perhaps on a daily, weekly, monthly, or yearly basis. What is a fact is that perhaps many more such severe and deliberate immoral acts are happening in various places around the globe, either by covert or overt state-sponsored activities or insurgent groups. What is also a known fact is that the insurgency cannot be totally prevented by force and state-sponsored terrorism or destruction of families or people groups. The insurgencies, be they in Afghanistan, Iraq, Palestine or Israel, can be analogous to teenagers who are in their rebellion stage and revolt against their parents' advice. Unfortunately, we have all seen how some parents tend to force their young boys (or girls) by physically scaring or slapping them in the face or hurting them to obey the parents' rules in the house. Of course, this is a period when the boys (or girls) are physically small and they might obey the parents simply because they do not have many other realistic options. What such parents do not recognize or realize is the long-term effects of such conditioning on the children as these young boys and girls will focus all their time on finding different means of "rebelling" against their parents and perhaps society in general. Eventually, they will be successful; and, thus at times, they will be causing harm to themselves and/or others. Furthermore, these young boys and girls will eventually grow up to be big boys and girls. In other words, a parent may not be able to physically scare, slap, or punish a 15-year old boy or girl who is now taller and bigger than the parent. What happens when they are eighteen or twenty years of age? It would be very difficult to slap a twenty-year old man or woman, would it not? One must remember that the twenty-year old can hit back hard and it will hurt. So, what works in cases of rebellion and insurgency is patience, collaboration, cooperation, and long-term care, not force and "my way or the highway" mentality. The same principles apply to insurgents in the political arena as well. Even with just cause and evidence, killing human beings or hurting them does not make the government or armed forces any better than the insurgents. Therefore, government agents and state-sponsored armed forces must be the "bigger" of the two by exercising patience and considering the long-term vision of eliminating violence instead of further legitimizing, breeding, or "feeding" it through force, intimidation and retaliations. We know that force, intimidation and retaliation do not work very well in the long-term as other alternatives in dealing with insurgents, so why not try real cooperation and collaboration to settle differences and reach a win-win outcome. The four Cs of cooperation, collaboration, commitment (to a common goal), and communication can be an important tool for negotiations in such processes.

Now, let us get back to the Russian invasion of Afghanistan. During the early summer of eleventh grade (1983), my mother, brother, and sisters decided to visit my other grandmother and my aunts for one week. They also lived in Logar, but in a different village called Rahm-Abaud (otherwise known as Zulm-Abaud), which is less than two hours away from Kabul. My uncle, Hammidullah had brought a letter from my Dad, who had moved from Pakistan to the United States, and he had asked us to move to Pakistan whenever we felt the time was appropriate. After two days and two nights of visiting my relatives, we were awakened at six o'clock in the morning by the airplanes and helicopters bombing and shooting down on everything they saw on the village next to my grandmother's house. Everyone was running away from the village as the helicopters were shooting down on us while bombing the next village. We stayed under the trees in the fields for about one hour until the bombing was over. We went to the bombed village to help them out, and saw their walls, houses, and gardens being shattered into pieces. The explosions of the huge and heavy, one-thousand pound bombs, had created some enormously huge holes in the ground. Mostly everyone had the opportunity to get out of their houses with the exception of few older people and children. Three people had died as the roofs and walls fell on them, and we were able to pull two people out alive, but injured, from under the broken houses. Next to the stream there appeared to be a bomb that had not gone off. As everyone gathered for a closer look, the adults came and told us to get away from it. Often, some of the bombs did not go off, and in some cases the pilots, intentionally, would not pull or turn off the safety latches before dropping them. After close examination, the Freedom Fighters discovered that it was not a bomb, but it was a large cow that had got blown away from the barn into the stream by the bombs. It was sad and very disappointing because many innocent people and animals died or became injured for no good reason. During the actual bombing, there were no

Freedom Fighters present in that village. Usually, the bombings killed many women, children, and elders who did not fight and could not get away from the houses fast enough. That day we came back to Kabul, and were very happy to have been alive. However, the situation in Kabul was not very safe either, but there were no bombings going on. Most fighting and Freedom Fighter attacks took place during nights and they lasted for only a brief period because the fighters would back away and spread out. About two months later in the summer of 1983, my uncle got out of jail three months early, for good behavior, because Karmel's government was attempting to "demonstrate" or show to the people that they were releasing prisoners. After Faqir's release from prison, we immediately (that night) started planning to move to Pakistan.

REASONS FOR THE INVASION

When the Soviets invaded Afghanistan in 1979, they also had troops present in many other nations such as East Germany, Hungary, Poland, and Czechoslovakia. So, their resources were scattered thin even as one of the superpowers of the world. As a matter-of-fact, the Russians had gone to Czechoslovakia eleven years before going to Afghanistan. The same general in charge of planning the invasion in Czechoslovakia eleven years earlier, Ivan Pavlovsky, was given the responsibility to mastermind Afghanistan's invasion as well. According to the Russian soldier, Vladislav Tamarov (1992), going to Afghanistan was not anything unusual, and being in one more country or one less country supposedly did not make much of a difference in their eyes. Perhaps this was also the mindset and thinking by some politicians in the United States in 2002 and 2003 as they consciously chose to occupy Iraq when they were still trying to assist the Afghan government rebuild Afghanistan. Consequently, the rebuilding process in Afghanistan was partially abandoned or, in some cases, totally ignored, and Iraq became another Vietnam for the U.S. Armed Forces. The 2006 issue of Time Inc. mentions that in the years since the Taliban were toppled, as the U.S. focused on its intervention in Iraq, Taliban fighters have emerged from the mountains to stage ambushes and challenge the nation's new administration. As of the fall of 2006, more than 300 American soldiers have died fighting in Afghanistan (Time Inc., 2006, p. 109).

For the Russians in the 1980s, it was not until the bodies of young Soviet soldiers kept going back to Russia in coffins that government officials thought this was one of their mistakes. The top Russian officials were not necessarily concerned about how many Afghans died, but they were concerned about their own soldiers and supplies. Tamarov wrote that many people from both sides got killed in massacres, "the massacres which we (*Russian soldiers*) defended their revolution from them, while they defended their land from us." The Russian soldiers did not get much training or education prior to coming into Afghanistan. After speaking with many of them in Kabul, I found out that not all Russian soldiers had graduated from school and many of them had dropped out of school. Besides being dropouts from high school, many of them were not well trained, and such levels of incompetency lead to many mistakes in a new culture, thereby unintentionally creating many unwanted enemies. Such levels of incompetency were not limited to the Russian soldiers, since many American soldiers in Iraq and Afghanistan have also made costly mistakes in the past few years, either because they are young and afraid or simply due to the fact that they are incompetent or not trained well. Some of the Russians were also afraid of being drafted into the army, and many did not want to volunteer to join the army. I had met some soldiers who had been conscripted into the army, and after four or five months were sent to Afghanistan. I was surprised to see how young these Russian soldiers were; most of them about 18 to 19 years of age in 1979, while I was about 13 years of age. Most of the Russian soldiers preferred to drink alcoholic beverages and they were given vodka to keep them happy. However, many of them bartered with the Afghans by substituting their weapons for Hashish and other available drugs. Because of the stress of having no control and not knowing why they were in Afghanistan, over sixty percent of them had resorted to drug abuse, which was a big downfall for them. The soldiers were not getting paid very much, and they had resorted to stealing jewelry, stereos, and even clothing from houses. In general, most of the soldiers just wanted to spend their two years and get back home alive. I do not blame them, because they were not in our country because of their own will, but rather they were fighting because a system of bad government and wrong decisions by incompetent or selfish leaders had forced them into it.

The 40th Army and the 103rd Airborne Division from the former USSR were sent to Afghanistan, perhaps, for many different, yet unclear, reasons. According to the Russians, they were invited by the Afghan leaders to help bring security and peace into the country. Brezhnev wrote, in a response to President Carter's request, that the Soviet Union had been invited into the country of Afghanistan, and they were performing their international duty of helping a neighbor (Lohbeck, 1993). However, the former Russian soldier and journalist, Borovik (1990), wrote that Babrak Karmal did not admit to inviting the Russians because, according to Karmal, he did not have the authority to issue the invitation. In other words, they were "proactive" and invited themselves to this foreign land as if it was their own. Brezhnev, perhaps, wanted to leave his legacy as the ruler who expanded Communism and the Soviet's territory or influence a little farther as previously planned by former Communists. The idea of making Afghanistan part of the Soviet territory must have sounded pretty good to the communist leaders, but they did not think about not being able to "swallow it" easily. The Russians also used Afghanistan as a testing site for their ground ammunition, air artillery, and chemical warfare. Of course, the American Army is also accused of being involved in similar experimentations both in Afghanistan and Iraq in the last four years. Such experimentations at a cost to the local culture and people must be abolished if we are to win the hearts and minds of individuals toward democracy around the world.

Some people argue that the decision to invade Afghanistan was because of the old Communist leadership, which included people like Brezhnev who did not want to change and was fearful of change. People claim that if Mikhail Gorbachev had been in power during the decision-making process, the Soviets would not have gone to Afghanistan. However, they did invade, and according to Vladislav Tamarov (1992), who served in the Soviet army in Afghanistan, Soviet troops went to Afghanistan for three reasons. The first and official reason was to satisfy the request of the Communist government. Second, Afghanistan is Soviet Union's southern neighbor, and putting soldiers there could assure security of Russia's southern borders. This was mostly told to the new soldiers entering Afghanistan. However, the main reason may have been to gain access to the Persian Gulf and the Indian Ocean. Third, the Soviet's smugglers needed drugs, gold, and precious stones, which were plentiful in Afghanistan. Tamarov mentions cases where zinc coffins were sent to the USSR filled with narcotics rather than dead bodies. Afghanistan also is a country that is full of untapped natural resources like emeralds, silver, gold, copper, rubies, diamonds, iron, natural gas, oil, uranium, coal, and many other such valuables that make it very attractive to outside nations. Afghanistan, itself, has not had the resources to take advantage of its natural resources; however, with advanced technology and research it can be turned into a major source of oil and natural gas. According to Jan Goodwin, Afghanistan's oil resources have been calculated to be equal to Iraq's, which ranked as the fifth largest oil deposit in the world. The existence of these natural resources had been tested and confirmed by many international geologists and researchers prior to the Russian invasion (Goodwin, 1987).

The reasons for the Russian invasion of Afghanistan perhaps vary from what has been mentioned publicly and may never become totally clear. Since, Afghanistan's location, in the heart of Asia, provides easy access to many other nations, it makes it very attractive for takeover by the superpowers. It is a country that has potential for many natural resources because the rocks and mountains have not been touched. Afghanistan has oil and gas which were among some of the first things being transferred into the Soviet Union during the invasion. Whatever the reasons were, the destruction will be felt for many years to come. One of the Russians soldiers, Tamarov, wrote that he found a TS-6.1 mine near some homes and then he found some flour near the houses and they destroyed the mine along with the barns, flour and the houses. He writes that they did not know why they did this, but for them it did not matter because they were in an alien nation and they did not know why they were there anyway. Afghans were fighting in a civil war, and the Russian soldiers were somewhat confused about their role in a country that did not want or appreciate their presence. One thing is clear about the Russians in Afghanistan, and that is their usage and testing of different arms, chemicals, and other military equipment. They also took advantage of the natural fruits such as oranges and lemons as they were being exported directly to Russia. The Soviet researchers had helped Afghans build orange farms in the Jalalabad area, and in return for their consultancy they were exporting the fruits to their country for at least ten years. It was rumored that most of what they had done for Afghanistan prior to their invasion had cost Afghanistan more than necessary. In some cases, their bills to the Afghans were supposedly two to three times higher than the actual cost. Perhaps their economic and military help always came with certain hidden costs as "there is no free lunch."

REFLECTIVE QUESTIONS FOR CRITICAL THINKING

1. Who are some of the influential leaders in Afghanistan? How have they impacted the behavior of people?
2. Describe Afghanistan before King Zahir Shaw became the ruler for 40 years.
3. What lead to the invasion of Afghanistan by the Russians?
4. What are some of the common mistakes that government officials and local leaders have made in Afghanistan during the past 40 years that lead to more

      conflict and suffering on individuals living at various cities within the country?

5. What are some common mistakes that the communist government leaders made before the Russians invaded?

6. What are some of the common mistakes that government officials made after the fall of communist government in Afghanistan?

7. What are some of the common mistakes that Taliban made while ruling Afghanistan?

8. Describe the history of political situation in Afghanistan in the past four centuries, and see if you can notice and discuss any patterns.

9. Compare and contrast the elements of the New Constitution created in 2003 by the leaders of the Interim Government with the original Constitution which was created in 1964.

10. Describe the benefits of Afghanistan's interdependent relationships with other countries and provide specific examples.

CHAPTER 3

FREEDOM FIGHTERS AND THE INVASION

The very name Pukhtun spells honor and glory,
Lacking that honor, what is the Afghan story?
(*Khushal Khan Khatak*)

Many people around the world did not think that Afghans would be able to survive for very long against a superpower, the former Soviet Union and the Red Army. The senior spokesperson for the State Department, Robert Peck, had said that the Afghans can never defeat the Red Army, and their only hope is a compromise for a diplomatic achievement. Of course, a diplomatic solution would have been the best solution for all parties. Seeing the power of the Red Army and its technological advancements perhaps made some people pessimists toward the victory of the Freedom Fighters. However, with the help of a strong faith and the Afghan people's determination, the Russians failed to accomplish their mission successfully in Afghanistan. Kaplan (1990) wrote:

> The Afghan Mujahidin, numbering over 10,000 were the first group of insurgents to drive out a Russian army since Czar Peter the Great began his empire's southward expansion three hundred years ago. The Mujahidin were attacked with more firepower than any Moslem group in the Middle East could imagine, yet almost never did they resort to terrorism.

While some international hostage situations have been successful strategies for terrorists and thieves, the Afghan Freedom Fighters did not want to put civilians in danger to deal with the Communist officials. As past hostage situations have shown, there can be many civilian deaths which may be inevitable in such circumstances. Similarly, while some militant groups in other parts of the world, supposedly, resort to bus bombings, bombings of public buildings, and other types of terrorist activities, Afghan Freedom Fighters were clear about protecting the innocent and directing their attacks during times when civilians were least likely to get hurt. This mentality, of course, put many limitations on their operation and sometimes avoidance of attacking certain Communist garrisons because of civilians living in the nearby villages. The Freedom Fighters had a policy of not hurting civilians when possible and, thus, stayed away from the practice of hostage taking which has often been used in the international arena (as demonstrated in Table 2).

While the Freedom Fighters were limiting their attacks only to Communist officials, and not necessarily their children or families, the Russians had a different perspective. Their perspective was to kill the whole village, if necessary, and scare the "living daylights" out of everyone. The Russians probably had the power and technology to bomb the whole country and kill every living thing while shattering some mountains into pieces. However, that destruction would have been a cost that even the Soviet Communists could not afford, and would not look very attractive to the rest of the world. However, killing almost every Afghan, which they nearly did, might have been their only chance of being successful in the invasion of Afghanistan. The people of Afghanistan were committed to losing their lives one by one in order to avenge their liberty and freedom. Some Afghans had lost part, or in few cases, all of their family members and had nothing to live for but to take revenge.

Table 2- International Hostage Situations

LOCATION	DATE	# HOSTAGES	DEATHS
Vienna, Austria, conference of OPEC	12-1975	70	3
Damascus, Syria, hotel	09-1976	90	4
Managua, Nicaragua, Congress	08-1978	400	14
U. S. Embassy, Tehran, Iran	11-1979	52	0
Mecca, Saudi Arabia	11-1979	300+	300
Dominican Embassy in Bogota, Colombia	02-1980	56	0
Justice building, Bogota, Colombia	11-1985	450	115
Achille Lauro cruise ship in the Mediterranean	10-1985	450	1
Hospital in Chechnya - Russian town of Budyonnovsk	1994	200+	100
Hospital in the Dagestani town of Kizlyar, in Chechnya	01-1996	3,000	N/A
Budennovsk hostpital in Russian Caucasus	01-1996	1500	150
LIMA, Peru-Tupac Amaru guerrillas in Japanese ambassador's house	01-1997	74	N/A
Saudi Arabia	03-2001	50+	3
Istanbul	03- 2001	120	0
Russia	07-2001	30	0
Istanbul, Turkey	05-2002	10	0
Moscow, Russia - Theatre.	10-2002	700	170
School Children and Teachers in Chechnya in 2004	09-2004	300	100+

Source: *News Reporting on Media, and Wall Street Journal, Jan. 8, 1997.*

The Afghan Freedom Fighters did their duty with vehement passion, commitment, and desire, which eventually led to the defeat of Russians. The Freedom Fighters had two choices, to win the war or to die trying and both choices were a sign of success and courage to them. What the Freedom Fighters lacked in unity, education, military discipline, and technology, they made up for in bravery, commitment to their mission, and pure hatred of being controlled by the Russians. The Afghan-Russian war will probably go down in history books along with the wars of Americans in Vietnam, Hitler in the Soviet Union as his troops were defeated in the brutally cold weather, and similarly for Napoleon in Russia. Now, let us see who these Freedom Fighters were and how they accomplished their primary mission which was to get the Russians out of Afghanistan and overthrow the communist regime.

THE FREEDOM FIGHTERS

Freedom Fighters in Afghanistan were considered to be all those individuals who were fighting, directly or indirectly, against the Russian army to protect the Afghan land and to gain liberty for the Afghan people, so they could exercise their rights however they desire. Afghans are comprised of Pukhtun, Hazara, Tajik, Baluchi, Noorestani, Hindu, and many other ethnicities. Pushtu is a language spoken by a large number of people in Afghanistan. The Pukhtuns are sometimes referred to as the Pathans who make up the largest ethnic group in Afghanistan. For Afghan people, courage and bravery are prime qualities as an Afghan song states, "better come home stained with blood, than safe and sound as a coward." Afghan *Mujahideen* (anticommunist resistance fighters) are commonly considered to be formally part of the resistance against the Russian government, who were threatening the religious beliefs and the liberty of all Afghans. The Western media has translated the term *Mujahideen* to mean those people who instigate *jihad* or "holy wars," as if a war can actually be "holy." According to Dr. Amir Ali, from the Institute of Islamic Information and Education, that term is not necessarily the correct Arabic meaning of the word *Mujahideen*. Sometimes, the two terms are used synonymously, because almost all Afghan fighters were Muslims who are considered to be Freedom Fighters since they were fighting against the Russians, who were a threat to their freedom and religious practices in Afghanistan. The word *Mujahideen* originates from the Arabic word *Jihad* which means striving or struggling to accomplish something. Afghanistan had some *Mujahideen* (Freedom Fighters) that were not Muslim. So, the word *Mujahideen* can refer to all individuals who are struggling or striving to achieve an end and not necessarily just those who were fighting with guns against Russians. Of course, the best form of jihad is to communicate and settle differences through effective dialogues and open discussions.

Robert Kaplan, journalist, wrote that he was able to see Islam objectively for the first time and concluded that "Afghanistan did not require a resurgence of faith, for the Afghans had never lost it. Unlike most other people in the east, the Afghans were psychologically sure of themselves." I most certainly agree with Kaplan that the Afghan war was more about keeping the people's freedom to exercise their religious freedom in their own land than about a resurgence of faith. Islam requires all believers to avoid eating, drinking, smoking, and sexual activities during the days of Ramadhan when fasting, with the exception of those individuals who are young, sick, fighting in a war, traveling, and women who are pregnant or lactating. Even though Islam does not require soldiers to fast during the month of Ramadan while on duty, most Freedom Fighters did so upon their own insistence.

The term "Freedom Fighters" is used here to describe all individuals that verbally, physically and nonverbally showed resistance against the communist party and the Russian forces. Kurt Lohbeck describes Afghan Freedom Fighters as "people who take the last rites of Islam before going to battle, for they are already dead and will remain so until they are killed and their souls are loosed. Or until they free their homeland." Afghans also knew that commitment and persistence had helped them defeat the British army three times and they could do this with the Russians. In 1842, the British army had about 4,500 soldiers, and only one person was able to escape Afghanistan alive. His name was William Brydon, a surgeon, who was injured by the time he got to Pakistan. Dr. Brydon retired in 1859 at age 48 and died in his native, Scotland, in 1873.

Afghans believe that when a person is fighting for justice, truth, liberty from invaders, and for the protection of the innocent, that person will be rewarded handsomely both intrinsically and in the eyes of their country. If anyone loses his/her life during this *jihad*, struggle, then she/he will become *shaheed*, martyr. Innocent Muslims who lose their lives during the crossfire's of a war are also considered to be *Shaheedawn*, martyrs. True Shaheedawn, according to religious beliefs, are guaranteed a place in paradise which is the kingdom of God. While most Afghans are considered to be Freedom Fighters, there were about two million *Shaheedawn*. In many cases, people did not have much of a choice about not taking a side. People were forced into going to the army or joining the Freedom Fighters. A Russian soldier, Vladislav Tamarov, wrote that the Afghan government had a different way of recruiting and choosing soldiers: current soldiers went into the villages and rounded up men and boys of "appropriate" age (in most cases between 15 and 45 years of age). So, most of the soldiers were in the military because they were required and forced to be there, and not necessarily because of their free will. I remember at age 16 the soldiers put me on one of their trucks because I could not find my student identification card. Luckily, I had not lost it, and it was in one of my books rather than my pocket, so I was released. Most people did not receive much military training; however, some individuals who volunteered were occasionally sent to Russia for training. Tamarov mentions Ahmad Shaw Masood, a well known Commander amongst Freedom Fighters, who had graduated from a Soviet military academy and after returning to Afghanistan, he joined the Freedom Fighters in Panjshir. Ahmad Shaw Masood, born in 1950, had also studied in France and spoke fluent French. Unfortunately, he was killed by an Arabic journalist and his cameraman, who blew themselves up during an interview with him a few days before the 9/11 attacks on the Twin Towers of New York City in the United States. These suicide bombers who killed Ahmad Shaw Masood were supposedly terrorists and/or people who were sent by the terrorists. Such incidents are not very heartwarming occasions as many of us throughout the world witnessed suicide bombers instantly change the lives of thousands of individuals when they hijacked several planes in late 2001. At 8:40 AM on September 11, 2001, I was at home in Lakeland, Florida getting ready to go to the office in Tampa. At that time, I was the Campus College Chair for the Graduate College of Business and Management in Tampa for the University of Phoenix (UofP) and usually went to work at about 9:00 AM. I was watching ABC News with Charlie Gibson and Diane Sawyer when they began showing a plane's crash into the Twin Towers of New York City. At that time they did not know what caused the first collision. It could have been an unfortunate accident or an enemy missile entering the building. Soon, it was mentioned that another plane had hit the Pentagon Building and this might be some sort of an organized attack from hijackers. While Charlie Gibson was discussing the crash, their camera was focused live on the Twin Tower buildings showing the smoke coming out of the building. As he was speaking, another plane hit the second tower which is when Charlie Gibson commented that I think another plane just hit the other tower and it might be an organized attack on New York City. After rewinding the tape, they showed it again and surely it was the second plane crash happening on live television before millions of viewers. As I saw the plane hit the building and split into pieces, my body began shivering and tears started flowing down my eyes as I was simply picturing the people inside of the plane and those inside the building. It was a sad moment, and it certainly impacted me very strongly, since the news became even more disappointing in the next few hours when the buildings totally collapsed as many were glued to the television channel. Like thousands of individuals around the world, I too had always been against violence since I lived through some terrible experiences in Afghanistan, and this occasion just made those thoughts and values even stronger. Besides impacting thousands of individuals, such tragedies impact the society economically as well. September 11, 2001 was a day that forever changed some ways in which global business is conducted. The impact is still felt today in the areas of security, transportation, and insurance coverage. There have been many new legislative acts in the United States, such as the Terrorism Risk Insurance Act and the Patriot Act of 2001, which have created new constraints producing permanent changes in international commerce.

Transitioning back to the situation in Afghanistan during the Russian invasion, some of the young men who were forced or encouraged to join the Communist army were able to get away from them, while others, unfortunately, did not have that luxury. So, many people were caught in between the two rival forces and, of course, many innocent individuals lost their families and lives, even though they did not choose to be involved with either side.

Most of the surviving Freedom Fighters were guided by different leaders in different groups but for the same purpose of eventually seeing a liberated Afghanistan. Different groups and parties were formed because their commanders had varying, and sometimes, conflicting views. For example, Kaplan (1990) said that Abdul Haq spent a few months with Jallaluddin Haqqani's group in Paktia and later separated to form his own group because he realized "how stupid some Mujahideen were." This, of course, is one person's opinion and the Freedom Fighters would have been successful regardless of Abdul Haq's contributions which were numerous around Kabul. However, Abdul Haq became an influential leader and completed many successful operations based on his perspective and experiences. Most of these leaders had a charismatic style that energized and motivated a certain number of individuals, but some lacked harmony and cooperation with other commanders who fought for the same purpose. While the decentralized decision-making systems were helpful and led to the defeat of the Communist regime, I believe cooperation and the integration of their diverse thinking and experiences would have been much more successful and beneficial. Ahmad Shaw Masood, a successful and strategic Commander, had said that making new parties, and further dividing the Freedom Fighters, would not be a good solution; and that is what he had been supporting all along which, perhaps, led to his enormous success. He was a well-respected Freedom Fighter and leader throughout Afghanistan, especially in the northern part of the country. His motto was "victory or death," which was the only option for the Freedom Fighters. He was one of the major commanders working with all the Freedom Fighters, but was formally a part of Jami'at Islami Afghanistan. Some of the large and organized groups were Harakat-e-Inqliab led by Mohammad Nabi Hohammadi; Hezbi Islami led by Hekmatyar and Khalis; Jabha-i-Nijat-Milli lead by

Sibghutullah Mojadidi; Ittehad led by Sayyaf; and Jami'at Islami Afghanistan led by Professor Rabbani. Most foreign leaders did not understand these parties, as McMahon, American Deputy Director of Operations to Afghanistan, referred to the seven parties as the "seven tribes" and called Younus Khalis the "tribal chief" (Lohbeck, 1993).

All the Freedom Fighters knew that unity would provide them a stronger force against the enemy; getting united was a different story. Agreeing about doing something and actually doing it requires different forms of courage and strategy. W. Bennett said that, "real bravery lies in deeds, not words." I read a story of how small creatures such as "mice" planned their strategy which is similar to what the Afghans were going through during the war. A cat was catching the mice by surprise and the mice were discussing how to avoid the cat. The old mouse, thought to be very wise, said, "Do as I say, hang a bell on the cat's neck and we will be able to hear it coming, then we can hide from it." All the mice agreed and they got the bell. The old mouse said now who is going to put it on the cat's neck? No one wanted to do it, and they all ran away to their holes. So, agreeing on something does not mean it can be done. Doing things as a team requires planning a strategy and agreeing on how to implement that strategy. So, the Freedom Fighters needed effective strategic planning. Strategic planning is simply determining where one is, where one wants to go, and then deciding and mapping a plan for how to get there efficiently.

When the seven-party alliance was completed, called the Islamic Unity of Afghan Mujahideen, many commanders did not agree with it because their decision-making processes had to be shared or they had to answer to someone. Many claimed that while they did the fighting in Afghanistan, people who sat in conference rooms in Peshawar made the decisions. This reasoning process, while valid and to the point, perhaps caused many killings and deaths in Afghanistan during and after the Russian invasion. Some of the commanders from the field were very strong and temperamental individuals who made decisions that were not questioned. However, making decisions, in a conference room, that affect other people who are outside one's level of influence, requires circumspection which takes time, patience, vision, intelligence, logic, and understanding. Unfortunately, most of the commanders were action-oriented because their combat success was based on actual fighting. So, the majority of these commanders would not be interested in structure, sharing, "red-tape," and authority. This fact, perhaps, is partially the cause of civil war in Afghanistan. Table 3 mentions the seven factions of the Freedom Fighters, along with some of the most influential leaders that were associated with each group during the 1980s. The Taliban, who are not mentioned as part of seven political parties, came into existence in 1995 with assistance from Pakistani officials and other outside connections despite the fact that there were many groups that worked against them. Table 3 only describes the seven major parties that fought against the Russians during the invasion since the Taliban had not officially formed during that era.

Although the overall purpose and mission of all groups were the same, there were some extremely different means of executing them and that generally brought weakness and dichotomies for the Freedom Fighters. The author has used the terms "enemy," "government army," "Russian soldiers," in this book, which refer to all Russian forces and Afghan soldiers representing the Communist government. It should be stated that not all soldiers in the government army were Communist.

People were forced to serve in the army regardless of their agreement with the government systems. Some individuals could not leave their families to become Freedom Fighters or refugees for economic, social, political, or other personal reasons; hence, they were forced to choose the option to serve in the army which represented the Communist government.

Table 3 – Freedom Fighter Factions during the Russian Invasion

Name of the party	Leaders
Jamiat-I-Islami of Afghanistan (Islamic Society)	Leader was Professor Burhanuddin Rabbani, former theologian and professor at Kabul University. Commanders Ahmed Shah Masood from Panjshir Valley and Ismael Khan from Herat were also with this party.
Ittehad Islami Afghanistan (Islamic Unity)	Leader was former university professor Abdul Rasul Sayyaf who used be together with Gulbuddin Hekmatyar. Most of his monetary support came from Arabic countries.
Hezb-I-Islami Afghanistan led by Hekmatyar (Party of Islam)	Led by Engineer Gulbuddin Hekmatyar who had many college aged supporters and was one of the dominant parties during the first years on invasion.
Hesb-I-Islami Afghanistan led by Khalis (Party of Islam)	Led by an Islamic scholar, teacher and journalist, Maulavi Younus Khalis. Some of the commanders were Abdul Haq, Jalaluddin Haqani, Abdul Qadir, and Qazi amin Wardak.
Mahaz-i-Milli Islami Afghanistan (National Islamic Front of Afghanistan)	Leader was Sayed Ahmed Gailani who is known for being strongly promonarch. Some of the Commanders are Rahim Wardak, Sharooq Gran, and Haji Abdel Latif who passed away.
Harakat-i-Inqilab-i-Islami Afghanistan (Islamic Revolutionary Forces)	Leader was Mohammad Nabi Mohammadi, clergy, who started the party before the communists became in power.
Jabha-i-Nijat-Milli (Afghan National Liberation Front)	Leader was Sibghatullah Mojadidi, professor of theology, who was a highly respected religious leader in Afghanistan and throughout Islamic Nations.

The Freedom Fighters mostly fought outside Kabul in an indirect form. Their attacks were strategically designed to eliminate or weaken the enemy and escape without any loss. Since most of their attacks were on the enemy garrisons (outposts), and they did not have transportation, they made sure they were able to get away quickly and aggressively. In general, most of the time they were putting pressure on the enemy in the form of either attacks on their outposts, ambushing convoys, and "stand-off" or commando actions against the Russian bases. Most of the Russian garrisons (outposts) included tanks, trucks, heavy and light weapons, some were supplied with helicopters, and a military crew of about 150 to 500 people that included Afghan soldiers (mostly Communist) and Russians. Some of the enemy flights were being flown straight from the Soviet Union, especially on the confrontations and bombings in the Northern parts of Afghanistan.

Uniting the fighters to aim at one common enemy was needed, especially during the beginning of war. Unfortunately, the Afghan leaders who were living in Peshawar could hardly ever meet together in a calm and friendly manner. Their meetings after a day or so would become somewhat chaotic and emotional as each leader tried to voice his opinion in a dogmatic fashion. They probably were under the assumption that the future of Afghanistan could be properly planned by one person and in a matter of just a few hours. Unfortunately, this frame of reference was too simplistic and perhaps caused the leaders to steer away from the exigency of the prospective civil war. Similarly, the Freedom Fighters in the field had guns and artillery, but all of the weapons were not aimed at the direction of the enemy simultaneously. In general, the smaller the number of parties in an area or village, then the greater will be the chances for cooperation and successfully implementing attacks. The decentralization of the Freedom Fighters in the field empowered them to make decisions situationally, which eventually lead to the defeat of communism. However, on the negative side, many mistakes happened, resources were wasted due to lack of effective synergizing and communication, and the division among parties brought about situations where people actually believed in the aphorism that "the enemy of my enemy is my friend." This type of a mind-set can be a challenging obstacle to overcome and, unfortunately, most Freedom Fighters had to deal with it on a regular basis. People were very selective about sharing known information about the enemy and the enemy's plans that could help others make better and more educated decisions. So, one of the most important tasks for the Freedom Fighters was trying to get all the different groups of Freedom Fighters to cooperate, and become coordinated while accomplishing a shared mission. Building strategic alliances between groups was a very difficult task, partially because of financial and psychological problems. This task becomes even more cumbersome when most of the fighting force is illiterate. Most of the formed alliances were not successful in the long-term because of personal biases, selfishness and disagreements. In some cases, the fighters and group leaders would want to spend more time defending and protecting their own valleys or villages as compared to other valleys that had more strategic importance in terms of military. So, such disagreements created animosity between people because the conflict was not always managed appropriately by the leaders. This lack of structure and ethnocentric thinking led to inefficiency and lack of discipline in the activities launched against the enemy. In order to eliminate this attachment of securing only one's own specific area or village, and to get everyone to fight for a common purpose, some leaders created Central Forces. Central Forces were units made-up of volunteers from different valleys, provinces, and cities who were willing to fight anywhere and at any place as decided by their leaders. Although, benchmarking was not used very widely, some programs received the attention of other groups because of the successful implementation. For example, Commander Masood from Panjshir was known for his creative militaristic strategies and transformational leadership. His plans could have been implemented in other areas with proper technology and the lack of ethnocentric thoughts; however, many obstacles stopped the proper uses of benchmarking activities.

It was the goal of unity that would drive Afghan Freedom Fighters toward national-joint-efforts and a common purpose, which was to drive the Russian Army out of Afghanistan and overthrow the communist government. The Central Forces' leaders would require all fighters to learn the idea behind strategic team fighting tactics and to become dedicated fighters with wisdom, determination, professional etiquettes, and the love of *iman* or faith. The Central Force team members were required to raise their level of knowledge and good manners by attending informal team classes on regular basis. This was the Freedom Fighters' remediation plan for the lack of general education and schooling within the population. The Task Force members were also highly encouraged to eliminate their habits of smoking cigarettes, so they could become better prepared to lead exemplary lives during the future of a liberated Afghanistan.

Table 4 - Examples of Actual Afghan-Russian Wars and Results

Location and date of the attack	Human Loss of enemy (communists)	Human loss of Freedom Fighters	Captured Products by Freedom Fighters
Rahm-Abaud , summer of 1981	Offensive surprise attack. 80 people killed and over 100 wounded.	4 people killed and several wounded	Several soldiers, over 200 light and heavy weapons.
Rahm-Abaud area in summer of 1982	None – This was offensive air attack on the village.	Three innocent villagers died while sleeping and one injured.	None- Freedom Fighter were not in the area at the time of bombing.
Khoshie in Winter of 1982	87 killed and many injured	4 people killed by the use of chemical gas.	None, This was an offensive attack by the communists.
Ferkhar on August of 1986-Leader – Ahmad Shaw Massod	113 people killed during two days of operations	Five people killed and eight were wounded	210 soldiers, 15 heavy and 213 light weapon as well as ammunition.
Nehrin on 11/11-13/ 1986.	More than 150 either killed, wounded or captured	22 people killed and 26 injured.	3 tanks, 8 heavy and 100 light weapons, and one Mi.-17 helicopter was shot down by DShKM.
Kalafgan on 7/7/87	40 people killed	three killed and 6 injured	115 soldiers, 2 heavy and 100 light weapons + ammunitions.
Keran on 10/29/87	29 killed	14 killed and 11 injured	266 soldiers, 13 heavy and 266 light weapons.
Sangcharak on 11/24/1987	00 killed	9 killed and several wounded	21 soldiers, 5 heavy and over 100 light weapons.
Pushghor on summer of 1985	More than 50	Not known	400 soldiers with their weapons.

STRATEGIC AND ENVIRONMENTAL FACTORS IN AFGHANISTAN

The large mountains (up to 20,000 feet high), hills, valleys, villages, roads, and cold weather are all factors that could hinder or help the Afghan Freedom Fighters. The Salang Tunnel which is about two miles and 10,800 feet above the sea level is an example of the large mountains. Salang Tunnel was built in 1964, and it shortened the distance between Kabul and the Northern provinces by 120 miles. The Freedom Fighters certainly did not have the technology to overcome the natural barriers of cold whether, high mountains, and dry deserts to fight more efficiently. They could not depend on the available electronically-operated technology, because most areas did not have electricity and the areas with electronic technology could not be protected from the destruction of bombs and buried in-ground mines. The Afghan ground, however, was mostly favorable for the Freedom Fighters. The mountainous valleys near flat land provided excellent opportunities for ground operations against the Russians and their army. The valleys start from heights of about 15,000 feet, which spread out for tens of miles and end in the fertile smooth and even lands. Most valleys were safe places for the Freedom Fighters and that is where most of their planning, education, and other such logistics were being taken care of with and by the leaders. Time's 2006 publication mentioned that:

> The British got their comeuppance in the mid-1800s: in 1842 a column of 16,500 retreating soldiers was reduced in seven days to a single survivor by the harrying Afghans. The Russians learned their lesson in the 1980s. Both discovered too late that the country's topography, a captivating tableau of high mountains, deep valleys and wide plains, is perfect for guerrilla warfare. Here, knowledge of the terrain is the most important weapon an army can have (Time Inc., 2006, page 57.)

Of course, unity of the Afghans across the various terrains can make it difficult for foreigners to conquer this nation. The Time (2006) article mentioned that "Only one cause seems to have ever united Afghans: resistance to foreign invaders. That instinct has deep roots in Afghan history: Alexander the Great first stumbled here, and Genghis Khan found it easier to reach accommodations with the Afghans than to conquer them." During the Russian invasion, the Freedom Fighters engaged in many different types of attacks on the enemy. Sometimes they targeted enemy outposts and garrisons by their artilleries and other heavy weapons. They also tried to plant mines on the army routes to cut their supplies and ambush their troops to cause more problems and casualties for the Communist regime. Most of the Freedom Fighters did not have official military training, but what they lacked in training and technology, they made up in commitment to their goal of revenge, and simple bravery. Most of the Freedom Fighters had suffered either a loss of property, home, parents, children, brothers, sisters, relatives or just pure liberty. Some of the Freedom Fighters had suffered bodily tortures and beatings that will be haunting them psychologically for the rest of their lives. These are some of the variables that contributed to the Freedom Fighters' vehement strife to defeat Communism.

The flat lands in Afghanistan are very fertile and the farmers produced most of their natural resources from these lands. Some of the common products are wheat, corn, potatoes, tomatoes, carrots, all of the green vegetables, and other needed natural products from the farm industry. Research has shown that the productions of food in the world grew steadily from 1961 to 1992 and at same time global food prices decreased. This was not the case for Afghanistan since during the Russian war (1979-1990), the production of natural products in farms had decreased because the farmers were not available or could not take care of the land for political reasons. At times, their crops were burned purposefully to reduce economic stability in the country, and at other times they were destroyed or stolen by other people passing through the area. This discouraged people to do large amounts of farming and in some cases the women were the only ones left to take care of the farming activities. As a result, over half a million people were not able to buy sufficient bread in Kabul as stated by Muhammad Ibrahim Wardag, Kabul's Mayor (Time, 1996). This certainly does not contribute positively to eliminating hunger and malnutrition in Asia, where about 100 to 400 million people were chronically undernourished in developing countries as reported by U. N. Food and Agricultural Organization.

Afghan people also have a tendency to keep domestic animals for milk, meat, plowing the land, and transportation purposes. These animals may include cows, sheep, goats, horses, donkeys, and in some cases camels. Bullocks (bulls) had been the main resource to farmers for plowing the land and most of the animals had been killed, so farming became difficult for them. Many people depended on farmers to provide them with natural resources and to keep food prices down. The Freedom Fighters depended on local communities, Mosques, and local alliances to provide food, shelter, clothing, and other supplies needed for their operations and educational activities.

Since the people of Afghanistan had gone in many different directions following heterogeneous leaders who could not always agree, people had sought the question of how could we eliminate all the bloodshed. One of the most common questions had been if the former King of Afghanistan, Zahir Shaw, could help settle this war peacefully by his involvement in the matter. Since, he had not been involved and actually may not have wanted any involvement for personal reasons, many of the Freedom Fighters' leaders disagreed with him being the solution. Some said that he does not have the experience or familiarity with the current situation in the country. According to an interview with commanders and leaders (Ahmad Shaw Masood and others) conducted by Abdul Hafiz, the reporter of Afghan News, some of the Freedom Fighters believed that continuing Jihad was better than finding a political solution in 1987. So, some of the Freedom Fighters were determined to fight and were not seeking alternative peaceful solutions. The truth of the matter is that Zahir Shaw was the King of Afghanistan for nearly forty years and managed to keep the country in a peaceful environment. That type of a record should certainly qualify him as an excellent candidate. He certainly was one great alternative to bringing people together, provided that he was physically capable of serving his country and people, and this alternative should have been sought and pursued to its fullest extent at the beginning years of the Soviet invasion. Many educated Afghans thought that if there was even a small chance of him taking or being able to take the responsibility, then we would have been able to avoid many battles during the civil war after the Russian army's departure. As it turns out, he was a huge part of the solution after the Taliban era, at least symbolically, in peacefully bringing the new interim government into fruition.

According to a report in Time magazine on June 24th of 1996, "no city has suffered more destruction in the 90's than the capital of Afghanistan." They further reported that there were 45,000 Afghans killed during a six-month period because of the civil war in Afghanistan. Because of this kind of human loss, any peaceful alternative was worth pursuing and continuously seeking. Zahir Shaw certainly had the experience to provide many intelligent solutions that could guide Afghan leaders to a path that possibly would have avoided further bloodshed. Hopefully, the new current democratic process established in Afghanistan with assistance from King Zahir Shaw can function effectively while strengthening the military, navy, and police forces so everyone can live peacefully.

AMMUNITION AND SUPPLIES

The Russians used GRAD and URAGAN "rocket launchers," which in Russia stands for "hail" and "hurricane," respectively. According to a Russian soldier, Tamarov (1992), the Soviet's aircraft included the jet-propelled MIG and SU and the AN airplane. The Soviets used MI-8 helicopters to transport their supplies and troops. They also used MI-24 helicopters to cover their army and their MI-8s because the MI-24s had accuracy and quick fire power. The Red Army further used DShKs, PTRC guided missile launchers, unguided NURS missiles, "bacuum" missiles called SHMELs (Russian for bumblebee), SCUD missiles, automatic Kalashnikovs (AKS-47 and AKS-74s), ashikis (machine guns), and mortars. The SCUD missiles could cover a distance of about two-hundred miles and the explosive power of many one-thousand pound bombs. Most of their weapons were easy to install and disassemble. For example, their Kalashnikovs were made-up of four pieces, and they were designed in such a way that they could not be reassembled the wrong way. Most Afghan Freedom Fighters preferred using their captured weapons until their supplies ran out.

The Freedom Fighters were not equipped with advanced technology; however, they were blessed with a strong will and bravery to fight till the last Afghan was breathing. The Freedom Fighters and refugees in Pakistan were always in need of warm clothes, good walking shoes, and other nutritional supplies to keep them comfortable and healthy. In general the highways were a good source of supplies (food, clothes, income, etc.) for the Freedom Fighters, because they were able to confiscate goods belonging to the government for themselves. Some of the Freedom Fighters had the luxury of using radios and other communication systems to keep in touch with each other. Their communication supplies were not very efficient, in general, because they were mostly using old, outdated and captured communication systems that were in poor condition. The Freedom Fighters did not have a continuous supply of guns and ammunition coming to them, most of their supplies and ammunitions were being delivered by horses, camels, donkeys, and human labor. Some of the supplies were carried on panniers used on horses, camels, and donkeys; while others had to be tied to the animals individually. It was not possible to carry equipment that weighed heavier than about 70 Kgs. because most horses could only carry up to that limit on the mountains. The Freedom Fighters did not have the luxury of having buses and military trucks because most of their traveling was done through the mountains where there were no roads built. In some cases where appropriate, they had captured trucks, motorcycles, bicycles, and tanks from the enemy, which they were able to use to their advantage. As soon as the equipment became a burden then they would burn it so the Russians and the Communists could not use them.

As the war progressed, the Freedom Fighters became better armed by capturing advanced weapons from the enemy and by receiving weapons from foreign countries that were helping them overthrow the communist government and defeat the Russians. Hand guns were not much use for the Freedom Fighters, and many were captured from the enemy. Some of them were brought back to Pakistan and sold for cash or exchanged for other supplies, ammunition, and weapons. They preferred the captured weapons from the enemy because, in general, they were light, efficient, and durable. Most of their old weapons had been replaced by the semi-automatic and automatic AK-47s, AK-74s, and PK machine guns which were captured from the enemy. During the late 1980s, the Freedom Fighters were receiving a few antiaircraft missiles at a cost of approximately $75,000 a piece. These stingers were able to destroy a Soviet helicopter or jet that cost about $4 million each. This was very helpful to the Freedom Fighters because they could stay in the battle-zone longer and not be afraid of the bombings.

Most of the Freedom Fighters had become experts in using weapons because they had to take care of the cleaning and other required maintenance. Table 5 presents some of the commonly used weapons during the Russian Invasion by the Freedom Fighters:

One of the steppingstone moments toward the success of the Afghan guerillas was when the United States started supplying the Freedom Fighters with the stinger anti-air-aircraft missiles that weighted about 35 pounds. These hand-held and hand-fired stingers could be fired from one's shoulder, and their use changed the military strategies of Freedom Fighters and their enemies. The Soviet planes had to avoid bombing many villages, and they usually had to fly high or release countermeasures to confuse and mislead the missile stingers. With these supplies the Freedom Fighters were able to destroy, on average, one Russian bombing airplane and helicopter such as the MI-24 (which cost about four million dollars each) every 36 hours toward the later years of the 1980s. The introduction of these stinger missiles to the Freedom Fighters was very helpful, and enormously costly, perhaps costing billions of dollars, for the Russians.

Table 5 - Weapons used by the Freedom Fighters in Afghan-Russian war

WEAPONS	CHARACTERISTICS AND POSSIBLE USES
DSchK (12-6m), APU-2 (14-6m) & ZPU-1	These are standard machine guns used for ground targets and against the Russians air artillery or forces.
DSchK	This was a very efficient weapon and most often used.
ZPU-1	Mainly used for anti-aircraft purposes.
82mm Recoilless rifles, 75mm RR, BM-1 and BM-12 (107 mm ground-to-ground rockets)	These are some of the heavy weapons used by the Freedom Fighters very efficiently. They did not have enough of these weapons.
82mm mortars and 122mm mortars	These weapons were captured from the Russians and were used very effectively. However, the Freedom Fighters did not have enough ammunition for them.
Mines and Mine detectors	Used for anti-personnel and anti-tank purposes. They did not have enough of these during the Russian Invasion.
RPG-7 (Rocket Propelled Grenade) and Chinese BM-12 (90 Kilos) Rocket Launchers	A very useful weapon which was used against tanks and other ground vehicles operated by the enemy. This weapon could also be used against concentrations of enemy troops as well as the low-flying planes and helicopters.
Anti-aircraft missiles	Used against the enemies helicopters and fighting planes. Not all Freedom Fighters had these missiles and more of these could have been very helpful for them. They were available after 1985.

The supplies from Pakistan to Afghanistan were transported using horses and camels which took about two weeks to one month, depending on the season and the destination. Having enough supplies was important to the fighting force and they knew that without ammunition, they could not go forward, so they would be going backward as a result because there was no cease fire or stand-still positions during their confrontations. At times, their confrontations were based on "kill or be killed" mentality, which caused some innocent people to be caught in between and die for no cause whatsoever. The distribution of supplies and ammunition did not always seem commensurate to the need, ability, and usage of different leaders. Some commanders and leaders were able to put their available resources to better use than others. However, these limitations were sometimes caused by supply chain disruptions.

REFUGEE CAMPS IN PAKISTAN

There were about 350 refugee camps in Pakistan, and most of them were set or built in wasteland and or hot deserts away from the city or water areas. Pakistan did not allow people to build mud houses, and refugees, regardless of weather conditions, were forced to live in the tents during the hot days of summer and cold months of winter. The conditions were so bad that 33% of Afghan children living in Pakistan's Refugee camps did not make it to age five. Many children died of heat, thirst, malnutrition, and bad living conditions that caused all types of diseases which could have been prevented very cheaply. I had visited Munda, Zakhil, and some of the other camps that produced temperatures of about 120 degrees. Many people left Afghanistan hoping that they would be taken care of in Pakistan; only to arrive there and find no help, while understanding that it was too late for them to return back home. Many people spent most of their income getting to Pakistan, while hoping that they would be provided with jobs or some type of basic food to live on temporarily. But that never happened, as most people were forced to live with their relatives and go hungry for days and some died of malnutrition. Most people had wished that they had stayed in Afghanistan and died with the bombs rather than live in such horrible conditions. I always asked my uncles, Hamidullah and Azatullah, why they did not take their wives and kids to Pakistan where they would be safer? Their answer was always clear by saying the living conditions were worse in Pakistan because they had seen it. They never moved from Logar even though they were forced to move into different cities because their houses had been searched and bombed many times.

The rations of water, wheat, oil and other necessities were not delivered on time, and some of the stored resources even went bad before they could get to people for usage so they had to be thrown out because of bad management. The management and distribution systems for resources had to be one of the worst. While people were looking for jobs and many thousands of children were dying of hunger and malnutrition, good food donated by the international community was getting spoiled because the delivery system and management was very ineffective. Sometimes people did not get their rations for months and some for up to two years, while at times they did not get anything. I suppose, since half of the world's 10 million refugees were Afghans and most of them lived in Pakistan, some chaos was expected. But what was going on in Pakistan was really disappointing as people were stealing and cheating to get rich, while other innocent people were losing their lives because they could not find jobs and food to eat.

ETHICAL AND MORAL CONSIDERATIONS

All human beings are born with a conscience, morality, work-ethics, and the desire to learn and do good in the society. However, other societal forces get in the way and direct peoples' action in the wrong or immoral paths. Some of these acts are caused by the "laws of the jungle" and the "laws of war," which are often understood as "kill or be killed." Most of the Afghans thought of the Russian Army and politicians as immoral and ruthless people who were pushy and would stop at nothing to invade the country. However, there were those who had personally interacted with the Russians, and thought of them as normal human beings that wanted to be moral agents to the society. I got to see many Russian teenagers when I attended Allowdean Elementary School, which was located across from the Russian Embassy on Darulaman Street. Some of the Russian families lived in the area, and some individuals took tours of the school, and we interacted with them during school hours before their invasion of Afghanistan. They were people like us, and they had eyes, ears, hearts, hands, and faces that went along with their names. The human conscience of a Russian soldier who fought in Afghanistan is best expressed in his own words, as he wrote:

> He (the Afghan Freedom Fighter) was holding his right leg, but the blood soaked through his fingers and flowed over his hand onto his sleeve. Intuition had saved me again this time: my kick had knocked his automatic out of his grasp a fraction of a second before he could press the trigger. The second kick was to his face. It sent him flying to his face. It sent him flying about six feet. I set my sights on his head, but something stopped me. "He is only a boy!" I observed and lowered my automatic. At the same moment, one of our guys let out a yelp behind me. Another bullet whistled by right next to me. Apparently, this Mujahideen was not the only one here. Again I aimed at his head, but again something stopped me. I saw how his hands were trembling; I noticed the horror in his eyes. "He is only a boy!" and I pressed the trigger (Tamarov, 1992).

There are many cases and stories such as this where people's moral conscience surfaced, but it was buried with the "laws of war." The Russian soldier, Tamarov, was 19 years old, and the Afghan Freedom Fighter was even younger in this situation. There were many young Afghans, age ten to sixteen, that had lost their families; therefore, fighting was the only way they knew of getting back at the enemy. During 1981 and 1982, I witnessed eight school children die on the streets of Darulaman, as they were hit by the speeding jeeps and trucks of the Russian soldiers and advisors. They did not even have the decency to stop and take the person to the hospital because they were afraid, drunk, or plain stupid. Some of the Soviets operated vehicles as if they were somewhat superior or "above the law," when driving in Afghanistan. Of course, today some U.S. soldiers and other officials operating in Afghanistan are accused of such inappropriate actions as well. Many of the young Afghan students, who lived far from school and, could not walk to school because of the long distance, had to take the buses which meant crossing the streets. The streets were not policed and there were no officers to arrest violators. However, the streets were full of military personnel who always searched people and conscripted young boys for military; but, they did not have the responsibility, experience, or authority to control traffic in the large city of Kabul. The issue of Russian soldiers operating tanks, cars, and trucks while they were heavily drunk was brought up to one of the Communist teachers in Allowdean Elementary School and he responded by saying, "things will get better." In 1985, an intoxicated Russian tank driver, who ignored the traffic signs and failed to stop at the intersection, killed sixty passengers as he ran into a bus (Goodwin, 1987). There were many moral dilemmas that were overlooked by individuals who did not know what they were doing in Afghanistan, did not want to be there, did not care about the system that took them away from their own country. Overall, the system created a situation where people were put in positions which they had no control over because of the "schatoma" (blinders) in their moral conscience. Maybe that is why Communism failed after causing much harm to many people in Afghanistan and around the world.

During the invasion, there were discussions initiated by the Communist government about a possible peace treaty or National Reconciliation toward bringing all the Afghan people together peacefully (Es'haq, 1987). The discussions for the National reconciliation did not get started because the group leaders did not think it was to their best interest. According to Es'haq, the Freedom Fighters saw this as a sign of weakness on the part of Communist government and the Russian army. The Freedom Fighters were under the assumption that the government's intention was to bring some cosmetic or physical changes to the communist government and that should be the end of things. The Freedom Fighters may have ignored to consider the possibility of other alternatives or may not have had any alternatives that were viable to all parties. The lack of openness and distrust among all parties involved may have prolonged a war which could have been resolved with peaceful means. Most of the decisions thus far had bad consequences, because many lives had been lost. There must have been "tough" ethical choices between many alternatives where each option could have been a "right" decision by itself. Often, the "tough" choices are not between a right and a wrong option, but they are decisions that are between many "right" alternatives.

Rushworth M. Kidder (1995) mentioned four models where people make "tough" choices between "right versus right" dilemmas. Those four models of right versus right models are: *"truth versus loyalty," "individual versus community," "short-term versus long-term," and "justice versus mercy."* For example a dear and close friend, who is a powerful and influential leader with the Freedom Fighters and to many others around the country, lets you know that he is thinking about joining the government (Communist) party on the assumption that if he cooperates with the Communist party, then they may come up with a joint solution that would solve all war problems peacefully. Now, you know that he is going to leave the Freedom Fighters and join the Communist party for a good intention, but the group leaders would be against this idea and prevent him from implementing his plan. What is the ethical action as you consider the four models of right versus right dilemmas?

- *Truth versus loyalty*: This is a situation where telling people the truth may violate ones promise to the loyalty of the country, group, or an individual. So, do you keep your loyalty to the group and tell the truth about him leaving, or do you stay loyal to your friend? What about your loyalty to all other Freedom Fighters?

- *Individual versus community*: Do you see the consequences of your friend's decision in terms of the individual (your friend) or the group (all Freedom Fighters)?

- *Short-term versus long-term*: In short-term, your decision may have deleterious effect on your party; however in long term there is the possibility of a peaceful solution to a big problem. Which one do you support?

- *Justice versus mercy*: Do you base your decision on the written rules of the law as agreed upon by the party members or do you base your decision solely on your friend's personal situation for which you have strong feelings and emotions?

These are difficult decisions and perhaps many of the Freedom Fighters faced similar situations at one time or another. At age sixteen, I remember during one of my trips to Logar, as I was traveling with several local Freedom Fighters, I met several young men who had ran into four other Freedom Fighters that had captured a communist soldier the day before and they were still interrogating him. This captured soldier was "supposedly" a young man about 21 years of age, who had been born in Kabul, and thought that the Freedom Fighters were all thieves and bad people as advertised by the Communist government. He was also an active member of Khad, government's secret agency. They had his hands and feet tied up and took all his outer-layer of clothes off during that cold winter day. He was asked if he believed in God, he replied "no." Then he was told that if he did not change his mind about God, they were going to throw him in the river which was covered with a thick layer of ice, but the current of water underneath the ice was still very strong. He still chose to "stick" to his original answer; then he was given another opportunity to change his mind, but he still said he did not believe in God and was always going to be a Communist since he believed in Lenin's philosophy. So, the four people, two holding his hands and two holding his feet were swinging him back and forth, back and forth as they finally threw him in the icy river. The ice broke, leaving a hole shaped like a human shadow which was supposedly very similar to the police's crime scene drawing on the floor during a murder; and the soldier was gone with the currents as fast as the eye could see. That is an extreme example where strong emotions were involved and the decision had to be made by few individuals, and it had to be made quickly, because they had no prisons or even food to feed captured prisoners. It was sad to hear about the situation. I was happy that I was not put in that situation to make a decision that determined whether someone dies or stays alive. I guess there was the assumption, on the part of his capturers, that upon his release, the soldier would go back to the army and start fighting against the Freedom Fighters; and, since he had been with the Freedom Fighters for a day or so he knew "too much." However, they were also serious about letting him live and work with the Freedom Fighters if he had said that he believes in God and will abandon believing in Lenin's ideology. I guess the young man (the captured solider) believed so strongly in the Communist ideology that he was willing to die for it, and he did. I always thought that throwing someone in the river is not the way to win a war, but apparently such acts happen more often in wars. For example, according to ABC News (January 12th 2005), an American soldier received six months of military prison time for drowning an Iraqi. The American Sergeant, who had ordered his soldiers to throw the Iraqis into the Tigris River, was sentenced to military prison, but did not get discharged. Prosecutors said that Zaidoun Hassoun, 19 years of age, drowned and his cousin, Marwan Hassoun, was able to make it out alive from the river. Marwan Hassoun had testified that he tried to save his cousin, but the current swept Zaidoun away. Marwan said the body was found in the river nearly two weeks later. The Army Sergeant had admitted that he had ordered his soldiers to throw an Iraqi man into the river in December 2003. According to ABC News, he claimed that the Iraqi man "had made a gesture of slitting his throat." He said he never meant to injure or kill the Iraqi by throwing him in the river. He supposedly ordered him thrown in the river to teach him a "hard lesson" about threatening U.S. troops. He said "I did not want them to think we were soft or weak." His commanding officers testified that he has been an outstanding soldier who tried to find non-lethal ways to deal with defiant Iraqis in the increasingly dangerous region. It goes to show that even "outstanding" individuals and/or their directions can go in the wrong path when one is being threatened or feels threatened. Furthermore, it shows that leaders must always carefully evaluate their directions to subordinates, as it could lead to unintentional consequences when carried out by others in the wrong manner.

On other occasions in Afghanistan, there were myriad considerations discussed among the Freedom Fighters in Afghanistan during decision-making about the attacks on the enemy posts. One of the major considerations would be the retaliatory bombing of the neighboring villages and provinces which are filled with many civilian families. People were concerned about women, children and the elderly civilians who may not be able to protect themselves, because they did not have weapons and did not want any involvement at all. One of the successful leaders in Panjshir was Commander Masood and his strategic planning was based on the overall success of the Freedom Fighters in general. His organized teams were designed to unite all fighters to be going in the same direction with a common mission. The leaders had to make tough ethical decisions about their short and long-term interests. They knew that sometimes they would have to take a temporary or short-term loss of resources or a competitive advantage in order to guarantee the survival of the fighters in the long term. Although not all leaders agreed on similar ends and means, most of them had to make sacrifices for the benefit of the society in general.

Some individuals were concerned about spying and morality during the war. People were reasoning that spying was acceptable as long as it was done for a just cause and purpose that was aligned with one's personal and professional values. Spying in the war can be simply described as letting your friends and family members know that they need to get out of their houses because the Communists are about to start bombing the village. Now, if a person in the army has this information, and he or she feels obligated to let his/her family members know, then spying would be aligned with his or her values, ergo an acceptable action. Other considerations and concerns involved the location and time of the attacks on the enemy outposts. It was important to consider the population of a village or valley before attempting to attack the Russian garrisons. Sometimes the attacks would result in Russians bombing the whole village where many innocent civilians and children would get killed. Some of the high-altitude bombers were flown straight from the Soviet Union territories to hit targets in Afghanistan. This was one area that the Freedom Fighters did not always have enough anti-aircraft missiles to protect themselves and the valleys full of innocent civilians.

COST OF THE AFGHAN-RUSSIAN INVASION

Tamarov talked about a Soviet training base in Afghanistan, and said that the base was where kind people were transformed into vicious ones, and vicious people became cruel. He also stated that the bases were places where young boys, 18 to 20 years of age, were transformed into murderers. In some cases, these young soldiers killed many innocent individuals who did not oppose their presence, but were caught in the middle of a chaotic battle. All government soldiers were taught that death in life is inevitable and the best way to conquer death is by directly confronting it. The Afghan Freedom Fighters were not afraid of death either, because they either won the war or went to heaven, so either choice would mean success or victory to them. Once in 1982, I met an old Freedom Fighter, who appeared to be 60 years of age, passing through Rahm-Abaud area to participate in an operation against the Communists in Chaur-Aussia, which is in the outskirts of Kabul. As we were sitting in the Mosque after the afternoon prayer, I asked him how long he had been fighting against the Communists? "Two months," he replied and then described vehemently what led him to his commitment to fight against the Communists until his last breath. After listening to his sad and recent biography, I found out that two of his sons were taken by the government officials and possibly were prisoners in Pul-e-charkhee jail; their whereabouts were unknown for over eight months, and they may have been executed. His other two sons had been killed by government officials during an operation, and his five grandchildren, wife, and two daughters-in-law had also been killed during the bombing of their village. He appeared to be a very wise and patient man who wanted to accomplish justice in an unjust world, and becoming a Freedom Fighter was one of the ways he could do this successfully. The war cost him everything, and there were many individuals whose lives had been shattered similarly during the first few years of the Soviet invasion.

I remember when my cousin Ghulam Jailani Haidari was killed by the government forces when they discovered he had been helping the Freedom Fighters. Jailani was 26 years old and had just graduated from the very prestigious four-year military college in Kabul. He worked for one year in the Kabul area and then was transferred to the Taliqaun area. About one month after his transfer to Taliqaun, one night, a family friend telegraphed us that Jailani had been injured and should be arriving at Kabul tomorrow. The next morning we looked at all hospitals in the city and did not find him, so we knew that something was seriously wrong and could not wait to start searching the next morning. As Jailani's dad, brothers, and some other family members were sitting at our house talking about the situation and deciding what to do, at about midnight, someone started knocking on the door. It was our family friend who had telegraphed, and had now brought Jailani's dead body. The news, although suspected, was difficult to take, and Jailani's dad fainted, but after about thirty minutes he recovered. The news was hard for everyone in the family, and we wished that no family had to go through such an unfortunate incident or loss. Jailani had been shot many times with machine guns from close range and the Communist officials had left him in a field. Somehow, the Communists had discovered that he had been building an alliance with the local Freedom Fighters and had been giving them supplies and resources, so they shot him dead at point blank range. Fortunately, the family friend, also serving as a colonel with the military, had heard about the situation and brought his body back to Kabul. The next day, we took Jailani's funeral to Logar at his final resting place.

COST OF WAR TO AFGHANS

Since the invasion of Russians in 1979, Afghanistan has become a massive burial ground. There are no cities, villages, or towns in Afghanistan that have not felt the destruction of war. Each and every city "appears" to have been built many centuries ago and/or destroyed by earthquakes even though they may have been built very recently. Each city that has been destroyed can be seen as an accurate microcosm for the entire country. Despite the Soviet Union's claim of clearing over 2,000 mine fields in Afghanistan, there are many of them still left to destroy the country for the coming years. About 22,000 villages are still planted with millions of mines that are designed to kill or maim people. As a matter of fact, soldiers and innocent people are still being injured by them. According to Gay Brenner, an American relief worker, a five year old, whose two legs have been destroyed by a mine, said that they were riding in a car with her two brothers and parents when the mine went off under them. She is the only survivor and will not be able to walk again as she did prior to the mine explosion. Most of these mines cannot be detected with instruments available to the people of Afghanistan. Approximately two million Afghans have died since the Russian invasion and more than two million others have become injured in different ways including mines. There are many Afghans who are living without their arms and legs because they had to be amputated. Amputations were very common during the war and in some cases doctors had to do it without anesthesia, which was not available to them all the time. While many patients died during this process, a few did survive, and perhaps would not have survived without the amputation. Injured Afghans usually died due to severe loss of blood because there were no medical personnel available to take care of them. Their best option was to travel to Pakistan, and that could take about one to four weeks depending on the location of the person in Afghanistan. The trip had to be made by horses, mules, and camels which are not very comfortable to an injured person. The Soviets had given orders to kill anyone who owned a gun and some people in the country towns were killed even if a hunting gun was found in their houses. Afghanistan is a country where many people owned hunting guns for going to the mountains and hunting. Guns were also used during wedding celebrations and other happy occasions by firing several shots into the air.

The inhuman methods of killing people continued until the Russian's last years of being in Afghanistan. According to Amnesty International, on January 16th of 1988, the Russian soldiers had gone to Kolagu village of Paktia Province and put 12 people in a Mosque, then, they burned it down to the ground. Only three people survived with major injuries. The killings are bound to continue as each of the 30 million mines left in the fields throughout Afghanistan keep exploding while civilians accidentally walk over them. In the last four years, and based on my observation of several cities in the Logar Province in December of 2005, some of these mines are being removed by Afghans, and hopefully this trend will continue until all of the country is a safe environment for everyone. About seven million Afghans left their homes and became refugees in other countries or provinces. For the past 30 years, the new generation who are ready to "run" the country has been born and raised in a war situation without appropriate "Afghani" education, teachings, food, or guidance. These teenagers have been forced to grow faster and lose their childhood in the process. Many of the children actually did lose their lives by picking up bombs that looked like toys. Most children have been forced to become mature adults, at a young age, both mentally and physically as a result of the war. According to Diana Sawyer's report in December of 1996 with Barbara Walters, there were over 35,000 widows just in the city of Kabul alone. Similarly, there are literally thousands of lonely fathers, mothers, orphans, husbands, and wives that will always remember this war and recall only bad memories. Since, most of the civil war activities had been taking place in the capital city of Kabul over eighty percent of the city has been destroyed by bombs, rockets, missiles, mines, and bullets. Borovik (1990) wrote that if the roads in Afghanistan could howl in pain, then he would prefer to be deaf. His statement tells much about the massive road destructions throughout Afghanistan. According to Congressman Wilson of the United States, it was "the blood of the most dedicated Afghan warriors that drove the Russians out." Of course, the blood of two million people can be a large cost to win anything this world has to offer, but Afghans and their allies probably thought this might be better than living under the direct influence of foreigners. Of course, nobody really thought the loss would be so great.

The rebuilding of Afghanistan will be a difficult task and requires cooperation of the East and the West. According to Democratic Congressman Charles Wilson of Texas, the United States should take the lead role, while getting others involved in the rebuilding of Afghanistan, to reward them for fighting the injustice of communist system that was imposed upon them. He says it is important to reward those who resist tyranny; with that in mind, developed countries should pour money into Afghanistan for its rebuilding process. While other Americans (i.e. Thomas Thornton- national security officer during Carter administration who became a professor at John Hopkins University) claim that the United Nations should play the leading role in the rebuilding of Afghanistan instead of the United States, although the United States should be an important contributor. It is good to see that the United States has taken a leading role, yet the U.S. still needs to do much more with regard to financial assistance for the rebuilding process. Although the Russian government claimed that they wanted to help the Afghans in the first place, they should be pressured by the international alliances into financially helping the Afghans to build their country. I believe the former Soviet Union wants to and should keep a good relation with the people of Afghanistan, because they will always be close "neighbors" and will need each other's understanding. As Mikhail Gorbachev once mentioned, he is not a "romantic," but rather a realist, and would like to keep good relations with the government of Afghanistan. Recently, Mikhail Gorbachev was one of the keynote speakers at the "2004 Living Leadership: Delivering Results the Right Way" held via live satellite interaction at Nova Southeastern University's Performing Arts Center in Fort Lauderdale on October 20th 2004. Mikhail Gorbachev was joined by people like Donald Trump, Peter Drucker, Jim Collins, Ken Blanchards, Larry Bossidy, Rosabeth Moss Kanter, and many others who spoke about the meaning of "living leadership" in the twenty first century environment. Of course, Mikhail Gorbachev taught the world that "government restructuring" and "political openness" are tasks for great leaders of this century who are willing to achieve extraordinary results through honesty and great character. These extraordinary leaders manifested that today's leaders must communicate with conviction, credibility, and compassion all at the same time. One facet cannot be substituted at the expense of the other without one's character and influence being damaged. Today, both government and corporate officials need to commit to leading by example, managing like a professional manager, and leading like a great leader.

COST OF WAR TO RUSSIANS

The Soviets incurred some severe losses as well since Afghanistan became their "bleeding wound" as described by Mikhail Gorbachev during 1986 in India. There is a Russian saying that states "measure your tile seven times because you will have only one chance to cut it." Perhaps, this Russian saying was not put into practice before the Soviet Union decided to invade Afghanistan. Therefore, they perhaps made the biggest military blunder by coming to Afghanistan. There were many Russian advisors and military personnel living in Afghanistan along with their families. Their families and children were limited to the government controlled boundaries in Kabul, mostly in Macroyon Apartments, and they were not allowed to travel around the city by themselves. Today, unfortunately, this is also the case for most United Nation and American contractors, soldiers, and members of non-governmental agencies (NGOs) that are working and living in Afghanistan. Macroyon accommodations were reserved for and limited mostly to Russian and Afghan communists. The Soviets eventually had about 150,000 thousand soldiers, advisors, and consultants present in Afghanistan. This number had increased and decreased at times but, it did not affect the stability of Afghanistan in a positive way. Nearly one million Russian soldiers and personnel have supposedly traveled through the mountainous lands of Afghanistan and have been affected by the war. Russians learned that increasing their soldiers was not beneficial, which in fact had been proven before, as the United States had about half million soldiers in Vietnam during their war and still did not succeed. Recently, Americans put over 250,000 soldiers and contractors in Iraq, but are still losing the battle and war. So, a large number of soldiers cannot necessarily eliminate conflict and insurgency during an occupation, at least not for any long-lasting period of time. The Soviet Union officially announced that they lost more than 15,000 soldiers, and more than 35,000 of their soldiers became injured in this war. A Russian soldier named Dmitri Khimich wrote a letter to journalist Borovik that he did not believe the figure of 15,000 soldiers being dead as announced by the government. Khimich wrote that by 1981, the first two years of entering Afghanistan, the number of dead Russian soldiers had reached 20,000. Several journalists report that over 50,000 Russian soldiers had been killed in Afghanistan and over 100,000 thousand had been injured. Of course, this loss was very small compared to their 20 million people who were killed during World War II when the Germans lost about 8 million people. During a visit to Kabul's *ChaurSadd Bester Hospital* (400 hundred-bed hospital) in 1982, my uncle said that there were over 1,500 injured people and most of them were Russians. This hospital, located in Kabul, was limited to active and retired military personnel only, and was made for 400 hundred patients. According to Russian officials, there were over 300 soldiers that were considered to be "missing in action." The Afghan invasion cost them heavily both financially and emotionally. The cost of the Afghan war to Russians has been estimated to have been about $12 million dollars a day, and about $40 billion for the entire duration of their stay, one decade. When compared to the invasion of Iraq by the Americans, this cost of $40 billion to the Russians is very small relative to the $400 billion just for first few years which Americans paid through their taxes. Today, an expenditure of half of this amount from the United States could create long-term peace and prosperity in Afghanistan, thereby eliminating poverty and insurgency. Nearly one million of the Soviet soldiers spent time in Afghanistan, and some probably have or will suffer the emotional and psychological consequences for a long time to come. Borovik (1990) wrote that during a war in Qandahar, a young Russian soldier started yelling, "Mommy, please take me back inside of you....Mommy, take me back inside of you." He also wrote about another injured Russian soldier who had written to his father, "You old ass, what the hell did you have to do it for nineteen years ago." He also wrote that "Afghanistan moves into your subconscious and haunts you day and night." Vladislav Tamarov (1992), a Russian soldier who served in Afghanistan at the age of 19 wrote, "Once, back home, I decided to count how many days out of my twenty months in Afghanistan I'd been on combat missions: 217 days. And I'm still paying the price for every one of those days." He further states that many American Vietnam veterans who have had excellent health facilities and hospitals in their service were pretty miserable because of the psychological effects of the war. He writes that by 1989 more of the Vietnam veterans died by violent accidents and/or suicide after the war than the number of soldiers who were killed in the actual war. The Russians are afraid of similar inevitable consequences for their soldiers who served in Afghanistan. Of course, the cost would have been much less for both sides if they would have learned their lesson and left Afghanistan in 1984, when the United Nation's General Assembly demanded their withdrawal by a majority vote. I suppose, just as some individuals are hardheaded and stubborn, so can be most determined groups of people and Communist leaders. They learn things the "hard way" as opposed to learning from others or simply learning quicker. Many people compare the Russian-Afghan war with the United States and the Vietnam War as they share some similarities. While Americans lost about 58,000 of their troops in Vietnam, Russians lost about 50,000 of theirs. However, the Afghans lost about two million people which is probably very small compared to the losses in Vietnam, whose population was about two and half times that of Afghanistan. The Soviet leaders had called their invasion to be "a national wound and a sin to impose Marxism ideology on the people of Afghanistan."

Moscow's killings have continued and will perhaps keep on happening as time goes on, but the place and location may vary. For example, since their conflict in Chechnya, there have been over 100,000 people killed in the ensuing war. Finally, at the beginning of 1997, according to Moscow, all the Russian troops had been withdrawn from Chechnya. Of course, just like many former Russians, I also have the habit of interpreting their sayings in terms of what they did not say that really counts. Also, hidden behind the wars, any war, would be the results or side-effects that follow many of the war participants and in some cases their families for the rest of their lives. Universally, there are the general psychological and physical breakdowns which result from the hardships and traumatic experiences of the war. According to a report in the Wall Street Journal on January 6th of 1997, research has shown that a substantial number of veterans from United States wars have constellations of serious symptoms, such as memory loss, fatigue, muscle and joint pain, headaches, stress, shortness of breath, palpitations, sweating, dizziness, disturbed sleep, fainting, not being able to concentrate easily, and forgetfulness. These are the general symptoms of any war, and will probably be haunting the Afghans, as well as Russian soldiers, for the rest of their lives. They will be suffering heavily from these symptoms, and unfortunately there will not be much help to them from their governments because they are struggling to survive in their economies. Some of these symptoms are also being seen in veterans of the Gulf War that includes about 697,000 Americans, 390 of whom lost their lives during the war. The same externalities are likely to be symptoms of soldiers fighting the Iraqis. The 2003 Iraq invasion has already cost Americans over 3,000 deaths, and around 25,000 injured soldiers and workers. According to a study by Harvard University researchers, as reported by ABC World News on November 25, 2006, the cost of taking care of the injured American soldiers from the Iraqi invasion will cost the U.S. government about $127 billion. The Harvard study assumed a continued but diminishing presence of American soldiers in Iraq. Some of these American veterans who are returning back from the Iraqi war are suffering from psychological problems and stresses; several of these veteran soldiers in 2006 have actually killed their wives, and the military began an investigation of how to help them deal with such post-war traumas and stresses. Of course, due to the widespread impact of the civil war, innocent Iraqis are paying a huge price as over 4,000 civilians in Iraq were killed just in the month of November 2006. Over one million Iraqis have now left their homes and have become immigrants or refugees due to the U.S.'s invasion of their country. There have been many human losses for the British and other coalition members' soldiers as well. Of course, there has been a huge loss for the people of Iraq as they have lost an estimated 50,000 people and perhaps around 200,000 people injured, ousted or jailed. These are huge costs for all parties involved and many innocent families will be feeling this loss for many years to come. Hopefully, there can be a quick, peaceful and honorable solution for American and coalition soldiers to leave Iraq and go home to their families. Israeli military soldiers have been causing much harm to the Palestinians for many decades now and recently (in mid 2006), with major help and approval from the United States, imposed their "military might" on the innocent people of Lebanon. However, Israeli political leaders soon learned that not only they had injured and killed thousands of innocent individuals, but they also lost "face" throughout the world by consciously and deliberately bombing residential areas and civilians. All governments and military officials need to realize that a war is always to be avoided as it is almost never the best alternative. I suppose if a country like the former Soviet Union, a world superpower at one time, could have had their priorities clear then Afghanistan would not have been facing these problems today. The Russian leaders finally figured out that their socialist system required one soldier to constantly watch the movements and whereabouts of one civilian in Afghanistan, which is very costly, and perhaps are part of the reasons for the breakdown of communism.

REFLECTIVE QUESTIONS FOR CRITICAL THINKING

1. What is a "freedom fighter"? Is this term based on a religious philosophy or general love of one's country? How is a "freedom fighter" different from a "Mujahid"?
2. Why would Russians want to invade Afghanistan as they did in 1979? What are some common reasons for such invasions?
3. The country of Afghanistan has suffered heavily and nobody would want to repeat this. Yet, every tragedy brings new learning and new opportunities for the future. So, what are some of the common benefits or learning from the 25 years of war in Afghanistan? What lessons should Afghans learn from the years of internal and external war?
4. What are some of the common costs associated with the Afghan-Russian war?
5. What role did twenty-first century technology play in the Afghan-Russian war during the past century?
6. What types of violations with regard to human rights issues were observed or seen in Afghanistan during the Afghan-Russian war?
7. Are there similarities in the Russian-Afghanistan invasion and the American-Iraq invasion? If so, how and what are they?
8. Discuss the strategies and reasons used for the departure of Russian soldiers from Afghanistan.
9. What can the American military leaders and soldiers have learned from the experiences of Russians in Afghanistan?

CHAPTER 4

AFGHANISTAN AFTER THE RUSSIANS' DEPARTURE

When you're wounded and left on Afghanistan's plains
And the women come out to cut up what remains
Just roll on your rifle an' blow out your brains
An' go to your Gawd like a soldier
(An 1892 poem: *"The Young British Soldier,"* as cited in Time Inc., 2006)

Someone once said that "The trouble with the future is that it usually arrives before we are ready for it" and this may very well have been the case with the Afghan Freedom Fighters. Dan Rather of CBS News said that Afghan fighters should be given all the credit for their bravery, determination, and persistence, because they fought in the war and they triumphed. Many people also believe that it is their bravery, determination, and persistence that caused riots and civil war as animosity among people dramatically grew during the invasion. I remember Reginald Denny, the truck driver, who was nearly beaten to death because of his skin color in Los Angeles during the 1992 riots. A year later, when he was still suffering the effects of the beating. Reginald Denny said even though racial biases can be very strong and leave long-lasting animosity between people, forgiveness is the key to peace. Anytime we want to end a conflict successfully, someone has to take the leadership role by being the first to stop arguing and realize the long-range vision while sacrificing short-term gains. Just like Dr. Martin Luther King, Jr. (from the United States), Mahatma Gandhi (from India), and Mother Teresa (India) who passionately advocated social justice without violence, we all should have such clarity of the future first and then discover means of getting there based on concrete self-chosen and principle-based universal values rather than emotional reactions. Perhaps forgiveness is the key to ending an unproductive cycle of hatred, while starting cooperative lines of communication to generate the best alternatives for everyone involved. People who make sacrifices and stop the negative tendencies or patterns are the real leaders; and Stephen R. Covey, author of *Seven Habits of Highly Effective People*, calls them "transitional" people. Afghanistan needs many transitional leaders who can willingly and voluntarily stop inter-racial or inter-group conflicts and begin living peacefully. After the defeat and departure of the Russian army, peace, quiet, growth, development, and celebration of the victory should have been the natural corollary of everyone's efforts, loyalty and hard work during the war. But, that did not happen and what did occur is the inevitable civil war, which had been prognosticated by many political analysts based on the Freedom Fighters' division into different and sometimes opposing factions. Even highly educated and intelligent Afghan leaders often used traditional fighting strategies to overpower and overthrow their opponents. These Afghan leaders were very effective during the Russian invasion because every person was aligned with a common and absolute vision or purpose to defeat the Russians. However, the leaders were not able to create peace in liberated Afghanistan, and this might be due to the lack of conformity to a single post-Russian purpose and mission. Maybe the future came before the Afghan people were ready for it, and as a result people were fighting among themselves. The antidote to this mentality and cynicism may be a new model or paradigm that seeks mutual benefit for all Afghans without resorting to physical or traditional wars.

Robert Neamann, former U. S. Ambassador to Afghanistan, during an interview, stated that there will be a war after the Russian's departure and all soldiers of the government should make their decisions to get out early. He was right because the civil war became more difficult than before and took many lives. The victory was looked at as the "perfect storm" of hurricanes Ivan, Charley, Frances, and Jean (which "hit" the state of Florida within a three month period in 2004) traveling with fast winds and high gusts covering a large area. Similarly, the tsunami disaster (underwater earthquake which caused water to travel at high speeds destroying homes and cities) in the Indian Ocean near the Indonesian island of Sumatra killed around 200,000 people in the first few weeks of 2005 off the coast of Sri Lanka, Indonesia and their neighboring countries (such as Thailand, Malaysia, India, Burma, and others). The tsunami was supposedly traveling at speeds of up to about 500 miles per hour at times. So, many individuals in its path did not have any advance warning, nor did they have a high chance of survival when caught unexpectedly. With the hurricanes, people in Florida knew days before that they were heading toward them, and they were bound to leave some destruction behind even though people were prepared for them to the fullest extent possible. The war in Afghanistan has caused ten times more deaths than the tsunami caused around the Indian Ocean. Both the tsunami and the war in Afghanistan have caused similar environmental destruction and psychological challenges for the local people. The tsunami can be seen as the war against the Russians and the civil conflict can be viewed as a lingering hurricane. In reality, this hurricane of civil war in Afghanistan was worse than anyone could have ever imagined. It was not traveling very fast because it was staying constant while traveling in a round-about way destroying everything that came in its path. This "hurricane," called "civil war," was predicted before the departure of the Russians, because true synergism did not exist among the Freedom Fighters, and in some cases, the pugnacious and voluble leaders would vilify their opponents when all else failed. This created much animosity and hatred among many of the Freedom Fighters during the Afghan-Russian War. The results are being witnessed even today, as some people are losing their lives in the process. When does the "perfect storm" or "hurricane" end, and how can the growth process begin are the questions in many minds and the focus of all Afghan leaders. We know one thing is clear, that self-centered and materialistic individuals do not make good leaders as Tertullian states, "He who lives only to benefit himself confers on the world a benefit when he dies." So, hopefully such benefits come faster for the people of Afghanistan as they attempt to rebuild the country physically and spiritually along with the psychological mindset of its citizens.

It appears as though the Afghan leaders may have experienced, and some may still be experiencing, the parable of the "boiled frog." Frogs seem to have a tendency to sense and respond to sudden threats but not the gradual forces that can take their lives. Peter Senge, author of the *Fifth Discipline*, says that if you put a frog in a container full of boiling water, the frog will automatically try to scramble out. But if you put the frog in a container of regular water and place the container on a stove and gradually increase the temperature, the frog will not do anything. As a matter-of-fact, the frog will sit there and die boiling, because he is so dizzy that he cannot even climb out of the container anymore, even though nothing has been restraining him from coming out. The struggles of some Afghan leaders for power, and proving that they are right, may have "blindsided" them, as the people of Afghanistan were being boiled to death like the boiled frog. Gaining the vision to see this gradual destruction of Afghanistan and its people requires slowing down and smelling the "roses." It is best to stop and find the right solution, and then execute appropriately as William Shakespeare said, "To climb steep hills requires slow pace at first." The war has been going on for nearly three decades, and people are still fighting to bring peace in Afghanistan. Fighting physically, with guns and other harmful technology to bring peace is an oxymoron regardless of whether it takes place in Afghanistan, Iraq, Palestine, Israel, or other parts of the world. The creation of peace requires common purpose, vision, integrity, and leadership that is not self-centered or materialistic, and challenging every citizen's mind by respecting and valuing their opinion. When Bruce Lee, actor and martial art expert of the 1970s, talked about the concept of "fighting without fighting," he meant that human beings can settle their differences by using their mind and learn new talents that further stretch the boundaries of the mind. Oliver Wendell Holmes said, "Man's mind once stretched by a new idea, never regains its original dimension." However, it may also be true to say that a man's mind once filled with hatred, evil, animosity, and revenge, may never be able to acquire peace (unless acted upon by an outside force) in a peaceful manner. So, each Afghan must come to peace with himself or herself before expecting peace with others. Each person should also try to forgive people of his/her past and educate him/herself about making the world a better place for the coming generations. Stephen Covey says, "We cannot lead others at any higher level of effectiveness than we are currently leading ourselves." So, as adults we are totally responsible for our learning, education, and actions. One should also stand for what is right as Confucius said, "To know what is right and not to do it is the worst cowardice." And Iman Ali, the fourth successor to the Prophet Mohammad (PBUH) has said, "Persist in your action with a noble end in mind...Failure to perfect your work while you are sure of the reward is injustice to yourself." It is every person's moral obligation to do what is right; however, it is also every person's obligation to do his or her homework and hear the alternative solutions before sticking with one's own point of view. Sometimes, it is appropriate and possibly necessary for the benefit of society to move from having a "point of view" to a "viewing point."

THE TALIBAN ERA

The word *Taliban* means "students" both in Persian and in Arabic languages. It originates from the word "Talib," which refers to one student. In the case of Taliban, who governed Afghanistan for a period of six years, the term implies "Students of Faith." The Taliban troops captured Kabul on September 27th of 1996. Their leader was *Mawlauna* Mohammad Omar, who became influential because of his charismatic style and religious background and involvements. Taliban also killed the last Soviet-backed President, Najibullah, 49 years of age, who was hiding at the United Nations compound in Kabul for more than four years. Taliban hanged Najibullah's body, along with that of his brother's, Shahpoor Ahmedzai who served as his security chief, publicly at the front of the presidential palace (*Arg*) in Kabul.

Amnesty International claims that 1,000 people were arrested and jailed in what it called a reign of terror (Spaeth, 1996). According to Spaeth's article in Time Magazine, some members of the Taliban group were forcing people from the streets to attend prayers at gunpoint. While everyone should be given the opportunity to pray and be spiritual, the act and its results are more powerful if it is self-initiated. Islam does not allow nor encourage the forcing of people into praying because it is the intention and not necessarily the ritual that counts most. As God mentions in the Quran, there are many ways a person can worship if his/her heart is in the right place. Worship could be in the forms of helping others who may need a helping hand, studying and/or teaching the spiritual literature, building places of worship, helping the poor and orphans, fasting, and many other helpful actions that are for the benefit of human beings. Spaeth also mentions that two foreign female reporters were forbidden to ask questions by Shir Mohammad Stanekzai, Acting Deputy Foreign Minister, because he did not want to hear their voices. Maybe these two reporters were asking the "tough" questions which the government did not have clear answers for; then again, all questions are "tough" and such officials better find the right answers; otherwise, peace would be very difficult to achieve and maintain.

Taliban banned women from working outside the house and closed girls' schools in Kabul. This action had given the Taliban a negative image and reputation because the country was, and still is, in need of an educated and experienced workforce. There were over 35,000 widowed women living in the city of Kabul in 1996, and many of them were the sole supporters of their families. Most people living in Kabul did not have the luxury of living off the natural products of agriculture because Kabul is a city of industry, manufacturing, and education. So, most people in Kabul do not own any land, and rely on the income from their jobs to support themselves. According to an interview with Diane Sawyer, Taliban officials claimed that all women who were working outside their homes would get paid without having to leave their home. Of course, this is a good thought and everyone can appreciate the official's good intentions, but the government itself was having difficulty trying to recover from the corruption and abuse from the war of the past few decades. So, providing payments for previously working women who were not working may be a very difficult and impossible task. Women made-up the most experienced portion of the workforce in Kabul, because most males became immigrants or could not work during the Communist government; so women had to support their families by being the only income earners. As a result, they became the experienced and most productive workforce in Kabul. Government officials had to understand that training new workers (males) would require time and money in many manufacturing and production jobs. All this would cause further delay in the development and growth process, which the country needed in order to recover from the devastating war and civil unrest of the past.

According to a report in Time Magazine on November 4th of 1996, about 600 men who were fighting for the Taliban, were captured by Ahmad Shaw Masood's forces and were being held in a Panjshir jail. Not all these prisoners were Afghans; 26 were Pakistani fighters who were fighting against the forces of the Afghan government that was driven out of the capital, Kabul, on September 27th 1996 by the Taliban. According to these captured Pakistani fighters, there were about 1,000 fighters from Pakistan who entered Afghanistan to fight for the Taliban. The motives of Pakistan's government, as stated in the Time Magazine article, would be to gain influence over its neighbor. This does not necessarily make sense, and may not be true because the former Prime Minister of Pakistan, Benazir Bhutto, had denied any involvement in this internal matter. It is also clear that their involvement would further increase the animosity between the people of Afghanistan. These captured soldiers might be Pakistan's citizens who had volunteered to fight and were getting paid by the Taliban officials and government. On the other hand, maybe they were organized by the Pakistani government to increase their influence and eventually turn Afghanistan into one of their states or provinces. Eventually, the Taliban government ended in late 2001 and was replaced with the members and officials from the Northern Alliance making up the "interim government." The 2006 publication from Time Inc. makes the following conclusion about the Taliban and their success in the reduction of opium poppies in Afghanistan:

> During their five years in power, the Taliban were more successful than any previous Afghan government in crushing the cultivation of opium poppies, the plant from which heroin is derived. While in power, the Taliban scorned the drug, though the opium crop has long been a primary source of revenue for the nation's warlords and farmers. But the Taliban's 2001 fall, and the subsequent flow of power to local warlords, has reopened the floodgates, and Afghanistan has resumed its traditional role as the world's largest supplier of heroin. Opium revenue amounts to some 35% of the national's gross domestic product. Despite a high-profile attempt by U.S. and officials in Kabul to eradicate producers, Afghanistan's 2006 harvest was reported to be the largest in history. United Nations authorities predicted it would amount to 6,100 tons, 92% of the world supply (Time Inc., 2006; p. 57).

THE ENDING CIVIL WAR

The civil war had continued between different factions in some part of the country and many people paid with their lives. According to the Wall Street Journal on January 6th of 1997, an air raid in Kabul killed four people and injured 32 others. At the same time a bomb in the busy streets of Kabul killed three and injured 37 people. While such killings were normal during the civil war era, it still happens today in some parts of the country while many individuals working with the existing administration are trying to bring peace to the country.

Current Afghan leaders and officials have done a good job of creating some security in Kabul (and many other provinces), so government and corporate employees can continue assisting the country in its development. These are brave individuals who have a vision of a brighter Afghanistan and have been willing to lose their lives for the country. While the country needs security and safety, there are still some individuals and groups of people that feel they need to continue living in chaos, as it may have benefited them personally in the past. As such, these individuals, along with others who oppose a functioning administration, are causing sporadic destruction and violence at times. The following are some of the unfortunate incidents that the current administration has had to deal with on a regular basis in 2004 (Pajhwok Afghan News, 2004):

1. The Pajhwok Afghan News reported that an Iranian woman and her three children who were kidnapped and smuggled into Afghanistan from her country were found by police in the eastern province of Laghman after an intensive operation.

2. On December 2nd 2004, tribal elders from eastern Nangarhar province vowed not to allow the US led coalition forces into their homes in search of opium. The provincial officials in the capital city of Jalalabad asked the Afghan government not to allow the coalition forces to carry out military operations on the basis of unverified reports and eye witness accounts. A tribal elder had said that there were no members of the Taliban or Al Qaeda in their province. He had further said that "Both the Taliban and Al Qaeda originate in Pakistan and they are there now – so the Americans should pursue them in that country." Another person had said, "The Americans must stop searching our homes on the basis of wrong information; they will have to suffer the consequences and pay the price." It appears that many people are bothered that the US military pursues any wrong lead they are given. As such, they should check out the information with Afghan officials before they barge into people's homes. The elders have said, "We are not going to allow random searches like the ones the US coalition forces carried out in the southern province of Helmand." One member had said that "If the Americans really want to collect opium they should buy it by paying for it -- -so no one will lose anything then." The Governor of Nangarhar, Haji Din Mohammad, said the US coalition forces do not seem to have a clear strategy or plan on how to go about dealing with the problem of poppy. "Their real aim is to hunt down remnants of Taliban and Al Qaeda, but their operations seem to be so haphazard and unsynchronized and that is why so many problems are caused," the governor said. The Afghan government has assured people that the previous mistakes of the US-led coalition forces will not be repeated.

3. The Jalalabad–Kabul highway was blocked by hundreds of angry demonstrators in late October 2004, protesting the detention of an Afghan woman and three men from the Bati-Kot district of Nangarhar province. The demonstrators lined the major road from three o'clock in the afternoon to eleven o'clock at night, chanting anti-American slogans. "Death to America"

– "We are ready to fight the Americans" – "Soviet troops were far better than the American ones, they shouted." They set vehicles on fire, and cracked the windows of cars, said a government representative in the Bati-Kot district. Unfortunately, the police fired their guns and killed one of the civilians. The female prisoner, Mahgul, held by the American forces in Jalalabad airport was released. The three men, Sayed Ahmad, Shabir Ahmad, Khan Mohammad, and the woman Mahgul were arrested following a series of operations in the district. The people of Bati Kot district say they were angered when they found that Mahgul had to leave her one-month old baby at home on the day of her detention on Saturday.

4. On October 28th 2004, the US led coalition forces detained 40 suspected Taliban members from the Dehrawood district in southern Oruzgan province in connection with the death of two US soldiers who were killed by an improvised explosive device (IED). Security officials believed the explosive device was planted by people working against the Afghan government and the coalition forces, and the attack was carried out during a routine patrol.

5. In October 2004, three Afghans working for a local aid agency were killed by suspected Taliban militants in the Deleram district of Farah province, during the early hours of Sunday morning. Four government soldiers were also wounded during the clashes when they rushed to apprehend the attackers. The raid took place when a group of men in three pick-up trucks attacked the Volunteer Organization for Reconstruction of Afghanistan. The attackers who managed to escape killed two guards and a cook during the dawn assault and the third guard was believed to be missing.

ABC News and the Washington Post, on December 5th 2004, reported that Pat Tilman, one of the United States' army personnel, had been killed on March 2004 as a result of "friendly fire" in the Southeastern region of Afghanistan. Pat was one of the well-known athletes from the National Football League (NFL) who left a very promising career in the NFL to help bring peace in the world. Supposedly, some soldiers had taken the wrong route and got lost. A rescue mission, including Pat Tilman, was going after them to help them find their way, when the soldiers fired on them thinking they were either Al-Qaeda or Taliban forces. This is where Mr. Tilman got hit and eventually died. Pat Tilman's case is one of many such unfortunate incidents that can happen during violence and war. For example, during the initial period when the Taliban had been overthrown from Kabul, four Canadian soldiers and pilots died when their plane was shot down by American forces through "friendly fire."

Despite such unfortunate incidents, the economy and the quality of life has improved in the last few years, and the people of Afghanistan can actually see the possibility of a much brighter future. John Foster Dulles, U.S. Secretary of State, once said that "The measure of success is not whether you have a tough problem to deal with, but whether it's the same problem you had last year." Luckily, these incidents are not the major problems that Afghanistan was facing just a few years back which means the country is progressively realizing its goal of becoming peaceful and independent in due time. Of course, being peaceful can come faster if all

Afghan leaders can talk with each other (instead of fighting) about their dreams and vision for the country and its relationship with the rest of the world. The people of Afghanistan make up the country and; therefore, should have input in where it is going and how it should get there. Consequently, Afghanistan can be much healthier if all of its members are healthy, educated and happy. To provide an analogy, let us say that Afghanistan is like a person's body, since a body are made up of many different parts (such as hands, feet, heart, head, eyes, stomach, knees, buttocks, etc.). If any of the parts in a person's body is not working effectively, then the person is likely to not function well. In order for the person to be productive and totally healthy, each part of his/her body must also be functioning as it is meant to perform. Of course, each part of the body is needed and each part has its own function and level of importance for different tasks and responsibilities. For example, without the capability and proper use of the eyes, one will not be able to see, read or physically recognize others. So, when it comes to reading and seeing, the eyes are critical for this task. Without feet, one will not be able to physically walk, and without the use of one's arms it would be extremely difficult to do much work (such as building a house, typing, writing, or playing a keyboard). Similarly, there are certain body parts that are not talked about as much as the eyes, nose, teeth, feet, and the ears but they are just as important to the health of the body as any other part. For example, without certain internal organs a person is likely to die or be extremely sick. And, similarly, without the anus or "asshole" a person is not going to be able to excrete solid waste or feces and will likely die in a few days or weeks. Imagine each part of the body and then think about its functions, purpose and responsibilities to the body or person. Overall, each body part must be taken care of and respected for its purpose and capabilities as together they make up the person. The same is true for people and their countries; this means that with a population of about 28 million people, Afghanistan has many heads, hearts, eyes, nose, teeth, feet, hands, arms, and even "assholes" that help it be what it is and what it can be in the future. While some of these parts do their jobs well and function properly, other parts may not do so at times because they probably were not taken care of well, not used at all, or they were perhaps overused; thus leading to an injury, disability, or a temporary strain of certain muscles. As such, first there must be a diagnosis and then perhaps an appropriate prescription to remedy the pain or offer therapy to effectively deal with the disability. In other words, the people of the various provinces make up the country of Afghanistan and every Afghan should be healthy, heard, involved, and capable of fulfilling their obligation and functions if the country is to be economically productive and prosperous.

While there may also be many repeated challenges for Afghan leaders, the country of Afghanistan is developing the needed infrastructure, so young people can go to school, entrepreneurs can do business, and investors can benefit from the massive opportunities available in the country, and so the leaders can work with their international colleagues on interdependent relationships toward the creation of a peaceful world. Hopefully, capacity building and higher levels of education will soon eliminate the problems of conflict among various factions as well as the animosity, drug trafficking, and internal turmoil which has devastated Afghanistan for the past quarter of a century.

WORK AND KNOWLEDGE MANAGEMENT

In Afghanistan, people work six days each week, just as students go to school six days a week, and the weekly holiday is Friday. Many of the jobs are created by the government sector as privatization is just beginning to come to fruition in Afghanistan. Today, construction and rebuilding of the country's roads employ many professionals and laborers. The government-owned factory, called Baghrami Textile Mill, is one of the largest employers in Kabul. This firm employs about 1,500 people and, according to some individuals, the working conditions are not up to standards. The noise has been reported to be very high and some people are supposedly still working without safety protection. The same working conditions seem to be true in most industries due to lack of qualified inspectors, rules, and means of enforcing the existing expectations. Both Afghans and non-Afghans are now able to come and work in Afghanistan because opportunities for business and entrepreneurship are endless. The major challenge for Afghan managers, leaders and officials in a democratic country is the effective management and distribution of knowledge to everyone in a timely manner using means appropriate for an environment where the level of functional literacy is low.

Of course, the use and study of knowledge management dates back to Plato's and Aristotle's time. The recent research and discussions surrounding knowledge management focus on the technology issue or the human issue. Today, knowledge management offers a unique concept considered by many in the industry as progressive and "soft" in application, primarily because of the intangible elements of knowledge, especially of tacit knowledge which is competence without awareness. One way to make tacit knowledge explicit is through sharing and collaboration; this sharing and collaboration might take place more effectively through story-telling sessions for most Afghan workers that have not had the opportunity to attend school or receive a high school diploma.

Effective knowledge management is the essence of true democracy, as well as the fact that each leader should strive for providing a fair and just environment for everyone to access and benefit from the information. Most developing economies are now focusing on the accumulation and free dispersion of knowledge to encourage and promote democracy. What exactly is democracy and how does it relate to knowledge management in various professions? According to research and experts on this subject, democracy generally consists of four basic elements and none of these elements can take place effectively without a good system for knowledge management and distribution to all relevant parties. First, democracy can be seen as a political system for choosing and replacing the government through free and fair elections. Second, democracy is defined through the active participation of the people, as citizens, in politics and the civic life of a nation. Third, democracy is about the protection of the human rights of all citizens living in a nation. Fourth, democracy is about the rule of law, in which the laws and procedures apply equally to all citizens that live in the country.

The dream and means of achieving democracy might vary in different cultures since their history as a people, their mores and economic realities will vary from one society to another. For example, "free and fair elections" require an effective system so all the right information is easily documented, disseminated and presented to a majority of the population if they are going to freely and fairly elect officials and vote for certain constitutional amendments. Some countries do not have such luxuries as free access to information through computers, websites, or libraries; therefore, they rely on the initiative and knowledge of the few to guide the majority and make fair decisions for their welfare. In developing economies, such as Afghanistan, Pakistan, India, Morocco, and many others, a large percentage of the population may not be able to read and write at a functional level. To be a little more gender specific, in many third world countries, over 60% of the female population may not have had the needed education to read or write. Consequently, when the information is available, it is of very little use to these individuals who are not able to make good use of it. Thus, knowledge management strategies might be very different for such cultures and may take the form of story telling and community socialization seminars.

While the rule of law should apply equally to all citizens, their creation and public education must be the responsibility of those who are effectively equipped to make such decisions. For example, it is not fair to expect a four-star military general to competently make technical decisions about a country's marketing website for attracting tourists from across the globe. Besides, there might be other individuals who are better equipped for decisions related to tourism and online communication as per their professional background and educational achievements. Similarly, experts in the tourism industry and online communication are not necessarily always the best individuals for decisions that relate to the security of government officials and people all around the country. So, knowledge management, as well as its creation and dissemination, must be left to the professionals and experts who are properly equipped for it. This is especially true of third world countries where community elders or "freedom fighters" are often expected to become politicians. One must remember that these community elders and "freedom fighters" may not be qualified to perform the required expectations.

Of course, what is also interesting is that people have different perceptions of certain professions and generally attach either less or more respect for people who are associated with such careers. According to a survey report on July 26, 2006 from the local affiliate of the American Broadcasting Corporation in Fort Lauderdale, Florida, people have a high level of respect for such professions as fire fighters, medical doctors, nurses, and teachers, respectively. Perhaps these professionals are given the highest level of respect because they have to earn their knowledge prior to being able to actually perform their tasks. Furthermore, individuals associated with these professions are also expected to keep up with the changing pace of information and new knowledge. Finally, they work hard to serve people, and what they do is often physically transparent to the naked eye. On the other hand, such jobs as those of lawyers, real estate agents, and business executives were ranked on the bottom with regard to respectful professions. While members of these professions also have high ethical standards and are encouraged to be responsible leaders in their field, they are often accused of taking care of themselves first, of selfishness and self aggrandizement. The citizens of the United States, where the survey was completed, form these perceptions from what they hear from television reporters and what they read in the newspapers. Such perceptions are formed when people read that business executives (i.e. those from Enron, Tyco, WorldCom, etc.), who earn millions of dollars each year, intentionally cheat stockholders by hiding the truth, manipulating their earnings, or "cooking the books" to show more profits. Of course, such examples of unfair practices and unethical dealings in developing economies are evidence that all nations need to work on the creation of a democratic culture through effective knowledge management in order for everyone to receive fair and just treatment.

Effective knowledge management can come best through Afghan officials and entrepreneurs. In other words, foreign contractors and non-governmental officials (NGOs) are not always the best persons to be responsible for such activities as they may not always consider the long-term impact of what they do or the cultural nuances which are part of the society. As concerned citizens, Afghan professionals through the Society of Afghan Engineers have actually highlighted some important and critical factors regarding the rebuilding of Afghanistan. First of all, the recent upsurge in violence and the increase in opium cultivation in Afghanistan is a direct result of the slow process of reconstruction and lack of involvement of Afghans in whatever is being planned, built and implemented. Second, empowerment and total involvement of professional Afghans in the reconstruction of their homeland should be the top priority in the rebuilding process. Third, developing human and infrastructure capacity inside Afghanistan is a must for sustaining the reconstruction and further economic growth and development in Afghanistan. Finally, ensuring the active participation of professional Afghans in reconstruction programs will have far reaching effects on improving security, stability, peace, quality of life, and prosperity in Afghanistan. Many of the alternatives implemented thus far have proven very costly for the entire world, especially for Afghanistan and the Untied States. As per the concerns and recommendations of Afghan professionals, the program for empowerment of Afghan entrepreneurs and skilled workers, at a minimum, should include making skill development and on-the-job training of Afghans part of the scope of each national and international project in Afghanistan. Furthermore, performance incentive packages should include enhanced salaries, spot bonuses, pay raises…for high performing employees and there should be provisions for rewarding high performing employees with scholarships and training through exchange programs. There should also be a process for facilitating the transformation of local NGOs into private Afghan-based businesses along with mandatory joint ventures and partnership of foreign businesses with locally owned Afghan business. Overall, there must be an active and sustained campaign against corruption, nepotism…and other forms of unethical conduct must be included as part of this program. According to Afghan professionals in the Society of Afghan Engineers, recommendations for sustainable capacity building and empowerment programs in Afghanistan should include the following:

- Short-term training programs including intensive courses, seminars, workshops, and conferences for those who have proper education, but were deprived of the opportunity to practice in their field and stay current with advancements in science and technology. With proper training, this category of Afghan professionals could make a significant contribution to the reconstruction of Afghanistan.

- Continuous education programs including evening classes to provide education accreditation and licensing opportunities for those who were deprived from proper education and experience. This training can be offered on campus or through long distance learning programs.
- Vocational training as required for the reconstruction projects must also be offered at strategic locations around the country.
- Formal education from elementary through university for the new generation must be the cornerstone of the government education policy.

The Afghan Diaspora can bridge the capacity gap and more effectively bring a successful resolution to the rising violence. The United States, in cooperation with Afghan Government and their international allies through the United Nations, must facilitate and encourage the return of non-partisan (apolitical) Afghan professionals, skilled workers and entrepreneurs living in the United States, Asia, Arabian countries, and Europe by providing relevant and rewarding incentives. According to the members of Society of Afghan Engineers, at a minimum, some of the incentives among other things could include:

- First choice employment opportunities for qualified Afghan professionals in projects funded by the United Nations, the United States and other international allies.
- Facilitating expansion of their businesses in Afghanistan.
- Mandatory joint venture partnership requirements with Diasporas-owned businesses.
- Employment and visa guarantees for those who need or want to return to the foreign countries where their families are located.
- Facilitating safe transfer of their funds for investment to Afghanistan.
- Comprehensive orientation programs.
- Continuous in-country public information campaigns aimed at preventing potential tensions between Diasporas and local professionals.

Of course, SAE and Afghan professionals recommend that the Diaspora must not seek political positions or interfere in internal politics of Afghanistan. Politically, they must remain neutral and strictly focused on the rebuilding and reconstruction of Afghanistan. As Afghan professionals, we ask for the international community's continued support in making sure Afghan experts and entrepreneurs are supported and empowered so they can increase the true capacity building of their people and country through effective expenditure, accountability and knowledge management.

EDUCATION IN AFGHANISTAN

Prior to the war, the literacy rate in Afghanistan had reached about 15% for males and 10% for females. So, the illiteracy rate for the general population was very high, about 88% throughout the nation. Education is important and a necessity no matter what form or shape it takes. Education can take place in both formal and informal settings. If education is not created in a purposeful and formal setting, then it most certainly will not happen effectively by itself. In the absence of a formal process, people nonetheless will learn and understand things by observation from the community. However, the depth of what they understand, and how they come to understand, may vary, and may take more time. Since, learning is strongly linked to doing and people learn best by doing, learning is inevitable because all humans choose to do things in order to be happy. We know that people learn what they really want to learn; so as children we should be guided to intentionally learn specific subjects because a good number of children tend to be egotistic. However, as adults we should seek to learn not only about the unknown in life, but also learn things we feel passionately strong about because it is through doing what one loves that happiness and joy surfaces in life. Purposeful learning is a type of formal education that is geared toward understanding the necessities of life in a systematic way with both short-and long-term goals. Education is about learning and, as human beings, learning is one of our most basic drives internally fueled and ignited. Learning is about enhancing our ability to make better decisions and execute effective plans. Human beings are designed to learn and absorb knowledge like a sponge absorbs water regardless of situational barriers. Based on my observations, Afghanistan's teachers, politicians, government officials, and religious leaders had this common understanding about learning and their attempts to better educate everyone in the country were being well-received prior to the Communist coup. More people were going to school, more people were graduating from high schools and colleges, and more people were receiving graduate degrees from well-known developed foreign nations. The competition among students in the education sector was intense because people valued, respected, and appreciated the educated members of the society. Additionally, living in the Afghan society was very rewarding for those with higher education, because they could serve their country in a better way. Afghan leaders used to emphasize the value of a good education and were on the verge of fully understanding and valuing interdependence.

However, the situation changed during the Communist coup and the Russian invasion. For a while, it appeared as though things were changing for the better as education and equality among all Afghans was being promoted. The People's Democratic Party of Afghanistan (Communist government) promised a nation of happy and satisfied farmers who could build the country for themselves as well as the coming generation of Afghans. The Communist government promised total equality between young and old, men and women, rich and poor, and between politicians and farmers. The reality of equality to the Communist regime meant taking land from its owners and giving it to the farmers who actually did the work. People could not own more than a certain amount of acres and those who had more acres than the law allowed had to simply give them up. I believe this was one of the first and biggest mistakes of the Communist regime. While most people believe in true equality, and would love for it to exist, the distribution of people's land to other individuals was not very smart nor true equality. To me, equality means having the opportunity to do or accomplish things and being fairly compensated. As a human being and a Muslim, I do believe in charity, helping those in need, helping orphans, and helping senior citizens. However, I do not believe in favoritism based on economic status by helping low-income families to become wealthier at a cost to other hard working families. Chances are that most wealthy individuals have earned their wealth through hard work, talent, and dedication as opposed to cheating, stealing, killing, and committing immoral acts. Therefore, taking their homes and land away would be unjust and fail promote equality, efficiency, and good work ethics. In the schools, students were told that better schools and education systems would be provided by the Soviet Union and everyone would get an excellent education. The only added thing in schools was more lectures about theories and philosophies of communism, the history of communism, and the "nightmares of capitalism." In reality, students were encouraged, and in some cases, pressured to join the Youth Organization of the Communist Party, and they later became full-fledged members of the Communist party at the age of sixteen and seventeen. Most of the individuals who joined the Communist parties in schools were sent to foreign nations such as Cuba, East Germany, Bulgaria, Czechoslovakia, Poland, Russia, and other socialist countries for a brief period as a reward. I had many classmates in Allowdin Elementary School and Habibia High School that went to some of these communist countries. The duration of these trips varied from one month to several years. These so called "education trips" included playing sports, having fun, some learning, watching movies, and many sessions of hearing about communism, Lenin, Marx, and their philosophies. Some of these young Muslim students, who are prohibited from alcoholic beverages, were given vodka and wine at times without their parent's consent. The adult students were mostly trained to become skilled military experts who could come back and fight along with the Russians. The Communists attempted to brainwash them through propaganda and misinformation about the Freedom Fighters, and how destructive they were to the country as well as other such lectures. Most of the men who were able to fight were sent back to Afghanistan immediately after their military training. Ahmad Shaw Masood, a well-known Commander in Jamiat-i-Islami Afghanistan who had also received some training in Russia, upon his return decided to fight against them and eventually became a powerful and influential Freedom Fighter in Afghanistan.

In the late 1990s, most of the female schools were closed as the government "temporarily" banned girls from attending school. One of the largest female schools in the country was Zarghona High School which served over 3,000 students; another one was Rob-e-'ai Balkhee High School, with a student enrollment of about 2,000. There were three other large schools in Kabul that were strictly designed for female students, which unfortunately were not being used for education during that era. However, according to an interview with the Taliban government officials, Diane Sawyer reported that females will be going to school and work once the government was able to provide them with the appropriate and necessary resources. Of course, that never did happen during their control since the international community did not provide much support to them. Today, many females and males are going to schools and do receive some education, which is not yet up to the high standards of quality as it was prior to the invasion because there has been a shortage of qualified teachers. Yet, it is believed that the education will get better as the rebuilding of Afghanistan continues, and the civil war ends throughout the country. The development has already begun and is progressing steadily in the positive direction. On September 19th 2004, the South Florida Sun-Sentinel published an article entitled "*Afghan teens find nothing to fear in South Florida stay*" written by a staff writer named Rafael Olmeda. The article was about three young Afghan exchange students who were in the United

States for one year to complete their education with American children while getting a "crash" course on the Western culture. Upon reading the article, I emailed the writer and made contact with the exchange students and visited with them two days later. The exchange students studying in South Florida schools were Abdulahad Barak (16 years of age from Qandahar), Khushal Rasoli (17 years of age from Qandahar), and Abdulahad Fazil (16 years of age from Char-asia of Logar). They were in South Florida until June of 2005 and then joined their colleagues back in Afghanistan to continue their schooling. They came to the United States along with 40 other Afghan exchange students who were dispersed throughout the various states living with American host families for the duration of their stay in America. Barak and Rasoli attended public schools while Fazil was accepted at a private Islamic school in Broward County. For the last few months of their stay in the United States, Fazil was also able to attend a public school to interact with more local people in regular high school classes. These bright and well-behaved exchange students were learning and enjoying their stay in the United States, and they were able to attend an Afghan wedding in West Palm Beach during November, visit Afghans in Orlando while visiting parts of Disney World attractions, and attended an Afghan gathering over New Years in Gainesville, Florida, where they met many of their countrymen and women. Of course, every Afghan living in Florida was thrilled to see them speaking so eloquently and intelligently about Afghanistan and their country of birth. The exchange students got an opportunity to meet with Dr. Fazil Najafi, Professor of Engineering at the University of Florida, and Engineer Zahir, a successful entrepreneur in Jacksonville, who advised them to make the best of this opportunity in the United States. Apparently, Dr. Najafi and Engineer Zahir were also exchange students to the United States when they were in high school, and offered helpful suggestions based on their personal experiences to all three of the exchange students. In 2005, there were 40 other Afghan exchange students from high schools in Afghanistan that were able to come to the United States and live with host families to attend one year of their schooling in this environment. Once again, four of these bright and spiritually competent students (Rafee, Khalid, Masood, and Ghani) were able to live with host families in the South Florida region and yours truly was able to visit with them on many occasions. They too had the opportunity to attend several Afghan gatherings and visit with Afghan families throughout the Florida region. They went back to Afghanistan in June of 2006 to continue their education back home. However, in August 2006, out of a new group of 40 Afghan exchange students five of them (Hasibullah, Mohammad Reza, Wajmah, Raubia, and Yagana) were once again housed with host families in the South Florida area. Thus far, I have been able to meet with all of them and they are truly enjoying their educational experiences in the Western environment, while spreading factual information about the needs of Afghan people in the community. These students are great role models as they speak several languages, are very articulate, earn excellent grades in school, model great behavior, dress according to the Afghan norms and customs, and always perform their prayers. While one of these articulate exchange students (Masood Jan) was able to speak and converse in nine different languages, all of them have been able to fluently speak Dari, Pushtu, and English. Many of them were also further able to speak and converse in other tongues such as Urdu, Turkish, Russian, and Arabic languages. It is understood and acknowledged that these exchange students have probably had a "slight" advantage compared to most Afghan teenagers who do not have access to educational facilities, competent and well paid educators, and or literate family adults who could "home school" them. Furthermore, these exchanges students were tested and "screened out" through a rigorous examination process from thousands of others who may have wanted the same opportunities. Since English fluency was a major element of the examination process to select the final group of eligible students for the exchange program, then perhaps these students would be expected to be great orators and master various languages faster than others due to their genetic or "developed" cleverness or aptitude regarding speaking and learning abilities. What is a fact is that if Afghan teenagers can be so articulate, intelligent and bright despite not having full access to modern technologies, classrooms, academic resources, and well-developed and comfortable educators, then just imagine how far they could actually go and what they could realistically achieve with the "advantage" of proper and up-to-date resources and not having to worry about civil wars, factional fighting and whether they will be able to live until high school graduation. These young exchange students are representing the true essence of what Afghanistan stands for and they are making many Afghans very proud through their character, hard work and great ethic. They are the future of Afghanistan, and if given proper educational opportunities, they can make Afghanistan a truly stable and developed country in the Asian region. Such progress and development opportunities offered to the future leaders of Afghanistan are great initiatives for the creation of a peaceful and educated country in the coming decades. Of course, these developments should not be limited to high school students since college students and the current adult population needs development as well.

While the Afghan children are getting better resources to receive their education, the world community, including young kids, is attempting to help them. An article written by Eileen Soler (2005) discussed how school children in Miramar, Florida, spearheaded a group that responded to a request to help children in Afghanistan. Students from Miramar High School, Perry Middle School and Nur-Ul-Islam Academy in Cooper City jointly working with the Miramar Police Youth Advisory Council raised money for buying school supplies and toys that were sent to DeKhuaja area of Afghanistan which is about two hours north of Kabul. About a dozen police officers, and Mayor Lori Moseley, donated their time to raise money, gather the supplies and ship everything for about 500 children to Afghanistan. Besides such assistance to children in primary schools, higher education schools are helping adults get the necessarily skills to plan, initiate and successfully continue as managers and entrepreneurs. Michelle Roberts (2005) discussed how business school training in Arizona helps Afghan women establish and expand lucrative businesses. Roberts (2005) expanded on the story of how 14 Afghan women participated in a special program that assists them get the education to expand and/or build new businesses in Afghanistan. The two-week training program at Thunderbird, the Garvin School of International Management, provides an overview of business school lessons covering marketing, strategizing, accounting, and the development of a business plan. The women have been paired with mentors who will continue to assist the mentees with their plans over the next several years. Since over 50% of the Afghan population will be women and the fact that there are over 70,000 widows today in and around the Kabul area, such training programs and mentoring assistance will equip women to start small businesses to support themselves and their children.

In 2003, at the Society of Afghan Engineers Conference at the Steven's Institute of Technology in New Jersey, I had a chance to meet Dr. Fiaez, Minister of Higher Education in Afghanistan. At that time, he mentioned that there is a strategic plan in place to provide quality education programs to all college students. He said that there were over 36,000 students at various universities in Afghanistan in 2003. Of course, this number is likely to be well over 50,000 college students by the end of 2007 as more refugees are returning home to complete their education. Furthermore, the government officials have been attempting to create more opportunities for students in the form of a community college system so they could attend classes locally during the first two years. Furthermore, Kabul University will soon have extended opportunities in the areas of computers, economics and architecture. In a video conference on January 7th 2005 and personal communication with the author in February of 2005, Dr. Ashraf Ghani, President of Kabul University at the time, said that his vision for the university includes a School of Engineering and Computer Science; a School of Architecture, Town Planning, and Environmental Engineering; and a School of Management, with a curriculum starting with economics and administration, and continuing with Management (public and/or private sector).

According Nikpai on February 1st of 2005, "Higher education in Afghanistan is expected to be revamped with international funding of $250 million" as per an interview with the current Minister for Higher Education, Dr. Sayed AmriSha Hasanyar. In his interview with Pajhwok, Dr. Hasanyar said the number of university students had increased by ten fold from the 4000 enrolled in the system during the time of the Taliban. As stated by Nikpai, it is conceivable that this number would go up to 1 million students in next ten years with the enrollment of 4 million in primary schools. To meet this demand, the Ministry would have to increase the number of teachers by thousands. Unfortunately, Afghanistan currently does not have the necessary modern education system. Compared to education systems elsewhere, Afghanistan's current resources and school system are partially outdated and lack a proper curriculum, textbooks and administrative system. "Basic facilities like laboratories, libraries and internet connections were also lacking (Nikpai, 2005). Initially in its first few years, the ministry along with appropriate personnel will begin reviewing the curriculum, launching administrative reforms and reconstruction. Its long-term plans for the next five years include construction of buildings, establishing laboratories and libraries, teaching and recruiting qualified professors and entering into agreements with international universities and expansion of provincial universities in Nangarhar, Balkh, Herat and Kandahar which are among the priorities.

It is fortunate to see that educated individuals, through their involvement in such important decisions as the education of thousands and millions of Afghans, are paving the way towards a brighter Afghanistan. While having an advanced degree on the part of each official is not a solution for all of Afghanistan's current and prospective challenges, it is an important initial step forward toward the development of each person's capacity to produce knowledge, make better decisions, and live in a more qualitative manner. It is also great to see that the new Constitution of Afghanistan has made the credentials of higher education a required consideration for selecting ministers. Such requirements will certainly encourage learning, creativity, and continuous pursuit of knowledge among all those who want to serve Afghanistan using their mental faculties through peaceful means. There are many individuals who have served their country through honesty and diligence over the past few decades without any formal education and they deserve consideration for some of the top positions. Certainly, the honest hard work of all individuals must be duly acknowledged and their services as advisors and other appropriate positions should be sought and used for relevant positions. It must also be considered that knowledge of war, skills of surviving a war, and guiding people to fight safely and strategically may not always transfer well to other jobs where the future of a country is being decided. While one might be perfectly prepared to manage and lead a group of people to a guerrilla type battle to attack the enemy who invaded the country, such skills are not necessarily transferable to leading people toward education, getting to work on time, and higher levels of mental development to effectively compete in the global marketplace. Of course, there are many commonalities between leading people to a battle and getting them to come to work for a good cause; however, the variables and the environments can change drastically. As such, professional certification and higher levels of current knowledge in each specific field are required if one is to appropriately lead Afghans toward productivity and better performance.

So, Afghan elders should use their years of wisdom and knowledge in every mentoring opportunity they get when leading younger individuals to become more competitive locally and globally. However, there might be cases when Afghan elders, as effective situational leaders, may have to voluntarily step aside and let the most knowledgeable person lead everyone as he or she might be better suited to make the people, the department, and the country of Afghanistan more competitive in today's global environment of business and entrepreneurship. There is always a right person with the right skills and management insights to lead people in specific fields. The key is to seek, recruit and retain such individuals by providing them with the right incentives and work environment. For example, a doctor might be a very wise person but he or she cannot be a good engineer without getting an engineering certification or the relevant experience. So, the doctor should do jobs that are in his or her field rather taking positions that require certain engineering skills. Similarly, a respected lawyer cannot function well as a doctor or as an architect since each of these fields requires relevant education and experience. Of course, Afghans should be familiar with this since usually the most learned and the most educated clergy is the lead person in the Mosque and not necessarily the oldest or the wisest person. Official rank, intelligence, level of wealth, body size, and one's overall status in the community does not necessarily determine who leads the prayer in the Mosque since the right person is one who has acquired the right education and certification about Islam, theology, spirituality, and/or relevant prayers for the community. In many cases, a young "Talib," "Hofiz," or "Imam" at the age of 25 is much more qualified to lead the prayers than a 60 year-old successful entrepreneur who is well respected in the community. Of course, the entrepreneur does not get offended if he is not asked to lead the prayer because he knows there is a person who has devoted his life specifically to being a "priest" and leading prayers. So, the priest is the best qualified person to lead the prayer. In this case, the entrepreneur can still get involved in the affairs of Mosque (Masjid) by being the general manager, finance director, media advisor or education director based on the size and location of the Mosque. For example, as the author of this book, I have a doctorate degree in business administration with specialties in human resources and international management which qualifies me to work and teach in these fields. These degrees and my nearly twenty-five years of management experience and training also qualify me to manage large departments, companies, businesses, and non-profit agencies. However, none of these degrees and years of experience qualify me to effectively function as an engineer, a nurse, a soldier or commander, a doctor, or a counselor to individuals with mental disabilities. So, I function best in the fields of consulting, directing, training, teaching, managing, speaking, leading, and coordinating small or large projects. In the Lakeland Mosque, I used to serve as the Education Director and sometimes I lead the prayer when the Imam, the Assistant Imam or other qualified individuals were not present. Despite these skills and academic qualifications, I could not be a good military commander since I know very little about fighting opponents and much of this little indirect philosophical or theoretical experience comes from earning a third-degree black belt in Tae Kwon Do. I received my experience and martial art belts at the American Tae Kwon Do Federation with Grandmaster Y. K. Kim while serving as an educational instructor with the World Martial Arts Research Foundation, founded by Grandmaster Kim in Central Florida. While the variables of sizing up an opponent, being prepared physically and mentally, practicing with discipline, and knowing all the rules might be similar to a battlefield, as a military commander I would quickly lose the battle to a very weak opponent. So, because I know this information I would not allow myself to be the commander since serving as a good solider and being led by a qualified commander could save my life and increase the likelihood of success for the team. The same analogy applies to the twenty-first century environment of global competition where the best survives and the weakest are pushed aside. Afghanistan needs the right individuals in the right jobs if they are to be a "relevant player" in the international community and successfully compete in today's global economy. So, the right individuals should be put in each job and they must be given the opportunities to serve their country in the best way possible. The same concept and principles apply to the selection of ministers and government leaders: the right person must be selected for the right job. The December 15th 2004 issue from Embassy of Afghanistan News reported that "The President is being advised by all Afghans to comply with the Constitution" which requires the consideration of advanced education for the selection of ministers. Such advice is good and hopefully all leaders will take this to heart as they select who should lead each ministry and each department. The existing choice of cabinet members certainly shows that diversity and higher education was considered and rewarded. Besides having the right education, the right candidates should be continuous learners since knowledge doubles every five to ten years as new information is being generated at an enormous pace. Of course, continuous learning is an important imperative for effective management and leadership regardless of one's country or work location.

As stated before, the facts must never get in the way of truth and peace as Afghans continue their progress and development. All the workers and leaders currently in Afghanistan are making great contributions with a noble end in mind...to improve Afghanistan. Afghans must continue achieving the three ingredients in the good life: "learning, earning, and yearning." Afghans have a choice and can "place" themselves in the categories of those individuals that are immovable, those that are movable, and those that move. Each Afghan has the choice to constantly "move" toward worthwhile and predetermined ethical goals with integrity thereby making his/her life, and that of their family members and colleagues more interesting and joyful throughout Afghanistan. Afghans and their country have endured much suffering but they are now healing and must continue this trend. Most Afghans know that being injured and defeated is often a temporary condition; however, giving up is what makes it permanent and Afghans cannot afford to give up. Each and every Afghan has the power for greatness because greatness is measured and determined by one's service to the community. Afghans and their country can be great once again so long as they continue to persist in their vision toward peace in a peaceful manner. Both formal and informal means of continuous education are critical factors in higher levels of thinking, better decision making, better treatment of people, equality, justice, fairness, and a better quality of life for the people of Afghanistan.

EDUCATIONAL NEEDS

Developing countries need resources, education, and training if they are to effectively transition and take full advantage of internationalization and privatization trends in this global economy. In the case of Afghanistan, based on personal visits to the country and research, this author feels that capacity building and leadership skills are best for new and incoming employees and managers in both the public and private sectors. These leadership and life skills can be used in any capacity, including with young children and adults in the community.

Stephens and Ottaway (2005) write that "Within the {Afghan} government there have been sobering private reassessments about the effort." They further stated that "The schools and clinical programs have been marked by a series of missteps and miscalculations that resulted in a flawed business model, inadequate supervision and poor execution." Some of this is probably due to the lack of comprehensive plans or insufficient number of inspectors. Stephens and Ottaway mentioned that "USAID did not, at the outset, have a quality assurance plan or adequate staff to monitor performance." Experts have concluded that "poor program design lay at the heart of the problems that have dogged this program." Others have said that the reconstruction effort has been "a highly successful program" that suffered from overly ambitious expectations (Stephens and Ottaway, 2005). In other cases, the international community's aid to Afghanistan has fallen short of what was promised or expected, and this has dramatically slowed down progress in educating and developing Afghans.

Margaret Coker and Anne Usher mention one example where international military officials contracted a firm to build a school but said that "no one from the military came back to inspect the quality of materials or the company's work." The next time that the villagers had seen the soldiers was weeks later at a ribbon-cutting ceremony. The military officials from the United States supposedly took pictures of the new building and then left (Coker and Usher, 2005). According to Coker and Usher, "Two years and $20,000 later, the locally made mud bricks crumble to the touch, and termites have infested the roof beams, leaving villagers with the morbid pastime of guessing when the ceiling will fall." It is reasonable for the local people to assume that the officials only care about photographs and marketing their achievements to the western Media regardless of the workmanship quality. Coker and Usher report that the "Use of inferior construction materials is just one of myriad complaints lodged by auditors and aid workers who are critical of U.S. efforts to rebuild Afghanistan."

According to Coker and Usher, "the U.S. Government Accountability Office (GAO) cited bureaucratic squabbles, poor planning, and a lack of coordination and oversight in the spending of U.S. reconstruction money in Afghanistan" for the slow progress. Coker and Usher concluded that the building and public works projects by the State Department and the Pentagon have had little impact on improving the country's long-term reconstruction. Afghanistan is ranked among the world's worst in terms of poverty, literacy and infant mortality, and the slow reconstruction endangers short- and long-term stability of the administration and the country. The reality is that it might have been easier to import skilled Afghan and non-Afghan workers from abroad and to train local people through effective leadership skills so they could take on more jobs and responsibilities. Leadership is a skill that all Afghans can use both in the workplace and in schools as they situationally develop their workers to take on more responsibility. Coker and Usher state that "improving primary education, by building schools, revamping inadequate curricula and training teachers, is a goal embraced by all international agencies working in Afghanistan." However, some of the U.S. government's most abysmal reconstruction results came in education. Coker and Usher mention that from 2002 till 2005, about 3,500 schools have been built or refurbished. Yet, according to the Education Ministry, another 2,000 schools will be needed if all children are to attend school. Initially, the USAID had projected that it would refurbish or build 286 schools by the end of 2004, but according to Coker and Usher, USAID "contractors had only completed eight by that deadline and refurbished about 77 others, with a coat of paint sometimes counting as a refinished school." Building the schools is important in preparing the new generation for strengthening both the private and public sectors.

Some international lending agencies such as the World Bank and nonprofit organizations have demonstrated better results than USAID (Coker and Usher, 2005). According to Coker and Usher, "CARE International, which has worked in Afghanistan for 44 years, built 40 schools in 2004, which in most cases cost between $10,000 and $20,000 less than U.S.-sponsored projects." Typically, the schools which have been constructed by USAID contractors tend to cost between $60,000 and $80,000. Coker and Usher conclude that "CARE's faster pace was possible in part because it already had relationships with Afghan villages and businesses with which to organize and build." Perhaps, building strong relationships with the local community, current workers, and the new generation of Afghans is a must if effective capacity building, education and leadership are to be practiced in the development of Afghanistan.

Currently there are many great thoughts regarding advancement of Afghanistan from Afghans who have passed on to their eternal life and those who are still living. During a face-to-face interview in May 2006 with Mrs. Frieda M. Zabuli, the widow of Mr. Abdul Madjid Zabuli who used to be one of the respected ministers in Afghanistan, she said, "I respected Mr. Abdul Madjid Zabuli from the day fate had crossed our paths between the years of 1955 and 1956 when I worked for him. But after reading his official correspondence, to government officials, upon his death my respect for him grew immensely." She spoke of Minister Zabuli's devotion toward the progress and opportunities for Afghanistan and where he thought the country could have been in the coming decades. Mrs. Frieda Zabuli continued by saying that "I knew his love for his country, his vision which was needed to build Afghanistan's economy from zero national income to an income of billions of dollars" through service, education and national productivity.

Mrs. Frieda Zabuli also mentioned that she knew of his desperate efforts in the 1970s to warn Afghan officials about the efforts of neighboring countries as well as the former Soviet Union and the United States desiring to find a way to the Pacific Ocean (warm water seaport route) through Afghanistan and Pakistan. In other words, Minister Zabuli had warned the people of Afghanistan that foreigners would continue their attempts to interfere in the affairs of the country in order to easily control it toward their own entrepreneurial and militaristic strategic plans. Of course, looking back over the last three decades, one can see that Minister Zabuli's projections did come true and foreign interferences combined with internal civil wars have led to total destruction of infrastructure in the country. Mrs. Frieda Zabuli said that despite Minister Zabuli's efforts, "nobody listened and it is frightening to learn how often only one man's opinion can stir things in such a way that war is the only option in the end." She stated that logic, reason and such calculated projections made by knowledgeable Afghans should not have been dismissed. According to Mrs. Zabuli, "One can learn of the short-sightedness of the leading government officials and also of the jealousy and greediness of higher ups" by reviewing the past, looking at what is happening in the present, and hopefully bringing about appropriate changes to impact the future. Since Minister Zabuli's projections were not listened to toward bringing appropriate changes, Mrs. Zabuli said "All this together made him more eager to promote education as he always wrote, and also told me often, that only education can make Afghanistan's future brighter."

In one of his letters to President Daud Khan during the mid 1970s, Minister Zabuli had advised: "Try to create such an ambience where narrow mindedness, selfishness and hostility are replaced by a sense of service and sacrifice for the progress and independence of the country, so that all people would sincerely participate in any effort for the progress of their homeland. Furthermore, until you have built a new house as a national shelter, you should not destroy the existing house, however uncomfortable it may be." Minister Abdul Madjid Zabuli meant that by pursuing the efforts to develop the country further (including education) the country would have reached a more secure position. And the president, Daud Khan, could then initiate the new reforms without causing internal turmoil in the country or among various ethnicities of people.

Mrs. Frieda Zabuli also knows that "One could talk and talk; unfortunately, people do not always learn from examples and some of the responsible ones are conditioned to only think of power for themselves." She stated that "If this mindset continues, then who cares for the people in remote places in Afghanistan, and who cares for their suffering?" While years of war has conditioned the culture of

Afghanistan toward safety and protection of one's own family and friends, there are also many great individuals in Afghanistan that do care for the people of their country in all regions and are putting their best talents forward to bring about equality, fairness, justice, and progress for the poor and rich alike through education and peaceful endeavors. As such, the international community should increase their assistance in enabling these individuals to create a strong foundation in Afghanistan through education so the country can become peaceful and an effective entrepreneurial player in the Asian region.

WOMEN IN AFGHANISTAN

Despite the popular belief by many foreigners, Afghan women have traditionally been equal partners in their cities and villages with their male counterparts. However, the Russian invasion tilted the scales to the male side as the lack of security, unsafe work environment, and the high mountains and ragged war situation made it difficult for women to remain equal partners. In the 1970s and 1980s, when I was attending school in Kabul, males and females attended the same classes and attended the same classrooms prior to high school. However, males and females were segregated during ninth, tenth, eleventh, and twelfth grades, due to their emotional and physical growth and/or level of immaturity at this stage. To reduce the psychological and emotional ties to sexual activities and thoughts, students during these grades attended separate schools. During college studies, after twelfth grade, the classes were mixed again because by the age of eighteen to nineteen most individuals are old enough to act responsibly. Historically, Afghan women were traditionally encouraged to stay home and take care of children, as influenced by other cultures in previous centuries. However, during the decades of 1960s, 1970s, and 1980s, these traditional views were changing as more women were attending schools and becoming part of the workforce in Afghanistan. Islam encourages education for everyone, knowledge and learning for everyone, and does not discriminate according to gender. However, Islam has set guidelines of how each gender is to dress moderately and act appropriately. *Chadari* (used for veiling or covering the whole body), which has been traditionally worn by some women in Afghanistan, is culture-based and not mandated by Islam. Women in Afghanistan were able to work along with men; however, there were biases by some individuals and groups of people who were conditioned to see women only as mothers and care-takers of the family. The education and equality of women in the decision-making process will be imperative in the growth of Afghanistan. Most women see things from a care perspective, while men generally approach situations from a predominantly justice orientation. The combination of these perspectives can effectively balance the recovery endeavors from the war and speedup the growth process. Past research has supported the fact that females have a higher sense of personal ethics than males. Gender makes a difference in the moral judgment of individuals, and often females approach moral issues from different perspectives than males, which are both needed for balanced decisions. Afghans have always prohibited people (both genders) from adultery and fornication, yet some young males who violated these rules were not punished as severely as the females. Such imbalanced and biased rules seem to be still present in many developed as well as developing nations. In the United States and European countries, females who are "close romantic friends" with many males simultaneously are at times referred to as "easy" (or sometimes whores), while their male counterparts who commit similar acts are not held to the same standards nor are they always victims of such labels. Certainly, there seems to be different and, at times, unfair standards applied for each gender, due to various reasons, around the world and Afghanistan is no exception.

The traditional feminine traits can improve the ethical environment of a country by bringing more sensitivity, caring treatment of citizens, more creative approaches to problem-solving, more effective relationship-building skills, creating greater trust in interpersonal affairs, and being supportive and understanding of others. In Afghanistan, men are usually expected to be head of the family, the leaders, the protectors, and the disciplinarians. Research has shown that women have been and can be great leaders, may be better protectors than men, as well as head of the households, and great disciplinarians, who can be very effective because they approach their decisions from a care and relationship orientation. On the other side, some women can also be less decisive. They can take more time to make decisions, and may even be naive at times. Conversely, men can be too decisive without enough information and too quick in the decision-making process without considering the relationship or its consequences on people. The best approach would be to combine the best traits of each sex to have a balance of the best characteristics from both sides. This will enable individuals to help each other by effectuating strong solutions to their personal and political challenges, while males and females could learn from each other. Experts mention some of the differences among males and females as they relate to moral dilemmas, and they are summarized in Table 6.

Table 6 - Male and Female Differences in Moral Reasoning

In solving ethical dilemmas, females are likely to:	In solving ethical dilemmas, males are likely to:
• Primarily respect feelings	• Primarily respect rights
• Ask "who will be hurt?"	• Ask "who is right?"
• Avoid being judgmental	• Value decisiveness
• Search for compromise to achieve fairness	• Make unambiguous decisions based on available data
• Seek solutions that minimize hurt	• Seek solutions that are objectively fair
• Rely on communication	• Rely on rules
• Believe in contextual relativism	• Believe in blind impartiality
• Be guided by emotion	• Be guided by logic
• Challenge authority	• Accept authority

We arrive in this world alone and, similarly, we will leave this world alone. However, in between our journeys, we interact with people, environment, space, cultures, and other natural forces which we may not fully understand. One of these natural forces is the gender differences, capabilities, and characteristics among human beings which have resulted in much happiness for many people and can make us all happy if we take advantage of these differences appropriately. Synergy, true and productive unity, lies in valuing and celebrating differences in our families, companies, and communities. So, depending on how we respond to each other's differences, our happiness and quality of life will be determined accordingly, regardless of how we reach conclusions. However, one thing is clear and that is both men and women are equally capable of making excellent decisions, and accordingly should be given equal opportunities to do so in order for everyone to be happy and productive as human beings.

One of the highest-ranking and most powerful women in Afghanistan during the Communist regime had been Dr. Anahita Ratebzad, a senior Afghan Political member. She had studied nursing at the University of Michigan in the 1950s. She earned her medical degree in Kabul and became a professor of preventive medicine. She had joined the Parcham party in 1965 during its infancy. She became a well-known figure during the Communist regime and served as the president for World Peace and Solidarity Organization and the Democratic Women's Organization in Afghanistan. She was a talented and well-educated individual whose hard work and dedication were perhaps on the "wrong side," of the Communist regime. I had heard some of her speeches in Afghanistan and her vision as well as mission seemed exemplary to many people throughout the country. She was a high-ranking politician in a male-dominated country (as well as the world for all practical matters) and that by itself required not only intelligence but also the charisma to function as a leader, which she did.

In 1995, the Taliban government banned women from going to school and to work in the city of Kabul. According to their representatives, this decision was only temporary, and females would be able to attend school and work after proper measures were taken to segregate men from women. This segregation would provide each gender the opportunity to educate themselves regardless of variations in the quality of education or physical environment during learning. As stated before, this never came to fruition. Now, the current administration has several women at high ranking positions in the cabinet and this is a good start toward bringing more equality between the two genders in Afghanistan.

DRUGS IN AFGHANISTAN

Islam has always prohibited drugs, alcohol, and all other substances that can hurt the body by intoxicating people, ergo altering their state of mind and decision-making. The "narco-mafia" economy is a major threat to the security and peace in Afghanistan. As such, the fight against all illegal narcotics in Afghanistan is one of the top priorities for the government and must remain until it is totally eliminated and/or under control. As a matter of fact, the government of Afghanistan held a two-day National Conference on Counter-Narcotics during December 8-9, 2004 where the President personally declared a "jihad" against illegal growth and sale of narcotics. All drugs are prohibited in Islam and in Afghanistan, including their use as pain killers, if other options are available. Islam is and has always been clear about its status on drugs. However, the problem in Afghanistan and Pakistan has been associated with the enforcement of these religious or government laws against drugs. In both Afghanistan and Pakistan, one can buy drugs just as easily as one can buy headache medicine. Although there have been times when the headache medicine has been outdated according to its expiration date, entrepreneurs nevertheless would try to sell it to those who cannot read. In December 2005 when I became ill in the city of Logar, a cousin bought some medication from the local pharmacy and several of the items were outdated by two years. Since the content and dates were written in the English language, most people do not notice the dates, nor can they always read the dates, and, thereby become victims of buying medications that might do more damage to their body than helping them get better. The widespread presence of drug trafficking is a world problem since it is the users in developed nations that finance these crops. However, one can easily find marijuana and related illegal drugs grown in Afghanistan. It is also possible that in the absence of a good, affordable healthcare system, many victims of the war will continue using hashish and marijuana to cope with emotional and psychological pains. This is, and will be, a common side effect of most war participants for Afghan and Russian soldiers since there is not much medical help available for them. There were many Afghans who had been tortured physically and psychologically, and lost many of their family members to the war. Many of them witnessed their families killed right in their presence. Some of these individuals give up hope and temporarily became insane; thus their only friend was the drug which provided them with the energy and escape from their past to fight whole heartedly against their enemies.

In the past, as well as the present, morphine and heroin have been used by medical doctors as pain-killers. This dilemma is still being debated in the developed countries, because some people would like physicians to be able to legally prescribe these drugs as pain-killers to their patients. While developing nations are able to control, reduce, or even eliminate their black-market drug activities, the drug lords and smugglers have been seeking new areas to supply their demands. I should mention that most Afghans do not swear, gamble, or smoke. Yet, I suppose some people used to play the lottery while they smoked; I guess they just do not swear (except for me but I do not smoke). Whatever the case, during the past decade or so, Afghanistan has become the place of "choice" to buy drugs which are refined and turned into finished products elsewhere. The farmers of Afghanistan are being offered better incomes, sometimes three to four times more, for their opium crops than their usual crops of wheat and corn. It was shown in the James Bond movie "*The Living Daylights*" starring Timothy Dalton, that the high ranking Russian Army officials were smuggling drugs to other Communist nations. The movie was not far from the truth because smuggling drugs has been theorized to have been one of the main influences (or reason) on the decision to invade Afghanistan. There have been many cases such as drugs that were seized in the Netherlands and in England that were originally shipped from Afghanistan to the Soviet Union and so on. According to the farmers in the mid 1990s, one kilo of opium paste would bring about $1,200 to the Afghan farmer and about four to five million dollars to the dealers in the United States. Most of these drugs from Afghanistan are bought by Pakistani dealers who sell them in different cities including, but not limited to, Peshawar. Ezatullah Zawab (2004) mentioned that much of the chemical products used for the production of illegal drugs in Afghanistan are being imported from neighboring countries like Pakistan. The anti-narcotics groups working with the current government has supposedly seized about 54 mobile heroin producing labs in 2003 and 29 in 2004 in eastern Nanagarhar's Achin district that borders Pakistan (Zawab, 2004). The interior ministry spokesman, General Mohammad Daud Khan, said it is "the responsibility of the border police to prevent smuggling of heroin producing equipment." Of course, this responsibility falls on the shoulders of everyone in Afghanistan and their neighbors.

During 1983 and the prior years, some people grew marijuana in their homes for its beauty and liveliness, while others would use it as a drug. Unfortunately, many Afghans became addicted to these drugs during the war as a way of forgetting their physical and emotional war wounds. The drug problem is not based on regions, cultures, gender, or any other elements because it is a universal problem which needs the help and cooperation of each member of this society to eliminate it. However, since Afghanistan has become a major supplier of illegal drugs in the past few decades, it is best to start the work there, by providing the needed resources to the current administration in their jihad against such activities. This drug addition problem is a huge concern for the current and future generations of Afghans as there are adult and children users of strong addictive drugs in Afghanistan. An article entitled "Afghan drug boom fuels child addition rates," distributed on November 27, 2006 through the afghaniyat@afghaniyat.com organization, by Sadeq Behnam and Sudabah Afzali from the city of Heart provides the following realities about this major problem:

> Doctors estimate that there are more than 2,000 drug-addicted children in the western city of Herat alone. Idris, 16, sells cigarettes for a living. Walking along the road in Herat with a wooden box hanging from his neck, he confesses that he had moved onto stronger substances. "I didn't want to become addicted, but I started smoking since I was selling cigarettes," he said. "Then I tried hashish with other kids. Now I can't work unless I smoke hash two or three times a day." Idris is an orphan who lost his family in fighting when the Taliban men were attacking the forces of local leader Ismail Khan back in the Nineties. Homeless, he sells cigarettes during the day and sleeps in city parks at night. There are many young people like him in Afghanistan, where families have been torn apart over decades of war.
>
> Nur Ahmad, 15, makes his living by shining shoes on the street. He, too, is alone: after his father was killed, his mother remarried but his stepfather threw him out of the house. "I started on snuff, moved on to cigarettes and now hashish." "Now I smoke hashish with my friends every night." Observers say that drug addiction among children has risen precipitously in recent years. This is especially true in western areas like Herat, because of the influx of returning refugees from neighboring Iran, where addiction rates are high. Dr. Abdul S. Shukur, of the Shahamat Centre, a non-government institution that helps combat drug abuse, told IWPR that he had seen a 20% rise in juvenile addiction over last year. "We have children between the ages of six and 16 at our centre," he said. There are many reasons why children start using drugs, said Dr. Shukur, including the lack of parental supervision, the large number of children orphaned by war, the return of refugees from Iran, and Afghanistan's booming illicit narcotics industry, which means drugs are readily available. Dr. Shukur

estimated that there are more than 2,000 drug-addicted children in the city of Herat alone.

A report issued by the United Nations Office of Drugs and Crime in late 2005 put the number of drug users in Afghanistan at 920,000, with 60,000 of them under 15. This year and next, opium and its derivative heroin will be even more plentiful, as poppy cultivation is on the rise despite eradication efforts sponsored by the international community. UNODC estimates that 60% more land was planted with opium in 2006, so that the harvest will hit 6,100 tons. "Afghanistan is increasingly hooked on its own drug," UNODC Executive Director Antonio Maria Costa said after presenting the latest estimates for cultivation and production in September. Abdul Hai Mahmudi, who heads the Khoja Abdullah Ansari orphanage in Herat, says homeless children are vulnerable to addiction and to exploitation as "mules" carrying drugs for the traffickers. "We have provided shelter for about 1,000 children, but that's only 20% of all the homeless children in the city. We just don't have the capacity to take them all." Adding that, some of the children in the orphanage were receiving treatment for their addiction. Mahmudi said homeless children are targeted by smugglers because they make good couriers and arouse little suspicion with the police. Nur Khan Nekzad, press spokesman for police headquarters in Herat, confirmed this. "We have caught ten children who were being used to smuggle drugs," he said. "Through them, we have been able to arrest the traffickers standing behind them."

Another cause of juvenile drug addiction is the widespread use of opiates to keep children quiet, said Juma Khan Karimzada, head of a charity that provides assistance to disabled children in Ghor, a province east of Heart. "The real reason for drug addiction in children is the high volume of poppy cultivation in the province." "Many parents use poppy paste to calm their children, and this then leads to addiction." Karimzada's organization is among several trying to combat the practice by getting the word out to parents, though the mosques and schools, but the problem persists. Other people, including children, become addicted while harvesting the poppy crop through their long exposure to opium. Mohammad Zarif, 17, who lives in the Braman district of Herat province, told IWPR that he became addicted while cutting poppy plants in nearby Farah province. "I'm not happy that I'm an addict," he said. "But I can't stop - there is no treatment for me. There is no real employment, either, and I do anything I have to in order to get food and drugs" (by Sadeq Behnam and Sudabah Afzali in November 27, 2006).

It is unfortunate to see that thousands of young minds are becoming addicted to these types of drugs in a society that cannot take care of them effectively through a good healthcare program. This is not just a problem for Afghanistan, but also a major challenge for humanity throughout the world. Perhaps what is required is a different manner of learning and proactively preventing such problems from becoming huge challenges before they actually happen. Perhaps there needs to be a major shift in consciousness about how we see such challenges when they are directly impacting us in "real time." Just because a problem is beyond our borders does not mean we do not have the obligation to fix it or prevent it from getting worse. While civilization has achieved many great things by working together using standardized technologies and educational avenues, we have not fully grasped the consequences of our collective actions that seem to impact everyone in the world, sooner or later. Perhaps we are now at a crossroad where we need to learn that our current practices in one part of the world could lead to many negative consequences for everyone in the coming decades, regardless of where they live or work. In today's interdependent world, maybe there is no room for mistakes or thinking in terms of one's own country or borders. As human beings, we need to increase our capacity for proactively anticipating and learning the consequences of our actions before they actually hurt a person. Everyone in the world needs to work as one global community by cultivating human potential of each being, thus creating global consciousness and synergy. True global consciousness and synergy can create a safer, healthier, and a more caring culture in each country. The widespread use and culture of addictive drugs by the young generation of people in Afghanistan should not become a reality of the country, and the world community needs to make sure this problem is prevented from taking place in such an environment. Afghanistan alone cannot effectively tackle this major world problem.

Of course, it is true that the government of Afghanistan has banned the cultivation of poppies, and this means that farmers will have to destroy their crops before they receive penalties or jail time for growing illegal drugs. According to Ezatullah Zawab, poppy farmers in Achin and Shinwar districts in the eastern provinces of Nangarhar destroyed nearly 170 acres of poppy growing land. The provincial religious leaders had announced the cultivation of the crop was against Islamic beliefs. As such, "The farmers themselves eliminated their poppy crops and the officials were not involved in it at all" (Zawab, 2004). Overall, Afghanistan must work "interdependently" with the international community to fight the trafficking of drugs. Afghanistan can join regional fighting against drugs with China and its other neighboring countries. For examples, according to the security officials from the six SCO nations at a meeting in the Tajik capital Dushanbe, without the involvement of Afghanistan, the Shanghai Cooperation Organizations' (SCO) battle against narcotics cannot succeed. Kazakhstan, Kyrgyzstan, Tajikistan, and Uzbekistan, all members of the SCO, are supposedly major transit routes for Afghan drugs. Some claim that China and Russia are heavily promoting the Shanghai Cooperation Organization (SCO) as a means of responding to the United States increased influence in the region.

The French government has been helping the people of Afghanistan by financially assisting Afghan poppy farmers to start growing cotton (Mohammadi, 2004). The United States government launched a $2.5 million reconstruction project for the elimination of poppy fields. According to Abdul Qadir Munsef, on December 13th 2004, "the governments of Afghanistan and the United Kingdom launched an Afghan Counter Narcotics Criminal Justice Task Force in Kabul on Sunday with the aim of accelerating the legal process by which drug offenders are tried and charged in the Afghan criminal justice system." Their plan is to train law experts, investigators, prosecutors, and judges by the end of 2005. Officials and experts from the United States, Canada, Norway, and the United Nations Office on Drugs and Crime

(UNODC) will be assisting in the design and implementation of the training program. According to Munsel (2004), "the training will be carried out by the International Institute of Higher Studies in Criminal Sciences (ISISC), the Italian-based Human Rights Law institute which is directly involved in rebuilding the criminal justice and the human rights legal system in Afghanistan." Dr. Rosalind Marsden, the British Ambassador to Afghanistan, said this action was another demonstration of the Afghan government's determination to tackle the drug trade. She added that in the past drug traffickers could be arrested but could not be prosecuted, in the absence of prosecuting and court structures. As planned, the comprehensive training program commenced in January 2005, and there are plans to develop a secure court and prison facility at Pul-e-Charkhi prison in east Kabul to deal with major drug trafficking cases (Musef, 2005).

The government of Afghanistan's five-pronged strategy of providing alternative livelihoods and substituting cash crops, emphasizing counter-narcotic law enforcement, and training, mobilizing Islamic institutions to revive religious prohibitions on production, trafficking or use of drugs, providing long-term economic development, and implementing forced eradication of poppy crops is slowly starting to work. Of course, Afghan farmers could not survive if they depended on the usage of their crops solely by the Afghan population. So, the foreign investors who buy these crops can now channel their income to legal investment opportunities in Afghanistan which offer generous incentives and payback. Afghanistan offers business opportunities in the reconstruction of its infrastructure, aviation, telecommunication, tourism, film and news industries, and natural resources such as the various valuable stones that are found in Afghanistan.

While narcotics are one form of illegal drugs in Afghanistan, alcoholic beverages are also illegal and they too should be banned. Munir (2004) stated that "Most traffic accidents are caused by drunk-drivers in the capital Kabul, although the sale and consumption of alcohol is illegal in the country." While the council of Ulamas (religious leaders) has voiced their concerns over the rise of alcohol consumption in the country, the government officials have paid more attention to dealing with the smuggling of narcotics than dealing with the prohibition of alcoholic drinks. Some Afghans living in Kabul say alcohol is readily available in many shops, and both locals and foreigners are sold beer and other alcoholic beverages. One natural consequence or corollary of a foreign military group and personnel living in a different culture has historically been to impact the local culture. Since there are thousands of NGOs, contractors and military personnel from the United Nations as well as the United States currently living and working in Afghanistan, the widespread use of alcoholic beverages might be their legacy to the country. Of course, this is probably one aspect of the Western cultures that Afghans do not need or want as it is against their beliefs and culture. Since there are bigger challenges and problems than the widespread availability of prohibited beverages facing the Afghan people at this time, hopefully the cultural legacy of the foreign contractors, NGOs, military forces, and their supporting personnel currently living Afghanistan will be better education, entrepreneurship, democracy, international competitiveness, effective communication, civility, industrialization, peace, and global interdependency. Besides Afghan leaders and government officials, the Western world should do what it can to improve the country of Afghanistan as many of these developed economies have to some extent contributed to the destruction of it in one manner or another. Author John Tirman's 2006 book, entitled *100 Ways America Is Screwing Up the World,* offers the following clear description regarding how some activities of officials and corporations from the United States has made the world a little worse over the past century and the past few years:

> What do George W. Bush, Wal-Mart, Halliburton, gangsta rap, and SUVs have in common? They're all among the hundred ways in which America is screwing up the world. The country that was responsible for many, if not most, of the twentieth century's most important scientific and technological advancements now demonizes its scientists and thinkers in the twenty-first, while dumbing down its youth with anti-Darwin/pro-"Intelligent Design" propaganda. The longtime paragon of personal freedoms now supports torture and illegal wiretapping—spreading its principles and policies at gunpoint while ruthlessly bombing the world with Big Macs and Mickey Mouse ears.

"Screwing up" the world includes causing animosity, hatred and fighting among the people of various societies or bringing a new culture that is not wanted or desired by the people of a country. Such undesired behaviors cause further hatred and animosity, thereby causing and/or extending civil wars. For example, the unfortunate reality today in Kabul is that for the most part, people living in the capital can get alcoholic beverages whenever they want them. Unfortunately, if this trend continues, then drinking alcohol may become a new trend among young Afghans. So, it might be best to eliminate this form of addiction at its root and ban its sale to Muslims. This should be done to respect the customs of the country, to make sure Afghans are not hooked on another "drug," and to respect the religious practices of people in Afghanistan. The current government has plenty of work ahead of them to heal the wounds of "maimed" and "injured" Afghans; so they do not have the time, nor do they have the resources, to deal with alcohol addiction issues. Therefore, officials "should take serious steps against the distribution and availability of alcohol, as they have taken against the smuggling of narcotics" (Munir, 2004). Perhaps some of the cultural changes in the country are due to the increase of alcoholic drinks, and it also extends to restaurants which serve alcohol in the city of Kabul. Perhaps, as the law enforcement agencies like the police and the government authorities in charge of law enforcement become stronger, they can do more to make sure this problem is rooted out at its source since Afghanistan cannot deal with this addiction as it already has plenty of wounds to heal for the next few decades. Taking care of the illegal drug trafficking is an excellent intention and hopefully each leader of Afghanistan and its surrounding countries can successfully deliver his or her intentions instead of simply becoming another "Mr. Meant to." As the following little poem points out, "Mr. Meant to" does not always deliver.

Mr. "Meant To" has a comrade
And his name is *"Did not Do,"*
Have you ever chanced to meet them?
Did they ever call on you?

These two fellows live together
In the house of never win,
And I am told that it is haunted
By the ghost of *"might have been."*

REFLECTIVE QUESTIONS FOR CRITICAL THINKING

1. How was work impacted in Afghanistan once the Taliban took over the official government?
2. What percentage of the Afghan population are women? What is the role of women in Afghanistan in the rebuilding process?
3. What are the literacy rates in Afghanistan and how do these rates compare with the literacy rates of Afghanistan's neighbors?
4. What are some best strategies to quickly educate both men and women of Afghanistan throughout the provinces so they can read, think critically and make sophisticated decisions about today's workforce technology?
5. What types of illegal drugs are grown in Afghanistan and discuss why Afghanistan is perceived to be producing the largest amounts of certain drugs?
6. What are some possible solutions to eliminate the drug trafficking problems in Afghanistan?
7. What type of impact can more education have on the "poor" people of Afghanistan?
8. What are some best strategies for providing equal working opportunities to women in Afghanistan?
9. What are some of the ethical challenges associated with the promotion of the "right" individuals into top positions?

CHAPTER 5

HUMAN RIGHTS VIOLATIONS

Makia, on December 16th 2004, reported that "Afghan human rights groups have demanded that the government respect human rights and values." These individuals, like many others in the country, want to ensure that the Afghan people can live in a secure and stable society that respects human rights. In 2004, the Civil Community and Human Rights Network, an "umbrella" group made up of 30 organizations representing human rights in Afghanistan, said that many Afghans do not even have access to basic human rights. Their concerns were that "armed men and commanders roam the provinces freely and warlords, working in the cabinet, make important decisions on the economic and social issues of the country" that impact the livelihood of ordinary citizens. Makia reported that "as a consequence, the people of the country are suffering instability and corruption." Some members are frustrated because they think "lip service was paid to the rule of law and that ministers boast about programs to improve human rights but no action is taken." While security and peace are critical steps to guaranteeing human rights across the country, more needs to be done by the international community to provide sufficient resources to the administration so they can ease the undue suffering and violations of human rights. Unfortunately, in many cases, Afghan women and children are the real victims of decades of war, disputes, and human rights violations. Fortunately, the Afghan government is speeding up the process of recruiting, training, and employing more educated police officers to assist in making the country safer.

According to Ibrahimi, "A thousand young men from the northern province of Kapisa have been recruited to train with the Afghan National police." The young cadets will supposedly "replace 'private militia-men' loyal to warlords and commanders who operate within the Afghan national forces." Some of the recruits include those who laid their arms down under the Disarmament Demobilization and Reintegration program (DDR), the national disarmament program introduced by the Afghan government and the United Nations. It is great to see that the recruits will receive a "salary" during their six-month training period, and it is strongly hoped that they will voluntarily join the police force after graduation. While the members of the Afghan National Army (ANA) initially received about $60 each month in salary during 2004, the Afghan National Police (ANP) members only received $20 a month. This year, I met experienced middle and high school teachers in Afghanistan that were earning less than $80 per month, and were forced to take a second job as a chef or a driver to earn enough money to support their children. What is interesting is that average hotel room in Kabul costs about $60 to $200 per night without many of the luxuries that are offered in most modern hotels. In the year 2006 and 2007, a two-bedroom apartment's rent inside the city of Kabul can cost about $400 to $600 per month. How can the local soldiers and police officers really live on their existing salaries? Of course, not that this is a good excuse, but a major source of increasing corruption in the country's law enforcement, including the police, is low salaries which need to be raised to match at least the minimal living standards in Afghanistan. Besides being the appropriate age, those who want to serve as police officers need to have completed a high-school education. Once accepted, they will then be comprehensively trained in the police academy for five years. A twenty-five year-old who gave up his guns and artilleries under the national disarmament program said: "I registered with the police commission because the Afghan police are here to serve its people day and night and I also want to serve the people" (Ibrahimi, 2004). The recruitment program hopes to have at least 62,000 officers serving in the police force. As of early 2005, about 31,000 trained police officers were serving throughout the provinces and the capital. Germany has promised to assist in the training of about 50,000 Afghan National Police (ANP) in 2005. The comprehensive training and education of the police officers should greatly assist in reducing some of the human rights violations in Afghanistan.

Julian Simon, an economist, said "The main fuel to speed the world's progress is our stock of knowledge, and the brake is our lack of imagination." The generation, creation, and application of knowledge by the common citizen will be the vehicles for the elimination of human rights violations in the recovering economy of Afghanistan. This vision of a peaceful country must be envisioned first and believed before its achievement can be realized. William James, psychologist from Harvard University, once said that "Most people never run far enough on their first wind to find out if they've got a second...Give your dreams all you've got and you'll be amazed at the energy that comes out of you." This dream of a peaceful society must be communicated and wanted by the majority of Afghans in order for it to become a reality. Dr. Martin Luther King, Jr., minister and activist, said that "Everyone has the power for greatness, not for fame but for greatness, because greatness is determined by service." As such, every Afghan must do his or her part in the achievement of this great cause to make sure every child, mother, wife, sister, brother, father, and others in the community are treated with dignity and respect.

Afghanistan is not the only country that is suffering from human rights violations. As a matter of fact, the entire world seems to have taken major steps backward in the past decade with regard to human rights violations, as there seem to be innocent people suffering and/or dying in Sudan, Rwanda, Chechnya, Palestine, Israel, Haiti, Lebanon, and Iraq. One of the major recent humanitarian challenges seems to have been in Darfur, Sudan. Nearly two million people were forced to leave their homes and become refugees in other areas while approximately 100,000 Sudanese individuals have been killed. The developed nations must do what they can to bring peace and stability to such devastated countries of the world, if they are all to live peacefully. One of the externalities of "war on terror" and "war in Iraq" seem to be that both democratic leaders and dictators feel like they can violate human rights and restrict civil liberties. The reality is that security and human rights must be achieved simultaneously, as one must not be at a cost to the other since the world needs both. As Amnesty International personnel have stated many times, security and liberty are not opposing values, as they can be seen as the "two sides of the same coin." In one of his messages in November of 2004, Chip Pitts, who is the Chair of Amnesty International USA's Board of Directors, said that "True security cannot be achieved without the preservation of human rights…The sooner the world realizes it, the better off we all will be."

It has been 28 years (beginning in 1979) since the Communist government and the Russian forces started a never-ending war in Afghanistan. They have destroyed many cities, villages, roads, bridges, hospitals, schools, irrigation systems, water plants, houses, and mosques through offensive and intensive bombing strikes. Rough estimates suggest that millions have died or been injured in Afghanistan as a result of the invasion and civil war following it. This, of course, is a great tragedy for any nation and for humanity in general. War is always a loss for the society in terms of human resources and physical resources, which further leaves destruction in the environment. The Afghan war is similar to many other wars; for example, during the first six months of war between Russians and the people of Chechnya in the 1990s, there were over 30,000 Chechen men, women, and children who died because of the brutal bombings. Furthermore, the bombings caused physical and environmental damage which obviously is not good for humanity.

According to the late Peter Jennings, ABC News Broadcast on November 22nd of 1996, the Sudan government violated basic and fundamental human rights by enforcing the strict or extreme interpretations of religious laws without any tolerance for anyone in the country, including those who are from different religions. In the North parts of Sudan, people are mostly Muslims (90%) and in the South there are many non-Muslims who are being forced into practicing the dominant group's rules and preferences. He further reported that there have been over one million Sudanese killed over the past decade because of their internal conflicts. Even in 2004 and 2005, the people of Sudan were suffering from internal conflicts and the world did very little to help them. For example, as stated previously, on November 08, 2006, the Israeli military terrorized a village of innocent Palestinians in the Gaza Strip as their artilleries hit several homes instantly killing twenty people, fourteen of them were from the same family and eight were children. Of course, many more innocent people were injured as well. If one looks at the definition or synonyms for the term "terrorism," one will find that it means intimidation, violence, bombing, terror campaign, and psychologically or physically harming innocent and unsuspecting individuals. While the victims of this Israeli military operation were all innocent Palestinian citizens, the Israeli officials did launch an investigation to see why the wrong village and homes were hit. Of course, an investigation is not going to heal the psychological and physical harms caused by such deliberate or accidental operation. The consequences of such deliberate or accidental activities are only the legitimization of more violence and conflicts. Of course, the Israeli army members are not the only one's terrorizing innocent individuals as many other official armies (such as that of the United States forces, former Soviet Union or Russian Army, as well as Pakistani Armed Forces) have been accused of hurting and killing innocent individuals. Of course, such actions terrorizing innocent individuals are only examples of few such activities that are psychologically and physically harming and intimidating people around the globe perhaps on daily, weekly, monthly, or yearly basis. What is a fact is that perhaps many more such severe and deliberate immoral acts are taking place in various places around globe either by covert or overt state-sponsored activities or insurgent groups. On the same day (November 08, 2006), a suicide bomber killed 40 Pakistani soldiers in a town near Peshawar when about 200 soldiers were completing their daily training regiment. Once again, of course, many more innocent individuals were injured and scarred for life. According to media reports, this suicide bombing was a response or retaliation to the strategic attack of the Pakistani government last month on a village that was suspected of "supposedly" housing insurgents that are supporters of Taliban. Such events make one think and reflect upon the question: Is violence really the only or best solution to settling differences and conflicts in today's diverse world? According to some military leaders' actions, be they state-designated or insurgents, from around the globe, using force and destroying innocent people's lives seem to be the most convenient way they know how to settle differences. If this is actually their best means of settling differences and conflicts, then the world needs to get new leaders and military officers as such activities tend violate the human rights of ordinary citizens and they further legitimize and breed more destructive thoughts for humanity. The violations of fundamental human rights appear to be ubiquitous in many developing nations where children, women, and other innocent individuals are feeling the effects physically and psychologically. According to an article in Time magazine, June 17th 1996, human rights members are prognosticating that about 200 million children are being forced into working full-time around the world - no play, no school, and no chance for an education that can make their lives a little brighter in the future.

These working age children from China to South America are being deprived of many opportunities, as their basic human rights are not being exercised. Harry Wu is a human rights activist who protests prison labor laws in China, and because of his efforts along with Liz Figueroa (Democratic Assembly of women in Fremont), former Governor Pete Wilson signed a bill that made it illegal for the state of California to purchase products made with slave labor in foreign countries. According to reports by Connie Chung, television reporter, and Time magazine, Pakistani children as young as eight years old were being paid 75 cents a day to make soccer balls. These are possible violations of slave labor, paying too low wages and denying children education, and denying their childhood experience based on the International Labor Organizations laws. However, Pakistani traditions permit young children working, which has been a tradition where "kids" are regularly working along their parents' side. Also, the International Federation of Football Association (FIFA) clearly forbids child labor in the making of soccer balls. All soccer balls are required to carry FIFA label approval which signifies regulation size, weight, durability, and fair labor standards. Reebok Corporation has taken a "proactive" step to commission a Pakistani manufacturer for building an exemplary factory that produces soccer balls while making sure that all international labor laws are being practiced and no young children are put to work. According to the United States former Labor Secretary from Bill Clinton's first administration, Robert Reich, in the 1990s, there were about 11,000 garment contractors in the U. S. that were paying their employees less than minimum wage who had often been working in "sweatshop" conditions. The Nike Corporation has had legal charges about its Indonesian contractors who supposedly failed to pay proper wages, fired many workers for trying to form a union, and at times for physically attacking employees. The Walt Disney Corporation of Orlando was criticized for making its Haitian employees work in sweatshop conditions while being paid about 28 cents an hour. This does not seem fair when compared to Disney's CEO, Michael Eisner, whose compensation totaled $15 million during the same time period, which equals about $7,100 per hour. Corporations and businesses are responsible for overseeing and extending specific rules and fair standards to their international subsidiaries to make sure universal human rights are not being violated. According to a poll of 1,004 adult workers by Business Week and a Harris poll, 95% of Americans believed that the role of corporations should not be just to make money. So, human rights violations appear to be taking a different form and shape in developed countries, such as the United States, but the psychological effects may be just the same as other violations with the exception of bodily injury and physical abuse cases. Violations of fundamental human rights during the war take a totally different form and they are very demeaning and unforgiving.

In addition to invading Afghanistan, the Russian-Afghan war resulted in many serious violations of basic human rights which included, but are not limited to, interrogations and killings of innocent people, torture, arbitrary bombings, many unfair trials, use of chemical warfare, etc. Many of these violations occurred during the Russian invasion and Communist government in Afghanistan. Most of these actions violated the international as well as Islamic human rights conventions and declarations. There were many cases where people had been taken away to join the military even though they had shown their student identifications, implying that they were teenagers and still in school. High school students were supposedly allowed to stay in school, but this law was not always followed. In some cases, the soldiers had thrown away students' identification cards and had taken them to the military without allowing them to tell their parents or families members. There were some cases where people were lost, and two weeks later their dead bodies came back from the military. During the war, there were tens of thousands of academicians, business-people, clergy, government officials, and other civilian citizens who were being imprisoned for long periods of time, without stating a reason or providing a just cause for their imprisonment. In some cases families were violently raided in the middle of the day or even at night by soldiers, and they entered people's houses without the consideration or respect for their privacy. The government intelligence officials (*Khad*) and military personnel did not seem to need just-cause or a court order to search people, houses, or even to destroy houses and to arrest or kill people. Government intelligence agents were implicitly given total authority to use all measures that infringed on basic human rights and dignity of individuals in the society in order to search for information. Most political prisoners never had the opportunity to see an official statement of their charges against them and were subject to unfair proceedings and subjective arrest and trials.

Due to such killings and lack of regard and respect for human beings, the only "fair" method of justice had turned out to be the "eye for an eye" rule, and consequently people took the law into their own hands. This bad situation caused many people to become full of animosity and bitterness against others in the community; ergo they joined opposing parties to protect themselves. Perhaps such inappropriate actions have been causing some Iraqi citizens to join or support forces that oppose the U.S. invasion of their country and the current administration. This consequence in Afghanistan brought about more insecurity on the part of the Communist government, and this kept increasing their rule of arresting people for no apparent reason. Most of the jails were filled to a point where rooms that were designed for 40 people had over 200 people in them at a given time. According to prisoners, some were sleeping so close together that people could hear each others' breathing patterns. Almost all of these crowded jails were filled with political prisoners, while thieves and other criminals were not being sentenced for justified periods, so there were few of them in jail. Many of the political prisoners were abused through various types of physical and psychological tortures, as they spent many sleepless nights in extremely bad living conditions and situations as part of their interrogation. The political prisoners had "zero" legal rights, and were at the mercy of the enemy each and every moment of their lives. The court systems did not allow any legal defense, legal procedures, and laws for political prisoners. Of course, this is probably very similar to the situation of prisoners being held in Cuba's Guantanamo Bay by the U.S. military forces. So defendants could not obtain any type of legal defense against them whether they knew the charges or not, and due process of law was not heard by most people during the Russian invasion. All decisions were subjectively decided by Communist officials and all decisions were final during and after the interrogations. In one situation, a 22 year-old college student, one of my uncle's friends, had been taken from school and interrogated for information by electric shocks and torture. He had received so many electric shocks, in different parts of his body that he could not control his biological muscles and bodily fluids to function as a normal human being. He was jailed with the absence of any physical evidence for over eight months during 1980 and 1981. The Communists were not able to get any information from him, so they finally decided to execute him and ease his suffering. This is not an uncommon or an extreme example of violations of basic human rights and abuses that were inflicted upon the people of Afghanistan. In some districts outside Kabul, the Russians had hanged, tortured, and burned children and women to get information about Freedom Fighters. In some cases, people's nails and toes had been taken out, while in other cases they were publicly humiliated and then killed. In one of the Russian attacks, while searching houses for Freedom Fighters and weapons, the Russians had supposedly taken several Afghan women with them, and then several hours later their naked bodies had been dropped from the helicopters. They did not stop at anything, and did whatever they could to make themselves feel victorious physically or psychologically. In 1987, a French journalist, Allain Guillo who had entered Afghanistan with the Freedom Fighters, was captured by the Communist government, and he reported horrors of torture, beatings, and extremely bad jail conditions after his release by the request of French President Mitterand.

During a general offensive attack with ground troops and air strikes by Russians and Communist government in Rahm-Abaud of Logar in 1981, a Freedom

Fighter from the Ahmad-Zaee Village got captured as he was trying to get away. He could not get away in time from the area because the Russians caught everyone by the "element of surprise." There were about 400 government and Russian soldiers, 80 tanks, 60 trucks, and seven helicopters which surrounded the village. There was no place to escape, and this Freedom Fighter did not want to confront the army, because he did not want innocent children and civilian people of the village to receive any harm. After about twenty minutes of interrogating him with physical abuses and beatings, the Russian leaders became impatient, and they started pulling his eye balls out of his skull while he was still alive. Then, they cut his tongue and lips in public to show others that they were not going to have mercy on those who did not cooperate. He was yelling so loud that four other Freedom Fighters, who were hiding a couple of blocks down because they did not want to start a war inside the village, heard the yelling and decided that they could not take the abuse anymore. Their emotions were high and their "blood was boiling," so they started fighting the Communist raiders by killing many Russians who were inside the village. Soon after, about 50 other Freedom Fighters from the next village came to help, and they attacked the Communists and Russian army from the outside, so the enemy was trapped in the middle and as a result suffered a huge loss of human resources. There were four Freedom Fighters and 80 government soldiers killed while many more people were injured on both sides. All this loss and aggravation could have been avoided if the vehemently violent Russian soldiers had not abused and tortured the captured Freedom Fighter as they did.

According to a Russian soldier who voluntarily surrendered to Freedom Fighters, the Russians were ordered to kill women, children, elderly, and drive over them with tanks as the commanders were laughing (Lohbeck, 1993). Lohbeck was one of the first journalists who videotaped the usage of napalm bombs by the Russians, as well as the symptoms of these chemicals that had been used by the Soviet troops. In one situation when he was in Paktia Province, the Russian helicopters had thrown a basketball type of bomb near them. He states that this was a napalm bomb because the area quickly converted into an inferno and the flame started spreading very quickly, like spilled liquid. One of the napalm bombs did not go off, and they stayed alive to talk about it. So, the Russians were finally caught "red-handed," lying about not using napalm in Afghanistan, by this brave journalist. Some of their chemical agents were referred to as the "liquid fire" which stayed on the ground, and upon touching it would burst into flames while killing and injuring everything around it. Goodwin (1987) mentions of 17 people killed, by chemical gases in Wardaug Province in 1982. These people had been killed, similar to my cousin and three others who were killed by the use of chemical gas in Khoshie village of Logar in 1982. Their bodies had been frozen, and many other animals had died near the area on top of the mountain. The Soviets did not care much for pervious international agreements of not using chemical weapons. According to Mohammed Nabi, the Afghan pilot who defected and brought an SU-7 fighter jet to Pakistan, there was a large-scale chemical weapons storage unit near Bagram in Kabul. They had over 120,000 chemical specialists, compared to United States' 6,000 and they had to do something with them. So, Afghanistan was an ideal place for them to perfect their chemical warfare. They also used the "butterfly" bombs, which had been banned in 1981 during an international agreement, signed and approved by the Soviets as well. The State Department in United States, had received reports of 3,000 people that died because of 41 chemical attacks in different parts of Afghanistan between 1979 and 1981. Russians did not stop at killing humans because they also killed cows, camels, goats, sheep, dogs, and all other animals kept by people. They killed one of our dogs in Logar during 1982, during one of their routine house searches because the dog was barking at them. Lohbech (1993) mentions a time where he went to take pictures of a village that had just been bombed and witnessed the corpses of over two hundred camels, cows, dogs, and other household animals. He said that all the animals had been shot by machine guns. Unfortunately, these are effects of war whether they are taking place in Afghanistan, Iraq, Palestine, Israel, Sudan, Chechnya or any other places in the world.

The following are some of the physical, spiritual, psychological, and emotional violations of basic human rights in Afghanistan during the Russian invasion:

1. People were jailed and detained for months without any charges, arrest warrants, or proof of illegal activities against them.
2. Some prisoners were left in a room with no bathroom, windows, or heating systems during cold winter days for weeks at a time.
3. Prisoners were burned with cigarettes on their shoulders, faces, and chests.
4. Some people were totally stripped out of their clothes, and then interrogated with much more abuse such as whippings and beatings.
5. People were threatened that their families would suffer harm if they did not talk, and in many cases these threats were carried out.
6. People's children and family members being killed in their presence to get them to "speak" and provide information...or else others would be killed similarly.
7. Political prisoners were housed in rooms and in quantities not suitable for human beings.
8. The arrested individuals could not exercise any rights to seek legal defense, to know why they were arrested, or to even defend themselves.
9. Some prisoners were scarred for life because the interrogators used scissors and knives on their bodies.
10. Many prisoners did not have any clothes provided for them, and had to live in the same clothes for months. Faqir, my uncle, wore the same clothes for 40 days.
11. Sometimes houses were raided and the soldiers would break windows, walls, and ceramic tiles were removed to search for documents and weapons as was the case in our house in Darulaman. They did not take responsibility or pay for fixing them even when the person was innocent.
12. Many dogs and other animals were killed as the army raided people's houses in all hours of the night because the dogs would be barking. We had a dog that got shot once, and he was living on three legs for two years. Two years later during another search, the Russians shot him about five times and he was dead. Many cows, chickens, sheep, goats, horses, donkeys, and bullocks were killed violently, as well to make their owners talk.

13. The raiders used to violate people's privacy by entering their bedrooms and sometimes abused women by forcing them into sexual acts and, in some cases, even young children were forced into such inhumane and unforgivable acts.
14. Young teenagers, sometimes as young as fourteen years of age, were conscripted and forced into fighting in front lines of the army without proper training and combat experience.
15. Young children were beaten and, in some cases, set on fire in front of their families to get information about the Freedom Fighters.
16. Young children who had run away from the soldiers were shot and killed on many occasions.
17. The Soviets used beautiful toy-shaped antipersonnel mines to specifically target children, and this was very cruel.
18. Young children had been held under water, so the parents would divulge information which they may or may not have had.
19. People were imprisoned, tortured, beaten, and finally released because they were arrested by mistake.
20. Chemical gas was used during some confrontations with the Freedom Fighters, and in some case by helicopters.
21. Mosques were burned and destroyed.
22. Criticism of government was totally prohibited, and a group of people caught talking negatively about government issues would be arrested.

There were many killings, massacres, tortures, and other human rights violations that had taken place in Afghanistan during the war and, unfortunately, the victims were usually young children. Jad Goodwin (1987) writes about how the Soviet army had massacred 1,500 people in Qarghaie district of Laghman, which is in the north-eastern part of Afghanistan. Most of these 1,500 victims were women, children, and senior citizens who could not run to get away. According to one of the survivors, who had hidden in the house because he did not want to be taken to the military, the Russian soldiers were very cruel. She quotes Shakeer Jamagul, who was a farmer in Qarghaie, as he described how his family was killed.

> Seven Russians came in armed with machine guns. I could see their faces; they were too young to have beards. They were laughing as they searched the house. Then, without saying anything, they raised their guns and fired, shooting my wife and my four children. My youngest son was sixteen days old, my oldest child seven years old...the soldiers took my wife's clothes and jewelry, our lanterns; they even took soap and candy. I found thirty one bullets in my house and everybody was dead (Goodwin, 1987).

Goodwin mentions another survivor, Mohamad Fazeer, whose wife and two daughters were killed and his two sons were burned alive by the Russian soldiers. There were many other cases where children and their mothers had been tortured for information and finally killed. The Soviets and the Khad members were operating in the country based on their own rules, where the rulers had guns and the power to do whatever pleased them. There were also many cases where mothers were shot in the back, while trying to hold on to their sons as they were being taken away by the soldiers to the army. If a person sees the soldiers shoot, kick, stab, and beat his mother, I cannot imagine how helpful this person will be to the Russians or Communist army. But this was real and people were forced to go to the front lines and fight as if they were being "watched" from behind. In many cases, these frontline soldiers did not receive any training either. Confucius in 500 B.C. said, "to lead an untrained people to war is to throw them away;" there certainly were many people "thrown away" during this Afghan-Russian war.

The Communist government did not allow people to express themselves freely, and this is totally denying people creativity, innovation, and the freedom to be themselves. As a matter-of-fact, many foreign journalists, at least ten, were killed while covertly attempting to report the news about Afghanistan. The secret agents (Khad members) would remind the government that foreign reporters were in the village, and the government helicopters would destroy that village by dropping bombs that would sometimes weigh up to one thousand pounds. In a democratic society, people can express themselves in a respectable manner, and that is just fine, meaning nobody gets hurt, and no one goes to jail as long as nobody is hurt or bothered. For example, during the 1996 Presidential campaign in the United States, David Brinkley of the American Broadcasting Corporation (ABC) television was covering the election, as he called President Clinton a "bore," and during a portion of the show where Brinkley did not know he was on the air, said the president would spout "goddamned nonsense" during the next four years. If a news reporter made a comment like that in Afghanistan during the Russian invasion, he/she would have automatically gone to jail. People should be open to speak their minds and criticize what is not working, while hopefully providing an alternative, as well. In October 2006, when Senator John Kerry told a group of high schools that they should study hard to receive a good education because they really do not want to get "stuck" in Iraq, he got criticized and cajoled to a point where he finally apologized to those American soldiers in Iraq that might have been offended by the use of his humor with these students in the United States. He made the point to students that those who do not get enough education will not have as many options and choices as they could have otherwise. So, while army is one alternative for learning and serving one's people and country, education in general is the key to having many options with regard to which career track one wants to follow for his/her livelihood, and this includes being in the armed forces.

Some of the Afghan Freedom Fighters were also reported to have taken actions that were based on false information. I remember when one of our neighbors, called Daiyron, who was originally from Laghmon, was punished by the Freedom Fighters. He had gone to Laghmon to visit his house and land, as the Freedom Fighters got a hold of him and asked him why his son was a communist. His son was actually forced to join the army because he was at the required age. He said that the Freedom Fighters had beaten him, and then tied his hands behind his back and threw him into a large river from the top of a hill. They shot at him about ten or fifteen times as he was going toward the water but the bullets did not hit him. He was able to swim nearly a mile with his hands tied up and got out on the other side where he hitched a ride to Kabul. He was upset because he was against the Communist government himself, but the Freedom Fighters wanted him dead. He and his brother theorized that maybe the situation was brought up because of their family animosity with certain other individuals.

THE EFFECTS OF PLANTED MINES

On March 26, 2005, four American soldiers were searching for a shooting range in Afghanistan when their truck drove over a land mine that was planted near Kabul area in the late 1980s when the Russians left Afghanistan. All four soldiers were killed. Such accidents and unfortunate incidents are hurting thousands of Afghan civilians and animals in the country each year. Luckily, officials in the current government are attempting to get international assistance in hopes of eventually safely removing all these killers. Afghanistan's Deputy Foreign Minister Haider Reza, an expert on landmine issues, attended the Nairobi Summit on Mine-Free World, which was held on November 29th -December 3rd 2004. Conference attendees discussed the sufferings caused by antipersonnel mines while prohibiting their use and requiring safe destruction of "leftover" mines by responsible states. According to Reza, Afghanistan remains one of the largest minefields in the world, and there have been over 2 million victims in the country. Afghanistan needs about one billion dollars to safely remove and destroy the millions of mines which are hurting unsuspecting children and working adults. The current administration, like their predecessors, has been concerned about destroying these unsuspecting killers.

In 1994, I met Afghanistan's Ambassador to United States, Abdul Rahim, at the Afghan embassy in Washington DC. After much talk about the past and present situation in Afghanistan, he showed much concern for the lack of children's education in Afghanistan. He mentioned that many of the schools have been destroyed; and Professor Burhanuddin Rabbani, President of Afghanistan at the time, along with other leaders, were positioning education as one of the most important factors in the rebuilding of Afghanistan. He further showed concern for the planted mines, which the Russians left behind, and asserted that the Afghans are doing their best to locate and disarm them before they take the lives of more innocent civilians and children. He give me a copy of a Persian book titled "*Stories Of Prophets For Children And Youth*" to read, and pass on to other Afghans, who can read the stories with their children as a way of remembering Afghanistan, while educating them about their Islamic heritage. Even though, Ambassador Rahim and his family were living in the United States, his conversation with me showed legitimate and widespread concern for the education of Afghan children throughout the world since he knew that education would be the solution to the future development of the country. Today, about thirteen years later in 2007, these efforts are fortunately still continuing and at a more rapid pace. Jan Goodwin in 1987 wrote that:

> When you have spent time, as I have, with Afghan women and men whose bodies and spirits have been destroyed by torture, when you have seen, as I have, so many young Afghan children who have lost their legs, arms, or eyes to mines disguised as toys, when you have stood rooted with fear, as I have,

while wave and wave of jet bombers reduce to dust the Afghan village you have been visiting, there can be no forgetting.

Having witnessed such psychological, emotional, spiritual, and physical destruction of current and future human assets in Afghanistan, it is impossible to sit still and forget about what happened, and is still happening, in parts of the country. According to the United Nations' estimates, there were 30 million mines in the fields of Afghanistan that are killing innocent individuals, most of whom are children. Reports have confirmed that during the Soviet evacuations, their soldiers had planted mines in bushes, trees, and so on. Consequently, the explosion of these mines has been the leading cause of death in Afghanistan after the Russian departure. Along with the planted mines, the Soviets had left over one billion dollars worth of weapons in Afghanistan, so people of different factions can hurt each other for a long time after their departure. Jan Goodwin mentions seeing Abdul, an eight year old, who had lost both of his legs up to the his hips after touching a small, four-inch mine that was shaped like a beautiful butterfly. She says he was determined to walk, and accomplished this by moving on his hands. Jan Goodwin also shows a picture of a ten year old boy named Jahan Zeb Khan in a hospital bed. Jahan Zeb went blind after picking up a Soviet bomb that was shaped as a toy. Most of these toys were designed to maim people and not necessarily kill. Their logic was that an injured person needs attention and taking care of, which will keep many more people busy instead of fighting. The "Bouncing Betty" mines were designed to explode at the waist level, causing injury to ones genitals and stomach area. The "Butterfly" mines are about 8 inches long, and they were the most common, and came in different colors to match and blend with the environment. Some of the most frequently used colors were green, light gray, and light brown. Other plastic mines were shaped like soccer balls, wrist-watches, dolls, and ball-point pens to attract and maim children. According to Robert Kaplan (1990), these mines have no self-destruct mechanisms and consequently will be killing people for a long time.

Nyrop and Seekins (1986) show the pictures of two boys who were victims of mines. The first boy, about seven years of age who has an innocent look on his face, has one leg, and is walking on crutches because of injury caused from a land mine. The second picture shows a young bald boy, about eight years of age and with a magnificent smile, who lost both of his legs while kicking a butterfly which turned out to be a mine. These pictures are everywhere in the discussion of Afghanistan and can bring a person to tears in one look because these boys are the innocent victims of a war that should never have taken place. Farhad is another 10 year old boy who lost both his legs because he stepped on a minefield in Kabul as he was gathering firewood for his family to use for cooking food (Time, 1996). This could have been me when I did the same thing in Kabul and Khoshie as a teenager, and it could have been any one of thousands of other young boys or girls. The article in Time Magazine also mentions Rahmat Khan, who was a school guard and went to pick up his hat as it was blown away by the wind and stepped on a mine, and lost both of his legs, as well. There is no scapegoat for these mines because the fighters arranged for them to be there and to kill or destroy animals and people. Unfortunately, the mines have been doing exactly what they were meant to be doing, but they are doing it to the wrong people and at the wrong time. So, the party members who fought long and hard to plant them for their enemy, must take the time to pull them out and destroy them safely, or at best sell them to another country whose leaders would like to turn their country into swampland. Saving lives is every person's moral responsibility, and preserving a life is a much more needed and valuable asset to Afghanistan than new buildings being built. If we do not find and eliminate these mines properly, then we are not only jeopardizing lives but also the environment. The environment is not going away, but we can help make it better, so people can live longer and more happily.

AMORAL MENTALITY LEADING TO IMMORAL ACTIONS

There are those individuals who claim that there is no ethics in politics, and there certainly should not be any ethics in a war. These are the people who are *amoral* individuals. *Amoral* means the absence of moral consideration while doing business or fighting a war. Amoral individuals may think strictly in terms of legal issues, and how they can earn the maximum benefit for themselves or their clients within those realms. There is nothing wrong with this mentality in a perfect world if there was such a world. Since we do not have and may never have a perfect world, amoral thinking may lead to immoral actions during certain conditions. Most people in a "just" war are usually fighting for a cause that is important to them. They may be fighting for personal freedom, liberation of their country, freedom of religion, or simply for the freedom of basic human rights. All these issues involve personal values, moral issues and principles, as well as personal ethics. We all judge situations based our own frame of reference, and reach moral conclusions according to our own personal ethics. Our own personal ethics may involve benefits to ourselves and/or to others. Whatever the case, our values need to be clarified and our actions should be aligned with our values, so we can strive for the appropriate results with appropriate means. By doing this, we can assure ourselves of consistency between actions, thoughts, and values. It is important to clarify our values prior to our actions, because our feelings and emotions involved around the issue can cause many of us to act differently according to the situation. The Russian author and soldier in Afghanistan, Tamarov (1992) writes "The explosion rang in my ears with an unexpectedly sharp force…Out of habit, my body reacted to it faster than my mind-in an instant, I was already lying in the bushes." He further states that one day as they were walking through a desert, they saw an Afghan walking and killed him immediately. Tamarov wrote:

> The man was probably one of those who were shooting at us…but maybe not. It is possible that he was simply returning home…We did not have time to think, is this an enemy or a friend? We only had time to pull the trigger…but maybe not. We shot at every shadow; everything that moved was a threat to us.

The body may be in pain physically and the best relief during a war might be to kill someone who just looks or acts like the enemy. This has happened many times in war situations in Afghanistan, and in some cases many thousands of people died because someone did not think things through his or her own personal ethics framework. Of course, similar unfortunate cases have supposedly taken place recently in Iraq and Lebanon as well, causing some individuals to not trust the army and coalition forces. Acting solely based on emotions can cause conflict between values and actions, which is not a very good leadership characteristic.

REMAINING OBJECTIVE IN THE FACE OF TRAGEDY

Realistically speaking, as human beings we are all driven based on emotions and unfortunately some individuals do not take the time to think things through and filter it through their cultural or personal values. When the September 11, 2001 attacks took place on the New York Twin Towers and the Pentagon, many people in the United States were very emotional and upset. Fortunately, not everyone was willing to act based upon their emotions. There were many people calling the radio stations and saying such things as the United States needs to just "bomb and turn Afghanistan and the middle-eastern countries into parking lots." Every decent human being is likely to be upset when an innocent person suffers or loses his or her life. As a matter of fact, one gets upset when energy and time are wasted or when damage is caused to non-living things such as a building. People get upset when kids hurt animals...many Afghans in Kabul and Logar used to yell and scream when young kids were bothering stray dogs. So, of course, people will get upset when terrorism impacts innocent individuals in one's backyard. However, one cannot let emotions drive major decisions. During the 9/11 attacks, the author was Campus College Chair for the Graduate College of Business and Management at the Tampa Campus for University of Phoenix. Because of so much emotion in the society and to make sure all employees were treated with respect and dignity during such a difficult time, the Campus Director, George Lucas, sent the following letter (email) to all employees:

> I know we all join our nation and the world in shock and disbelief at the senseless acts of destruction and violence perpetrated on our country...!
> We truly are engaged in a noble vocation. We change lives. We prepare our students to support their families and help their organizations become more productive. We equip them with attitudes and skills that help them become better members of their communities and citizens of our nation.
> In T.H. White's book *The Once and Future King* that tells the story of King Arthur, there is a passage that captures an important aspect of the healing process-- and it's something we of the Faculty can help accomplish. If you will recall, Merlin the Magician was the boy-Arthur's teacher and guide. The wise Merlin counsels a despondent Arthur. "The best thing for being sad," replied Merlin, beginning to puff and blow, "is to learn something. That is the only thing that never fails. You may grow old and trembling in your anatomies, you may lie awake at night listening to the disorder of your veins, you may miss your only love, you may see the world about you devastated by evil lunatics, or know your honor trampled in the sewers of baser minds. There is only one thing for it then--to learn. Learn why the world wags and what wags it. That is the only thing which the mind can never exhaust, never alienate, never be tortured by, never fear or distrust, and never dream of regretting."

I ask you to join in redoubling our efforts to help our students learn so that they will achieve their life and career goals. It is easy to get in a rut and find oneself simply going through the motions--I know from personal experience. If there is anything good to come out of this awful tragedy, it will come because we acted courageously in response. That courage may take many forms--but one sure way is to do what we are called upon do each day more reflectively, with more preparation and care and with more of an eye to the good ends we want to achieve.

I also ask that you help educate our students to think critically about these events. Particularly it is important for us to help them understand the difference between the actions of "evil lunatics" as described by Merlin, and the great majority of peace-loving adherents to Islam who are our colleagues, students, and neighbors. The backlash we are seeing against innocent people is unconscionable and unacceptable. As educators, we have a responsibility to help others see those difficult moral distinctions and must be indefatigable in our defense of the basic truths upon which our civilization is centered.

On a practical note, I also ask that we all be sensitive to our students of differing religious faiths and those who are called into military duty. The University's policy is that we do not penalize our students who are observing religious holidays, such as the current celebration of Rosh Hashanah by members of the Jewish faith. Additionally, your campus will be communicating procedures regarding those called up to military duty. If you have questions about these issues, please be sure to contact your Campus College Chair or Director of Academic Affairs.

Thank you for your dedication and devotion to our students and to the important work we do together. I am proud to say that I am a member of the faculty of the University of Phoenix and to be able to call all of you my colleagues.

Professor Lucas's letter to all employees and faculty members was very powerful as it was written with rational thinking and objective decision-making. Such is the quality of great leaders who are able to keep calm and allow such calmness to become contagious through their effective communication. Another good example is Mr. Tamim Ansary's letter and thoughts (see below) which show a rational thought process in terms of the consequences of one's actions. His letter also points out some of the bigger issues that government officials should consider when they decide how to combat terrorism on a global scale.

A gentleman by the name of Gary T. in September 2001 forwarded the letter from Tamim Ansary to many individuals connected to the cyberspace and it received much attention as he was invited to, and the letter was shown, on the Oprah Winfrey show. Gary said, "The following was sent to me by my friend Tamim Ansary. Tamim is an Afghani-American writer...He is also one of the most brilliant people I know in this life. When he writes, I read. When he talks, I listen. Here is his take on Afghanistan and the whole mess we are in."

"Dear Gary and other readers:
I've been hearing a lot of talk about "bombing Afghanistan back to the Stone Age." Ronn Owens, on KGO Talk Radio today, allowed that this would mean killing innocent people, people who had nothing to do with this atrocity, but "we're at war, we have to accept collateral damage. What else can we do?" Minutes later I heard some TV pundit discussing whether we "have the belly to do what must be done."

And I thought about the issues being raised especially hard because I am from Afghanistan, and even though I've lived here for 35 years I've never lost track of what's going on there. So I want to tell anyone who will listen how it all looks from where I'm standing.

I speak as one who hates the Taliban and Osama Bin Laden. There is no doubt in my mind that these people were responsible for the atrocity in New York. I agree that something must be done about those monsters.

But the Taliban and Bin Laden are not Afghanistan. They're not even the government of Afghanistan. The Taliban are a cult of ignorant psychotics who took over Afghanistan in 1997. Bin Laden is a political criminal with a plan. When you think Taliban, think Nazis. When you think Bin Laden, think Hitler. And when you think "the people of Afghanistan" think "the Jews in the concentration camps." It's not only that the Afghan people had nothing to do with this atrocity. They were the first victims of the perpetrators. They would exult if someone would come in there, take out the Taliban and clear out the rat's nest of international thugs holed up in their country.

Some say, why do not the Afghans rise up and overthrow the Taliban? The answer is, they're starved, exhausted, hurt, incapacitated, and suffering. A few years ago, the United Nations estimated that there are 500,000 disabled orphans in Afghanistan--a country with no economy, no food. There are millions of widows. And the Taliban has been burying these widows alive in mass graves. The soil is littered with land mines, the farms were all destroyed by the Soviets. These are a few of the reasons why the Afghan people have not overthrown the Taliban. We come now to the question of bombing Afghanistan back to the Stone Age. Trouble is, that's been done. The Soviets took care of it already. Make the Afghans suffer? They're already suffering. Level their houses? Done. Turn their schools into piles of rubble? Done. Eradicate their hospitals? Done. Destroy their infrastructure? Cut them off from medicine and health care? Too late. Someone already did all that.

New bombs would only stir the rubble of earlier bombs. Would they at least get the Taliban? Not likely. In today's Afghanistan, only the Taliban eat, only they have the means to move around. They'd slip away and hide. Maybe the bombs would get some of those disabled orphans, they do not move too fast, they do not even have wheelchairs. But flying over Kabul and dropping bombs would not really be a strike against the criminals who did this horrific thing. Actually it would only be making common cause with the Taliban--by raping once again the people they've been raping all this time.

So what else is there? What can be done, then? Let me now speak with true fear and trembling. The only way to get Bin Laden is to go in there with ground troops. When people speak of "having the belly to do what needs to be done" they're thinking in terms of having the belly to kill as many as needed. Having the belly to overcome any moral qualms about killing innocent people. Let's pull our heads out of the sand. What's actually on the table is Americans dying. And not just because some Americans would die fighting their way through Afghanistan to Bin Laden's hideout. It's much bigger than that folks. Because to get any troops to Afghanistan, we'd have to go through Pakistan. Would they let us? Not likely. The conquest of Pakistan would have to be first. Will other Muslim nations just stand by? You see where I'm going. We're flirting with a world war between Islam and the West.

And guess what: that's Bin Laden's program. That's exactly what he wants. That's why he did this. Read his speeches and statements. It's all right there. He really believes Islam would beat the west. It might seem ridiculous, but he figures if he can polarize the world into Islam and the West, he's got a billion soldiers. If the west wreaks a holocaust in those lands, that's a billion people with nothing left to lose, that's even better from Bin Laden's point of view. He's probably wrong, in the end the west would win, whatever that would mean, but the war would last for years and millions would die, not just theirs but ours. Who has the belly for that? Bin Laden does. Anyone else?" (Tamim Ansary, September 2001).

Although, there is no evidence that members of Taliban government had any involvement in the 9/11 attacks, Mr. Tamim Ansary is certainly entitled to his opinions and the possible solutions to the dilemma he bravely reflected upon at the time. While you (the reader) and I (the author) may not necessarily agree with portions of his assertions or statements (since the general public does not have access to any real evidence showing the perpetrators of the attacks), he did write a very powerful letter to make emotionally-charged individuals reflect and think twice about their words and, more importantly, actions. His letter also points out some of the bigger issues that all international leaders should consider when combating poverty and terrorism on a global scale. I mention "poverty" because it seems to go hand-to-hand with terrorism. Many individuals say that if the world community tackles the issue of eliminating poverty, then terrorism may also be wiped out as a natural corollary of it.

RECOMMENDATIONS

Dr. Abdul Sattar Sirrat, former delegate of King Zahir Shah to the Bonn Conference and advisor to the Saudi Arabian government and professor of Islamic Studies at Kabul University, mentioned that "The people of Afghanistan wish to have two basic human rights: security and self-determination" (Sirrat, 2004). Dr. Sirrat further mentioned that these two objectives can be achieved by the following steps:

1. *First*: Providing the opportunity for the people of Afghanistan to choose their political national system by their own free will.
2. *Second*: Peace and security throughout the country should be restored by the disarmament of illegal armed groups by the U.N. peace forces and a national security force should be created by establishing a neutral and professional Afghan military committee.
3. *Third*: Foreign interference from anywhere should stop by any possible means.
4. *Fourth*: The international community should honor its legal and humanitarian obligations to rebuild Afghanistan without any interference in the political life in the country.

Ultimately, such security and prosperity must come from the self determination of all Afghans to work hard and keep peace within the country. There is the story about the ant and the grasshopper which applies here to the people of Afghanistan as they rise to the occasion and speed up the recovery process. The ants worked hard all summer and gathered food for their winter. As they were preparing to make a meal during the winter, a grasshopper came by begging for food from the ants. The ants asked him, "What did you do during the summer?" The grasshopper replied, "I was too busy singing and did not have the time to gather food for winter." The ants said, "if you spent the summer singing, then you should spend the winter dancing." You see, "God helps those who help themselves." Afghans and their friends have to rise to the occasion and build a civilization that they can be proud of in the coming decades. "Asia is not going to be civilized after the methods of the West. There is too much Asia and she is too old" (Rudyard Kipling, 1865-1936). They must persist in rebuilding Afghanistan toward a brighter future and constantly improve every process.

All individuals are human beings that represent a diverse group of people and organizations with an astonishing history of commitment to peace and civil rights. It is the human being's special cognitive ability that makes them intelligent creatures that are different from other mammals. It is also that special ability that has allowed human beings to acquire rapid development from generation to generation as compared to animals. Furthermore, it is that special ability that allowed human beings to realize their wrongdoing and thus to pave the way toward eliminating slavery, killing and abusing young girls, discriminations based on color, selling of children, killing of animals violently, and so on. I believe it is that special ability of human beings that will end these human-inflicted violations of morality and basic human rights. However, this endeavor will require each and everyone of us to do our part in defending the rights of those who need our help; and accordingly to help stop, educate, and guide those who are committing these violations. It is every person's moral obligation to make this world a better place for him or herself. It is through living certain basics guidelines that we can help all involved parties simultaneously which can rapidly abolish these violations. Each person can individually start learning, understanding, visualizing things mentally, and expressing themselves in a better way that is exemplary to others so they can benefit from it. We cannot change other people's views or ideas, but we have total control over our own actions and that is where change has to start. The Quran says, "You are accountable for none but yourself; he that goes astray cannot harm you if you are on the right path. To God you shall all return, and He will declare to you what you have done." We have the freedom to control and choose our actions, and we need to be the change, which we would like to see in another person, in order for things to improve in this world. It takes a mature individual to concentrate on his/her own abilities to keep doing good for others, and to forgive the mistakes and bad intentions of his/her enemies. Yet clearing one's mind by forgiving others is important to one's psychological health and to personal victory. Aristotle said, "I count him braver who overcomes his desires than him who conquers his enemies; for the hardest victory is the victory over self." One may not be able to control the world and make huge changes, but one should not let that interfere with things that he/she can do. One should always focus on accomplishing things which are at his/her proximity and control, while keeping in mind that "things which matter most must never be at the mercy of things which matter least," as Goethe, the German philosopher, stated. Once a person is going in the right direction, getting there is just a matter of time, patience, and perseverance. One must stick to the plan and keep following one's deeply held values and principles of good conduct. The concept of "Stick-to-itiveness" can mean getting great results in life.

> The fisher who draws in his net too soon,
> Will not have any fish to sell;
> The person who shuts up the book too soon,
> Will not learn any lessons well.
> If you would have your learning to stay,
> Be patient-do not learn too fast;
> The man who travels a mile each day,
> May get round the world at last.
> (Unknown)

The story of the "crow and the pitcher" can show how patience can be instrumental if accompanied with strategy. One day there was a thirsty crow who saw a pitcher of water. The water was low in the pitcher and the crow could not reach it. The crow tried to tip it over, and it also tried to break it in order to get some water out of it, but with no success. The pitcher was too strong. Finally, the crow started thinking about other alternatives. He saw stones laying nearby and started throwing them into the pitcher until the water was high and he was able to drink out of it. So the crow said, "There is always a way out of hard places if you have the wit to find it." When there is a will, there is a way. One must always be loyal to the vision and one's destination, so long as they are aligned with universal principles and values. Then one should find the means to achieve the vision efficiently regardless of the risks involved.

Two brothers fighting against the Russians in Afghanistan were very close and loyal to each other. One of them became injured, and the other asked the group leader if he could go over and bring his injured brother from the battlefield. The leader replied, "He is probably dead, why would you risk your life to bring in his body?" Finally, the leader agreed with the brother and said he could go. The healthy brother finally brought his brother, and as he came back with his brother on his shoulder, the injured brother died. So, the leader replied, "There, you see, you risked your life for nothing." The brother replied, "No, I did what he expected of me and I have my reward. When I crept up to him and took him in my arms, he said, 'big brother, I knew you would come - I just knew you would come.'" Personal and professional loyalties involve certain obligations, and these obligations need to be carried out despite the risk involved.

Loyalty that applies to one's vision and future development of a country must start at home with the children, parents and older relatives. An old man lived by himself, and he was widowed. He finally became ill and could not take care of himself. He had three sons, and they each came by and visited with their dad for about an hour and left. As he got sicker, the kids came less often. So, one day, he put a whole bunch of broken glass in a wooden box and started guarding it really closely. His sons asked him what it was, and he said it should be guarded really closely. The sons started taking turns living with him because they did not want the box to be stolen. They thought it was full of gold. So later when the old man died, they opened the box and discovered broken glasses. They were very disappointed, but they discovered that it was for the box that they took care of him, otherwise they may have neglected him until the day he died. The responsibility of taking care of parents and children should not change with age or physical disabilities. We should provide them with unconditional love no matter what the situation might be. It has been said that most senior citizens are children for the second time, and caring for them may mean taking care of them like a little baby.

While taking care of family members is one obligation, Afghans need to treat their peers, countrymen, and neighbors with kindness and good hospitality, as such forms of kindness are contagious. Once upon a time, two men were traveling together on the mountains of Afghanistan when a bear came across them. One of the travelers, the athletic one, ran away without consideration for his companion. The companion yelled "please help me," but he did not come down from the tree to help him. So, he just threw himself on the ground and pretended to be dead. The bear came and sniffed him all around, but he kept still, and did not take a breath. So, the bear went on its way because bears do not touch dead bodies. So, his friend came down and asked what did the bear whisper to your ear? He replied "he told me not to travel with a friend who deserts you at the first sign of danger." It has been said that "Misfortunes test the sincerity of friendship." Friendship is like filling a cup of water, where it gets filled one drop at a time, and it is the last drop which makes it run over. So, in personal relationships, we should make many deposits and it might be the last act of kindness that makes someone's heart run over to make them a real friend for life. Friendships should be constantly replenished by making many deposits day in and day out. We should always seek to be with old and new friends. One should never make new friends at the expense of an old friend.

What is disappointing with regard to the violation of human rights is that often governments and state-run agencies are accused of taking part in such activities through torture and initiation of conflicts among various people groups. At times, the state-run agencies are accused of actually poisoning, killing, and executing whistleblowers, journalists and their own members who have defected. If these state-run agencies are not held responsible for having and withholding higher standards, then how different are they from actual thieves, gangs, terrorists, and warlords. For example, the Russian authorities were accused of poisoning the Ex-KGB spy in late November of 2006. Litvinenko fell ill after someone slipped the poison in his food or drink at a sushi restaurant. Alexander Litvinenko, a former KGB agent, who had been an outspoken critic of Russian government authorities, died two weeks after the poisoning on November 25, 2006. Of course, the Russian government and President Vladimir Putin officially denied any involvement in the poisoning. Litvinenko was supposedly following leads in the murder of Anna Politkovskaya, a Russian investigative journalist who was gunned down Oct. 7 in her Moscow apartment building. The poison used to kill Litvinenko interferes with the cardiovascular and nervous systems, attacking the vital organs. According to experts, a deadly dose of thallium can be no bigger than an eraser head on a pencil; thallium, an odorless and tasteless lethal metal, seems to be a poison of choice in the world of espionage. The government of Iraq during Saddam Hussein's regime has been accused of using it. The CIA, from the United States, is also believed to have hatched a plan to lace the soles of Fidel Castro's shoes with it; and according to media reports, the apartheid government of South Africa considered poisoning Nelson Mandela with it while he was imprisoned on the Robben Island. With regard to the death of Anna Politkovskaya, the Executive Director of Amnesty International USA, Larry Cox wrote the following in his letter to members on November 27, 2006:

> She was brutally murdered in the elevator of her apartment building for speaking out against torture. Anna Politkovskaya - a dedicated journalist, human rights defender and mother of two - worked tirelessly to expose human rights abuses in Chechnya and other regions of the Russian Federation. Politkovskaya faced intimidation and harassment from Russian and Chechen authorities due to her outspoken criticism of government human rights violations, including disappearances and killings of civilians. At the time of her assassination, she was preparing an article about the alleged use of torture by authorities in Chechnya. She was found shot dead in the elevator of her apartment building in Moscow in the middle of the afternoon. Even back in 2001, Anna was receiving death threats when AIUSA organized a press conference to promote her first book. For more than five years, she chose to go right back into the heart of danger, a "small corner of hell," as she called it, to shine a light on horrific human rights violations that others did not want to face (Executive Director of Amnesty International, USA).

The world has much work ahead of it in order to eliminate human rights violations and all instances of such violations must end if we are to live peacefully. Pope John Paul II, who died on April 3rd 2005, once said that when human rights are violated wars begin; and, when human rights are restored wars can end. There are still many conflicts in this world and the leaders must work hard toward eliminating such tragedies. Of course, Afghanistan is only one of many places that need everyone's immediate attention. The next few pages provide the content of two actual letters that were sent by the Human Rights Watch (Asian Division) in December 2004 to President Karzai (Kabul) and Donald Rumsfeld (Washington) about the current situation in Afghanistan along with recommendations (Adams, December 2004). Some of the names from the letter, in this book, have been purposely replaced by this author with (*Xxx Xxx*) in order to keep discussion and reflections objective.

LETTER BY THE HUMAN RIGHTS WATCH-ASIAN DIVISION TO PRESIDENT KARZAI

HUMAN RIGHTS WATCH
An Open Letter to President Hamid Karzai
December 3, 2004

Congratulations on your election and inauguration as Afghanistan's first directly elected president. By taking part in presidential elections, Afghans overcame intimidation from regional warlords, threats from the Taliban, and tremendous logistical difficulties. Your victory gives you the mandate to realize the oft-stated wish of Afghans to live in peace and security after nearly three decades of conflict. We at Human Rights Watch wish you success in meeting this challenge.

Over the last three years, we are aware that as Afghanistan's interim and then transitional president you acted in many cases to safeguard human rights and protect vulnerable persons and groups. As you assume your new position, we ask that you give an even higher priority to protecting the rights of all persons in Afghanistan, regardless of gender, religion, or ethnicity. In particular, we urge you use the position granted to you by the Afghan people to press for the rule of law, the prosecution of human rights violators, and an end to the insecurity and warlord rule still plaguing much of the country.

Human Rights Watch has been monitoring Afghanistan for over twenty years. We would like to take this opportunity to bring to your attention several areas of special concern reflecting our investigations around Afghanistan: the need to weaken warlord rule; ending impunity and strengthening the rule of law; promoting international support for human rights protection and enhanced security; curbing abuses by U.S. forces; promoting women's rights; and preparing for upcoming parliamentary and local elections.

Ending the Rule of Warlords:
You have echoed in numerous public statements what hundreds of Afghans have told us over the last three years: that insecurity and criminality associated with regional warlords and factional militias constitute the most serious impediment to the well-being of the Afghan people. Afghanistan's booming drug trade has only increased the power of warlords. Today, three years after the Taliban were ousted, armed groups controlled by warlords use violence and create fear against much of the Afghan population. In previous administrations some warlords even assumed positions at highest levels of your government.

We recognize that the warlords' usurpation of power was due in large part to realities on the ground and decisions of political and strategic expediency by the United States and its other coalition partners. Now that you have a popular mandate as the elected leader of the Afghan people, we hope that you will choose a new cabinet and appoint new government officials whose power does not derive from the strength of arms and who are committed to civilian rule in Afghanistan. The process of disarming these armed groups and reintegrating them into Afghan society should be a top priority for your new administration.

We applaud your efforts so far to sideline some of these warlords from government, in particular your dismissal of *Xxx Xxx* as governor of Herat and *Xxx Xxx* as governor of Qandahar , and your decision not to have *Xxx Xxx* run as your vice-presidential candidate. We urge you to use the occasion of naming a new government to accelerate the replacement of warlords and their proxies with civilians committed to the rule of law.

We urge you to take appropriate steps against warlords and others outside of government who use unofficial authority to improperly interfere with democratic processes and institutions. Specifically, we call on you to speak out against and disarm the forces of *Xxx Xxx*, the head of the Ittihad-i Islami faction and the Daw'at-e Islami party. *Xxx Xxx* has no government post but has used his power over the Supreme Court and other courts across the country to curtail the rights of journalists, civic society activists, and even political candidates. He also controls militias, including forces recognized as the 10th Division of the Afghan army, which intimidate and abuse Afghans even inside Kabul. We ask that you express public opposition to *Xxx Xxx's* activities, explicitly state your opposition to such misuse of unofficial authority, and move expeditiously to disarm and demobilize armed forces associated with Ittihad-i Islami and other unofficial forces.

Dismantling the power of the warlords requires speeding up the process of disarming, demobilizing and reintegrating the tens of thousands of Afghans who carry arms as part of militias (as called for in the December 2001 Bonn Agreement). Disarmament of militias has been largely symbolic: in most rural areas local commanders have retained their forces, and use them to commit abuses against local populations. This process has progressed far too slowly, largely due to obstructionism by warlords and the failure of the international community to challenge them. With your election, you have the opportunity to focus the necessary international attention on finally ridding Afghanistan of unauthorized guns and gunmen.

Ending Impunity and Strengthening the Rule of Law:
Afghanistan continues to face a crisis of impunity. Numerous officials in local and national posts—including several senior military and police officials, as well as district and provincial governors—have been implicated in ongoing and past human rights abuses and other crimes. Very few of these officials have been brought to justice.

Some of the abusers who now threaten Afghanistan's security gained widespread notoriety and public opprobrium during Afghanistan's long and bloody civil war. Warlords like *Xxx* and *Xxx* are implicated in serious human rights abuses during the bloody battles that destroyed much of Kabul in 1992-95. General *Xxx Xxx*, now a military commander in northwestern Afghanistan, is also implicated in atrocities in Kabul during that period, as well as in Mazar-e Sharif and northwestern Afghanistan in 1997 and after the ouster of the Taliban. Armed militias loyal to these leaders continue to commit human rights abuses to this day.

In addition, there are numerous police officials, army troops, and intelligence agents in your own government who are further implicated in current abuses.

There are also numerous former Taliban leaders implicated in past and current human rights abuses. We are aware that your government is currently negotiating with some of these leaders, and that it is possible some may be brought into your government.

As a matter of urgency, we urge you to create a commission that would let all senior government posts, preferably in collaboration with the Afghan Independent Human Rights Commission, with the power to sideline persons from government service who face credible allegations for past or recent abuses.

With regard to crimes of the past, we urge your office to work with the Afghan Independent Human Rights Commission to investigate the creation, with parliamentary approval, of national mechanisms to promote accountability, so that the persons involved in serious war crimes and crimes against humanity can be called into account for their atrocities. It is clear that there is strong sentiment among Afghans for making the most serious criminals of the past answer for their crimes.

Ultimately, however, the best way to address impunity is to strengthen institutions which uphold the rule of law, including the police, the judiciary, prosecutors, and the Afghan Independent Human Rights Commission. Accordingly, we strongly urge you to seek greater support from the international community to accelerate efforts to improve and professionalize the police force, judicial and correctional systems. Simply put, persons who violate the law need to be prosecuted and fairly tried for their crimes, and your government should work to reform the institutions—police, judicial, and corrections—to make this possible.

In addition, we urge you to appoint judges who are adequately trained in civil law (as distinct from religious law), devoted to improving the judicial system, and committed to upholding human rights standards and the rule of law. We are deeply troubled by the fact that the current chief justice of Afghanistan's Supreme Court, *Xxx Xxx*, and his deputy chief justice, *Xxx Xxx*, lack any training in civil law. More troublingly, they have abused their authority by targeting journalists, civic activists, and even presidential candidates. They do not appear to act independently, the first requirement of a judge, instead making political judgments in close collaboration with warlords like *Xxx Xxx*.

Seeking Greater International Support for Afghanistan:
International actors, including the United States, have committed considerable resources to helping Afghanistan rebuild, but there is much more they can and should do. We urge you to use the mandate you have received from the Afghan people to be a more forceful—and, if necessary, more critical—interlocutor with the international community.

Over the past three years, key international actors have used your public silence or diplomatic phrasing to justify inaction or strategic mistakes that did not take into account the best interests of the Afghan people. One specific disappointment has been that NATO, as the lead organization in the International Security Assistance Force (ISAF), has failed to satisfy its repeated promises of providing the adequate number of troops necessary to bring security to most of the country. As a result, reconstruction and development projects in many areas have not gotten underway, and efforts to disarm militias have gone too slowly.

Small Provincial Reconstruction Teams, consisting of coalition troops, have been deployed to some areas, but their numbers are too small and their area of coverage too large to provide adequate security. To make matters worse, the mandates given to both ISAF and coalition Provincial Reconstruction Teams are vague and do not include explicit instructions for commanders to assist with human rights protection efforts or disarmament programs.

At the same time, from its inception the United Nations Assistance Mission in Afghanistan (UNAMA) has deployed an inadequate number of human rights and political affairs officers outside of Kabul—officers who could help protect vulnerable persons and groups, monitor elections, and maintain pressure on commanders to meet their obligations to disarm their militias. The United Nations has an obligation to address this problem.

We hope that you are able to use your new mandate as Afghanistan's first directly elected president to ensure that international security assistance to Afghanistan fully meets the needs and concerns of the Afghan people.

Curbing Abuses by U.S. forces:
We urge you to take all necessary steps to ensure that foreign forces on Afghan soil, particularly U.S. forces, conduct military operations in full accordance with international human rights and humanitarian law, for which they remain obligated. As we have raised previously, U.S. forces in Afghanistan appear to act without regard to any specific body of law. U.S. forces continue to conduct military attacks and arrest operations in many parts of the south that lead to unnecessary civilian death and injury, as well as resentment at the local level. U.S. forces continue to arrest and hold Afghans at detention sites around the country, incommunicado and indefinitely, without regard to and in violation of Afghan law. Allegations of physical abuse continue to be raised, and the U.S. military's response to such allegations remains inadequate.

The Afghan government is responsible for human rights violations committed on its soil, even if committed by foreign armed forces acting on its behalf. The U.S. government, moreover, cannot evade its responsibilities under international law because they are occurring outside the United States. We urge you as an immediate step to seek a clarification from the United States that appropriate Afghan and international law will be applied to all arrests and detentions occurring in the country, whether carried out by Afghan or foreign forces. This will require, among other things, that the U.S. forces overhaul their detention policies, in particular, by allowing visits by the AIHRC and family members of detainees, as well as by legal counsel or other representatives. We also ask that appropriate Afghan authorities investigate claims of abuse by U.S. and other coalition forces in Afghanistan.

Increasing Support for the Rights of Women and Girls:
We urge you to increase your government's political and material support for the rights of women and girls, who have suffered disproportionately over the last 25 years of instability. Today, women and girls continue to suffer from major inequalities in educational and work opportunities, as well as severe social restrictions.

We call on you to appoint a cabinet that is more representative of women, and to work to mainstream women's involvement in your government. Women should be given meaningful opportunities to serve in all ministries, in particular powerful ministries like interior, foreign affairs, and defense. We also call on you to strengthen women's representation at the local level by appointing more women to local government positions.

In addition, we call on you to appoint a minister of education who will work to equalize educational opportunities for women and girls across Afghanistan— not only in elementary levels but through the university level.

Preparing for Parliamentary and Local Elections:
The October 2004 presidential election was an important and historic step forward, but political rights in Afghanistan remain at risk. Upcoming parliamentary and local elections, scheduled for next year, will be a vital test. Regional leaders and warlords continue to dominate political processes at the local level, and many politically active people have told us that they are afraid to run as candidates for fear that their lives will be in danger.

We urge you to continue your efforts to prevent and address threats made by local leaders against politically active persons, and we urge you to speak out against repression by local leaders and in favor of free expression and pluralism, so that everyone in Afghanistan—even people who criticize you or warlords—can enjoy their political rights. We ask that you take special care to ensure that political groups operating on your behalf set a good example by scrupulously respecting human rights.

We urge you to press the international community to increase and expedite the logistical and security support necessary for successfully carrying out parliamentary and local elections, including by ensuring a sufficient number of impartial international and domestic observers.

We believe that you would agree with us that the protection of human rights and political freedom is ultimately the best recipe for stability and peace in your country.

Human Rights Watch wishes you success in carrying out the historic responsibility entrusted to you by the people of Afghanistan.

Yours sincerely,

Brad Adams
Executive Director, Asia Division
Human Rights Watch

LETTER BY THE HUMAN RIGHTS WATCH TO DONALD RUMSFELD

HUMAN RIGHTS WATCH
An Open Letter to US Secretary of Defense Donald Rumsfeld December 13, 2004

Donald Rumsfeld
Secretary of Defense
1000 Defense Pentagon
Washington, DC 20301-1000

Dear Secretary Rumsfeld,
We are writing to you regarding U.S.-administered detention facilities in Afghanistan. We are troubled by new allegations of serious abuse by U.S. military personnel and by the failure of your office to make public the results of investigations into past abuses and take adequate steps to hold abusers accountable. In most cases of which we are aware, the Department of Defense has launched criminal investigations only after particular abuses received media attention. These investigations have proceeded extremely slowly and in excessive secrecy. An internal Pentagon investigation of detention operations in Afghanistan, conducted by Brig. Gen. Charles H. Jacoby, has been completed, but remains classified, unlike similar reports on abuses in Iraq.

Six detainees are now known to have died in U.S. custody in Afghanistan—including four known cases of murder or manslaughter—and former detainees have made scores of other claims of torture and other mistreatment. Some of the cases took place over two years ago. Yet to our knowledge, the U.S.

government has conducted only a handful of criminal investigations, and has charged only two people with any crime in these cases.

The government's failure to hold its personnel accountable for serious abuses has spawned a culture of impunity among some personnel. And as you know, some of the personnel involved in earlier abuses in Afghanistan have now been implicated in later abuses in Iraq.

Over nine months ago, in March 2004, we issued a report, "Enduring Freedom": Abuses by U.S. Forces in Afghanistan, focusing on arrest and detention procedures by U.S. forces in Afghanistan. The report documented cases of U.S. personnel arbitrarily detaining civilians, using excessive force during arrests of non-combatants, and mistreating detainees. Detainees held at military bases in 2002 and 2003 described being beaten severely by guards and interrogators, deprived of sleep for extended periods, and intentionally exposed to extreme cold, as well as other inhumane and degrading treatment.

The report discussed three deaths known at the time to have occurred in U.S. custody: the death of a detainee in Asadabad in June 2003, and the deaths of two detainees at Bagram airbase in December 2002 which were ruled as homicides by U.S. military pathologists.

The detention system in Afghanistan continues to operate outside the rule of law. The United States continues to hold Afghan detainees in legal limbo and in many cases incommunicado, in violation of U.S. obligations under the laws of armed conflict and applicable Afghan law. There are fewer recent complaints about the central detention facility at Bagram air base, where serious abuses had occurred in the past. However, allegations of abuse and arbitrary detention continue to surface at forward operating bases, such as those near Gardez, Khost, Urgon, Ghazni, and Jalalabad.

New Developments:

Since the publication of our March report, several new cases of serious abuse have come to light. Through 2004, the Afghan Independent Human Rights Commission (AIHRC), a government-appointed body with a proven track record of credibly reporting on human rights conditions, has received numerous complaints about mistaken arrests, arbitrary detention, and mistreatment and beatings of detainees by U.S. forces. Human Rights Watch's interviews with former detainees bolster these reports of ongoing abuses.

Human Rights Watch has also learned of additional detainee deaths that were not documented in our March report. We call on you to take action to ensure full accountability for these cases:

• A new case from 2002. Just last week, new evidence emerged of a previously unpublicized alleged murder of an Afghan detainee by four U.S. military personnel in Afghanistan in or before September 2002. This is the earliest known death of a person in U.S. custody in Afghanistan. According to internal Department of Defense documents, recently released to the American Civil Liberties Union as part of a Freedom of Information Act request, the Army Criminal Investigative Command opened an investigation on September 26, 2002—over two years ago—into charges of "Murder," "Conspiracy," and "Obstruction of Justice" in conjunction with the case. The document states that "CPT (captain) [name redacted], SFC (Sergeant First Class) [name redacted], SSG (Staff Sergeant [name redacted], and SSG (Staff Sergeant) [name redacted] murdered Mr. [redacted] after detaining him for following their movements in Afghanistan." To our knowledge, the government has not prosecuted any of the four personnel implicated. The report indicates that the case was "closed" and that a "4833" was received in the case—presumably, a Commander's Report of Disciplinary or Administrative Action, known as DA Form 4833—which suggests that a final disciplinary or administration action has taken place. Yet we know of no court martials that have taken place with respect to this "murder." We call on you to explain what disciplinary or administrative actions were taken by the Department of Defense in this case and the basis for these measures.

• A new case from 2003. Another death in custody was uncovered in September 2004 by researchers with the Crimes of War project, a non-government organization. The findings were later published in the Los Angeles Times (September 21, 2004). Jamal Naseer, a soldier in the U.S.-backed official Afghan Army, was killed in March 2003 after he and seven other soldiers were mistakenly arrested by U.S. forces and taken to a base in Gardez. Their case was investigated by the United Nations office in Gardez, the office of the Attorney General of the Afghan Army, and the Crimes of War project. The investigations showed that U.S. forces severely beat Naseer and the other soldiers while in custody. Numerous witnesses who saw them at the time (including U.N. representatives) described them as having wounds and heavy bruises. The surviving detainees themselves allege that U.S. forces punched them, kicked them, hung them upside down, and hit them with sticks or cables, among other abuses. Some said they were soaked in cold water and forced to lie in snow, and shocked with electricity on their toes. The Army Criminal Investigative Command opened an investigation into this case in May 2004, but to our knowledge it has not reached any results and has not charged any one in connection with the death or the abuses against the seven other soldiers held with Naseer. We request that you publicize the results of this investigation and initiate appropriate prosecutorial and administrative measures against those responsible.

• A new case from 2004. Another detainee died in U.S. custody in September 2004. Sher Mohammad Khan was arrested on September 24, 2004 during a raid on his family's home near Khost in which his brother, Mohammad Rais Khan, was shot and killed by U.S. forces. Sher Mohammad Khan died sometime later the next day at a U.S. military base. Military officials in Khost told journalists that he had died of a heart attack, and that the Khan family were "bad guys." As noted above, Khan died within hours of being taken into U.S. custody. Khan's family has told investigators with AIHRC that the body was bruised when they retrieved it from U.S. forces. We urge you to order a thorough investigation to determine the circumstances of Sher Mohammad Kkan's death, release the results of his autopsy, and allow representatives of the AIHRC to discuss the case with U.S. investigators.

Earlier Cases:

In addition to the three deaths in custody cited above, we remain concerned about the three cases described in our March 2004 report. Two men, Habibullah and Diliwar, died at Bagram air base in December 2002. Another, Abdul Wali, died in June 2003 at the Asadabad airbase.

There appears to have been little progress in these three other cases. A full investigation into the two deaths at Bagram was only launched in March 2003, after the New York Times (March 4, 2003) reported that the deaths had been ruled homicides by Army pathologists. (Lt. Gen. Dan McNeill, who was the commander of U.S. forces in Afghanistan at the time, had ordered an investigation into the two deaths in early 2003, but the investigation did not result in any findings of criminal behavior, and recommended no court martial.) The investigation by the Criminal Investigative Command dragged on without result for over a year and a half. The U.S. military command in Kabul promised that they would share the results of investigations with the chief U.N. representative in Afghanistan, Lakhdar Brahimi, but to our knowledge never did. Army investigators also told Human Rights Watch repeatedly over 2003 and 2004 that the investigation was "almost finished," but failed to provide any information about its findings.

The Criminal Investigative Command finally completed a classified report on the deaths in May 2004, recommending that 28 personnel be prosecuted in connection with the deaths. The crimes identified in the report included negligent homicide, maiming, maltreatment, assault consummated by battery, conspiracy, and dereliction of duty. According to the Washington Post, which obtained a copy of the report and cited its findings in an article on December 3, 2004, other abuses discussed in the report include "slamming prisoners into walls, twisting handcuffs to cause pain, kneeing prisoners, forcing a detainee to maintain 'painful, contorted body positions,' shackling the detainee's arms to the ceiling, and forcing water into the mouth of the detainee 'until he could not breathe.'"

None of these allegations were made available to the public in a timely manner. Only in October 2004 did the Criminal Investigative Command finally announce publicly that it had recommended the 28 persons for prosecution in connection with the deaths at Bagram. Yet even now, the case appears stalled: several of the interrogators named in the report were first recommended for prosecution much earlier, in December 2003, yet remain uncharged. The Criminal Investigative Command to date has charged only one person in connection with the deaths. When Human Rights Watch inquired about the cases last week, Public Affairs Officers refused to offer any further information.

Human Rights Watch has also learned that Capt. Carolyn A. Wood, the head of the interrogation unit at Bagram from July 2002 to December 2003, is not among the 28 recommended for prosecution. According to an internal Department of Defense report by Maj. Gen. George Fay and Lt. Gen. Anthony Jones (the Fay-Jones report), Capt. Wood drew up the harsh interrogation techniques that interrogators later used at Abu Ghraib, techniques which she had previously approved in Afghanistan, according to an Army lawyer who testified before Congress in May 2004. In August, a former Bagram interrogator told a Knight-Ridder journalist that at the time of the two deaths screams and moans could easily be heard from interrogation rooms at Bagram, and that Wood must have been aware of the abuse, as the interrogation rooms were near her office. In any case, by virtue of her position, Capt. Wood should have been aware that abuse was taking place. We are concerned that, as at Abu Ghraib, the U.S. government appears more interested in blaming abuses on low-level personnel than in investigating the role of commanding officers and civilian officials.

As for the case of the June 2003 death of Abdul Wali, in Asadabad, we are troubled that over a year passed before the military took action on the case, and that the government sought an indictment in the case only after the Abu Ghraib photos became public. While a federal court in North Carolina indicted David Passaro, a CIA contractor, in June 2004, Defense Department documents released to the ACLU indicate that the Criminal Investigative Command "reopened" the investigation into the Asadabad death on May 25, 2004, only after the Abu Ghraib scandal surfaced. This suggests that the United States had no intention of prosecuting anyone in the case until after the bad publicity from Abu Ghraib. We are also concerned that Passaro might not be the only person responsible in the death: Afghan witnesses allege that other U.S. personnel were with Passaro during the interrogation period. The CIA generally has not adequately responded to allegations that its personnel have tortured persons captured in Afghanistan.

To our knowledge, the government has not recommended any prosecutions with regard to other allegations of torture and mistreatment. Released detainees held in facilities in Bagram, Qandahar, Jalalabad, Asadabad, Gardez, and Khost have made serious allegations to Human Rights Watch, as well as to U.N. and Afghan officials, about numerous other cases of ill-treatment from December 2001 to the present. We know of no prosecutions initiated in connection with any of these allegations.

We are also concerned about new allegations of serious abuse at U.S. forward operating bases—smaller military posts in remote areas. Released detainees have provided both Human Rights Watch and the AIHRC numerous new complaints in 2004 about the behavior of Special Forces soldiers, who often work alongside CIA personnel and operate at forward bases, sometimes without coordination with Afghan government officials or other U.S. forces on the ground. Reported abuses include beatings, sexual humiliation, and exposure to cold. There appears to be no effective mechanism for monitoring the conditions at remote locations maintained by Special Forces or CIA teams. One Army detective, talking about his difficulties in conducting investigations at the Gardez forward operating base, told the Los Angeles Times (September 21, 2004): "We do not know what unit was there. There are no records. The reporting system is broke across the board. Units are transferred in and out. There are no SOPs [standard operating procedures] . . . and each unit acts differently. . . . Gardez is the worst facility—it is three or four times as bad as any other base in Afghanistan."

Inaction and Lack of Transparency:
In our March 2004 report, we called on the United States government to, among other things:
◊ End incommunicado detention practices that facilitate mistreatment.
◊ Fully and impartially investigate allegations of mistreatment of detainees in detention at all U.S. facilities in Afghanistan and make public the results of those investigations.
◊ Take disciplinary or criminal action as appropriate against all personnel responsible for mistreating or otherwise violating the rights of detainees.

It is clear that the U.S. government has fulfilled none of these recommendations. The United States continues to detain persons in Afghanistan without any recognized legal process. There is no access to these sites by family members of the detained, legal counsel, or representatives of the Afghan Independent Human Rights Commission. Many detainees, especially those held for long periods at forward operating bases, are never seen by representatives of the International Committee of the Red Cross (ICRC). Three former interrogators who worked in Afghanistan in 2002 and 2003 told a journalist with Knight-Ridder (August 22, 2004) that it was standard operating procedure in 2002 to hide some detainees from the ICRC in Afghanistan, sometimes for several months—a practice that violates the Geneva Convention. (This practice was also used in Iraq, according to Fay-Jones report, and the Pentagon report by Maj. Gen. Antonio Taguba.)

To date, the government has charged only two people in connection with detainee abuse in Afghanistan, while six deaths and scores of other claims of torture and mistreatment are reported to have occurred. This reveals a large-scale failure of accountability within the military. (By way of comparison, we note the relative speed of prosecutions in the case of two Air Force pilots involved in the friendly-fire death of four Canadian troops near Qandahar in April 2002: both were charged four months after the incident.)

Your office has also failed to publicize the results of investigations into detention sites in Afghanistan. In May 2004, Lt. Gen. David Barno, the chief of military operations in Afghanistan, announced that Brig. Gen. Charles H. Jacoby would conduct an in-depth investigation of U.S. detention sites in Afghanistan, report back to Gen. Barno in June, and that your office would publicize parts of that report. But you have failed to make public the findings of the Jacoby report, which was finished almost six months ago.

In June 2004, we wrote to Gen. Jacoby, soon after he was appointed by Gen. Barno to conduct an investigation into mistreatment allegations in Afghanistan. We offered to brief Gen. Jacoby or his staff. Gen. Jacoby replied in a letter of June 12, 2004 that he would be unable to meet because he was focusing all of his "available time and efforts" towards the investigation. We were disappointed that Gen. Jacoby's investigation did not include discussions with Human Rights Watch staff, who had written the only public report about U.S. abuses in Afghanistan and were in a unique position to provide information for his investigation. We have also tried to raise detention issues in other meetings with your staff—meetings to discuss other human rights issues in Afghanistan—but have not received adequate feedback or acknowledgement about our concerns.

The Afghan Independent Human Rights Commission has repeatedly requested meetings with the staff of Gen. Barno to discuss their findings and concerns. They have also repeatedly asked Gen. Barno's office for access to detention sites, but have as yet received no response. U.S. military personnel outside of Kabul, approached by Commission staff seeking to discuss detention cases, have treated the staff rudely—in some cases even threatening them with beatings or arrest. In a recent interview, a senior military official in Kabul told journalist James Rupert (*Newsday*, November 14, 2004) that the U.S. command in Kabul is not sure if Commission members are "good guys." The suggestion that the AIHRC is not trustworthy, or that their access to detention sites might be a security threat, is without merit and insulting to AIHRC. The U.S. government has on several occasions pointed to the work of the AIHRC as evidence of progress in Afghanistan. U.S. officials from other departments meet regularly with the AIHRC, and the U.S. government helps to fund its work. We would also point out that, in Iraq, the Iraqi Ministry of Human Rights has access to Abu Ghraib and other U.S.-run detention sites.

The Importance of Accountability:
We strongly urge you to immediately correct these problems and take action to restore a sense of accountability among forces deployed in Afghanistan. Under the Geneva Convention, the United States is obligated to investigate grave breaches, such as willful killings, and prosecute those responsible. Beyond this legal obligation, the United States must restore accountability to prevent future abuse. We note again that some of the interrogators and military police who ended up being implicated in the Abu Ghraib scandal (members of the 519th Military Intelligence Battalion and the 377th Military Police Company) were earlier involved in deaths and abuse in Afghanistan. A senior Army lawyer, Col. Marc Warren, testified in Congress in May of this year that Capt. Carolyn Wood brought interrogation procedures to Iraq that were developed during the 519th Battalion's service in Afghanistan. This suggests that some of the later abuse in Iraq was preventable. Had the investigation and prosecution of abusive interrogators in Afghanistan in 2002

proceeded in a timely manner, it is possible that the abusive techniques might have been abandoned, and that many of the abuses seen in Iraq could have been avoided. It also suggests that past failures to establish accountability may be leading to further abuses today.

We strongly urge you to take the necessary steps to correct the problems noted above. We request that you:

◊ Issue a clear policy on interrogation applicable to forces in Afghanistan, repudiating all methods that violate international, U.S. and Afghan law.

◊ Order the public release of the Jacoby report.

◊ Order the U.S. military command in Afghanistan to meet with representatives of the Afghan Independent Human Rights Commission to facilitate their access to detention sites and allow them to share their findings and concerns with you.

◊ Ensure that criminal investigations into abuses and deaths of detainees in Afghanistan include investigations into the relevant actions of senior commanders and Department of Defense officials.

◊ Ensure that persons recommended for prosecution are brought to justice in a timely and transparent manner.

We would be happy to meet with you or your staff to discuss any of these matters further.

Sincerely,

Brad Adams
Executive Director
Cc: Porter Goss, Director of the Central Intelligence Agency

Kofi Annan's Lessons Learned and Recommendations[1]

The principles of collective responsibility, global solidarity, the rule of law, mutual accountability, and multilateralism are essential for the future conduct of international relations (Annan, 2006). Prior to leaving office as the Secretary General of the United Nations at the end of 2006, Mr. Kofi A. Annan offered several universal principles that can be extremely useful for reflection and strategic planning toward the creation of equality, justice, peace, and fairness for all. The five lessons can be retrieved from the United Nation's Website (http://www.un.org). The following are Mr. Kofi Annan's lessons, recommendations and reflections offered to an audience in the United States (December 11, 2006):

What a pleasure, and a privilege, to be here in Missouri. It's almost a homecoming for me. Nearly half a century ago I was a student about 400 miles north of here, in Minnesota. I arrived there straight from Africa – and I can tell you, Minnesota soon taught me the value of a thick overcoat, a warm scarf... and even ear-muffs!

[1] Speech by the Secretary-General Kofo A. Annan, Truman Library; December 11, 2006; retrieved on December 14, 2006 from the United Nation's Website. See Annan, 2006.

When you leave one home for another, there are always lessons to be learnt. And I had more to learn when I moved on from Minnesota to the United Nations – the indispensable common house of the entire human family, which has been my main home for the last 44 years. Today I want to talk particularly about five lessons I have learnt in the last ten years, during which I have had the difficult but exhilarating role of Secretary-General.

I think it's especially fitting that I do that here in the house that honors the legacy of Harry S. Truman. If FDR was the architect of the United Nations, President Truman was the master-builder, and the faithful champion of the Organization in its first years, when it had to face quite different problems from the ones FDR had expected. Truman's name will for ever be associated with the memory of far-sighted American leadership in a great global endeavor. And you will see that every one of my five lessons brings me to the conclusion that such leadership is no less sorely needed now than it was sixty years ago.

My *first lesson* is that, in today's world, the security of every one of us is linked to that of everyone else. That was already true in Truman's time. The man who in 1945 gave the order for nuclear weapons to be used – for the first, and let us hope the only, time in history – understood that security for some could never again be achieved at the price of insecurity for others. He was determined, as he had told the founding conference of the United Nations in San Francisco, to "prevent, if human mind, heart, and hope can prevent it, the repetition of the disaster [meaning the world war] from which the entire world will suffer for years to come." He believed strongly that henceforth security must be collective and indivisible. That was why, for instance, he insisted, when faced with aggression by North Korea against the South in 1950, on bringing the issue to the United Nations and placing US troops under the UN flag, at the head of a multinational force. But how much more true it is in our open world today: a world where deadly weapons can be obtained not only by rogue states but by extremist groups; a world where SARS, or avian flu, can be carried across oceans, let alone national borders, in a matter of hours; a world where failed states in the heart of Asia or Africa can become havens for terrorists; a world where even the climate is changing in ways that will affect the lives of everyone on the planet. Against such threats as these, no nation can make itself secure by seeking supremacy over all others. We all share responsibility for each other's security, and only by working to make each other secure can we hope to achieve lasting security for ourselves.

And I would add that this responsibility is not simply a matter of states being ready to come to each other's aid when attacked – important though that is. It also includes our shared *responsibility to protect* populations from genocide, war crimes, ethnic cleansing and crimes against humanity – a responsibility solemnly accepted by all nations at last year's UN summit. That means that respect for national sovereignty can no longer be used as a shield by governments intent on massacring their own people, or as an excuse for the rest of us to do nothing when such heinous crimes are committed. But, as Truman said, "If we should pay merely lip service to inspiring ideals, and later do violence to simple justice, we would draw down upon us the bitter wrath of generations yet unborn. " And when I look at the murder, rape and starvation to which the people of Darfur are being subjected, I fear that we have not got far beyond "lip service." The lesson here is that high-sounding doctrines like the "responsibility to protect" will remain pure rhetoric unless and until those with the power to intervene effectively – by exerting political, economic or, in the last resort, military muscle – are prepared to take the lead. And I believe we have a responsibility not only to our contemporaries but also to future generations – a responsibility to preserve resources that belong to them as well as to us, and without which none of us can survive. That means we must do much more, and urgently, to prevent or slow down climate change. Every day that we do nothing, or too little, imposes higher costs on our children and our children's children.

My *second lesson* is that we are not only all responsible for each other's security. We are also, in some measure, responsible for each other's welfare. Global solidarity is both necessary and possible. It is necessary because without a measure of solidarity no society can be truly stable, and no one's prosperity truly secure. That applies to national societies – as all the great industrial democracies learned in the 20th century – but it also applies to the increasingly integrated global market economy we live in today. It is not realistic to think that some people can go on deriving great benefits from globalization while billions of their fellow human beings are left in abject poverty, or even thrown into it. We have to give our fellow citizens, not only within each nation but in the global community, at least a chance to share in our prosperity. That is why, five years ago, the UN Millennium Summit adopted a set of goals – the "Millennium Development Goals" – to be reached by 2015: goals such as halving the proportion of people in the world who don't have clean water to drink; making sure all girls, as well as boys, receive at least primary education; slashing infant and maternal mortality; and stopping the spread of HIV/AIDS. Much of that can only be done by governments and people in the poor countries themselves. But richer countries, too, have a vital role. Here too, Harry Truman proved himself a pioneer, proposing in his 1949 inaugural address a program of what came to be known as development assistance. And our success in mobilizing donor countries to support the Millennium Development Goals, through debt relief and increased foreign aid, convinces me that global solidarity is not only necessary but possible. Of course, foreign aid by itself is not enough. Today, we realize that market access, fair terms of trade, and a non-discriminatory financial system are equally vital to the chances of poor countries. Even in the next few weeks and months, you Americans can make a crucial difference to many millions of poor people, if you are prepared to save the Doha Round of trade negotiations. You can do that by putting your broader national interest above that of some powerful sectional lobbies, while challenging Europe and the large developing countries to do the same.

My *third lesson* is that both security and development ultimately depend on respect for human rights and the rule of law. Although increasingly interdependent, our world continues to be divided – not only by economic differences, but also by religion and culture. That is not in itself a problem. Throughout history human life has been enriched by diversity, and different communities have learnt from each other. But if our different communities are to live together in peace we must stress also what unites us: our common humanity, and our shared belief that human dignity and rights should be protected by law. That is vital for development, too. Both foreign investors and a country's own citizens are more likely to engage in productive activity when their basic rights are protected and they can be confident of fair treatment under the law. And policies that genuinely favor economic development are much more likely to be adopted if the people most in need of development can make their voice heard. In short, human rights and the rule of law are vital to global security and prosperity. As Truman said, "We must, once and for all, prove by our acts conclusively that Right Has Might." That's why this country has historically been in the vanguard of the global human rights movement. But that lead can only be maintained if America remains true to its principles, including in the struggle against terrorism. When it appears to abandon its own ideals and objectives, its friends abroad are naturally troubled and confused. And states need to play by the rules towards each other, as well as towards their own citizens. That can sometimes be inconvenient, but ultimately what matters is not convenience. It is doing the right thing. No state can make its own actions legitimate in the eyes of others. When power, especially military force, is used, the world will consider it legitimate only when convinced that it is being used for the right purpose – for broadly shared aims – in accordance with broadly accepted norms. No community anywhere suffers from too much rule of law; many do suffer from too little – and the international community is among them. This we must change. The US has given the world an example of a democracy in which everyone, including the most powerful, is subject to legal restraint. Its current moment of world supremacy gives it a priceless opportunity to entrench the same principles at the global level. As Harry Truman said,

"We all have to recognize, no matter how great our strength, that we must deny ourselves the license to do always as we please."

My *fourth lesson* – closely related to the last one – is that governments must be *accountable* for their actions in the international arena, as well as in the domestic one. Today the actions of one state can often have a decisive effect on the lives of people in other states. So does it not owe some account to those other states and their citizens, as well as to its own? I believe it does. As things stand, accountability between states is highly skewed. Poor and weak states are easily held to account, because they need foreign assistance. But large and powerful states, whose actions have the greatest impact on others, can be constrained only by their own people, working through their domestic institutions. That gives the people and institutions of such powerful states a special responsibility to take account of global views and interests, as well as national ones. And today they need to take into account also the views of what, in UN jargon, we call "non-state actors." I mean commercial corporations, charities and pressure groups, labor unions, philanthropic foundations, universities and think tanks – all the myriad forms in which people come together voluntarily to think about, or try to change, the world. None of these should be allowed to substitute itself for the state, or for the democratic process by which citizens choose their governments and decide policy. But they all have the capacity to influence political processes, on the international as well as the national level. States that try to ignore this are hiding their heads in the sand. The fact is that states can no longer – if they ever could – confront global challenges alone. Increasingly, we need to enlist the help of these other actors, both in working out global strategies and in putting those strategies into action once agreed. It has been one of my guiding principles as Secretary-General to get them to help achieve UN aims – for instance through the Global Compact with international business, which I initiated in 1999, or in the worldwide fight against polio, which I hope is now in its final chapter, thanks to a wonderful partnership between the UN family, the US Centers for Disease Control and – crucially – Rotary International.

So that is four lessons. Let me briefly remind you of them:

1. *First*, we are all responsible for each other's security.
2. *Second*, we can and must give everyone the chance to benefit from global prosperity.
3. *Third*, both security and prosperity depend on human rights and the rule of law.
4. *Fourth*, states must be accountable to each other, and to a broad range of non-state actors, in their international conduct.

My *fifth and final lesson* derives inescapably from those other four. We can only do all these things by working together through a multilateral system, and by making the best possible use of the unique instrument bequeathed to us by Harry Truman and his contemporaries, namely the United Nations. In fact, it is only through multilateral institutions that states can hold each other to account. And that makes it very important to organize those institutions in a fair and democratic way, giving the poor and the weak some influence over the actions of the rich and the strong. That applies particularly to the international financial institutions, such as the World Bank and the International Monetary Fund. Developing countries should have a stronger voice in these bodies, whose decisions can have almost a life-or-death impact on their fate. And it also applies to the UN Security Council, whose membership still reflects the reality of 1945, not of today's world. That's why I have continued to press for Security Council reform. But reform involves two separate issues. One is that new members should be added, on a permanent or long-term basis, to give greater representation to parts of the world which have limited voice today. The other, perhaps even more important, is that all Council members, and especially the major powers who are permanent members, must accept the special responsibility that comes with their privilege. The Security Council is not just another stage on which to act out national interests. It is the management committee, if you will, of our fledgling collective security system. As President Truman said, "the responsibility of the great states is to serve and not dominate the peoples of the world." He showed what can be achieved when the US assumes that responsibility. And still today, none of our global institutions can accomplish much when the US remains aloof. But when it is fully engaged, the sky's the limit.

These five lessons can be summed up as five principles, which I believe are essential for the future conduct of international relations: collective responsibility, global solidarity, the rule of law, mutual accountability, and multilateralism. Let me leave them with you, in solemn trust, as I hand over to a new Secretary-General in three weeks' time. My friends, we have achieved much since 1945, when the United Nations was established. But much remains to be done to put those five principles into practice. Standing here, I am reminded of Winston Churchill's last visit to the White House, just before Truman left office in 1953. Churchill recalled their only previous meeting, at the Potsdam conference in 1945. "I must confess, sir," he said boldly, "I held you in very low regard then. I loathed your taking the place of Franklin Roosevelt." Then he paused for a moment, and continued: "I misjudged you badly. Since that time, you more than any other man, have saved Western civilization." My friends, our challenge today is not to save Western civilization – or Eastern, for that matter. All civilization is at stake, and we can save it only if all peoples join together in the task. You Americans did so much, in the last century, to build an effective multilateral system, with the United Nations at its heart. Do you need it less today, and does it need you less, than 60 years ago? Surely not. More than ever today Americans, like the rest of humanity, need a functioning global system through which the world's peoples can face global challenges together. And in order to function, the system still cries out for far-sighted American leadership, in the Truman tradition. I hope and pray that the American leaders of today, and tomorrow, will provide it. Thank you very much.

REFLECTIVE QUESTIONS FOR CRITICAL THINKING

1. It has been reported that there were physical, spiritual, psychological, and emotional violations of basic human rights in Afghanistan during the Russian invasion. What are some of the specific violations and discuss the long-term impact of such actions (violations) on the society.
2. The laws of physics tell us that "for every action there is an equal and opposite reaction." How does this statement relate to human rights violations and violence? Is there a link between the two? Discuss and provide specific examples.
3. There are many forms of human rights violations that people are experiencing today throughout the world. Describe some of the common international human rights violations based on what you have read or heard through the media.
4. What are some of the negative impacts coming from the mines which are still planted at various parts of Afghanistan?
5. Who should remove the mines which are scattered throughout Afghanistan?
6. What are the responsibilities of the World, the Russians, and the United States in assisting with the removal of the mines in Afghanistan? Be specific and justify your reasoning with concepts, examples, and theories. Discuss what may happen if these mines are not removed in a fair manner.

7.   What are some of your recommendations for making sure that human rights are not violated in Afghanistan? Provide specific action-oriented steps.

8.   What are some of the critical issues raised by the "Human Rights Watch" group in the letter sent to President Karzai?

9.   What are some of the critical issues raised by the "Human Rights Watch" group in the letter sent to Donald Rumsfeld?

10. What can the international community do to reduce and/or eliminate human rights violations throughout the world in the 21st century?

11. Mr. Kofi Annan's five lessons are important for all managers, leaders, politicians, economists, educators, and spiritual experts. Which of the following are important in your profession and discuss the reasons for the important:

   a.   *First*, we are all responsible for each other's security.

   b.   *Second*, we can and must give everyone the chance to benefit from global prosperity.

   c.   *Third*, both security and prosperity depend on human rights and the rule of law.

   d.   *Fourth*, states must be accountable to each other, and to a broad range of non-state actors, in their international conduct.

   e.   *Fifth, we* must be working together through a multilateral system, and by making the best possible use of the unique instrument, such as the United Nations.

12. The fourth recommendation from the U.N. Secretary General which states that "*Governments must be accountable for their actions, in the international and domestic arenas.*" "...As things stand, poor and weak states are easily held to account, because they need foreign aid. But large and powerful states, whose actions have the greatest impact on others, can be constrained only by their own people." Name five nations that can be considered to be the "large and powerful states," and discuss what can they do to create a better world for all?

13. Mr. Kofi Annan states that "But large and powerful states, whose actions have the greatest impact on others, can be constrained only by their own people, working through their domestic institutions...I mean commercial corporations, charities and pressure groups, labor unions, philanthropic foundations, universities and think tanks – all the myriad forms in which people come together voluntarily to think about, or try to change, the world. None of these should be allowed to substitute itself for the state, or for the democratic process by which citizens choose their governments and decide policy. But they all have the capacity to influence political processes, on the international as well as the national level. States that try to ignore this are hiding their heads in the sand." What do you think Mr. Annan is trying to see in the last part of his statement about "...hiding their heads in the sand." Discuss and reflect using examples.

CHAPTER 6

BECOMING REFUGEES: BIOGRAPHICAL JOURNEY

I, Ghulam Bahaudin Mujtaba, was born in 1966 at the village of Khoshie, which is in the Logar province adjacent to Kabul--the capital state of Afghanistan. Khoshie was a small village made up of about 1,000 families and a population of several thousand people. It was surrounded by mountains and high hills. Khoshie is located right in the middle of the valley. It is sort of like having a whole village in the Grand Canyon, U.S.A. There were beautiful trees, gardens, mountains, farmlands, animals, and good-hearted people that knew each other fairly well. Most people know each other on a first name basis. Starting at the age of three, my grandfather used to take me to the Mosque (Masjid) each and everyday. One morning, at age five, he did not wake me and left for the Masjid alone. Soon, my Mom woke me up and I remember running to the Mosque without any shoes and the snow was about one foot high. The Mosque was about a quarter of a mile away, and I did not want to miss the prayer and the lesson of learning prayers and reading the Quran. I got there and joined everyone for the prayers.

Life in Khoshie was calm and nice, similar to the city of Mayberry in the famous Andy Griffith's television show. There were no soldiers, and the mayor did not carry a gun because everyone respected the law and those who represented the government. The most serious altercations and disagreements often resulted in a fist-fight until some elder stopped it. The mayor knew most people by name, and was very respected by everyone in the community. As a young boy, I thought he was very strict and a bit gruff; however, he was not malevolent or malicious in anyway. His presentations and speeches seemed very honest, and his answers to one's questions did not appear to be equivocal, instead they were concise and to the point. As a result of seeing these government officers, I always thought that having a civil servant's office position required knowledge, honesty, character, integrity, courage, and the ability to be able to interact with others by being clear and consistent in one's words and deeds. I also thought one had to be a good example to others, and to model the type of behavior one expected of others in the community. A leader to me was someone who could lead his/her followers to the right path by showing a vision, strong character, good communication skills and excellent strategies. As General H. Norman Schwarzkopf said after the Gulf War "Leadership is a potent combination of strategy and character. But if you must be without one, be without the strategy." I thought most people in Khoshie were exemplary and possessed strong character, but were not always concerned about using deceitful tactics, ergo political strategies were not apparent in the physical environment.

I lived in Khoshie until I was six years of age. When my father came back from the United States, after completing his two years of graduate studies at the University of Cincinnati in Cincinnati, Ohio, we moved to Kabul, where he was teaching at the College of Engineering, Kabul University. I started first grade at age six, and was considered and perceived to be "different," in terms of language, from others according to most of my classmates and teachers. The kids in Kabul used to laugh at my accent and the way I spoke. I always thought something was different about the way they spoke and pronounced certain words. I thought it was all interesting and loved the interaction with everyone very much. Since I was born with a condition known as "genetic nystagmus," many people noticed my rapid eye movements and wondered if I was confused, crazy or about ready to pass out. "*Nystagmus,*" according to medical dictionaries, is basically an involuntary, rapid, rhythmic movement of the eyeball, which may be horizontal, vertical, rotatory or mixed, i.e., of two varieties. Mild cases do not need any medications but severe cases usually require treatment and or medical prescription. Since I have a mild case of this neurological disorder, it does not always impact my vision, sight, or thinking. As a matter of fact, most of the times I do not notice nor feel that my eyes are moving from side to side or up and down. As a matter-of-fact, I did not even know it was a medical condition until the age of around twenty-seven when I visited an optometrist for an eye exam. Anyhow, kids in Kabul did often treat me "differently" because of my eye condition, accent, and the words I used since I had learned them in Khoshie. Such treatments only get noticed when there is a pattern of it over time and through many individuals. I remember thinking that perhaps I was different simply because I was from the country and maybe my abilities were not the same as the kids from the city. However, it all changed one day when a balloon salesperson during the *Nawrooz* (New Year's Day) carnival and celebration made a very profound statement to me. This crippled little old man was selling these colorful small, medium-size, and giant bright balloons at the carnival for different prices. Since he had graduated from the "street smarts" school of entrepreneurship and marketing, every few minutes he would release one of the big and bright balloons into the air so more kids would notice and persuade their parents to come and buy the balloons. As a seven year-old boy, I was watching how he always released one of the big and bright balloons which would rise to the sky as if there was no limit to its journey. While he released several of these giant balloons during the few minutes I was watching, I became curious of why he did not release one of the tanned small balloons resting on the bottom section under all the other colorful large ones. I perhaps associated this small balloon which seemed "different" from the others and somewhat "out of place" with my life in Kabul. So, I asked my grandfather whom I called *ShawAgha Jaan* (actual name Ghulam Sarwar) why the person was not releasing the small balloon. He said he did not know but I could go and ask my question from the salesperson. So, I went near him while pulling down on his sleeves and said "sir, if you were to release that small balloon in the corner section into the air, would it go up and rise like the rest?" He looked at me and my grandfather for a few seconds and then said one of the wisest and most influential things I have heard anyone ever say to me. His statement basically translates into, "Son, it is not the size nor the color that makes a difference in the journey toward the sky...because it is what is inside that makes it go up as if there was no limit for them in this universe." He released the small-tanned looking balloon while finishing up his sentence and surely it kept going up...and up until it became lost in the blue skies of mountainous city of DehMazang, Kabul. It made me think that I too could be as good as anyone else since the genetic Nystagmus and "country / rural" accent were only external characteristics and internally I was the same as others.

While the reflective thinking was good, I was not into reading and doing my homework all the time and as a matter-of-fact, I avoided it as much as I could. However, my dear mother was always there to make sure I got them done, and sometimes she would spend hours reading and doing my schoolwork with me. I was not concerned much about earning good grades and being really neat about the homework. I do remember when I received my report card at the end of first grade. I went to school late in the afternoon since I had forgotten that it was report card day. When I got to Allowdin Elementary School, Mrs. Saidah Jaan was in the principal's office, and she looked at me and congratulated me for passing the first grade. I was very happy, and then she told me I ranked 31st in the class of 36 people. The ranking did not mean much to me, because I had passed first grade and was going to second grade. I said good-bye to her as she kissed my forehead. I took the city bus, telling the driver that I was going to second grade and came home safely. My parents were proud of me for passing the first grade and I was on "top of the world" for the next two months enjoying the winter break. Nonetheless, I was still pushed and forced by my mother to read second grade books and to be prepared for the next year.

For the next few years, I became aware of the importance of ranking but I still did not do much studying to get good grades. I wanted to know enough of the material to pass the tests and to make teachers happy and to stay out of trouble. For the most part, the school system in Afghanistan conditioned students to memorize the material rather than actually think about it and practice what was being learned. I was lucky because my mother pressured me and spent time with me to make sure I would get the homework and readings done. So, in most cases, I did well in school because Mom was with me every step of the way. Actually, after the third and fourth grade, other students were seeking my help and guidance for their homework because my rankings were in the top five or so in each grade. It was not until ninth grade that I finally ranked number one in my class and then I knew that everyone was truly proud of me. I must say that the extrinsic rewards of being ranked in first place were fantastic. However, intrinsically, I was not really satisfied because my grades did not accurately reflect my natural talent. However, the grades did represent my ability to know what was going to be on tests, memorizing them, and doing well in most cases. At this time, I was very good at doing the homework, turning in neat and clean assignments, and on top of it, I was a well-behaved teenager who always acted politely around most people. During the eighth grade, my Dad had become a refugee in Pakistan and I had to be a good example to my younger brother and sisters and to the community in general. I was expected to be good and I was...for the most part. So everything I did had to be "good" because it represented an image of me and my family to the public in general. My actions were geared toward accomplishing results based on my understanding of what the public thought was good. Also, because of the internal turmoil and civil war, the school environment was no longer very good and some of the teachers did not seem to care if students received proper education or not. Everyone was trying to make a living, stay alive, and get by. The school system and the economy were not strong enough to withstand the many vicissitudes of the unstable government and the presence of the Russian military in the country. Consequently, doing well in school was not the focus of teenage students, who worried about being safe and saying the right things as to not offend the government officials.

ESCAPING AFGHANISTAN: MAKING THE JOURNEY TO PAKISTAN

A week later after Faqir (the author's uncle) was released from the Pul-e-Charkhie jail, where he served a two-year sentence for supposedly working with the Freedom Fighters, we packed up and left for the village of Rahm-Abaud in Logar in late 1982. Rahm-Abaud is where my mom's brothers and cousins could help us move to Pakistan. Myriad considerations went into our decision to move to Pakistan and proceeding with circumspection was a necessity to everyone's survival. We could not tell many of the relatives, family friends, classmates, and neighbors at Kabul about our plans of leaving the country, as that would put them in danger with the Communist government. Not only would we have put their lives in danger by telling them about our plans to escape, but we also would have put our own lives in danger. So, we had to leave and disappear once and for all without anyone knowing what happened to us. We came to Zulm-Abaud to my grandmother's house, where the government did not have much control over the people or their activities most of the time. Freedom Fighters came, lived in the city, and passed by almost everyday. People basically lived by their own rules of respecting others, respecting the environment, and practicing the Golden Rule. My uncles, on my Mom's side of the family, Hammidullah and Ezatullah, were both Freedom Fighters in the Logar province. They traveled back and forth from Logar to Pakistan to carry weapons for themselves and others, so their lives were highly peripatetic. We all gathered at my grandmother's house at Zulm-Abaud (Rahm-Abaud) and rented two jackasses (donkeys), two horses, and three camels from the movers who helped people cross the border during evening and night hours through the mountains. The camels and horses were expensive based on the local standards, about 3,000 Afghanis each ($60 at that time). While the Afghan economy was not very strong at that time, the value of Afghan money drastically decreased even further in the next 18 years (1983-2001) due to the turmoil and strategic meddling of outside forces who wanted to defeat the Russian government. Kaplan (1990) wrote, "For years already, in one of the CIA's most successful covert operations, millions of counterfeit Afghanis had been printed in order to wreck the Kabul regime's economy and allow the Mujahidin to buy weapons and ammunition on the open market on the Northwest Frontier."

Continuing with the trip, my two teenage sisters rode on donkeys, while the two younger sisters, brother and Mom rode on the camels. The two horses were loaded with food, clothes, and blankets to cover ourselves during nights on the cold mountains. My uncles and I were going to walk because we did not want to spend more money renting another horse. The trip usually took about three days and three nights walking in the mountains of Afghanistan to get to the border of Pakistan. We started our trip about four o'clock in the afternoon and said our final good-byes to all family members in *Zulm-Abaud* (officially known as *Rahm-Abaud*). The walking was fast-paced, and sometimes in the middle of the night, we had to jog parts of the time because we were too close to the government garrisons (outposts). At about two o'clock in the morning of the first night, we got shot at a couple of times by the Russian tanks that were approximately three miles away from the mountain we were crossing. They were shooting air-shots since they could not see where people were traveling, sometimes missing us by miles because the night was dark and they could not pin-point the exact location or path of the travelers. However, we were certain that they could hear people moving and the animals making noise, despite the fact that we were all trying to be very quiet. This walking thing, after so many hours, was getting on my nerves because I was tired and my legs were not cooperating as much toward the dawn hours. We had to travel up and down the paths to get past these high mountains which at times were very cold. Although we were traveling in the fall, some mountains still had snow on them. Towards the morning, I was tired and somewhat sleepy, as well. The traveling was taking its toll on me during the first night, and we still had two more days of traveling to do in order to get to the border. Things were not looking good for me. However, the morning was bright, and I knew we were going to have to stop somewhere to eat and rest for a few minutes. The guides wanted us to get far from the danger zones, so we traveled till about eleven o'clock in the morning. When we came to the rest area, everyone ate first, and then went to sleep…I just went directly to sleep. About three o'clock in the afternoon, we got up and continued the trip to make it a bit closer to the border. By now, my bones were hurting, my feet were tired and I was hungry. The five hours of sleep appeared to have made me more tired and lazy. I was good at eating while traveling so I "pigged out," and ate anything that was in my backpack while walking for the first few hours on this afternoon. Then it got dark, I ran out of water, and stopped eating. My brother's funny camel had a mind of its own, as it used to get away from all the other camels. At times, he used to yell "help...I am going away from everybody." My brother, Mustafa (Parwaiz), was only ten years old at the time, so just like every other young person riding on camels, he was tied up on the top of the camel for his own safety. At times, the kids would be sleeping on top of the camel while we were traveling. My brother and four sisters were all "good sports" about the trip. My sister Nilofar, who was nine years old at the time, got sick on the way and was vomiting, possibly due to stress or the fearful conditions, but she got better on the last day when we got to Pakistan. My youngest sister, Farzana, was only seven years of age at this time and she acted like a mature person. She never cried, and never said that she was tired despite the fact that we were all tired. Despite the difficulties and challenges, I was so proud of my sisters and my brother for being so brave and not complaining one bit.

During the second night, we were on top of a huge mountain, and going through the sides on top of the mountain was the only way out, because there was another outpost of Russian soldiers in the village nearby. We were supposed to cross a bridge connecting one side of the mountain to the other, near its highest point. It must have been about two o'clock in the morning when we got on the bridge. The sky was dark and the flat bridge (no side walls) may have been about eight feet wide and fifty or sixty feet long and about five hundred to one thousand feet above the ground level. As we were crossing the bridge, one person and one animal at a time very carefully, a scary and unexpected thing happened. When my brother's camel was crossing the bridge and was at the other side near the end, the camel's back foot suddenly slipped. The strong camel was doing a good job of holding on and trying to fight the fall. All of us men quickly got to the camel and started to pull the camel upward. Mustafa, my brother, nicknamed Parwaiz, was tied up very well on top of the camel and the camel's fall would have meant his fall as well. My mother started yelling really loud, "get Parwaiz off the camel....get Parwaiz off the camel and do it now," while crying as loudly as she could. My uncle, Faqir tried to grab his hands but he could not separate him from the camel. We tried to cut the ropes off, but that was not working either because we did not have a strong hold on my brother, he was too far for us to reach his whole body. The best hope was to pull the camel up. Then the miracle happened as all five men tried to help the camel get up, the camel got up and Mustafa (Parwaiz) was safe. All these efforts during this scary slip took about two horrifying minutes before the danger was over, but it is these few short minutes that still scares the daylights out of me, as each time I imagine the moment and the alternative consequences. For that miracle, our family will always be appreciative of God and his miracles. Because of the noise and everyone yelling to get Parwaiz during the quiet night, the Russian army could hear us, and started firing many bullets toward our direction, but we quickly got out of the area, and luckily nobody was hurt.

There are many high mountains in Afghanistan, and these kinds of slips were not unusual, and many of the people paid with their lives. There had been many reporters who lost their cameras and luggage during similar slips in different parts of the country. We were all happy that Mustafa (Parwaiz) was not hurt and I was amazed at the courage and bravery shown by him, my mother, and sisters, as they were calm, polite and were not complaining one bit about anything related to the hardships of the trip, or being afraid. Their perseverance and fortitude inspired the best in me as I overcame the fear of not making the trip safely to the end. No matter how hectic the trip became, they maintained their placid expressions. For a while, it appeared as though the pendulum of my mind was swinging to the positive (making the trip) and negative (doubts about making the trip safely with good health) sides rapidly. As my focus increased on the circumstances surrounding me personally, I noticed that my body became weaker both physically and psychologically. I was translating my physical pain and weakness into negative consequences for the whole trip, and that caused the pendulum to stay on the negative side as my doubts were getting stronger and stronger. However the pendulum of my mind was strongly affected to stay at the positive side by my family's bravery, courage, and my role to keep them that way. I knew that I had to transcend my doubts for them and for myself in order to enjoy being successful in our endeavor to eventually see Dad and to be together. So, I put my faith into God, said a few prayers, and believed that God was going to provide us the will and ability to complete this journey successfully. Soon after, I had both the will and the ability to only hear the words of God and build a schatoma to all the negative thinking and apparent fear surrounding us which brought doubts into my mind.

Now, in the middle of our journey, my inner strength and motivation was great and the pendulum stopped swinging and stayed at the positive side, as I detected and extirpated the sources of the weakness. Then my concern was not just about making the trip, but also to make it with enthusiasm, and the least amount of hassles for the family during the trip. The next two days and one night went well and we finally got to a province called Teri-Mangal, which is a liberated province in Pakistan located on its border to Afghanistan (it never has had government control and decisions are made by village elders and chiefs). Looking from the top of the mountain down into the valley showed a crowded, noisy, dusty, and an old ancient city that was full of people throughout the valley. The picture was not pretty at all. The walk from top to the bottom of the valley was a very slow process because the camels and horses could not travel well down the hill. Also, the route which we were traveling on was a very narrow trail along the mountain, zigzagging left and right, which had the appearance of continuously making U-turns down the hill. This is basically where we left our guides, since we were able to take the bus from here, and the guides would go back to Logar while carrying weapons on their horses, camels and donkeys for the Freedom Fighters.

Teri-Mangal is full of Pathans, one of the largest ethnic tribes in the world that has been living in both Pakistan and Afghanistan. Everyone communicated in Pushtu, and most Afghans did not face the language barriers of going into a foreign nation. Living around the borders had become very dangerous for both Afghans and Pakistanis during the invasion. We were warned not to stay there long because the Communists would bomb this area at various times. Some years there were over 600 violations of Soviet and Afghan pilots going through the borders and entering Pakistan's land. During these violations, communists bombed many areas in Pakistan trying to damage Freedom Fighter refugee camps and training centers. About four hundred people from Pakistan (in the cities of Teri-Mangal, Saddar, and Parrachinar) had died because of such bombings during the Russian invasion.

LIFE IN PAKISTAN

We stayed in one of the hotels on the border during the fourth night, and the next morning we rode the bus to Peshawar which took about ten hours or so. In Peshawar, we met more friends and relatives who helped us find a house to rent as we settled in the city. The people of Peshawar were very nice, and many of them spoke Pushtu which was our second language. So, we could communicate well with them. However, it did not take long for us to find out that the level of bribery and corruption was very high in Pakistan. One time, a friend of mine and I were going to the city as the police got onto the bus, and asked my friend to stand up. He stood and the police searched him and planted a small piece of marijuana in his pocket. Then he asked him why he was carrying drugs with him. My friend said I am sorry as he slipped fifty rupees quietly in his hand. The police officer slapped him and said "do not carry this stuff again, you little dumb Afghan." I asked my friend why did you take that lie and you know he put that in your pocket? He said it happens all the time and the best thing to do would be to give them some money because that is what they are looking for since they are not paid well. The alternatives are not very good choices and finally you are going to end-up paying someone anyway, so you may as well do it now and eliminate the "red tape" and many hassles in the middle.

While in Pakistan, we received mail from my father, who worked in the United States. Dad would send us money for food, rent, and other expenses every month or so. About eight months after staying in Pakistan my uncle, Faqir, went to cash a check from my Dad as he usually did, that was sent to us from the United States. Well, that night he did not come home, so my other uncle (Farooq) and I went to the city to see if anyone could tell us what happened to him. The city shops for cashing checks were closed and nobody knew where he was. First thing the next morning, we went back to the shops looking for him and finally one of the shop owners (entrepreneurs) told us he had seen my uncle being carried to jail by the police because he was carrying American dollars with him. Soon we found out which jail, and saw him there. Faqir said it appears that carrying dollars in this city in Pakistan is against the law. I said but you were carrying a check with you and not American dollars. He said well, I guess, they just wanted money (bribe) and I did not read their signs right as I should have. By this time, everything had been documented and many more people had to be paid off in order to get him out. They put him in jail, treating him as a criminal; they made him work in jail by grinding hot peppers and other labor intensive work. He was in jail for over a month before we were able to find the right people to get him out. The system was very corrupt and people were not treated fairly, because most officials wanted money. It eventually cost us about $500 at that time to buy his freedom from jail. Their custom of bribery was not geared specifically to the immigrants, so it could not amount to xenophobia. Usually the residents were asked for payments as well, if they wanted someone to get their paperwork done quickly, bypassing the red-tape. Jan Goodwin (1987) wrote about the level of corruption and her endeavor of trying to enter Afghanistan while she was stopped by Pakistanis and jailed. She confirmed that bribing the officials in Pakistan was, usually, one of the best ways of getting out of the problem which should not have existed in the first place. They gave her a hard time in Peshawar and ordered her not to go to Afghanistan, as all foreign reporters were supposedly prohibited from going there. However, her determination and bravery provided her the impetus to enter Afghanistan the hard way, and she finally did. Bribery was not something that people liked, but it was the only way that they could get one out of government trouble quicker than the other fair alternatives or methods. Maybe that is why Pakistan government had, in the mid 1990s, earned the number one rating for being the most corrupt country in the world. To me, it appeared that bribery was ubiquitous in Pakistan's bureaucracy, and people could not avoid it. I think the people of Pakistan, which include many intelligent, religious, and honest people, want a just and fair society; however, the implementation and enforcement of those fair and just laws can be costly and difficult in such a corrupt environment. Today, according to many individuals, the work environments in some official government departments in Afghanistan are similarly corrupt as certain officials are open to accepting payments to process paperwork.

Within ten to twenty-five miles from the city of Peshawar, there are cities such as Daray Adam Khel, which was a center for international purchase and delivery of drugs, weapons, and other such activities. In such cities, one could find and purchase some of the most advanced military weapons, and have them delivered, for the right price. Over all, the cities of Peshawar and Islamabad were nice and filled with many people that were very wise and helpful to the Afghan refugees. I think we will always be appreciative of their efforts for welcoming and helping about four million Afghans to their country. Pakistan had been nice to its neighboring Afghans probably because they wanted to be "good sports" or perhaps for economic reasons or both. The United States encouraged President Zia to continue their assistance to the Afghans by supposedly pouring nearly $7.4 billion into Pakistan's economy and military through 1991 (Goodwin, 1987). Goodwin further estimates that United States spent about one billion dollars to aid the Afghan Freedom Fighters economically and in terms of military aid. During the ninth month of our stay in Pakistan, our visas and passports were approved through the U.S. Immigration and Naturalization Departments and we left for the United States.

JOURNEY FROM PAKISTAN TO THE UNITED STATES

From Islamabad of Pakistan, our plane left, and we switched planes in London. Then we were in New York, where our immigration paperwork for coming to America was finally completed. During the flight, I was wearing traditional Afghan clothes and people kept looking at me. I kept thinking that I must be very special because of all the attention. Then I figured out that it was the traditional clothes that everyone was looking at suspiciously. When people started talking to me, I was very polite and tried to speak back, but it was difficult to understand them since everyone spoke English. After four hours of waiting in New York's airport, we flew to Atlanta, and then to Fort Myers, Florida where we finally met with Dad after three and half years of being apart. I remember Mom being really mad at my Dad and she would not even give him a hug or talk to him for leaving us behind for three and half years. I said Mom this is not the time to be mad at Dad; it is time to look forward to the future and catch up on everything that has been happening. Finally, we got home to Cape Coral which is near Fort Myers.

A week later, we started going to school, starting in April of 1984. My two sisters and I started going to Fort Myers High School, where they had a special English as a Second Language (ESL) Program for students who came from non-English speaking countries. Mrs. Vanna Crawford was the head instructor in the program and she had a very good way of getting her students to learn English. The first day we all went to our homerooms and did not know what was going on or why I was in that classroom. I went where they took me and sat where the teachers told me to sit. I spoke very little English and understood even less. About twenty minutes later, the principal, Mr. Wiseman, came and took me to my sister Anisa's homeroom, where she was a little upset and crying because she was not sure what to do or what was going on. I tried to be supportive to her because she was young (fourteen years old) and this was a totally new experience for her. I stayed with Anisa for about one hour, and we tried to figure out what the teacher was saying, but not much was registering in our minds. After about a week or so we knew where to go and who to listen to and who our teachers were. It took me about two months to figure out what to say when the teacher in the homeroom called our names. Of course, most of the time when he got to my name, he said "OK you are here" so I knew that my name was very difficult for them to pronounce just as their's were to me. For the first two months, when the teachers called my name, I answered "yes," and later I figured out that the common word was "here."

GOING FROM A "CLEAN UP BOY" TO A "MANAGER"

Two months later in the summer of 1984, I got my first temporary job doing landscaping work earning minimum wage which was $3.25 per hour in 1984. This job was basically farming and required shoveling and digging the ground all day long in the summer days of nearly 100 degree weather and planting trees to make the streets of "hot" Florida beautiful. I was able to do a good job while I was employed there for a short duration and, thus, learned that farming and physical labor was not easy. On the first day of the job, I had previously made an appointment to take my written driver's license exam. I started my job at seven o'clock in the morning and worked very hard until four in the afternoon. At this time I knew my Dad was coming to pick me up for the test, so I started washing my hands to be ready. The pain of hard work and manual labor was present in my arm muscles and fingers as they kept cramping up each time I moved them. I was tired and thought that I was definitely going to fail the test, so I told my Dad that maybe I should take this test some other day. He said, "Oh, do not worry about it, it is just a test." Anyhow, I took the test and luckily passed it on the first attempt. My Dad was very proud and he let me drive the car for about one-sixth of a mile as soon as we got out of the testing facility. For the first time, I really felt happy, because Dad made me feel like I did not let him down, and even not passing the test would have been all right with him.

After about a month, my temporary employment at the landscaping job was over and I had to start looking for other employment opportunities. Within a month, I got a job at the Jefferson World Stores (retail outlet) working in the garden section to assist customers and keep the plants fresh every day. They probably offered me the job since I had some experience with landscaping and because the garden section did not require as much interaction with customers as other parts of the store. This job paid $3.50 each hour and I had to dress up and wear a tie to work every day. So, I went to high school at about 7:00 am and packed my work tie and clothes in the school bag so I could go directly to work after school each day. I would take the city bus from the Fort Myers High School neighborhood to go to work and then Dad would pick me up from work at about 10:00 pm. I enjoyed working indoors learning about the various plants, taking care of the plants, and helping customers with their gardening needs. The managers were very customer-oriented and showed great leadership skills. My colleagues were very nice and helped me learn English words and phrases since they liked my work ethic. I sort of grew to like this job and had aspirations of eventually going into retail management when I finished college. This job lasted three months because the company went bankrupt and we were all laid off.

Then, I was unemployed for about another month but I was able to study more for school since twelfth grade courses had tons of homework and I was preparing for college entrance examinations, as well. So, the month went by very quickly and eventually I was hired at the Danish Bakery of Publix Super Markets at their Cape Coral Parkway Store (#110) in the city of Cape Coral. Once again, I began going directly to work everyday after school. This job was paying $3.75 each hour…the lesson I learned then was that with every job change I was making more money per hour. I reported to work on the first day at about 3:30 p.m. and a beautiful female salesperson by the name of Tricia said "Welcome, you must be the new clean up boy." So, now I knew my new title was "clean up boy." She wrote my name on a time card and asked me to "punch in" and start working. She took about five minutes to show and tell me that I had to wash the dishes (there seemed to be several "tons" that needed washing), take the trash out to the dumpster, and mop the floors. As such, my official training was over in about five minutes…of course, I could go back and ask any questions and she would check on me later to make sure I was doing things right. As a side note, I am happy to say that the training requirements changed drastically over the years and Publix does have a very comprehensive employee training program. Taking care of the sanitation in the bakery department was basically my daily routine, which often took about five to six hours each day to complete all the tasks well. I was able to finally meet Wayne, the Assistant Manager at the Bakery Department, a few days later on the weekend. However, the manager named Mr. Bob Manfredo was on vacation at this time. Wayne showed me how to do a few other jobs besides washing the dishes and mopping the floors on Saturdays and Sundays. So, on Saturdays and Sundays I was able to work about eight to twelve hours since there was more work that could be done. Since I needed the money, I welcomed all the extra work and responsibilities. Two weeks later, the manager was back from vacation and I got to finally meet Bob. He was a tall, dark and handsome looking fellow that looked like a typical Afghan or Italian person. He turned out to be very impressed with my flexibility, work ethics, commitment, and performance over the first few weeks. So, he gave me a 50 cent raise as I was going on my fourth week of work at this Bakery.

I was very happy and was really impressed with Bob's style of management and leadership. Anyhow, since I did not receive much training I did not know when I would be paid. During week six, Bob asked me if I had received my checks yet and I said no. He said I could go and pick them up from the front office cashiers as they keep everyone's checks. So, he took me to the front office and they had five checks for me and Bob said "wow, what are you going to do with all that money?" I said I was probably going to give it to my Dad for household expenses. He said "if your Dad does not need it, then do not spend it all in one place because you can invest your money in Publix stock." As it turns out, that was the best financial advice anyone could have given me at that time. The next month, I did invest one thousand dollars in Publix stock and if I had continued that trend each month during my employment with the company, I would have become a millionaire much faster. Anyhow, that is the strategy that Bob and his brother John Manfredo used, while working with Publix, to become financially wealthy and retire as multi-millionaires before they were fifty years of age. Today, as young men, they enjoy their retirement while watching their money grow every year. John Manfredo was also a Bakery Manager with Publix Super Markets and was promoted to Supervisor in the Central Florida region. I ended-up working with Mr. John Manfredo as well in the Orlando area when I moved there to attend school at the University of Central Florida (UCF).

I continued working with Publix and learned many new skills besides washing dishes and mopping the floors. As a matter-of-fact, I learned to bake breads, cookies, birthday cakes, wedding cakes, pastries, and about four-hundred total varieties of baked goods. I also learned customer service, management and leadership skills with my colleagues. After high school and while attending college, I was given a full time job in the company as a Baker and began receiving full benefits. On my days off from my own store, I volunteered to cover for other bakers and managers in the cities of Cape Coral, Fort Myers, Naples, and Port Charlotte when they were on vacation. I began getting more and more calls to cover for managers when they needed a day off or when they were short staffed. I enjoyed learning and working about 50-70 hours each week even though some weeks were very tiring as I was attending college classes at the same time. Eventually, I moved to Orlando and transferred my job there performing the same tasks helping managers in over twenty different locations. During my time in the Central Florida area, I worked in nearly 20 different stores with hundreds of different individuals who provided an exposure to different means of getting the job done more efficiently. As a matter of fact, I worked in the cities of Oviedo, Ocala, Sanford, Altamonte Springs, Kissimmee, St. Cloud, Winter Springs, Tampa, and Orlando to assist various stores with their needs. Working in different stores and cities also provided me the opportunity to get to know diverse employees and managers from various cultures which were all very interesting and motivational. Orlando, in the early 1990s, was ranked as the number one multicultural city in the State of Florida by studies conducted through the Orlando Sentinel personnel. Three years after starting to work with Publix as a "clean up boy," I was promoted to an Assistant Bakery Manager earning a good salary each year. The salary was great and much higher than college graduates because managers often worked very hard, some weeks putting in as many as 70-80 hours. This was great for the author since college tuition was high and living in Orlando was expensive as I could barely afford it on my hourly salary. After four weeks as an Assistant Manager, once again, I was promoted to a Bakery Manager at the Altamonte Spring Publix Store (#194) in Central Florida while receiving around a 30% increase in compensation. Once again, this was a great increase in salary because managers needed the skills of ethics, service and value delivery, management, showing high commitment, and leadership skills to make the department a success. I managed a team of 23 employees, reported to several bosses in a matrix structure, and we produced nearly one million dollars in revenue each year. I was responsible for hiring, development, retention, and performance appraisals of employees in my department. Furthermore, I was responsible for daily, weekly and yearly projections of sales revenues, expenses, raw material, supplies, and net profits. In this matrix or dual-structured organization, the bakery managers had to report to the store managers, district managers, and their own departmental supervisors who monitored both the quality of the product as well as the sales and payroll increase. Managers had to keep all superiors happy and, to the extent possible, their ideas and visions implemented. Sometimes it was difficult to successfully meet the desires of everyone since they had conflicting visions and thoughts on how to increase product quality, sales, bottom-line profits, and keep customers coming back to the store for all of their retail shopping needs. Some of the bosses would visit the department on a weekly basis while others would come by once every month to say hello and thank employees for a good job. Overall and over time, I had earned their respect and they served as great mentors and coaches so our department could be the best it could become based on my observations, research, and recommendations.

During my first year as a manager, my team and I, in the bakery department, were able to increase sales by over 30% and net profits by over 220% from the prior year. I had an experienced Assistant Manager, name Ed Zebraski, who had previously been a manager with the company for many years. He had chosen to step back to the assistant manager level due to health reasons. Also, I had a full-time employee name Marlene who had been a manager with Publix for many years and had now chosen to step back to forty hours of work to spend more time with her family members. Beside these two experienced individuals who were of tremendous assistance to me as their new manager, I had many other experienced bakers and dedicated employees who respected me as a manager and worked very hard to produce quality products and provide superior service to our customers. The technical and people skills I had learned from my previous managers, colleagues and mentors such as Bob Manfredo, Charlie (Kiss) Kovar, Patricia Grover, Sing Dang, Teresa Rice, Jim Pirone, and Barbara Barker had all prepared me to be a good manager. Also, with John Manfredo as my immediate supervisor and mentor in Orlando, I had access to great leaders when I had questions or concerns. Mr. John Manfredo was always kind enough to provide "the tips" I needed to be an effective manager and leader. Mr. Manfredo was a skilled analyst of people's likes and dislikes who listened to people and observed their behaviors to effectively motivate them as per their needs and desires. My other great mentors in retail management and people that I looked up to in this Fortune 100 organization were Walter Marshall, Terry Simpson, Herbert Waschul, Tom McLaughlin, Roy Raley, Jim Sexton, the late Henry Pileggi, and Ed Crenshaw, to name a few.

So, I had worked my way up the hierarchy from a "clean up boy" to a "manager" in less than three years with this organization which employed nearly 100,000 individuals at that time. I worked as a manager in different locations taking different regional responsibilities for the training of other managers whenever opportunities presented itself. At this time, I was completing my masters and doctorate degrees at nights and on weekends besides working about 50-60 hours each week as a manager. After the completion of my doctoral dissertation in 1995, I was promoted to a Training Specialist in the Management Development Department of Human Resources at the headquarters of Publix in Lakeland, Florida. In this position, which was tremendously enjoyable, I was responsible for the development, designing, and delivery of leadership and management training for all Publix executives and managers. Over the years at Publix, which has been repeatedly ranked as one of top 100 best companies in America, I had the pleasure and honor of working with some very honest, kind-hearted and intelligent entrepreneurs who have made the firm one of the premier companies in the world. Once again, I attempted to study the most successful people on the support side to see what traits made them great trainers and leaders for nearly 125,000 employees in the company. While asking for the advice of my previous mentors when needed, I also became an admirer of the skills demonstrated by many new individuals who were there to make sure I was a great "management trainer and developer." Each person served as a teacher or mentor to me in his or her own way since I observed their behaviors and listened to their advice. I capitalized on their wisdom and avoided their mistakes or traits that did not match my style. For example, Frank taught me that we can have a good sense of humor and integrate fun into the classroom in order to increase learning and retention. Annisa and Anthony (known as Amp) taught me that diversity management requires more than just seeing the physical differences in people by getting to know the needs, desires, wants, and challenges facing each person because of his or her unique characteristics. MaryLou, Max, and Ruth showed me how to facilitate emotional issues of leadership and management with a high level of professionalism by being a living example of what we preach. David (whom we lovingly called "Gator Dave" since he was a huge fan of University of Florida's football team) taught me the art of story telling to keep the audience hooked and active on the material. David Richard showed us the impact of brain-based learning, blooms taxonomy and how various adult learning skills can be used to effectively teach and facilitate based on higher levels as per the learner's level of readiness. Similarly, many other colleagues had great lessons for me either by their wisdom, by what they said or simply by how they acted to various aspects of adult education and leadership. For nearly six years working in the improvement systems and human resources department of Publix, I worked on different long-term projects to develop and coach company managers or executives so they could be successful leaders in their departments and regions. I eventually retired from there as a senior training specialist and a coach to executives at different regions. I stayed with Publix Super Markets for over sixteen years and very much enjoyed it.

I had begun teaching as an adjunct college professor in 1996 and thoroughly enjoyed it as I was dealing with working adult graduate students. The retirement from retail environment, was a transition into academia by taking a job as a Campus College Chair for Undergraduate Business Programs in the city of Tampa, Florida, which ended up being very fruitful. So, in a matter of about twelve years, I had gone from being a "clean up boy" to becoming a university professor and then a college director a few years later. I am not telling you all of this to impress you but I am discussing it because it impresses me as I went from a person who was not sure about his abilities as a young boy in a new culture to a person who progressively kept going toward his dreams by taking advantage of every opportunity that was afforded to him over the years. A person does not have to be a genius or a "rocket scientist" to achieve his or her dreams. However, a person has to learn that having an interdependent relationship with others can have huge dividends for all parties. Such progressive success also goes to show that good guidance from parents and colleagues as well as persistency, patience, and value-based goal setting do make a difference. Of course, I am humbled to have had great colleagues, friends, mentors, bosses, and parents who showed confidence in my commitments and trusted my abilities to live up to their expectations. Academically, there were many individuals at

Fort Myers High School, Edison Community College, University of Central Florida, and at Nova Southeastern University who left great impressions on me and helped me get where I am today. At the university level, I did not get an academic director and professor's position simply due to my own abilities, although that is an important part of it, since many individuals guided me to get there through their mentorship. Of course, getting there is one thing, but staying there is a totally different variable. Staying there requires doing a good job and helping others discover their hidden talents while providing them opportunities to apply them toward worthwhile endeavors. One cannot achieve his or her dreams without helping others while capitalizing on their talents and efforts through interdependent relationships and candid expectations. Hundreds of other great individuals helped me as colleagues, employees and faculty members in the programs and departments which I was responsible for making sure students are treated with respect and dignity and that they receive the highest quality education in the most effective manner. These are the great heroes that provided thousands of undergraduate and graduate students quality education, and I thank them for their commitment to the education industry.

Education is one of the best industries in which to work since there are great opportunities for learning and for helping others learn. For example, at Nova Southeastern University (NSU) students, staff, and faculty members are offered many opportunities to personally develop their management and leadership skills. Everyone can attend lecture sessions by some of the leading authorities in the local community as well as nationally and internationally known speakers. Everyone has many great opportunities to attend sessions on Life Management, Stress Management, Leadership, Entrepreneurship, etc. while meeting some of today's leaders. "Life 101...Personally Speaking Welcomes Max Weinberg" is one of such opportunities for learning how to manage life and its conflicting goals. Max Weinberg, drummer for Bruce Springsteen's E Street Band and music director for *Late Night with Conan O'Brien*, was the guest for NSU's "Life 101...Personally Speaking." This informal interview and question and answer session was held in the Rose and Alfred Miniaci Performing Arts Center on NSU's main campus. Of course, tickets were free to NSU students, staff and faculty and staff members. Also, in the past few years, at NSU we have had the opportunity to personally meet people like Jack Welch, Clarence Thomas, Larry Bossidy, Paul Hersey, Richard Wagoner, H. Wayne Huizenga, Fred DeLuca, the Dalai Lama, L. Paul Bremer III, and many other world renowned leaders. Each leader brings a message of hope, leadership, strong values, and/or a great character in society.

For example, the Dalai Lama brought a message of hope and compassion to us at NSU. His Holiness the 14th Dalai Lama of Tibet, Tenzin Gaytso, came to Nova Southeastern University on September 18th 2004 to address students, faculty, and members of the public. Approximately 10,000 students and people from the local community attended the event which was held in front of the Alvin Sherman Library, Resource and Information Technology Center. NSU President Ray Ferrero, Jr. conferred an honorary Doctorate of Humane Letters on the exiled Tibetan leader, citing his unflinching support for human rights. The Dalai Lama spoke movingly on "Universal Responsibility," addressing the crowd in English with occasional assistance from his translator. His theme was simple: "Human affection and loving kindness, I believe, are the most important values." He urged us to keep compassion in our hearts, "because in the long run it's the only way." After his speech, the Dalai Lama took questions from audience members, and then blessed a Tibetian prayer wheel donated by philanthropist Albert Miniaci, Jr. The prayer wheel is now on display at the Alvin Sherman Library, Research and Information Technology Center. At his request, the Dalai Lama met personally with five NSU students after his speech. "You are of the 21st century and this century belongs to you," he told them. "Do what is necessary to make a difference."

NSU's Farquhar College of Arts and Sciences invited L. Paul Bremer, III at their distinguished Speaker Series on Thursday, February 17th 2005 to speak about and discuss his experiences and thoughts on "Iraq and the War on Terrorism." Mr. Bremer was the former civilian presidential envoy to Iraq and he left his position once the interim government selected their Iraqi cabinet members. Speakers such as Paul Bremer, Jack Welch, Dalai Lama, Richard Wagoner, and Paul Hersey tend to show, through their presence, the impact of great leadership and how students can make the best of their education while attending college and after their graduation. These distinguished lecture series and other events are offered to all those who are a part of NSU and those who seek growth in a variety of areas such as leadership development, ethics, and diversity. So, it is great to be involved with the education industry…even though the income generation opportunities are limited and not as good as the private sector.

Let me backtrack for a minute on the schooling aspect…after graduating from Fort Myers High School in 1985, I immediately started going to the only college that was available in Fort Myers. After completing an Associates of Arts degree at Edison Community College in Fort Myers, I moved to Orlando and enrolled at the University of Central Florida during the summer term of 1987. Throughout the college years, I worked an average of about 50-60 hours each week in order to pay for schooling, apartment, insurance, and other such expenses, while getting corporate experience. At the University of Central Florida in Orlando, I received a Bachelors of Business Administration in 1991, and that is when I enrolled in the Master of Business Administration program at Nova University. After completing the MBA program in 1993, I continued my graduate studies in the Doctoral Program at Nova Southeastern University in the areas of management, international management, and human resources management. Finally my studies were completed during 1996, and this was the beginning of a life-long journey toward learning the meaning and purpose of life.

Now, I am able to focus my energy and time on what matters to me personally, instead of trying to focus only on what is relevant from an educational and materialistic perspective or financial welfare. Getting a higher education has opened my mind as well as many new doors and opportunities. It is well worth the difficulties of having to balance life's other important roles and activities in order to attain the education one wants to achieve. Washing dishes to put myself through school was a small price to pay but very much worth it for learning the English language and the needed people skills to be successful socially and professionally. Overall, going to Edison Community College at the time cost me about $5,000 each year. Attending the University of Central Florida along with the expenses for apartment, car, insurance and other day-to-day expenses cost me about $20,000 each year. The masters of business administration (MBA) degree at Nova University cost me about $15,000 and two years of studying at nights and weekends while missing family gatherings and birthdays. The doctorate degree at Nova Southeastern University was the most expensive, yet the most valuable as well, as it took four years of studying and a financial burden of about $50,000 to complete. However, working at Publix Super Markets for sixteen years, teaching classes at NSU and UofP to adults, and writing this book on Afghanistan was "priceless." There are some things in this world that money cannot buy as they need to be personally experienced and reflected upon. No, this is not a credit card sponsored advertisement but a true message from the heart. I am glad to have had such great opportunities to work with talented individuals and organizations while learning to make small contributions to their successes along the way. I understand that as a "supposedly" small nine pound baby (I fully understand that nine pounds is not exactly small), my parents, relatives and eventually colleagues and peers had to help me get to a point where I could be independent and eventually interdependent. So, I needed much support and assistance to get to interdependency and it is also true that I'll probably need the same level of cooperation as I depart this world. Of course, this life cycle is true of all human beings and in between the beginning and ending stages, many of us have this great window of being able to support and assist others to make this society a better world for everyone. Making this world a little better is a good intention and hopefully we all will be fortunate enough to do our part before the window of opportunity closes its doors.

LEARNING TO SPEAK ENGLISH

Most Afghans tend to speak Persian and Pushtu while some are also able to speak other local languages, as well. I learned to "converse" in Urdu for simple items while living in Pakistan but did not really learn the language since some people in Pakistan could also speak English, as well. I understood a little English since it was a requirement in school starting with seventh grade. However, I had never spoken the English language, so I did not have any practice beyond using a few words with hotel personnel in Pakistan. It was a totally new world when I boarded the plane for the United States since from there on, I did not meet many people who could speak Persian or Pushtu. So, my family and I were forced to learn the local language, fast, if we were to successfully attend school and do well in preparation for college. However, the real learning of the language (such as the cultural norms, nuances, accents, and implied meaning that accompany phrases) did not occur until after the basics were learned. English, as far as we know, is the most widely used language in the history of the planet. One, or more, in every six human beings (over one billion) are able to speak it. More than half of the world's books, and three-quarters of international mail is supposedly written in English. It has been said that of all languages which exist in the world today, English has the largest vocabulary – perhaps as many as two million words – and one of the noblest bodies of literature.

Nonetheless, it has been said that English is a complex, yet crazy language as the following examples have been gleaned from the sayings and writings of many creative individuals. For example, it was a hard lesson to learn that there is no egg in eggplant, neither pine nor apple in pineapple, and no ham in hamburger. For the first several months, we avoided eating hamburgers thinking they had "ham" in them. Of course, ham is pork (which is prohibited in Islam) and hamburgers are made from beef which is eaten by Muslims. Besides, there is no dog meat in "hot-dogs" which do not look like dogs nor are they made for dogs. I also learned that English muffins were not invented in England and French fries did not originate in France. However, I think the "French Kiss" which is practiced in every nationality may very well have come from France…we can certainly give them credit for it. Sweetmeats are candy, while sweetbreads, which are not sweet, are meat. Most native speakers in the United States tend to take English for granted and do not necessarily think of such complexities. You see, when we explore the paradoxes present in the English language, we find that quicksand can work slowly, boxing rings are square, public bathrooms have no baths, and a guinea pig is neither a pig nor from Guinea. Bathrooms are refereed to as "John" by some Americans and as "Box" by some of the British, while others call it "lady's room," "powder room," or even "restroom." I do not know too many English speakers that actually "rest" in the bathroom. Somebody posed the question of "why is it that a writer writes, but fingers do not fing, grocers do not groce, humdingers do not hum, and hammers do not ham?" Why is it that one can tell a baker that his bread is tasty, but should not always really tell him that his "buns" are to die for? How is it that the word "read" can be used with the same spelling for both the present and past tense?

Of course, I have seen other interesting aspects of the English language but, like many native speakers, I do not think much about it now as I speak much more fluently. Another creative individual asked, does it not seem loopy that you can make amends but not just one amend, that you comb through the annals of history but not just one annal? If you have a bunch of odds and ends and you get rid of all but one, what do you call it? Someone said that "sometimes I wonder if all English speakers should be committed to an asylum for the verbally insane." In what other language do people drive on a parkway and park in the driveway? Fly on a runway and run on a highway? Recite at a play and play at a recital? Ship by truck and send cargo by ship? Have noses that run and feet that smell? How can a slim chance and a fat chance be the same, while a wise man and a wise guy are opposites? How can overlook and oversee be opposites, while quite a lot and quite a few are alike? How can the weather be hot as hell one day and cold as hell the next? Well, you will certainly notice more of such nuances as you hear them each day. How is it that one can keep a record of files in the court of law, buy a record to play a specific song, and make a record to do something tomorrow? You have to wonder at the unique lunacy of a language in which your house can burn up as it burns down, in which you fill-in a form by filling it out, and where your alarm clock goes off by going on. These examples show that English, like other languages, was created by people over time; and it reflects the genius and creativity of the human race (which, of course, is not really a race at all). That is why, when stars are out they are visible, but when lights are out they are invisible. And why, as someone questioned, when I wind up my watch I start it, but when I wind up this paragraph I end it?

Besides such complexities of the English language, pronunciation makes a huge difference, as well. Many of the little differences in how words are vocally said can be difficult to notice when one is initially learning English. Words like bread, breed, breath, and breadth can all be perceived to be similar in sound unless one is pronouncing it slowly to a new English learner. For example, I had a classmate in Edison Community College that I kept calling "Dog" for about the first two weeks. Finally, he said "are you calling me Dog? I said "yes." He said "why" and I said "you told me that was your name." He replied "it is not dog, it is Doug." I could not really tell the difference in pronunciation between "dog" and "Doug" but knew there was a slight difference. Another student in my calculus class at Edison Community College once borrowed my calculator during the start of the class. About ten minutes later, I asked another classmate his name and, since the teacher was lecturing, with a low volume I said "Hey Dick, I need my calculator back." He asked "What did you call me?" I answered "Dick." He said "Why?" I said because that is your name. I was wrong because his actual name was Seth and the classmate (named Vonn) had just set me up to call him a bad name. I feel more confident now, but during my first few years in the United States, I must have been pretty gauche. However, my ability to converse easily, although sometimes without perspicuity, about mundane matters, with friends and classmates has helped me considerably in pronunciation of words in the English language. I still wonder why is it that people named Robert are called Bob and those named Richard are often called "Dick"? What is even more confusing is that many of the nicknames are gender neutral that can be used for either boys or girls. For example, names such as Pat, Chris, Leslie, Carol, Morgan, Kelly, Terry, Jerry, Sam, and Jamie are used for males and females. Of course, it takes some enculturation before one finds out that "Pat" can come from Patrick (male name) or Patricia (female name). Similarly, "Chris" can come from Christopher (male name) or Christina (female name). I am still confused why so many people name their dogs "Spot" which usually is a synonym for a mark, location or dot. Then again, such curiosity and its fulfillment are the essence of life and it must continue based on priority and importance.

REFLECTIVE QUESTIONS FOR CRITICAL THINKING

1. What are some common reasons for why people left Afghanistan during the late 1970s, 1980s and 1990s?
2. Why do you think people left their homes in Afghanistan after the 9/11/2001 attacks on the Twin Towers in New York City?
3. The Russians left Afghanistan in 1989 but people were still leaving the country in the 1990s. Why and how could such migrations have been prevented by the ruling governments?
4. What were some of the challenges associated with migrations to Pakistan, Iran, or other countries during the Russian invasion?
5. What were some of the challenges associated with internal migrations (moving from one city to the next or from one province to another)? Provide specific and real examples.

6. What challenges did refugees face when they got to camps in Pakistan or Iran? What caused these challenges and how could have they been prevented?
7. How were Afghan refugees treated in Pakistan and Iran?
8. What role did the Afghan leaders living in Pakistan play in making sure that refugees received the best treatment and services once they left Afghanistan?
9. Did Afghan refugees face any form of discrimination in foreign countries? Describe your thoughts and provide examples.
10. What are some reasons for success stories of Afghan refugees who became well educated despite many hardships?
11. What are some of the reasons for why some Afghans have become successful entrepreneurs?

CHAPTER 7

RELIGIOUS AND SPIRITUAL BELIEFS

Since the majority of Afghans are Muslim, and they have been brought up with Islamic beliefs and values, it is best to review some foundational elements related to the religion. *Islam* implies submission to the One, and only One, God who is the creator of everything in the universe. Anyone who accepts this submission to God and accepts Mohammad as the Messenger of God is considered to be a Muslim. A Muslim uses the Quran to study the ways of God and the teachings of his Messenger, Prophet Mohammad (Peace Be Upon Him), who died in 632 A.D. Prophet Mohammad is the last of all the Messengers of God, which included Jesus, Moses, Abraham, and other Prophets. Prophet Mohammad lived from 570 - 632 AD and the collection of his sayings and guidance are called *Hadith*. The *Quran*, words of God, was revealed to Prophet Mohammad (PBUH) because he is the last Messenger of God. The Quran, the book of God, is every believer's guide to the truth and justice, because humans can be misled by "Satan" or the various temptations of the world. Islam is an egalitarian religion where everyone is created by God and can be taken away by God. So, each person is born equally, meaning nobody is born better or worse in the eyes of God, and each person may spiritually leave this world differently depending on his/her beliefs and deeds. Muslims are monotheistic and believe that God is the creator of universe and is omnipotent, fair, and merciful.

ISLAMIC PRACTICES

The word "Islam" in Arabic means peace. Muslims often greet each other by saying *"Assalam-u-alaikum,"* which basically means "peace be upon you." In this respect, Islam is very similar to other practices or ways of life. For example, in the tribes of northern Natal in South Africa, they greet each other by saying *"Sawa bona,"* which means 'I see you,' and the other person would reply by saying *"Sikhona"* meaning "I am here." The concept is that by acknowledging that you are seeing the person, you bring them into existence. In Islam, the proper reply for *"Assalam-u-alaikum,"* would be *"Wa`-alai-kum-Assalam"* which means "and peace be unto you." Islam is about the universal unity of every human being on earth, and does not discriminate based on race, culture, ethnicity, country of origin, or any other societal factors which one cannot change. Islam is a way of life as it has imposed a complete ethical code that expects honest, fair, generous, and respectful conduct and behavior from its members in all situations. This code also prohibits waste (all kinds), adultery, gambling, usury, alcoholic beverages, and eating certain meats (i.e. pork). Each and every Muslim is responsible for his or her own actions to God. Each Muslim declares his/her faith toward the one God, should pray daily, practice almsgiving, fast during the month of Ramadhan, and make pilgrimage once in a lifetime if financially and physically capable.

Table 7- Five Duties of Muslims

FIVE DUTIES OF EVERY MUSLIM (The Pillars of Faith)	
1	To make the profession of faith: there is only one Supreme Being (known as God) and Mohammad is God's Messenger (prophet).
2	To pray five times each day while facing Mecca.
3	To give a percentage of one's assets to charity (almsgiving) for those in need.
4	To fast during the month of Ramadan from dawn to dusk each day.
5	To make at least one pilgrimage to Mecca if at all possible physically and financially.

There are two major factions of Islam, called Sunni's and Shia's. Both factions believe in God and have the same major values. In Afghanistan, Sunni and Shia practiced their religion often in the same Mosques, homes, cities, and provinces. The personal differences among the two factions were fully respected as they were based on each person's personal beliefs which did not hinder others. Table 8 presents some of the common beliefs between the Sunni and Shia.

Table 8- Sunni and Shia Muslims

SUNNI	SHIA
• Orthodox (Conventional - accepted in usage) • Practice tends to be staid (quite, sober) and simple. • Are deterministic	• Believes in 12 *imams*, perfect teachers, who guide the faithful from paradise. • Practice tends toward the ecstatic • Affirm human free will

WOMEN IN ISLAM

According to a 2006 publication by TIME entitled "*The Middle East: The history, the cultures, the conflicts, the faiths*," "When Islam swept across the Middle East in the 7th century, it profoundly changed the place of women in Arab society— for the better. At a time and in a place where women were generally regarded as slightly less valuable than livestock and infants, girls were routinely buried alive, Islam actually outlawed female infanticide, made the education of girls a sacred duty and established a woman's right to own and inherit property." The TIME publication also states that Islamic leaders even decreed that sexual satisfaction was an entitlement for women.

In accordance with Islam, women can work, attend school, and go to defensive war, similar to their male counterparts. According to Islamic teachings, women, while in the presence of others, should be modest. In Afghanistan, most women chose to wear *chadari* - which has been borrowed from the ancient Persian culture. *Chadari* provided women privacy and at times protection from thugs, criminals, and rapists. However, during peaceful times, it was not a common occurrence for many Afghan women. When I lived in Afghanistan, some women went to school and worked wearing pants, skirts, and professional work attire, as they do in most modern countries. The TIME publication mentioned that the covering of the head and body which is mandated by Islamic tradition "may seem a symbol of oppression to the Western eye, but to many women who wear it, it represents freedom from unwanted sexual advances as well as pride in Islam."

During a divorce with no circumstantial evidence, generally women are granted custody of their boys until age seven and their girls until the age of nine. Then the husband is allowed to seek custody.

JIHAD AND ISLAM

In most Western societies, people are being challenged with many mind-boggling questions about jihad and moral issues in Islam. The lack of education and understanding of such topics has brought misinterpretation of these terms and many other such Islamic views. The media has concentrated on wars and extreme forms of government in many Islamic countries in developing nations, where subjective and cultural views are being interpreted for Islamic rules. There are many reports that are examples of wars and other unfortunate cases which the media interpret as being instigated by Muslim extremists and totally ignore other variables, such as freedom, rights, liberty, and other societal or environmental conditions of those countries.

For example, in 1979, the Communist government and the Russian forces started a never-ending civil war in Afghanistan, which was interpreted as the work of Mujahideen, who are mostly known as Islamic soldiers. "Rough" estimates suggest that over two million people died in Afghanistan because of this war, which is a great tragedy for a developing nation and for humanity in general. This destruction is often seen as the work of Islamic soldiers by the media; and that portrayal is not totally accurate because people who are not religious also fought in the war since they too did not want to be controlled by outsiders. Islam allows defensive war just as people of other faiths are also encouraged to defend their country and people. The Afghan war is similar to many other wars. For example, during the first six months of the war between the Russians and the people of Chechnya, there were thousands of Chechen men, women, and children who died because of the brutal Russian bombing. This war was also seen as the work of the Mujahideen, while the fact of the matter is that the people of Chechnya, who happen to be Muslims, want their freedom. So, their war is about wanting freedom and independence.

The term "jihad," in the Arab language, means struggling or striving to accomplish something. As children, we struggle to crawl, walk, and graduate from high school. Musicians, movie stars and politicians strive to increase their popularity with members of the society. The term "jihad" can apply to Muslims as well as non-Muslims with the same application, meaning efforts exerted toward accomplishing something.

In most areas, the term "jihad" is generally communicated as "holy war" which is not the correct meaning of the term. This translation has been generally popularized by century-old propaganda through the media. According to Islamic literature, starting a war is discouraged and considered to be unholy, unless it is inevitable. The Quran and the Hadith (teachings of Prophet Muhammad) use the word "jihad" in many different contexts and the following are some of its applications and explanations (Ali, 1994):

1- *Recognizing God and loving God unconditionally.* All human beings are generally conditioned to recognize and build an attachment to the physical and what is in the proximity of our vision and senses. God (Allah) is the creator of the universe and at times many of us have a propensity to ignore and not recognize him. The Quran says the following to all who believe in God:

> Believer, do not befriend your fathers or your brothers if they choose unbelief in preference to faith. Wrongdoers are those that befriend them. Say: 'if your fathers, your sons, your brother, your wives, your tribes, the property you have acquired, the merchandise you fear may not be sold, and the homes you love, are dearer to you than God, His apostle and the struggle for His cause, then wait until God shall fulfill His decree. God does not guide the evil-doers. (9:22-24)

2- *Resisting societal pressures.* Many individuals who commit themselves to serve the one and only God and to put Him above all else, often feel the pressures from others. It may be difficult to resist such pressures and strive to stay committed to God over all other things. The person who has converted to Islam from his/her family religion, may feel the pressure designed to make him/her go back to the original religion. The Quran (25:52) says: "Do not yield to the unbeliever, but strive against them by this (Qur'an) most strenuously."

3- *Always remaining on the straight path.* Sometimes Muslims will be harassed and bothered by others. It is the responsibility of each Muslim to strive and struggle for a life that is truly Islamic. The Quran (22:78) say: "Strive for the cause of God with the devotion due to Him. He has chosen you, and laid on you no burdens in the observance of your religion (faith)......."

It is the responsibility of Muslims to migrate into other lands if they are being pressured by non-Muslims. They should move to an area that is peaceful and tolerant where they can continue to strive for the cause of God. This is what Prophet Muhammad (PBUH) and his followers did when they were boycotted socially and economically to pressure him to stop his message of God. They did not stop their belief in God, but struggled and strived for His cause, and eventually they achieved moral victory. The Qur'an (4:96-8) says:

> The angels will ask those whom they carry off while steeped in sin: "What were you doing?' 'We were oppressed in the land,' they will reply. They will say: 'Was not the earth of God spacious enough for you to fly for refuge? Hell shall be their home: an evil fate. As for helpless men, women, and children who have neither the strength nor the means to escape, God may pardon them: God pardons and forgives.

4- *Striving for righteous deeds.* Often people are forced to choose between competing interests, so choosing the right decision becomes a jihad as one tries to make his/her decision. In the Quran (29:69) God declares: "Those that strive for God's cause will surely be guided to God's paths. God is with the righteous."

Prophet Muhammad (PBUH) had encouraged many Muslims to strive (participate in jihad) by serving their parents, to make a pilgrimage to Mecca, to stand for truth, and continually serve God and abandon evil deeds.

5- *Having courage and steadfastness to convey the message of Islam.* It takes courage and consideration to stay a true Muslim and to educate and invite others to the way of God. God has praised many people in the Quran who have passed His message to others. In the Quran (41:33) God's message is: "Who is better in speech than he who calls others to the service of God, does what is right, and says: 'I am a Muslim'"

We should remain strong in the face of pressures and material interests. God has declared his message in the Quran (49:15) by saying: "The true believers are those that have faith in God and His apostle, and never doubt; and who fight with their wealth and their persons for the cause of God. Such are those whose faith is true."

6- *Defending Islam and the community.* Defensive fighting is allowed by the Quran and it should be done to defend and protects one's family, property, and community. God says in the Quran (22:39):

Permission to take up arms is hereby given to those who are attacked, because they have been wronged. God has power to grant them victory: those who have been unjustly driven from their homes, only because they said: 'Our Lord is God'.

And the Quran further says (21:90-93):

Fight for the sake of God those that fight against you, but do not attack them first. God does not love the aggressors...Fight against them until idolatry is no more and God's religion reigns supreme. But if they desist, fight none except the evil-doers.

7- *Help allies.* God has further encouraged everyone to help allied people who may not be Muslims, as did Prophet Muhammad when Banu Khuza'ah became his ally. God has also encouraged Muslims to fight for what is right and defend those who cannot defend themselves. Muslims are to remove treacherous people from power whenever possible. The Quran (8:57) states: "...If you fear treachery from any of your allies, you may fairly retaliate by breaking off your treaty with them. God does not love the treacherous..."

The Quran further states (2:216): "Fighting (defensive) is obligatory for you, much as you dislike it. But you may hate a thing although it is good for you, and love a thing although it is bad for you. God knows, but you know not..."

God has further encouraged all believers to strive for continuously educating, informing, and conveying the message of God to others in an open and free environment. It is also the responsibility of all individuals to free people from tyranny and exploitation by oppressive systems as did Prophet Muhammad (PBUH). We should all keep in mind that Islam did not spread by the use of force, swords, or guns. Islam has been and should be spreading through the use of reason, knowledge, self- discovery of God, and continually educating and informing others about the ways of God. Quran (2:256) declares:

> There shall be no compulsion in religion (Islam). True guidance is now distinct from error. He that renounces idol-worship and puts his faith in God shall grasp a firm handle that will never break. God hears all and knows all.

MORALITY IN ISLAM

There are several important and difficult moral issues which many organizations and societies are facing today. Since specific rules and regulations cannot solve certain problems, and they surely are not able to provide direction to the right path, we need to refer to religious belief systems, because such fundamental foundations would be one solution to living a moral life. Learning more about these scriptural beliefs can help us grow mentally, psychologically, spiritually, and in the mundane social mainstream.

Human sexuality: In Islam, the only valid sexual relationship is that of a legitimately married couple. Islam does not limit the age at which one can marry. The specific time of marriage period depends on one's physical (sexual) and mental maturity. Muslims have been encouraged by the Prophet Mohammed to get married when they are sexually mature, so they can avoid committing sins. Those who cannot or do not want to get married, can fast to help him/her totally abstain from inappropriate sexual temptations and activities. All sexual activities outside a marriage are prohibited. Homosexuality is prohibited in Islam. It is considered to be in the same league as fornication and adultery which are sins because they are illicit. Homosexuality defeats the purpose of bearing children in its natural order, which is one of the main elements of having a sexual relationship. The Quran emphasized that humanity has been created in pairs (man and woman), and any deviation would destroy this natural order; so homosexuality is not allowed.

Birth control, as suggested by Muslim legal scholars, is allowed, and people may use their own choice of birth control. It is encouraged that people not use birth control because they are afraid of not being able to take care of their children since God will provide and help in this matter.

Abortion in Islam is acceptable during the first four months of pregnancy, which is a period that begins with the last menstrual period. After the first four months, abortion of any type is prohibited because the embryo becomes a person at this time. It is after four months that most of the human organs and the brain with its cortex are formulated, and they thus function as a person. Most Islamic scholars agree that abortion is reprehensible; however, it is not sinful if undertaken within the first four months of conception.

Drugs and gambling: All alcoholic beverages and drugs which prevent the mind to function normally are prohibited in Islam. The Quran (5:90) says: "O you who attain to faith; intoxicants, games of chance and idolatrous practices and divining the future are but a loathsome evil of Satan's doing; shun them, so that you might attain to a happy state (of life)." Islamic work ethics have always encouraged hard work, personal commitment, and efforts for accomplishing things and receiving things. So, gambling and drinking alcoholic beverages would violate these conditions because they are unproductive and they cause the mind to function abnormally. Since all gambling activities and "games of chance" are not productive, they are discouraged in Islam and this prohibition includes biding on games, lottery, and all other forms of gambling.

HUMAN RIGHTS

Islam does not discriminate based on any physical differences such as nationality, race, color, or gender. In Islam, all human beings are substantially the same, and no persons should be discriminated against based on their physical appearance, ethnicity or place of birth. All human beings are the same, and thereby related to one another to form a community as friends, family members, brothers, and sisters. A country may have geographical boundaries and may be located in any part of the Earth, Islamic rules and guidelines regarding human rights and privileges are not restricted to such limitations. Islam has clarified some universal rights that are basic and applicatory to all humanity without regard to circumstances or man-made territorial borders. These rights apply to all human beings, whether a person is Muslim or not, these rules should be obeyed for the sake of the society in general. Human life is sacred in all of its forms, and human blood should not be spilled without justification. The Quran (5:32) equates killing of one person without just cause to the killing of entire human race.

> Whoever slays a soul not to retaliate for a soul slain, nor for corruption done in the land, should be as if he had slain mankind altogether and whoever saved a human life shall be regarded as though he had saved all man-kind (5:32).

Islam does not allow anyone to mistreat women, children, older people, or people who are sick or wounded badly in any sense whatsoever. As a matter-of-fact, Islam encourages respect for women, feeding the hungry, treating the injured, and educating children without considering their religious beliefs or cultural backgrounds. The fundamental human rights in Islam are things that have been granted to all people from God, and not from an ad hoc task force or a legislative assembly that has been appointed by human beings. Things that have been, or will be, created by people can be taken away just as easily as they were created because they can prove to be harmful in different situations or as time changes. However, in Islam, human rights are fundamental to all human beings and they are granted to everyone from God. They will always stay unchanged and will be applicable universally, regardless of race, gender, nationality, and so on. All Muslims have to accept, live by, and enforce these fundamental human rights. No one (Muslim) should deny them, change them, violate them in any situation or circumstances because the verdict of Quran (5:44) for such a person or society is clear: "Have no fear of man; fear Me, and do not sell My revelations for a paltry end. Those who do not judge by what God has sent down are the disbelievers (5:44)."

The following human rights for an Islamic State have been stated and clarified by the Islamic scholars, World Assembly of Muslim Youth (WAMY) and the Institute of Islamic Information and Education (IIIE):

1. *The Security of Life and Property*: When Prophet Mohammed (PBUH) addressed the Farewell Hajj, he said, "Your lives and properties are forbidden to one another till you meet your Lord on the Day of Resurrection." Prophet Mohammed (PBUH) has further stated that, "One who kills a man under covenant (i.e. Dhimmi = non-Muslim citizens of a Muslim state) will not even smell the fragrance of Paradise."

2. *The Protection of Honor*: The Holy Quran (49:11-12) says: I) You who believe, do not let one (set of) people make fun of another set. II) Do not defame one another. III) Do not insult by using nickname. IV) Do not backbite or speak ill of one another.

3. *Sanctity and Security of Private Life*: The Quran has laid down the injunction, I) Do not spy on another (49:12). II) Do not enter any houses unless you are sure of the occupant's consent (24:27).

4. *The Security of Personal Freedom*: Islam has laid down the principle that no one can be or should be imprisoned without being proven guilty in an open court. Arresting people on the basis of subjective suspicions, imprisoning people without proper court documents, and without giving people a reasonable opportunity to defend themselves is not permissible in Islam.

5. *The Right to Protest against Tyranny*: In Islam, all powers belong to and come from God, and people have only been empowered with this trust. Everyone who becomes a recipient of such a power has to stand in an "aweful" reverence before his people towards whom and for whose sake he will be called upon to use these powers. This counsel was acknowledged by Hazrat Abu Bakr (Khalifa), who said in his very first address, "Cooperate with me when I am right but correct me when I commit error; obey me so long as I follow the commandments of God and His Prophet; but turn away from me when I deviate." Also, people can protest against government's tyranny, because the Quran (4:148) says, "God does not love evil talk(harsh words) in public unless it is by someone who has been injured thereby. God hears all and knows all. Whether you do good openly or in private, whether you forgive an injustice- God is forgiving and all-powerful."

6. *Freedom of Expression*: Islam says that everyone has the right to freedom of speech and the right to express themselves, so long as it is for the propagation of virtue and truth, and not for spreading of evil and wickedness. Islam does not allow the propagation of evil and wickedness under any circumstances. Islam does not give anyone the right to use abusive offensive language as means of criticism.

7. *Freedom of Association*: Islam has given rights to people to associate with whomever they choose to and to form parties or organizations. This right is subject to certain general rules and must not be formed for evil or wickedness.

8. *Freedom of Conscience and Conviction*: Quran (2:256) says, "There should be no coercion in the matter of faith. True guidance is now distinct from error. He that renounces idol-worship and puts his faith in God shall grasp a firm handle that will never break. God hears all and knows all." On the contrary, most totalitarian systems deprive the individuals of their freedom. Indeed, this undue exaltation of the state authority curiously enough postulates a sort of servitude, of slavishness on the part of human beings. In the past history, slavery meant total control over another man and today it has been totally abolished, but in its place totalitarian societies impose a similar sort of control over people.

9. *Protection of Religious Sentiments*: Islam has also given people the right that their religious sentiments will be given due respect, and nothing will be said or done which may encroach upon their rights.

10. *Protection from Arbitrary Imprisonment*: The Quran (35:18) says, "No bearer of burdens will be made to bear the burden of another. If a laden person cries out for help, not even a near relation shall share its burden." In Islam, people are not to be arrested or imprisoned for the offenses of other people or other societies.

11. *The Right to Basic Necessities of Life*: Islam has given rights to the needy individuals who may be in need of help financially, socially, psychologically, or physically. The Quran (51:19) states, "And in their wealth there is acknowledged right for the needy and the destitute."

12. *Equality Before law*: All individuals have been given the right to absolute and complete equality in the eyes of the law.

13. *Rulers are Not Above the Law*: Prophet Mohammed (PBUH) has clearly stated that none can be above the law. Even if family members of the King commit a crime, they should be punished according to the law.

14. *The Rights to Participate in the Affairs of State*: Islam says that all leaders of the government should be elected by the people of the society without coercion. The Quran (42:38) says, "...And to conduct their affairs in mutual consent among themselves..."

Islam tries to achieve these human rights, and many others mentioned in the Quran, by providing certain legal safeguards, but mainly by asking all human beings to transcend the lower level of animal life, and to be able to go above and beyond the mere ties fostered by the kinship of blood, racial biases, linguistic arrogance, and economic privileges. Islam invites people to learn to reason with each other, and speak by speaking a language that is understandable to both parties.

CHALLENGES FACING AFGHAN MEN AND WOMEN

While Islam has provided clear guidelines for both men and women, there are some cultural practices in Afghanistan that have created challenges for the growth or education of women. While the number of young girls going to school in Afghanistan has increased in the last few years, there are still some people in the Afghan society who believe their daughters should not be educated. This view is partially culture-based and to some extent due to the insecurity which is still present at times. In the rural cities, girls are less interested in schooling because of their families' reluctance to have them educated and the shortage of schools in their villages (Samsor, 2004). The government officials, and many of the local school administrators, have launched a promotion to entice children to attend school despite the fact that they face some parents who do not want to send their daughters to be educated mostly due to safety concerns in the environment. In some cases, young kids (both boys and girls) do not go to school because of rules and policies that require certain books and uniforms. For example, a ten-year-old girl, Nahida, stopped going to school and said: "My father died last year and the teacher told me to wear a black uniform, but we could not afford it." Samsor states that there are nearly 4 million Afghan boys and girls attending school, and out of these 30 percent are girls. However, approximately one million girls, in the seven to thirteen age ranges, have been deprived of an education for various reasons. Yet, since late 2001, the number of girls and boys going to school has quadrupled. One of main reasons for girls not attending school is because they have no sufficient and well-equipped school facilities. It is very difficult for young boys and girls to study under torn tents in the freezing cold weather. Many officials believe the reason more girls do not come to school is because of the weak economy, insecurity and the lack of investment in the schooling system.

Another major problem facing young women that get married is the fact that they are often alone for many years with their in-laws without much support from the husband. According to Zubair Babukarkhail (2004), for example, Fatima's husband has been working abroad for nearly eight years to support their family and four children. Fatima only sees her husband every two years. Added to this challenge of having a distant husband is the fact that women have to defend themselves in the family disputes and quarrels. Fatima says: "I am harassed by my in-laws when my husband is abroad...My husband is like a protector and a guardian and when this protection is not there I become vulnerable" (Babukarkhail, 2004). It has been a tradition for many Afghans to travel to far away countries in search of earning money and economic stability. Some leave their wives at home to take care of the kids and stay away for years to be able to send money home to their families. Yes, some travel abroad to earn money for their *dowry*, which is a gift of money or valuables given by the groom's family to the bride before the wedding can take place. Dowry is a cultural tradition that is still being practiced by some families. Hopefully this practice, in its current format, will soon disappear in all areas of the country. Sometimes, young males get into debt after having to pay out huge amounts towards their dowry, as requested by the bride's family.

Unfortunately, the necessity to work abroad in order to save money for a dowry has created huge social pressures for family life, especially for some young men and women. Some men are stressed because they often have to earn large amounts of money before they can get married, and women face other challenges as a result of such practices. Of course, most women would feel unhappy when their husbands leave them for long periods of time to work in foreign countries. This loneliness and separation can lead a young person to depression. The other sad element is that some in-laws may treat the new brides as domestic servants which can be a huge blow to one's self-confidence...further leading to worse cases of depression. According to Babukarkhail, there have been reports of newly married women trying to kill themselves by taking poison or trying to shoot themselves. Sadly, a newly-married girl's life gets worse when she has to live with her in-laws, under such bad conditions, without her husband. So, Afghan males have to be careful, and plan accordingly to not leave their wives by themselves in a bad environment when possible. While some women may complain to the family elders or to the government officials, there are perhaps thousands of women who are in the same situation as Fatima, but only a handful are courageous enough to come forward and talk about their situation. Many young people today disagree with the dowry system, and believe the tradition was imposed many centuries ago by "other" foreign cultures. Many Afghans say that they are unhappy about the "bride price" imposed by some elders. Many young men tend to say that "The bride price is too high in our area so we are forced to go abroad to work." Yes, Babukarkhail states that other Afghans think that the custom of demanding a "high" dowry for women is rooted in values of an uneducated society: "In comparison to most of our women the men are ignorant and they impose such strict values in the name of religion."

Reports, according to some relief workers, confirm that the number of Afghan women committing suicide and setting fire to themselves because they cannot bear their lives has risen dramatically in the last few years. Furthermore, it is estimated that more than 50% of all marriages in Afghanistan are now "arranged." The term "arranged marriages," for adult males and females, usually implies that the male's family or representative initiates or makes a request (the occasion is known as *khaustgaurrie*) to the female's father, mother or other family members for her hand in a marriage to the designated "boy" or "groom to be." Once the request has been made, then the girl's family is supposed to speak with her to see if she wishes to be married at this time and whether she wants to marry this "boy" or not. If she agrees, then, and only then, the girl's family will give candy to the boy's family, implying that they can be engaged to be married. Depending on how well the two families know each other this process might take from a few weeks to several months before the girl's family says "yes" or "no" to the request. If the girl wants to marry someone else or is expecting another family to make a request for her hand in marriage to their son, then she will respectfully decline the request by saying "no" or the fact that she is not ready to get married at this time as she wants to continue her education or take care of her mom, dad or an elderly grandparent. In areas where educational facilities and opportunities are not available, most girls tend to get married at a younger age, provided that they are healthy. In many cases, girls are engaged and married off around the age of 18, some much younger. Unfortunately, in some cases, a good number of the "arranged marriages," that are not to the satisfaction of the girl or bride are to settle debts or feuds between family members or even tribes. Despite the fact that this is not a cultural or religious intention, such acts cause "women" to be regarded as commodities rather than wives, sisters and mothers. Due to such perceptions, conditioning and a few abusive men, some women are treated like slave workers by their families and husbands. Since many are not able to attend schools, they remain uneducated and their only options are limited to bearing children, taking care of the children, and/or doing house chores. While household chores or taking care of children are good tasks for both males and females, what makes women stressed and depressed is the manner in which some males treat them. The fact is that over 300 Afghan schools were burnt down in 2006 or simply closed after threats from opposition groups, leaving hundreds and thousands of students nowhere to go for an education. Such insecurity is not limited to children and girls as adult women are also negatively impacted. Due to security reasons, the overwhelming majority of women in Afghanistan are still encouraged to cover their entire bodies and faces. As a matter-of-fact, even the United Nations personnel had supposedly circulated a memo to all their staff in Afghanistan, advising women to cover their heads in Kabul.

According to some professionals in Afghanistan, as cited by Christina Lamb in her November 2006 article, "Women do not have liberation at all. People in power, whether in government, parliament or governors, are warlords and...are no different in their outlook..." According to many Afghans, as cited by Lamb, "The West talks of Afghan women having freedom and going outside without a burqa but I tell you the burqa was not the main problem for women. Look at the high rate of suicide among our women. The real problem is security and more and more are returning to the burqa." Kabul, which has been like an oasis of calm, has unfortunately become a jumpy place where working people live behind high walls, concrete blocks, wires, and sandbags after several suicide bombs have rocked the city. Aside from such the worsening security throughout the public offices, the other main problem facing the country of Afghanistan is the widespread corruption. Perhaps due to low salaries and lack of trust, public institutions are either very weak or nonexistent. Reporters have stated that where public institutions do exist, they are often so corrupt that people wish they were not there. Christina Lamb states that it is common to see people "offering bribes to get relatives lucrative posts or arrange for them to be let off crimes." In a male-dominated society with such conditions present, professional women are against a "tide" that will require major forces to block and overcome as officials search for equality and synergy.

Many Afghan and non-Afghan professionals are often shocked by the lack of basic development when visiting Afghanistan. Even the universities and ministerial offices are not up to par, lacking basic necessities. According to Christina Lamb, in her Sunday Times article, U.K., on November 10, 2006, there is a huge gap between the reality on the ground and the "remarkable progress" claimed by most western diplomats who sit in fortified compounds behind guards and concrete blocks in Kabul. Christina claims that the only area in which the country could really be said to have made remarkable progress in the last five years is in growing the poppy. Under the U.S. and British supervision, Afghanistan has become the world's biggest opium producer. Christina Lamb, in 2006 claimed that last year Afghanistan produced 6,100 tons — 92% of world supply.

GUIDELINES FOR A PRODUCTIVE LIFE

1. Start off each day with a prayer (waking up Supplications), thanking God for waking up in good shape.
2. Put your Creator (God) first in your life by doing that which enhances the quality of life for you and others while passing through this world.
3. Broaden your horizons- learn 5 New verses from the words of God, travel to pray Far in the mosque / community with others to brighten your day, take up a booklet having supplications and read them.
4. Pray and read inspiration material after sunrise for mental development.
5. If someone says something mean to you, see what you could do to make sure you are not the cause of it (if you are the cause, apologize and correct immediately); otherwise, just shrug it off and dismiss it in a friendly, laidback manner, and pray that God shall forgive them.
6. When you get angry, remember God, and how short and worthless life is to waste in being Angry.
7. Remember that you can never have too many friends, but you can have few quality friends that help you fulfill the purpose of your Creation (i.e., live for the sake of eternal happiness and to create eternal happiness for you and others in the society).
8. When you're happy, try to share your happiness with others and thank God for that, and pray its continuation.
9. When something bad or embarrassing happens to you, just think that it could always be worse, remember the reward of patience, and thank God that it's not worse than it is.
10. Do something extra of goodness once in a while, like feeding / assisting a poor person, or helping senior citizens and orphans.
11. Never stop believing that you can win God's love and thus work for it. Then you can win the love of God's slaves / creations.
12. Spend some time thinking of God's amazing creations and how they are miracles that make life interesting and a joy. Then appreciate God's miracles!
13. Always love those who love God unconditionally thus are doing the "right" things. This way you will ensure that you live for Him and love for Him thereby making our society a little better because of your existence.
14. Find the righteous ways to express yourself, and if you think that what you are about to say shall cause no benefit, maintain silence (this is tough) while you search for better solutions and learn.
15. Every now and then, give yourself a break. Play sports, give time to your family, friends, but always remember God and watch that He is watching and expecting you to make something of yourself and to use your time in this world purposefully.
16. Pray for blessing to come to your enemies, and pray to God to guide them to the right path.
17. Hug your parents, kiss their hands and heads and obey their wishes so long as they are making our society a little better.

18. Smile to everyone, for your smile makes a big difference to him or her and you will be rewarded for your efforts both now and in hereafter.
19. Forgive those who meant bad wishes, forget what cannot be changed and smile to make life a little better for those around you.
20. Tears are for all human beings (not those who are weak or in distress) with feelings remaining in them. Do not restrain your tears when remembering God and His creations.
21. When people criticize your actions and efforts, revise your actions as appropriate and see if they are pleasing to God. If they do please God (hence are creating a better world for everyone), then ignore critics and remember how some of the best leaders (i.e., Mother Teresa, Mahatma Gandhi, the Prophet and the Sahaba) were criticized, made fun of and/or even physically harmed, so have patience.
22. Read the words of God daily and try to have a schedule for reading portions of it with complete meaning and personal reflection in your life every month (or on a weekly basis) on a regular basis as per your schedule. Read the words of God with the observation of its meaning, intentions and application to your life (instead of just passing your eyes through the words).
23. Do not let popularity go to your head, for it never lasts and you may lose from it more than gain.
24. Never look down on anybody, for they may be better than you in God's eyes. Remember, the human eye, appearances and first impressions can be very deceiving.
25. Send wise words and statements to all brothers and sisters with the intention of having a healthy society with everyone living in harmony. You will be rewarded today, tomorrow and in the hereafter.

A colleague of mine by the name of George Lucas used to say, "Take the easy path, and life is difficult. Take the difficult path, and life is easy." These words are actually a part of the ancient Samurai's philosophy, sometimes referred to as "Sho-ri e no Michi," or "The Way to Victorious Life." Just like Dr. Lucas, I am a great believer in these very old, time tested principles because they focus on honor, truth, and a peaceful existence through internal strength as well as a strong, external presence.

Do you want victory? Do you believe that you can face the challenge? In fact, there are many practical ways to apply the Samurai philosophy to accomplish your goals and successfully meet all challenges. It might be useful to take a moment and reflect on the following twenty-one precepts taken from ancient Samurai philosophy.

1. Know yourself.
2. Always follow through on commitments.
3. Respect everyone.
4. Hold strong convictions that cannot be altered by your circumstances.
5. Do not make an enemy of yourself.
6. Live without regrets.

7. Be certain to make a good first impression.
8. Do not cling to the past.
9. Never break a promise.
10. Take personal responsibility in life, and do not depend on others to take care of you, guide you, or make you happy.
11. Do not speak ill of others.
12. Do not be afraid of anything.
13. Respect the opinions of others.
14. Have compassion and understanding for everyone.
15. Do not be impetuous.
16. Even little things must be attended to.
17. Never forget to be appreciative.
18. Be first to seize the opportunity.
19. Make an extraordinary effort... and drive yourself beyond what you think you were capable of by extending your vision.
20. Have a plan for your life.
21. Never lose your "Beginner's Spirit," or the freshness and excitement that you bring to any new endeavor as a beginner, and the fundamentals that you can return to in order to find the solutions to your problems.

Hopefully you believe in these fundamental precepts because they can make an enormously positive difference in your day, and in your life. It can eliminate some of the personal and professional conflicts we fight off and experience each day. You see, "Fighting is for fools, yet few realize that those who do it well need not do it at all." In my personal opinion, this is probably one of the "great secrets" in life. If you think about it, it is really true for all situations we encounter, is not it? Such is the real key to physical, emotional, psychological, and spiritual training. Individuals who condition themselves to be victorious in battle, often seem to completely avoid conflict, yet still reach their goals quickly and decisively without engaging in the daily battles that others may think are simply unavoidable in life. Do you know anyone like that? Here is another way to think about it... do you happen to know the "four things to know" for professional success? Four things to know for success in business are know your customer, know your product, know your market, and most importantly, know yourself. If we train hard regularly and use all of the resources available to us, we will "know" everything necessary to avoid conflicts and emerge victorious. You can make these guidelines a daily habit by consciously thinking of them and doing them for about twenty-one to thirty days.

WHAT "I" HAVE LEARNED

There have been many great lessons about character and living a good life which should be repeated by watching and learning from others. Of course, religious leaders like Mohammad and Jesus as well as other leaders like Mahatma Gandhi, Martin Luther King Jr., and Mother Teresa have had great lessons for everyone and the following are a few that have been cited (Leadership, 2004):

What have I Learned?

1. I've learned....that the best classroom in the world is at the feet of an elderly person.
2. When you're in love, it shows.
3. I feel better about myself when I make others feel better about themselves.
4. Having a child fall asleep in your arms is one of the most peaceful feelings in the world.
5. What we have done for ourselves alone dies with us. What we have done for others and the world remains and is immortal.
6. One sincere apology is worth more than all the roses money can buy.
7. Words harshly spoken are as difficult to retrieve as feathers in a storm.
8. Being kind is more important than being right.
9. You should never say no to a gift from a child.
10. I can always pray for someone when I do not have the strength to help them in some other way.
11. No matter how serious your life requires you to be, everyone needs a friend to act goofy with.
12. Sometimes all a person needs is a hand to hold and a heart to understand.
13. Life is like a roll of paper towels. The closer it gets to the end, the faster it goes.
14. We should be glad God does not give us everything we ask for.
15. Money does not buy class.
16. It's those small daily happenings that make life so spectacular.
17. Once a relationship is over, if you experienced more smiles than tears, it was not a waste of time.
18. Under everyone's hard shell is someone who wants to be appreciated and loved.
19. Never humiliate another person. Always give him an honorable way to back down or out of something and still save face.
20. To ignore the facts does not change the facts.
21. When you plan to get even with someone, you are only hurting yourself.
22. The older I get, the smarter my parents become.
23. Love, not time, heals all wounds.
24. I always think of the right thing to say when it's too late.
25. To gather all the crumbs thrown my way. They soon form a lovely, thick slice of life and memories.
26. Everyone you meet deserves to be greeted with a smile.
27. No one is perfect until you fall in love with them.
28. Opportunities are never lost; someone will take the ones you miss.
29. When you harbor bitterness, happiness will dock elsewhere.
30. It is just as wrong to be rude to a child as to an adult. In fact, it may be more unforgivable.
31. One should keep his words both soft and tender, because tomorrow he may have to eat them.
32. A smile is an inexpensive way to improve your looks.
33. I cannot choose how I feel, but I can choose what I do about it.

34. Nobody wants to know what you're doing until you're doing something that you do not want anyone to know.
35. Everyone wants to live on top of the mountain, but all the happiness and growth occurs while you're climbing it.
36. It is best to give advice in only two circumstances; when it is requested and when it is a life-threatening situation.
37. The less time I have to work with, the more things I get done.
38. Life is tough, but there is always help.

BEING HAPPY

Happiness and success can be synonymous when they are based on long lasting universal principles such as the law of the harvest which states that one reaps what he or she sows. I truly believe that happiness and success are the progressive realization of worthwhile and predetermined goals. There are many means to being, and progressively becoming, happy and the following are some of the secrets of happiness as suggested by experts.

- Know what makes you happy.
- Friendship is more important than money.
- Direct your life so that it has purpose and meaning.
- Stay away from watching too much television.
- Have worthwhile and meaningful goals that are attainable.
- See the world as a positive place.
- Age is not something to dread.
- Stay in touch with your spiritual beliefs.
- Be open to new ideas.
- Do not be harsh with those you love.
- Possessions do not equal success.
- No two relationships are the same.
- Think about improving the future.
- Help others.
- Exercise regularly.
- Develop bonds with family and friends through shared activities.
- Laugh often.
- Appreciate animals.
- Get sufficient sleep.
- Take turns and share.
- Bad times pass.
- Join like-minded people.
- Be prepared for death.
- Life events are a matter of perception.
- Be friendly with your neighbors.
- You can choose what you think is important.
- Have fun and a good sense of humor.

- Think about happy times in the past.
- Enjoy routine days.
- Money does not buy happiness but doing good can result in it.

Use check marks to evaluate your current practices with regards to the above secrets of happiness. Place a check mark beside those areas you would like to improve. For each item you checked, write down your ideas about what changes you would like to make in your approach to the issues.

REFLECTIVE QUESTIONS FOR CRITICAL THINKING

1. What is Islam and how can it impact one's behavior?
2. Why is it that some people in Western cultures tend to perceive Muslims to be associated with terrorism? Is this true or not? How can such perceptions be removed, reduced or eliminated?
3. How does Islam relate to people who are not Muslims? Can non-Muslims successfully live an Islamic country?
4. What is the true meaning of Jihad and have you ever been involved in Jihad? What was or is your aim in this Jihad?
5. What is Jihad and how are students, teachers, medical doctors, nurses, computer operators, masons, laborers, librarians, politicians, lobbyists, mothers, and other hard working Afghans involved in Jihad on a daily basis?
6. What does Islam say about cheating, bribery and killing of innocent individuals?
7. What does Islam say about terrorism and suicidal activities?
8. What is dowry and how was this practice started? Why are people practicing this system of paying for the bride? Who is to receive the dowry and for what purpose? What functions does dowry serve?
9. What are life philosophies that you live by each day as a human being, as a professional, and as a spiritual leader?
10. What are some suggestions for effectively dealing with the stresses of twenty-first century's professional life?
11. What are some of the profound spiritual lessons that you have learned in life?

CHAPTER 8

THE CURRENT REALITIES

"With love you can persuade a Pushtoon to go to hell, but by force you cannot take him even to heaven."
(Khan Abdul Gaffar Khan)

The Communists in Afghanistan made the mistake of partnering with the Russian army and forcing people into learning and practicing socialist ideologies. People were expected to attend literacy courses, volunteer work programs were actually done through forcing and threatening people, and people were expected to comply to the rules of land reform which led to total chaos and inequality. However, the Russian invasion of Afghanistan did bring partial unity to most Afghan citizens, who are made of up many different ethnicities and backgrounds. Nyrop and Seekins (1986) wrote that, "Scholars studying Afghanistan quip that if Afghans were not fighting the soldiers of another country, they would be fighting each other." This became true, as can be seen from the ensuing civil war after the Communist defeat. Afghanistan has not come up with a system where every ethnic group has equal power in the decision making process according to their ratio or size. The Constitution in 1964 recognized every citizen as an Afghan; however, generally only Pukhtuns were considered Afghans *de facto*. Some of the ethnic groups that are small in members have been treated unequally according to personal biases. Historically, position status has played a major role in Afghanistan, and has contributed to much of the dissatisfaction with the *status quo*. For a peaceful Afghanistan, the unity and equal treatment of every Afghan is a necessity and prerequisite, and Afghans need to determine whether they want to build their country or wreck it by being self-centered.

Professor Burhanuddin Majrooh, an Afghan scholar, in 1984, prognosticated and said that one of his greatest concerns was that the Freedom Fighters would win the war before they were ready to run the government (Lohbeck, 1993). Unfortunately, Professor Majrooh did not live to see the departure of Russians, because he was killed in Peshawar during the 12th day of February in 1988. He had published a report showing that people supported the return of Zahir Shaw, the former King, to lead the Afghans. Borovik (1990), who interviewed Sayed Ahmad Gailani in London while he was visiting his family, mentions that Gailani was one of the Freedom Fighters' leaders that spoke in favor of Zahir Shaw. While it is not known whether Zahir Shaw would have been a good choice or not because of his physical challenges, many people think he had the ability to unite Afghans peacefully and to create a voting system where people would vote for the candidates of their choosing.

The people of Afghanistan are used to war, and the new generations of young people are brought up with war, and that is what they know best since they can do it very well. Changing this situation and replacing it with a new and productive working environment requires visionary, creative, honest, committed, dedicated, and charismatic leadership. This leadership would require a visionary strategy that is seeking a peaceful Afghanistan to ensure social justice, freedom of religion, freedom of speech, and adherence to basic human rights as put forward by Islam and the United Nations. This leadership would require the integration of all ideas and talents of Afghans into the direction of caring for all humanity, having strong values, and practicing global "brotherhood." Kaplan (1990) quotes one of the Afghan Commanders who had said, "You have to make even the weakest and the stupidest people feel they have an important job to do. That way everyone will help you." I believe this commander has the right thoughts, but is on the wrong track if he is only following the Machiavellian paradigm. There are no weak people, and there are certainly no groups of people that can be categorized as stupid (there are always exceptions on an individual basis). All individuals should be striving toward accomplishing something moral and valuable; ergo, having a mission and working to accomplish that mission should be the issue and not necessarily helping the commander or leader. The truth of the matter is that sometimes the leaders can be immoral, and consequently they may be going completely in the wrong direction. An obvious example of this would be Adolf Hitler, who was a very influential "elected" leader at the time, yet with what is now considered "immoral thoughts" by many people in society, as his followers slaughtered thousands of innocent individuals. People just followed his directives, and did not question his mission or purpose in the long-term. Chances are that many people would not have agreed with him; ergo, not follow or support his cause if they were encouraged to think for themselves based on their universally held moral values. So, people should feel important because they are working toward accomplishing a good cause, and not necessarily because they are helping another commander achieve his/her egotistic goal. All individuals should feel good about their contributions, whether big or small, because it is the "little things" that make a society successful. When one thinks about how all the little things have accomplished big results, one cannot help but to conclude that there are no little things. Everyone and each person can do his/her part in the recovery and rebuilding of Afghanistan.

Some people say that the future leadership of the country belongs to those people who have fought in the war during the Soviet invasion. While the victory and work of the Freedom Fighters must be appreciated and commended, this theory totally ignores all those people who did not have the opportunity and therefore could not contribute to the liberation efforts. I believe the future of Afghanistan belongs to all Afghans who would like to see the country grow and become an industrialized nation that is known for its creativity, innovation, bravery, and beautiful sceneries. I honestly believe that guns are not the solution to a peaceful country; however, people, reason, logic, and sound investment in the education of every young, middle-aged, and mature person are the solution to a peaceful environment with true universal values. It reminds me of the maxim that says, "You can lead a boy to college but you cannot make him think," and "you can lead a horse to water but you cannot make the horse drink." So, it is possible to make someone act like he/she believes in God, but one cannot "make" a person have true faith in God and enjoy all the spiritual, psychological, and personal benefits of both worlds. The true belief and faith has to come from within, and that is the essence of Islam. Islam has always encouraged and recommended honesty, education, strong work ethic, and reasoning with all people. As parents and adults, we are totally responsible for educating and training our youth with strong values, morals, and true universal teachings. While parents must take responsibility for the proper upbringing of children, adults are one hundred percent responsible, and capable of making their own choices and decisions based on sound reasons and logic, which leads to commitment in one's faith and values.

There are many destructions because of the war, and immediate improvements will be needed to achieve progress: finding and destroying all mines and bombs planted in the ground, getting schools built and operational for both children and adults, electric plants working, water supply systems built, communication systems working, sanitation programs and transportation routes put in place, and getting the roads fixed as they have been damaged heavily by tanks, bombs, and time. While all of these are taking place, the workforce will also need education, training, and good leadership.

THE "DIVIDE AND CONQUER" STRATEGY

The United States' and the United Kingdom's government officials have often been accused of causing much animosity among the people of developing economies, including Afghanistan over the past thirty years. Regardless of whether these accusations are based on facts or misinformation channeled by "dirty" politics, many people in developing economies perceive them to be true. The people of developing economies see the reality of their lives and the destruction of their work environment through the continuous fighting and animosity among people. Some blame this on the strategies of the Western world's objective of spreading capitalism in other environments as this will benefit their corporations and bank accounts. Some experts go as far as to claim that globalization of Western capitalism in third world countries can be similar to economic terrorism. Such experts state that globalization does very little for the third world countries when all the profits from the global businesses are being distributed back among the richest people (stockholders) of the world in the Western societies. Furthermore, such forms of globalization cause the poorest of the poor entrepreneurs to go out of business as they cannot possibly compete effectively with the giant international corporations. While the war about globalization is one story, there is another debate that some Afghans have had regarding the animosity among their people which has come to surface over the past thirty years after the invasion of the country by the former Soviet Union soldiers and the fact that now there are many United Nations staff as well as military personnel from the United States. These foreign soldiers from the Soviet Union, United States and United Kingdom have often been blamed for purposely and strategically causing animosity among people based on their ethnicities and religious beliefs using a "divide and conquer" paradigm. The following few paragraphs are some edited thoughts and actual statements that have been debated among various Afghans in the online internet forums during December 2006. The original statements have been partially edited and altered by removing the names of individuals and references to specific ethnicities as some reflections were "emotionally charged" and considered extremely "subjective." Nonetheless, the views presented provide a partial picture of current thoughts and views of some Afghans about their different people groups as well as how they see foreign interventions in the politics of their country.

One writer mentioned that Pashtuns have not treated Uzbeks, Hazaras and other Afghan minorities negatively; in fact some people came from Uzbekistan and in a little while ended up being "Khans" (rich entrepreneurs, and landlords) with large plots of property. As to the Hazara situation it goes much deeper than language differences. During the pacification period a war took place between Hazaras and Pashtuns led by Amir Abdul Rahman, which created many miseries on both sides. Consequently, Pashtun and Hazara Afghans suffered. But then after 1992, Hazaras, Tajiks and Uzbeks jointly worked against the Pashtuns. Sure, Afghans (be they Hazaras, Uzbeks or Pashtuns) have shortcomings, but they should not let those limitations become the perpetual nonsense undermining the Afghan culture and their "Afghan" identity.

A second person stated that I was twelve when I left Afghanistan and I know what we did to some minorities in Afghanistan. My uncle (a Pashtun fascist), used to beat up a pregnant poor minority woman and her "disabled" brother who was pulling a cart for living. By the way, as a result, she had a miscarriage. This was all because the uncle's dinner was not ready on time. This uncle was an extremist and a fascist who happened to be part of the majority and, thus, had certain "unearned" privileges which he abused and used to cause pain and suffering to innocent individuals. Extremism is bad, ugly and always causes more headaches than anything else. As a matter of fact, there is a guy, considered an extremist by some individuals, sitting in the American Whitehouse, but on the opposite side of many people from the developing world. We all can feel the pain he has brought to the people of Afghanistan as well as the Iraqis. If Afghanistan was as powerful as the U.S. and certain "extreme Afghans" were the Defense Secretary and President, I can imagine the degree of pain and hardship those individuals would bring to the rest of the minorities in Afghanistan as well as their neighbors. There are many so called well-educated Afghan-American guys that have received higher education certificates from perceivably good institutions, but have not really been "educated," since a college diploma fulfills only one dimension of life's lessons in leadership. Call me a traitor, an inadequate Afghan, or whatever that brings you comfort, but some educated extremists' picture of reality is much distorted. With a fascist-like approach, I can guarantee that extremists will face one "wall" after another in their attempts to force their ways on others in today's global world (just see what has been happening to the poor people of Iraq and Palestine). Such extremist individuals from developing economies are significantly limiting themselves; and, as such, others will continue to think for them using a "divide and conquer" strategy.

Another contributor said that my ancestors have tumbled down from Mountains of Paktia, and I am proud to be a Pashtun. However, I am ashamed of how my people, for centuries, have treated Afghan minorities (i.e. Turkmans, Hazaras, Uzbeks, Hindus, and others). With this in mind, how can I demand respect, sympathy or love from those that "I" have once crushed? Only now that I am getting leveled with bombs and being jailed, I am pushing my pride aside and appealing for help. Moreover, some of the socialists and communists wanted unity amongst different races and ultimately peace around the world. On the other hand, United States' agenda is driven by capitalism and globalization of the Western paradigm, so dividing people and creating chaos to achieve their goals is not unlikely. The country of Iraq is an example of this "divide and conquer" strategy, as the foreign forces from the United States and United Kingdom seem to have created animosity among people based on their religious ideologies. If I am recalling correctly, America consulted with Britain before sending troops to Afghanistan and Iraq. Britain's policy of divide and conquer is obvious to all; isolating people based on religion or race is exactly what America has done in Afghanistan and Iraq. I think we should recognize our wrong doings from the past and try to unite with our fellow Afghans to build our country. In today's complex world, how can one make the claim that "you are either with us or against us!"? We all know that this black and white approach does not work. We should recognize that there is no one to help Afghans and they have no one to blame, but themselves for falling victims to the "divide and conquer" strategy of outsiders. Of course, due to the U.S. intervention and their removal of a functioning government, Iraqis are now in a similar boat and must get themselves out of it using carefully-thought out strategies and teamwork among their diverse populations.

THE BLAME GAME

Sometimes, we cause our mind to see only what we want to see. This characteristic is considered being closed-minded. At other times, we purposefully see what we want to see because we may be threatened by the reality. So, often some individuals run around gathering false evidence to support their thoughts and subjective feelings. When it does not work, they blame the situation on others rather than trying to take responsibility for their actions and choices. I remember hearing the story of the person who lost his axe and suspected the neighbor's boy had stolen it. Every time the boy walked and talked, his actions appeared like a person who had stolen an axe. The whole day went by and every time he saw the boy, the boy's actions appeared as though he had stolen the axe, further confirming his previous thoughts. The next day he found his axe, which was lying near a tree in his own yard. Then he saw the boy and the boy did not appear as a person who had stolen an axe. Often, we make decisions based on incomplete information while nonetheless supporting it on our "gut feelings." The boy had not changed at all, because he was not aware of the situation. However, this person's perspective had changed, and thus he saw the boy differently because he had found his axe and was not suspecting him anymore. Similar to others around the world, this is the essence of many of the Afghan people's problems because they made decisions based on rumors and not actual facts. Although, "word of mouth" is very strong in any culture, and Afghans have always relied on it for information in the past, it should not be used to judge people's actions in severe circumstances.

Some Afghans have been divided into different factions of religious and ethnic groups. They either see things from their own perspective or none at all. This dichotomy of seeing things as either good or bad, "black or white," us or them, positive or negative, has had many bad consequences in the rebuilding of Afghanistan. So far, it has either slowed the process, or may have prevented some of the rebuilding, as some people are still fighting about how to rebuild it, and who should be in charge of rebuilding it. People are blaming things on others instead of taking responsibility for their actions. They play the "blame game" similar to children, and unfortunately they have not grown out of their blaming habits. At one time, most of the blame usually was directed toward Gulbudin Hekmatyar, the former leader of Hezb-i-Islami Afghanistan. He was reported to be somewhat outspoken and usually attempted to be credited for being the leader of a group that started the war against Communists. He further claimed that it was his people that first started attacking the Communists' garrisons, killed the first Communists, captured the first Russian soldier, and so on. I cannot say he was wrong because during the first two years of the invasion, a good number of the active Freedom Fighters (students and civilians) in Kabul supposedly belonged to his group. His party members, mostly students from high schools and universities, were charismatic and very active at the beginning; ergo, Hekmatyar achieved much popularity during the first few years. Much of the media considered his attempts to be properly credited but some recognized his efforts as egocentric and selfish. Of course, the facts are only known to God, as human beings we should always try to be fair, honest, and truthful while striving to seek justice. Hekmatyar's aggressiveness should not have been viewed as evidence of him ordering the killing of other Afghan leaders and commanders, especially in the absence of any real evidence. However, the blaming continued and became worse when the rumors passed on from person to person, as the real issue, usually, became ten times worse than the original instigator had stated. In one case, a certain Commander had told journalists that Sayed Ahmad Gailani did not have to unite with others because, regardless of Afghanistan's future, he has a way of making a living in Germany or other nations. This line of reasoning and logic comes from shortsighted individuals who do not see the long-term vision. Many scholars of management are of the mindset that those individuals who do not "have" to work will be some of the most valuable and productive employees that an organization could have, since they can speak honestly without being afraid of being laid off. It is important to have people who clearly express themselves and state how they feel without being pressured. In general, when people feel threatened about making the wrong decision, or if they feel others in higher authority would disagree with them, then they may not state exactly how they feel. They would either try to comply with their dogmatic superiors or "sugarcoat" their opinions simply into "lip service" to make everyone happy. So, if Sayed Ahmad Gailani or others who did not have to work and continued to be actively involved in the struggle against the Russian Armed Forces, then they probably were doing their personal duty or obligation, because they vehemently wanted to drive out Russians. They were Freedom Fighters because they wanted to feel good and serve their country in the best ways they knew.

Some of the Freedom Fighters were being played against each other in Pakistan by the involvement of many active members of the KGB and KHAD. They would commit crimes and make them appear as though one of the Freedom Fighters' leaders or commanders had ordered the crimes. About five hundred killings of Afghans and Pakistanis in Peshawar were credited to be the work of KGB and KHAD members. The Freedom Fighters should have discredited the messages by punishing or even arresting the messengers because often KHAD members started the rumors. According to Waseel, defected finance director of KHAD, assassinations, instigating rumors, and continually killing people in Pakistan was part of their campaign to create chaos among the Freedom Fighters as well as the people of Pakistan (Lohbeck, 1993). In 1983, while I was living in Peshawar, three Afghans were killed near an Afghan camp, and it was assumed to be the work of rival Freedom Fighters. In management training, it is being said that "when you assume anything, you basically make an ass out of you and me." It is also important that one should attempt not to "judge a book" simply by its "cover" because it can be very misleading. Another example would be the explosion on April 12th of 1988 which happened in Pakistan. This was one of the major explosions at the main ammunition warehouse, where supplies were kept before they were distributed to the Freedom Fighters. The explosion took place in the Islamabad area and killed more than a dozen people. While the truth about the instigator of the explosion was never found out, the Freedom Fighters were putting the blame on each other, rather than trying to analyze the situation and find the truth. Of course, some of the foreign journalists wrote about the explosion being the work of top military figures in Pakistan, who may have stolen the Stinger missiles along with other weapons from the Afghan Freedom Fighters. Lohbeck (1993) wrote, "It seemed convenient that the major ammo dump in the country (Pakistan) would blow up just days before an American military audit." The rumors and backstabbing strategies had become widespread and common among different groups. This further promoted bad morale among the many Freedom Fighters who did the actual fighting in Afghanistan. In some cases, while preparing to fight the Communists, the Freedom Fighters would start fighting each other which made the enemy more powerful during their attacks. Because of the unorganized and heavily corrupted government system in Pakistan, many people tried to capitalize on the situation, and then hide their corruption by eliminating the evidence. It is similar to stopping the message by the way of killing the messenger at all costs. In a corrupt system, people's morale will be very low and work is without commitment or integrity; ergo, many accidents and damage may occur. The Wall Street Journal reported, January 13th of 1997, that gas cylinders aboard a truck leaked in a populous area of Lahore and killed 30 people while sending more than 900 people to the hospital. This is one example of many, which is sad and unfortunate, that can happen when people are not committed to their jobs. It was this type of a corrupt environment that may have contributed to much of the blame and animosity between the Freedom Fighters, some of whom are still experiencing conflict. However, the people of Afghanistan cannot afford to, and should not, blame others for their hatred toward each other and should not look back but only forward. Afghans cannot change the past, but are partially in control of the future. As we know, tomorrow's success comes from today's learning and efforts.

Of course, it is true that all Freedom Fighters meant to do well for the people of Afghanistan, and they have done much productive work. However, times have changed and today their duty is not to fight each other but to answer their call of duty by building Afghanistan. It is clear that every Afghan has good intentions, but good intentions do not "cut it" if they are not acted upon. Today, the past Freedom Fighters have an opportunity to build the country they wanted during the invasion, which I am sure was not a country in civil war. Benjamin Franklin said, "Work while it is called today, for you know not how much you may be hindered tomorrow. One today is worth two tomorrows; never leave till tomorrow that which you can do today."

The blaming game is not limited to the politics in Afghanistan since people in other countries, such as the United States, also hold their leaders responsible for their actions. For example, on December 16, 2006, a petition was distributed to people around the globe using cyberspace email addresses and newsgroups to impeach the United State's President and Vice President for some of their actions / inaction. The following is the actual letter or petition:

Hello,

I just signed this petition; I invite you to do the same:
http://www.afterdowningstreet.org/petition

TEN REASONS TO IMPEACH GEORGE BUSH AND DICK CHENEY
I ask Congress to impeach President Bush and Vice President Cheney for the following reasons:

1. Violating the United Nations Charter by launching an illegal "War of Aggression" against Iraq without cause, using fraud to sell the war to Congress and the public, misusing government funds to begin bombing without Congressional authorization, and subjecting our military personnel to unnecessary harm, debilitating injuries, and deaths.
2. Violating U.S. and international law by authorizing the torture of thousands of captives, resulting in dozens of deaths, and keeping prisoners hidden from the International Committee of the Red Cross.
3. Violating the Constitution by arbitrarily detaining Americans, legal residents, and non-Americans, without due process, without charge, and without access to counsel.
4. Violating the Geneva Conventions by targeting civilians, journalists, hospitals, and ambulances, and using illegal weapons, including white phosphorous, depleted uranium, and a new type of napalm.
5. Violating U.S. law and the Constitution through widespread wiretapping of the phone calls and emails of Americans without a warrant.
6. Violating the Constitution by using "signing statements" to defy hundreds of laws passed by Congress.
7. Violating U.S. and state law by obstructing honest elections in 2000, 2002, 2004, and 2006.
8. Violating U.S. law by using paid propaganda and disinformation, selectively and misleadingly leaking classified information, and exposing the identity of a covert CIA operative working on sensitive WMD proliferation for political retribution.
9. Subverting the Constitution and abusing Presidential power by asserting a "Unitary Executive Theory" giving unlimited powers to the President, by obstructing efforts by Congress and the Courts to review and restrict Presidential actions, and by

promoting and signing legislation negating the Bill of Rights and the Writ of Habeas Corpus.

10. Gross negligence in failing to assist New Orleans residents after Hurricane Katrina, in ignoring urgent warnings of an Al Qaeda attack prior to Sept. 11, 2001, and in increasing air pollution causing global warming.

Source: CACabrera@aol.com.

WIN-LOSE MENTALITY

When the Russians were present, the Freedom Fighters had a common enemy who held the power of the government. However, with the Russians' departure, Jihad for Islamic values was over; the civil war began and the war continued between different groups in Afghanistan. Many of the leaders were very successful during the Russian invasion, because people followed their direction as long as it was directed toward getting the invaders out of their country. However, today many of those leaders will have to earn people's trust in order to get followers. So, leadership will require a new vision for the country, and better skills to accomplish that vision as opposed to doing it by military activities and killing the enemy, because there will not be any enemies (at least not common ones in the form of invaders).

During the presence of a common enemy (Russians), almost everyone had this "win/lose" mentality. The Freedom Fighters had to win, and the Russians had to lose, which was the sole objective of the struggle (resistance against the Soviet invasion), because they were perceived to be a threat to Islam and the freedom of Afghanistan. So, the win/lose way of thinking is very strong in the Afghan culture now, and it has created many obstacles that need to be extirpated before we can expect a peaceful environment. This way of thinking made the civil war ineluctable, and it is bound to continue unless some drastic measures are taken to educate everyone differently. The best solution may be the continuous emotional, psychological, and spiritual education and training to help everyone see a perspective of a win/win mentality and the benefits thereafter. Albert Einstein said, "the significant problems we face cannot be solved at the same level of thinking we were at when we created them." It appears that Afghans have created or developed a vision of dichotomous mentality, and they thus think in halves; either you are right or you are wrong, either you are good or bad, you either get positive results or negative results. This leads one to think that milk is always white and no other milk would be appropriate for me, my family, or my country people. The side effect of this mentality is that it totally ignores all other varieties of milk that are available or that could be available, such as chocolate milk mixed with cocoa powder, and all varieties of tasty yogurts that are produced from milk but are not necessarily white. There are yogurts that are flavored with blueberry, cherry, raspberry, blackberry, strawberry, chocolate, peach, mint, and many other great and creative varieties, because someone stepped out of the box and said there could be many options of yogurt than just plain white.

So, we need to begin doing things differently in order to expect and get different results. Someone said that if you have always done it the same way, it is probably wrong. It appears that many of today's Afghan leaders are doing things differently (in a positive direction) and it is hoped these differences will bring security and prosperity to the country during the coming years.

HUMAN DEVELOPMENT AND CORRUPTION[2]

In their role of developing Afghanistan, the private sector officials must be able to regulate themselves and operate according to the highest industry and international standards if the country is to benefit from a speedier recovery. The problems associated with corruption are of great concern to the Afghan people. The purpose of this section is to offer background information on national corruption, to introduce the concept of human development as a statistically significant factor in corruption, and to discuss the implications of these findings to the rebuilding of Afghanistan. Private sector officials should benefit from this material by becoming aware of the relationship between corruption and human development, and to create ethical standards and codes of conduct for all of their employees and colleagues.

The problems associated with corruption are of great concern to the Afghan people, so much so, that President Karzai addresses it specifically in his forward to the National Human Development Report of 2004 (Saba & Zakhilwal, 2004). *Corruption* is the misuse of public office for personal gain; this includes bribery, kickbacks, coercion, and related activities which provide unfair advantage to one party over another. Corruptive practices undermine fair trade, waste resources, defraud the public, and increase human suffering (Vogl, 1998). While the measurement of corruption has been calculated on a national level for quite a number of years (Internet Center, 2002), the explanation for the reasons behind these figures have yet to provide a comprehensive model for a thorough understanding of corruption. As mentioned above, the purpose of this section is to offer background information on national corruption, to introduce the concept of human development as a statistically significant factor in corruption, and to discuss the implications of these findings to the rebuilding of Afghanistan. "A better understanding of the causes of corruption would help in the design of policies to overcome it" (Kacapyr, 2001, p. 671). It is during this rebuilding time in Afghanistan, that the local and national governments are designing policies and practices which can be specifically formulated to consider the impact of human development on corruptive practices.

National Corruption

Corruption can hurt and slow the growth process of an economy. "The World Bank now identifies corruption as the single greatest obstacle to economic and social development because it distorts the rule of law and weakens the institutional foundation on which economic growth depends" (www.worldbank.org/publicsector/anticorrupt; as cited in Davis & Ruhe, 2003, p. 276). In an attempt to

---

[2] Contributed by Randi L. Sims, Nova Southeastern University. Originally published in the *Society of Afghan Engineers Journal*, Vol. 3, Num 1; Pages 47-56 (March 2006).

better understand national corruption, the Internet Center for Corruption Research, a joint venture of Transparency International, gathers survey data on the perception "of the degree of corruption as seen by business people, risk analysts and the general public" (Internet Center, 2002, p. 1). The Corruption Perceptions Index (CPI) ranges from a high of 10 points for a country considered 'highly clean', to a low of 0 for a country considered 'highly corrupt'. While the Center considers as many as 16 surveys for each country, a minimum of 3 surveys are needed before a country will be included in the CPI report (Internet Center, 2002). Wilhelm's (2002) research supports the validity of the CPI. Afghanistan has only recently been included in the study of corruption by the Internet Center for Corruption Research (2005). A first time score of 2.5 was reported for Afghanistan for 2003, this score is associated with a highly corrupt nation. This measure was based on only two surveys, one fewer than the organization considers a minimum standard for reliability. It is hoped that future reports will increase the number of surveys gathered in the study of Afghan corruption. For now, this number can be considered a starting point in the study of corruption in Afghanistan.

Human Development

Human Development refers to the ability of a nation's people to be able to lead full and productive lives. This includes not only their ability to earn a living wage, but more importantly to the personal choices they have that impact their lives. "The most basic capabilities for human development are to lead long and healthy lives, to be knowledgeable, to have access to the resources needed for a decent standard of living and to be able to participate in the life of the community" (Fukuda-Parr, et al., 2001, p. 9). Money is only a means that enlarges the choices of people. Human development is measured as an index from zero to .9999. There is not an automatic link between income and human development. For example, both Costa Rica and Korea have had recent improvements in human development scores (both over .800), yet the people of Costa Rica have achieved this level of human development with half the yearly income of those people living in Korea. Similarly, Pakistan and Vietnam have similar yearly incomes, yet Vietnam outscores Pakistan on the human development index by nearly .200 (Fukuda-Parr, et al., 2001).

Given that Afghanistan has been largely unstudied by the United Nations over the past two decades, not all statistical measures have been available in order to properly compute the human development index for the Afghan people. As such, Afghanistan has been excluded from many United Nations Development Program Global Reports. The human development index for Afghanistan for 2003 is 0.346 (Saba & Zakhilwal, 2004). This figure is quite low, with only five countries in the world scoring lower on human development (Burundi, Mali, Burkina Faso, Niger, and Sierra Leone; Fukuda-Parr, 2004). Comparison of Afghanistan's level of human development to its neighboring countries demonstrates quite a disparity. In 2003, the human development index for Tajikistan was reported as 0.652, for Uzbekistan as 0.694, for Turkmenistan as 0.738, for Iran as 0.736, and for Pakistan as 0.527. It is not just wealth that leads to these differences in human development between Afghanistan and its neighbors. For example, Tajikistan reports similar per capita

Gross Domestic Products (GDP) to that of Afghanistan (US$193 versus US$190) yet the human development index for Tajikistan is nearly twice the level reported for Afghanistan (Saba & Zakhilwal, 2004). The difference in human development measures between Tajikistan and Afghanistan are primarily due to the differences in adult literacy, considered at age 15 and above, and life expectancy. Tajikistan reports over 99% of its adult population as literate, while Afghanistan reports less than 29%. The life expectancy at birth is 44.5 years in Afghanistan and 68.6 years in Tajikistan (Saba & Zakhilwal, 2004). Education and wellness are key factors in a people's ability to lead full and productive lives and to be a contributing part of their community. As demonstrated by the human development success of the Tajikistan people who live on similarly low levels of income, money alone is not the key to improving the human development of the Afghan people.

As the citizens of Afghanistan work towards the rebuilding of their country, they face many difficulties in obtaining basic resources needed for living a long and healthy life. These basic resources are commonly provided by local governments (clean water, food, healthcare, education). If there are problems with corruption within the public service departments of the local governments, then the residents and businesses are not able to fairly access these basic services. For example, 60% of Afghan households do not have access to safe drinking water. Compare this figure to neighboring Iran, where only 8% of its people do not have access to safe drinking water (Saba & Zakhilwal, 2004). Government initiatives to address this problem must ensure that corruptive practices do not interfere with the fair and equitable distribution of this important resource. Poor and unsafe drinking water and inadequate sanitation methods are a leading cause of illness and death among the Afghan people. It is easy to see why a safe, adequate, and uncorrupt water distribution system must be a top priority among the public service sector, yet the Afghan Operating Budget for 2003 allots 2.4% of its funding to three departments associated with water distribution and public works (see Table 9).

Table 9 - Afghanistan 2003 Operating Budget[3] (in Millions Afs.)

Ministry	Budgeted	Percentage of Total
Ministry of Education	3,445.8	15.7
Ministry of Health	1,065.2	4.8
Ministry of Irrigation and Water	88.0	0.4
Ministry of Water and Power	159.1	0.7
Ministry of Public Works	270.3	1.2
Total of all Ministries	22,006.0	

Similar corruption problems might also interfere with the distribution of health care. If medical personnel are not assigned to outlying areas, receive fair compensation for their services, or face inadequate medical supplies and equipment, then rural citizens will continue to suffer from one of the lowest life expectancies in the world. A child born today in Afghanistan has a 46% probability of dying before

---

[3] Data Source: Saba & Zakhilwal, 2004.

age 40, while a child born today in Iran has only a 7% probability of dying before age 40 (Saba & Zakhilwal, 2004). The Afghan Operating Budget for 2003 allots 4.8% of its funding to the Ministry of Health. For more specifics, one can always glean the most recent data (year 2003) available for both Human Development (http://hdr.undp.org/statistics/data/indicators.cfm) and Corruption Perception (http://www.icgg.org/corruption.cpi_2003.html). Only those countries where data was available for both indexes were studied for this research. Data from Afghanistan for the year 2003 (Saba & Zakhilwal, 2004) was included as a reference, although missing from both the formal Human Development and Corruption Perception Reports because of limited data availability.

Prior research (Sims, 2005) has found that countries with low human development scores also report lower scores on the CPI, an indication of greater national corruption since lower scores on the human development index are an indication of fewer life choices, less involvement with the community (and thus perhaps government officials), and lower levels of literacy/knowledge. When the general public has lower levels of development, the political leaders and providers of public service may have an easier time in continuing their corrupt activities unquestioned by their citizens. Using available data, a correlation coefficient was calculated to determine the statistical relationship between Human Development and Corruption Perception. The results of the correlation ($r = 0.704$; $p = 0.00$; $n = 131$) indicate that there is a statistically significant positive relationship between how a country scores on the Human Development Index and the Corruption Perception Index. Higher levels of corruption (indicated by lower scores) are related to lower levels of human development.

Study Discussion

Research results indicate that Human Development is significantly related to measures of National Corruption. The measure of Human Development accounts for more than just income or purchasing power of the individual. This index allows a comparison of the ability of people to lead full and productive lives and to participate in their community. Since there are significant differences in costs of living and expectations of wealth by region of the world, many traditional measures of wealth do not provide a good picture of the actual impact of these figures on a person's life and choices. Money is only a means by which to allow individuals to make decisions for themselves. Life expectancy and education (which includes adult literacy) are also components of Human Development (Seyoum, 2001). The results of this study indicate that as Human Development scores increase, so do the scores on the Corruption Perception Index (lower scores on the CPI are an indication of corruption). Thus, countries with longer life expectancies, higher education and literacy, an adequate living wage, and the ability of its citizens to participate in their community, are less likely to suffer from increased levels of national corruption. Programs designed to reduce national corruption should consider the level of human development achieved by the citizens of the nation in question. It may be that an indirect route to improvements in national corruption would be to implement policies and practices that improve the human development level of the people. It may be better to fund education, health care, and opportunities for small businesses than it would be to only fund anti-corruption policies which are often ineffective. When citizens are well-educated, well-fed, and have access to adequate healthcare, they have the opportunity to live full and productive lives. They may also have the energy, sophistication, and interest in their local and national governmental officials and providers of public services. Citizen interest in the behavior of officials is not a priority when they have to worry about food for their families. Who better than to improve the level of national corruption than the citizens of that nation? It is the local people who are most hurt by corruption and who have the most to gain when corrupt activities are halted. International regulations against corruption have largely been ineffective and routinely exclude the involvement of the average citizen (see Sandholtz & Gray, 2003 for a summary of recent anticorruption movements).

This study utilizes country-wide measures and does not account for individual variations within specific countries for any of the measures. This study uses only one measure of corruption and only one measure of human development for each country. It is unreasonable to assume that all officials within one country have the same propensity for corrupt behavior as it is to assume that all citizens have achieved the same level of human development. Using the country as the unit of analysis does not permit for individual differences, but it does allow for generalization. This is the opposite of what can be concluded when the unit of analysis is at the individual level; much available data on individual differences, with limited ability to generalize. It is suggested that anti-corruption policies should be formulated with the understanding that human development is a significant factor behind national corruption. The findings of this study demonstrate the major importance of human development on the reported perception of national corruption. As such, improvement in education/adult literacy, life choices, and citizen involvement in the community should be considered when implementing anti-corruption policy and procedures. Mandating national change is not an easy task, especially when dictated by international agencies outside of the country in question. It is better to involve, educate, and empower the citizens of the nation in the improvement of their own homelands. The recent advancements in human development in Costa Rica and Korea may serve as examples (see Fukuda-Parr et al., 2001).

Over the past several years, school enrollment of Afghan children has increased and today, many parents, and even the children themselves have come to realize the importance of education in the success of the Afghan nation. The Government of Afghanistan has allotted 15.7% of its operating budget to the Ministry of Education, an increase from 10% of its operating budget in 2002. Even with these great strides in enrollment, problems still exist in educating the youth. As many as half of the children in Afghanistan are currently not attending school (the figure is much greater in rural areas, where in some regions as many as 80% of the children are not enrolled). Access and funding for school buildings and associated educational supplies remain scarce in many rural communities. In addition, some parents fear (and not without cause) that the schools are unsafe and withhold their children's attendance (Saba & Zakhilwal, 2004). There is little doubt among researchers and scholars that the key to improvements in the human development of the Afghan people lies within their education. Well-educated people have greater earning capacity, more choices in the places they live, a stronger voice in local and national government practices, and offer more back to their own communities in terms of holding jobs that provide services to others (medical and educational fields for example). The improvement in the lives of the well-educated bring improvements to the lives of those in their surrounding areas by providing health care, clean water and sanitation, additional educational opportunities, and a stronger voice. It has been said that "Ignorance is what has destroyed this country and education would rebuild it" (Salarzai; as cited in Saba & Zakhilwal, 2004, p. 28).

Ongoing corruptive practices within the public sector have enormous implications on the security of the Afghan government. Citizens unhappy with the fair, equitable, and timely distribution of pubic services can resort to revolts and other negative behaviors which offer nothing to the rebuilding of this nation. As popularly believed by many experts "Corruption is eroding people's confidence in the government" (Zaman, as cited in Saba & Zakhilwal, 2004, p. 161). As such, the government of Afghanistan must work quickly to overcome even the perception of corruptive practices. Unemployment is high, yet it is the very employment of the citizens in the building of public works (schools, medical facilities and infrastructures like roads and water distribution systems) which will lead to great strides in both human development and the reduction of the perception of corruption.

There are several areas in which corruption needs to be reduced and can be reduced, especially where organizations such as the International Monetary Fund (IMF) and the World Bank are largely involved. These organizations are helping nations eradicate corrupt officials at the national and local levels in order to combat corruption at the international level by providing incentives through monetary aid. There are several ways that corruption can be combated, including having the IMF and World Bank insure that all bank loans are used effectively and efficiently, while other financial institutions can prevent fraud in projects that they finance. The international legal system should provide measures to criminalize bribery, eliminate tax deductibility of bribery as a form of business expense, as well as increasing the transparency of public procurement. The international legal system should also enforce sanctions on countries that fail to comply with agreements and treaties in regards to anti-corruption measures. International institutions need to fight corruption at the macro level, while at the same time; the national governments must contest it at the national and local levels in order to manage corruption. This can be seen in countries such as Singapore, where there are very low levels of corruption amongst the government officials, citizens, local officials, and multinational corporations due to the strict enforcement of penalties that exist for such crimes. If other nations followed the example of Singapore, then they too can provide a safe haven for their citizens and international investors, as well as attract high levels of foreign direct investment. MNCs from developed and industrialized nations can also deter corruption with their international managers through auditing practices that "prevent the establishment of 'off the books' or secret accounts," as well as preclude the development of documents that contain improper records of transactions made by international managers. There are several other forms of preventing corruption;

however, combating it effectively lies in the hands of national governments that must enforce anti-corrupt regulations at the local levels.

The grand epidemic of corruption has manifested within different environments, where its existence in the political and economic realms has quietly spread. International managers from western based societies are not equipped to learn the ins and outs of engaging in it and neither are societies within the developed and developing countries. Yet, it is the people of these countries who have been caught in this vicious cycle. There are several policies that have been conceived among different Presidents, officials and international organizations, but the enforcement of these prescriptions have been weak to nonexistent. Fingers are constantly pointed at one another by different nations and their people, but all can be blamed for corruption in one form or another. Until policies and regulations are enforced, this epidemic will continue with its fate, where not only will nations be affected, but most importantly, its poor, who will pay the ultimate price. Afghan leaders must create a "just" and "fair" public system that serves everyone equitably in order to gain the trust of each citizen in the country.

SUGGESTIONS AND POSSIBILITIES

Many people are wondering about the solutions to the world's liberty, security and safety as the turmoil of civil wars, terrorism, suicide, and the general animosity toward capitalism has drastically increased in the past decade. Whatever the solutions may be, we do know that they are not easy, since the solution involves cultures, beliefs, and diverse traditions. As such, there are no panaceas for such complex and deeply rooted problems unless the world unites and jointly works on the solutions. Terrorism, insurgencies, and suicidal tendencies for liberation causes cannot be eliminated simply by one or two countries working against the world. As they say, in a fight between you and the world, bet on the world, because it is going to win every single time. The solution of security and peace in Afghanistan lies in the hands of the local leaders and the people of the country. The long-term solutions to cultural animosities and civil wars almost never lie with the outsiders; however, honest outsiders can assist in setting up the infrastructure for a speedy development. However, real long-term success with regard to political stability and economic development must come from within and not from without. The leaders can attempt to speed up the process of economic recovery, while the local citizens of Afghanistan can speed up the process of learning faster and better than others to prepare themselves for global competitiveness through knowledge acquisition and entrepreneurship. One of the guests (retired General Wayne Downing discussing the issue with other retired American generals and military analysts) on NBC's "Meet the Press" with Tim Russell, during December 13th of 2004, said that the Americans cannot make Iraq secure since the security of Iraq depends on the local people. General Wayne Downing said that even if the entire United States military personnel, made up of approximately 3 million individuals, were to be transferred to Iraq, they could not guarantee long-term security. So, the solution to the world's security, liberty and prosperity does not rest on the shoulders of the Europeans, the Russians, or the Americans, but rather it lies on the shoulders of unity, and how well the diverse leaders lead the local people in each situation.

There is a theory which states that 'if you always do it the way you have always done it, then, you will always get what you have always got.' If Afghan people keep doing what they have been doing after the Russian's departure, then most likely they will continue to be mired in the thick mud of war so deeply that they will not have the energy to pull themselves out when there is no one left to fight with. Afghans must believe in the existence of new options and alternatives about settling their differences. They need to eliminate the mentality of dichotomous thinking in terms of good or bad and win or lose because there might be better options available that can satisfy the needs of everyone. Each Afghan needs to believe in the theory of self-efficacy, which states that one can achieve what he or she sees possible and sets out to do. People with high self-efficacy expectations are healthier, more effective and generally more successful in life when compared to people with low self-efficacy.

Henry Ford said, "You can take my factories, burn my buildings, but give me people and I will build the business right back again." In Afghanistan, the factories of the past may be gone, houses destroyed, many people uneducated, and natural resources covered under the mountains without the technology to make use of them, but there are still people who can and will make a difference by hard work and perseverance. People are the common denominators of success in many different countries that have had virtually no natural resources. An example is Japan, as they received their independence from the British the same year as Afghanistan during 1919, which has no natural resources but is becoming the financial center of the world. Singapore is another example of a country which has become one of the leading economic powers in southern Asia without natural resources. It is not the amount of gold, gas, atomic or chemical weapons, and a superb military force that will determine the success of a country. The one thing that will be the greatest asset to a country will be its people and their educational systems, which will enable them to generate knowledge faster than others. "In oneself lies the whole world, and if you know how to look and learn, then the door is there and the key is in your hand. Nobody on earth can give you either that key or the door to open, except yourself" (J. Krishnamurti). Afghanistan has the potential to be one of the economic powers in the world in the next three decades if the proper education systems are built to support the knowledge generators. Afghanistan has untapped natural resources that can build it economically in the short-term and intelligent people who can make it become the world's knowledge center. Afghan leaders need to predict the future by inventing it and by stopping to redesign the past, or even designing Afghanistan similar to other countries. Afghanistan has its own special descriptive qualities that are different from other countries; these characteristics must be seen and respected in order for peace and development to take place. The problems and aggravations are mostly in the past; however, we have many of the symptoms, originating from past problems, still affecting the solutions; therefore, we have to start fighting the symptoms by attacking its causes as a team. Afghanistan faces a whole new generation of teenagers that will be leading the country, who have been acculturated with animosity, revenge, and war throughout the past two decades. The new generation of leaders should attempt to embrace retro-acculturation where they can cherry-pick the best values from eras of the pre-war generations, war generation, and post-war generation, and integrate them into their own values in order to create a knowledge generation culture.

I remember hearing the stories of "The vineyard" and "The unity of sticks" from my grandfather who used to advise us not to fight with each other as kids and do what we are told because their directions had a good purpose. My grandfather said that a farmer called his sons before he was about to die and said 'I am about to die, I just wanted to let you know that I have hidden some gold (treasure) in the vineyard and it is all yours after I die.' The farmer died and the sons started digging all over the vineyard to find the gold, but they had no luck. However, in the coming summer, they had the best crop of grapes ever. They sold it and become very happy. The excellent result was because of their hard work and digging under the vineyard. He said there is almost never any treasure without toil, and hard work pays off in the long run. I succinctly remember one winter, when I was 13, in Jalalablad, and my grandfather told me the story about the importance of sticking together because I was fighting with my uncle who was a few years older than me. Grandfather said that another farmer asked his sons to stop quarreling with each other about how to succeed against their enemies. However, he did not succeed as the kids continued their quarreling, so he asked them each to bring a stick. His five sons each brought a stick and the old farmer put them together and asked each son to try to break them by their hands or across their knee. None of them were able to break it. So, the farmer took each stick separately and broke them one by one and explained, "United as brothers no one will be able to win against you; separately, even an old man like me will break you easily. So, he told me that unity is a strength which is greater than the sum of its parts and very difficult to defeat. Then he went on to explain his war experiences, and how Afghans defeated the British several times because they fought as a team and for the same purpose. According to him, teamwork was the key in the success of each family member and each citizen in the country. Now, I know what he meant, and thus the importance of working as a unit and toward a common vision. As such all families must come together and work toward the rebuilding of Afghanistan. Of course, "Coming together is a beginning, staying together is progress, and working together as a team is success" states James Miller- author of *The Corporate Coach*.

To hope for any kind of a bright future in Afghanistan anytime soon, we need to have and appoint leaders who can avoid self-serving political strategies, and focus their efforts toward accomplishing what is best for the people of the country. Some leaders focus on promoting their own influence while others focus on protecting the borders and soils of the country which is not nearly as important as caring for the lives of those who live on that soil. People must be given a voice and heard in matters that affect their livelihood. People must also be educated to see the future more clearly, not only in terms of their own well-being, but also in terms of everyone in the society. The secret to a truly empowered society, where people can make informed decisions, would be to share information with everyone so they can become better educated. When people are prepared to think for themselves, and are members of an autonomous society, they will be contributing more to themselves' and their people's wellbeing. According to Ken Blanchard, John Carlos, and Alan

Randolph, authors of the book titled *"Empowerment takes more than a minute,"* the most productive people are those who do what makes sense to them. They use the example of training and selecting *"Seeing Eye Dogs"* for the blind. It was determined that the best dogs for the job were those that did what their masters told them, but only if it made sense to the dogs. For example, if the owner wanted to cross the street, while cars were coming and commanded the dog to do so, the dog should not go along with the master because it does not make sense to get run over. So, Afghanistan needs leaders that would help everyone become educated, liberated, and leaders that would let them appoint government officials that are "people-driven" instead of self-centered and power motivated. These leaders should stick to the path and not give in to the pressures of the warlords, outsiders and other rival forces when they are not benefiting all people. What is right must be done even if nobody is doing it, and what is wrong should not be done, even if all others are on this path.

The American comedian George Carlin says "there is nothing wrong with the planet. The planet is fine...it has been here for 4 1/2 billion years. We have been here for about 100,000 to maybe 200,000 years. And we have only been engaged in heavy industry a little over 200 years; 200 years versus 4 1/2 billion. And we have the conceit to think that somehow we are a threat? The planet is not going away. We are." We have lived for only a short period of time and how long we live is determined by the way we live and how we interact with others. Also, the decisions we make today are going to determine the quality of our future and the future of the coming generations. The civil war, or any type of war for that matter, most certainly does not provide the conditions or environment where people can take care of themselves by using the natural resources to their advantage. In the civil war, the natural resources of the environment were being compromised and wasted throughout Afghanistan because the war and the system of production and consumption are not designed to benefit anyone today nor in the future. Afghanistan's human resource asset has been diminishing at a very rapid pace, and this needs to stop in order for the country to grow and become stable. In a country that is in need of growth and economic stability, one needs to design a system that considers one's relationship with the environment, and then possibly adjust one's views appropriately. This way of thinking would require new and creative ideas, critical explorations and thinking, pragmatic considerations, and openness to innovative ways of thinking by all leaders.

All individuals have their own learning styles, while some learn from experiencing a task, others can learn the same task from books, mentors, watching or hearing it from others, or even from learning the theory behind accomplishing the task. While some people use their kinesthetic abilities to learn a task or a concept, others may learn the same task by using their spatial, intrapersonal, rhythmic or even their linguistic abilities to learn and understand the same task or the concept. This means that while some people learn best by reading or seeing the future based on theoretical basis, most people learn from hands-on activities and experience. Since, most people learn to eat, crawl, walk, and talk by personally experiencing it, then learning from experience becomes one's dominant and powerful learning style. Although most primary and secondary school programs are highly formal and strictly coordinated, much of the higher education is heuristic. As a result, learning by trial and error becomes normal for most people and sometimes it can be costly.

Experience, of course, is a very powerful tool for learning...it is sometimes the only way. I remember when I first got promoted to a manager in a Fortune Five Hundred company in my early twenties. I was young and eager to get things done my way, and no management book could influence me to do otherwise. I was concerned with numbers and becoming the number one department in sales and profits. I was very aggressive without a deep understanding or concern for interpersonal relationships. I wanted people to accomplish things and give one hundred percent just as I did. Time changed my feelings about my approach as I learned that people have different styles of doing, learning and accomplishing things.

When Bill Clinton first became the president of United States, he tried to push his thoughts and feelings into the market in a rushed manner, and regrets doing it as he did. Seagal and Horne (1997) wrote about President Bill Clinton who was quoted in *LA Times Magazine* saying:

> I think a lot of the mistakes I made early on in this office, which led to some not very favorable press, were legitimate mistakes, but they were more mistakes of process than product. I think if you started any vast enterprise like this and you really tried to push your 'product' to market in a hurry - your processes would not have quite worked out. Particularly if you were in town...I think I should have started a little more slowly and spent more time just in interpersonal relationships with people than I did. But I was in a hurry to get started.

Seagal and Horne (1997) categorize President Clinton as an emotional-objective person because emotional-objective people have a desire to get started and want things to get done before resting or taking a break. There is nothing wrong about different personality types; however, it does help to understand our learning styles and improve on our weaknesses while capitalizing on our strengths. In general most people learn best by being involved or through visuals. Being involved means experiencing the situation, and possibly reaping rewards or suffering as the results of our "trial and error" type of learning. The problem with this type of learning in a war situation is that sometimes it may be too late when you have learned something. Carolyn Wells said that, "We should live and learn; because by the time we have learned, it's too late to live." Many times people in leadership positions make decisions but they do not see any immediate results and that can be difficult for some people because they assume that their actions are still good and they continue defending their position. As leaders, people must have a clear vision of the future and must create safeguards to avoid any loopholes and shortcomings. This requires getting "feedback" from all team members in such a way that no one is being punished for being open and honest. Leaders must be careful about criticism during a brainstorming session, otherwise people will not be encouraged to speak their minds and become safeguarded. So, it is extremely important that all leaders look for other ways to confirm their thoughts besides "trial and error," because their decisions can affect many people whose lives are being put on the line.

A leader's moral rectitude, creativity and charisma can affect all citizens in a positive way if it is purposefully directed toward them or a general vision. A leader cannot survive or even become a great leader without the involvement of all relevant stakeholders. One time I attended a Jazz Concert on December 8th of 1996 that was held at Bartow Civic Center which is in the state of Florida. I was mesmerized by Mr. John DeYoung's, Conductor, creativity as he got an audience of approximately 1,500 people involved in the music. At one time, he said most of you have musical instruments with you and now is a good time to use them. He asked everyone to pull out their car keys and pocket change and play along by shaking them according to his direction. He was also able to get everyone involved in singing some of the songs with the sixty piece band, as he was giving direction at various points. Of course this required prior planning and creativity on his part as the leader of the band. By involving the audience, everyone enjoyed the concert, and perhaps many of them will return again because they were part of the team and had a good time in the process. Political leaders can use similar innovative methods to involve people and challenge them to do the best they can for their people and country. Without people's input and creativity a leader's positive influence can disappear very quickly and that would be unfortunate for visionary leaders.

Most of the foreign nations have not been putting enough effort or resources into helping Afghanistan because it has been involved in a civil war. At times, the United Nations and other influential nations put scant efforts to help ameliorate the condition in Afghanistan, because it is being perceived to be complicated, extremely religious, too far out of the way, and *fait accompli*. There are too many heavy and light weapons available in the country which should be gathered, controlled, or destroyed. It is not in the interest of anyone, especially foreign nations, if those artilleries are not eliminated. When Russia was seen as a superpower and a threat in the world, Afghanistan was a method of weakening its stance and most nations favored the Afghan war against the Russians because the enemy of one's enemy can be one's friend, and Freedom Fighters were certainly an enemy to the former Soviet Union. Also, some nations may feel threatened and would not interfere until those weapons are all used up or destroyed, while other nations may not want to put their personnel in jeopardy by sending help to a country that is continually combative and not peaceful. So, the burden of improving the situation falls solely on the shoulders of all Afghans who live inside and outside the country with those who are able to do their part in moving the country forward financially, economically, psychologically; and in terms of production, manufacturing, education, and training; and finally in terms of industrializing the nation for exporting and importing purposes into the global arena to take advantage of economies of scale. And let us hope that the number of projects our country's leaders are planning in both the private and public sector will ameliorate the living conditions of all Afghan people throughout the country.

We all are members of nations, and most of us have some type of an imagination about a great nation. Most often, when we live in a satisfying nation or society, we have a tendency to forget about all the good things and focus on the negative aspects of it by dwelling only on the shortcomings. We totally forget to enjoy what it has to offer and where it could go if our energy was focused on doing something positive and not negative. This is what happened to all Afghans who wanted change during King Zahir Shaw's monarchy, and focused on the negative aspects of his regime by fighting his system. We had forgotten that we were living in an environment where people could practice their religious beliefs, learn, run a business based on their capabilities, and do as one pleased, as long as it was within the boundaries of respectable human acts. We had forgotten that we had a country that was learning in a total sense of a learning community. We had forgotten that great nations are not born but built over time by learning, cooperation, initiative, responsibility, and successful interdependent relationships with other nations. We had forgotten that Afghanistan was a country by itself and separate from others. We had forgotten that Afghanistan could not be converted into Saudi Arabia because the people of each culture have different values and practices. We had forgotten that Afghanistan could not afford a foreign or civil war because it was still developing and growing. We forgot that we had liberty, freedom and peace and took the system and government for granted by creating and dividing the people of Afghanistan into communist, socialists, fundamentalist, liberals, and others.

Now, as Afghans, we are paying the price for our own actions or the actions of previous generations. However, we cannot blame the previous generations since that would be wasted energy, and we cannot blame others since that also leads to animosity and wasted energy. So, we need to start building our lives and then prepare to help others in Afghanistan. We need to succeed as individuals in our own private souls and families before we can succeed with others in the political and social worlds. Otherwise, one would be sacrificing his or her own soul and individuality for popularity and material gains in the social mainstream of a "dog-eat-dog" environment. So, let everyone learn to live ethically, deliver good value through great service to others, and to be effective leaders in all types of situations facing them in Afghanistan. With people's input nationally and internationally as well as hard work, and creativity, the negative circumstances can be turned around which will be a good thing for Afghans. The future is getting brighter for the people of Afghanistan as can be seen from the building of relevant relationships with the international community. The following paragraphs highlight a few examples as officials in the government of Afghanistan have been working to involve people from the United States in the rebuilding process.

President George W. Bush's wife, First lady Laura Bush of the United States of America, visited Afghanistan on March 30/31, 2005 to emphasize support for education, especially for the education of women, and announced millions in grants to Afghan educational institutions. Mrs. Bush told an audience of about 400 at Kabul University that "It's an extraordinary privilege to celebrate the incredible progress made by the Afghan people over the past few years, with women now being teachers, doctors, businesswomen and ministers" (EA, 2005). Her trip and involvement emphasizes that Americans are committed to the participation of women in society, not just in Kabul but throughout Afghanistan. The previous First Lady of the United States, Senator Hillary Clinton, announced the launch of the New York Partnership for a Green Afghanistan. This is an initiative to replant trees to revitalize Afghanistan's orchards, nurseries, woodlots and greenbelts. According to the Embassy of Afghanistan (EA) in the United States, "the people-to-people tree-planting program is designed to help Afghanistan regain its historic position as the 'orchard of Central Asia' and support Afghans as they rebuild their orchard, vineyard and forestry businesses." As an initial step, the Global Partnership for Afghanistan has promised to develop family-owned orchards, nurseries and woodlot businesses encompassing about 70,000 trees at the initial stage.

According to Afghan Embassy (March 31, 2005), during a visit to Kabul on March 17, Secretary of State, Dr. Condoleezza Rice mentioned that "the terrorist attacks of September 11, 2001, were, in many ways, a joint tragedy of the American and Afghan people as they resulted, in part, from the United States' failure to continue support in Afghanistan during the turbulent period following the Soviet army's withdrawal." She mentioned that the American people have "learned the hard way what it meant to not have a long-term commitment." Dr. Condoleezza Rice pledged that the United States government would not repeat the mistake of abandoning the people of Afghanistan, and will continue to assist them in the rebuilding process. Economic assistance will help the Afghan people to move beyond their years of civil war while embracing true freedom and democracy. Of course, Afghanistan needs and welcomes all the support they can get from the international community. President Karzai said that "Afghanistan and the international community have to join hands in order to provide the Afghan people with alternative livelihood" (EA, 2005). An example of "joining of hands" is the establishment of better educational facilities in the country. On March 21st 2005, President Hamid Karzai inaugurated the construction of Afghanistan's first private university known as The American University of Afghanistan. It is schedule to open in 2006, while providing courses for 1,100 undergraduates in subjects including management, communications, and liberal arts. All courses are scheduled to be taught in English (EA, 2005).

WORKING IN AFGHANISTAN

There are many Afghans who have gone back home to rebuild their lives and to assist in the rebuilding of Afghanistan. However, others have chosen to stay in foreign countries perhaps due to the occasional violence that is still impacting people in some regions and since their children are attending school in these foreign nations, or because the right jobs or opportunities have not become available to them in Afghanistan. However, thousands of Afghans, residing in foreign countries, are willing to serve in whatever capacity they can to assist their people back home. As a matter-of-fact, many individuals have volunteered as much as three to five weeks of their time each year since 2002 to assist the government in Afghanistan. Some people have been volunteering to gather relevant resources from around the world for the people of Afghanistan, while others are assisting in Kabul or other provinces to rebuild the infrastructure. A good friend of mine, Wali Jaan, left his Masters studies at Florida Atlantic University (FAU) in the area of political science to work with the transitional government in Kabul. He spent three months in Kabul and then came back to be with his family in Boynton Beach, Florida. Of course, he had to support his family so he had to come back and continue his work. During his time in Kabul, Wali was able to assist the administration in many areas, especially in gathering educational opportunities such as scholarships for Afghan students in the countries of Japan, Germany, Austria, France, and the United States just to name a few. Wali Jaan speaks several different languages, and he is a multinational person since he has lived in over five different countries, which enabled him to communicate effectively with people of different ethnicities. Wali mentioned the realities of working in Afghanistan where the infrastructure of government departments are now being built, and where the quality of life is not the same as living in developed nations. However, he immensely enjoyed his service to Afghanistan and decided to look for opportunities to work with Afghan agencies either in Kabul or other international locations. Shortly after his arrival to the United States in 2003, he was able to join a branch of an Afghan Agency, in New Jersey, where he continued his service for the people of Afghanistan. Today, he is working as an Afghan Ambassador to one of the Arabic countries.

In the early part of January 2005, I had the opportunity to interview an exemplary Afghan who had spent six months working in Afghanistan. I interviewed Dr. Mahmoud Samizay for an article publication titled "Entrepreneurship and Development in Afghanistan," which was published in the Journal of Applied Management and Entrepreneurship (JAME) in their April issue. I will share some of material from the interview with permission from JAME, but the full article can be read in the April issue of JAME. Dr. Mahmoud Samizay is another expatriate Afghan who got the opportunity to assist in the development process in Afghanistan. In 2004, he served as an advisor to the Ministry of Urban Development and Housing in Afghanistan, and in the last year he spent six months in the Afghan city of Kabul. Dr. Samizay was scheduled to return to Afghanistan around March of 2005 to continue assisting with the development process. I visited with Dr. Samizay in December of 2005 again at Kabul University during the Society of Afghan Engineers' conference, and he was still very active with various tasks and committees in the rebuilding process. The rich and diverse experiences of Dr. Samizay serves as an example of thousands of expatriate Afghans with similar credentials who can assist the current leaders in Afghanistan, if and when the right opportunities are presented to them. Dr. Samizay was born in Kabul and after finishing the French High School of Lycee Estequlal in Kabul in 1976, he went to the former Soviet Union where he earned his master's degree and Ph.D. in Urban Construction and Town Planning from the Kiev State Technical University of Construction and Architecture in 1989. Dr. Samizay worked on his Doctorate of Science in the same university in Ukraine. His Ph.D. topic covered the future development and strategic plans of large cities. He conducted an extensive study on socio-economic, climatic and town planning characteristics of Central Asian countries with similar conditions as large Afghan cities. In addition to teaching town planning courses as part of his academic program during his stay in Kiev, Dr. Samizay received firsthand knowledge of culture, history, and language of former Soviet Republics, particularly those in Central Asia. Dr. Samizay moved to the Washington, D.C. area in January 1992. Later, he entered another Ph.D. program in the School of Information Technology and Engineering at George Mason University in Virginia. During the academic years at George Mason University, one of his interests was the building of a Geographic Information System (GIS) model of Afghanistan and a GIS database.

In 1997, Dr. Samizay carried out a feasibility study on modular houses built by German based Buck Technologies Company with a group of George Mason University experts. He was employed by the Exxon Mobil Corporation as an analyst and then as a system technologist at the Exxon Mobil Research and Engineering company between 1999 and 2003. His duties included analysis of fuel marketing, project design, graphic design, and building of real time optimization models. Since October, 2003, he has worked at SRA International Inc. as an IT expert and geo-political analyst on Afghanistan. Dr. Samizay was assigned as an advisor to the Ministry of Urban Planning and Housing (MUDH) by Afghanistan Reconstruction Development Services in May 2004. The program is funded by the World Bank. He was directly involved in the design of National Urban Program consolidated strategy, in writing proposals for the establishment of an Information Technology and GIS group within the ministry, in the MUDH Resource Center, and in reform and restructuring within MUDH. He coordinates the links between MUDH and international donors for implementation of urban projects, particularly the Kabul Urban Reconstruction Project funded by the World Bank. Dr. Samizay participated in capacity building within the MUDH as key element of reform and reconstruction of Afghanistan by teaching computer programming and GIS applications. He is the author of a book titled "*The Art of Urban Planning in Afghanistan*" both in the English and Russian languages; and a CD ROM titled "Encyclopedia of Kabul." A number of his articles have been published in American, Russian and Afghan magazines. The articles cover the problems of Afghan urban planning traditions and town planning of large cities. Dr. Samizay is an active member of the Society of Afghan Engineers and runs the Afghan-Info.com web site. The following are some of my questions (author) and his answers from the interview about his thoughts on developments in Afghanistan.

Bahaudin: You spent the past six months working with the interim government of Afghanistan. When did you initially leave Afghanistan and how many times have you returned back home? How would you describe your personal experience and observations? Was your experience different from your expectations?

Samizay: I was working as an advisor to the Ministry of Urban Development and Housing (MUDH) during the period of May 1st through October 30th of 2004. My first part of the contract with the Afghanistan Reconstruction and Development Services lasted for two months. I believe any assignment in Afghanistan is challenging and worthy. The country desperately needs native Afghan professionals and the participation of Afghan expatriates in the rebuilding process of the country, which is very important. Working in Afghanistan was a big experience for me in terms of understanding the people's mentality, possibilities and work environment. It is not always smooth. It is challenging to work in conditions where you have to start everything from scratch. Ordinary people appreciate your job and help. It is nice when you see people respect you and your expertise; although, some people judge you negatively because of differences in salaries. The experts should be involved in specific assignments based on each ministry's needs; although, it is not always possible to work within one's area of expertise. Sometimes, the advisor is involved in too many unseen routine tasks that distract him or her from the main assignment. In my case, I was involved from advising on technology issues to design of projects, writing proposals, helping capacity building by teaching computer programs and GIS applications, coordination of short term scholarships for employees, participation in the advisory board of the Ministry, and field research.

Bahaudin: You mentioned that you enjoyed your trip to Afghanistan and working with the ministry officials. What made your trip enjoyable and how have you contributed to the welfare of the Afghan community?

Samizay: First of all, I think it is nice when you work in your own native country and see that people respect you and need your expertise. It is more enjoyable when you see that you are doing worthy jobs for an individual or for an entire organization. The leadership of the ministry understands this and welcomes Afghan professionals from outside who want to help the country. I try to teach the MUDH staff not only technical elements or features but relevant responsibilities and discipline as well. I tried to share my experiences, which I received from other countries, with colleagues. I advise people to think in a new way, based on current realities facing Afghans. We cannot live like before as the variables impacting life have changed drastically. I came to the conclusion that we cannot push forward the process of rebuilding without making changes in the life and living conditions of local citizens. The distribution of salary is an issue among local professionals and those expatriates or foreigners who come from outside while receiving much higher salaries. For example, a professional engineer with a salary of 2,000 Afghanis per month has little to no incentive to do a productive job in his/her field because of such very low wages. In most cases, these individuals can earn twice as much if they work as laborers instead of working in their own fields. So, a major contribution to the welfare of the country would be to make the salaries fairer for the local professionals. In any case, I enjoyed my time in Kabul and I look forward to returning there soon to continue assisting with the development process in Afghanistan.

Bahaudin: Who are some of the government officials that you met and thought were both visionary and enthusiastic about the future of Afghanistan? Can you describe what made their vision relevant and realistic for the people of the country?

Samizay: I had close contacts with many high ranking authorities including the ministers and deputy ministers within the Afghan government and other international agencies. Generally, the vision of government officials is enthusiastic. To be honest, the vision of each authority figure seems to be a bit different depending on who they are and where they come from. While this offers diverse perspectives, it can also waste resources when not managed effectively. I'm not saying that only certain professionals are good and others not as they all seem to work very hard. We have many local and expatriate experts who work very hard and truly believe in the future of Afghanistan. Many of the current high level authorities are very courageous and enthusiastic as they fight against corruption and do their jobs honestly. These are mostly professionals and experts with years of work and life experiences in the United States, Europe and other developed countries. I hope to see more Afghan professionals return to the country and participate in the rebuilding of Afghanistan. I strongly believe that only Afghans can best rebuild Afghanistan in a speedy manner, since they are likely to be familiar with the diverse cultures, languages and mores of each province. I worked with two ministers of Urban Development and Housing: the Honorable Mr. Gul Agha Shirzoi and the Honorable Dr. Abdullah Ali. I had discussions with the Minister of Finance, Dr. Ashraf Ghani; Kabul municipality authorities; head of mission of World Bank (WB); UN Habitat and Agha Khan cultural foundation in Afghanistan. They are very optimistic about the future of Afghanistan and its rebuilding process. Lack of qualified people within the country is unfortunately slowing down the rebuilding and recovery process from the nearly 30 years of war. The capacity building must be one of the priorities in every Afghan organization, and the ministers agree with this being the country's number one objective for the development of the workforce.

Bahaudin: Afghanistan is going through an infrastructure development process at this time. What is the status of development and progress in terms of business and management in the country thus far?

Samizay: Unfortunately, not enough progress has taken place in the rebuilding process of Afghanistan by the Afghan government. Part of this is due to lack of sufficient infrastructure, resources and funding. The key issue for economic development of the country is the creation of new job opportunities in both small and large cities. The Afghan government and private businesses have not been able to make it successful so far. The process of rebuilding of old factories and enterprises seems to be extremely slow. The private sector is busy with the import and export of goods, instead of building new plants and factories to improve the capacity of the workforce in the country. Having a strong economy is an important factor for the security, welfare of population and stabilization of the political situation in the country. Large projects including rebuilding of infrastructure are generally run by foreign companies or non-governmental organizations (NGOs). There is either very little or no quality control mechanisms for the implementation of projects. The biding for projects is not always fair, and the local workforce and technical staff are not always hired by foreign companies as they bring outsiders. As a result, you see very little impact of projects on the economic situation of the local population. In most cases this is true for the road projects. The government must establish a mechanism for quality control of projects, monitoring and evaluation of projects, participation and training of local employees. In the National Urban Program (NUP), which is one of the 12 Afghan Government National Priority Programs (NPP), we defined six main sub-programs: Urban Governance and Management, Urban Upgrading, Land Development, Preservation of Heritages and Historical Sites, Urban Infrastructures and Services and the last one is Water Supply and Sanitation. The NUP has more than $1.3 billion (USD) to spend over the next 10 years. It needs a team of qualified people to design separate urban projects and implement them. Of course, most Westerners have heard Walt Disney's philosophy of "If you build it, they will come." This is true of entrepreneurship and modernization of Afghanistan as well. As such, once the roads are built along with sufficient infrastructure for electricity and technology usage; then, national and international businesses will invest in new markets, which will speed up the rebuilding process.

Bahaudin: How would you describe the leadership in the new government and their vision for Afghanistan?

Samizay: As you know, President Karzai promised to push for reform within the government after the October elections in 2004. In his pre-election agenda, President Karzai declared that the new government will not be a coalition of different groups or warlords, but the ministries will be run by qualified professionals. As can be seen from President Karzai's selection of cabinet members in December 2004, many of the newly-appointed ministers and high ranking officials are terminally qualified individuals who received their masters and doctoral degrees from diverse countries around the globe. It is also good to see that there is a high level of ethnic diversity in the new cabinet and the fact that three of the newly appointed ministers are women. The hard work of such a talented, diverse and qualified cabinet members will certainly encourage the minority and female populations to get involved in the development of Afghanistan. I very much hope that the government will always consist of qualified experts, professionals and honest people. The "new hope" must end the era of warlordism and regional power in the country if successful development is to continue.

Bahaudin: How would you describe the current government's entrepreneurship philosophy? What are they doing to attract more international businesses to invest in Afghanistan?

Samizay: I believe security will be one of the priorities for the new government and international forces in the country. Without the security, I'm not sure how the foreign companies can be encouraged to participate in funding and running of major projects that require their presence within the country. Clear and fair laws for investment must be passed by the Afghan government to provide a guarantee for free business activities in Afghanistan. Then, the government should create a mechanism to control and monitor the flow of money and implementation of projects in Afghanistan. In other words, Afghanistan needs a powerful auditing agency to make sure there is integrity and fair accounting practices in each organization. Ministries need to have clear vision of their mission and create real projects with outputs for funding by international agencies. We included this concept in the design of National Urban Program (NUP) projects.

Bahaudin: Is the Afghan workforce ready for the progress envisioned by the government leaders? If not, what are your recommendations? How can the international community and other expatriate professional Afghans assist in their development?

Samizay: Unfortunately, the Afghan workforce has not been fully involved in all levels of the rebuilding process. There are a number of facts to point out. The government must clearly outline its vision on rebuilding. The working mechanism between international donors and Afghan government, in terms of funding of projects and their implementation, is still not understandable for everybody at the level of the ministries. Most of the government organizations, including MUDH, could not absorb the available money allocated by Ministry of Finance and International agencies. Simply, MUDH could not create urban projects for funding. As a result, MUDH has lost a significant amount of allocated budget and funds for the current fiscal year. This is true of most of the other ministries as well. The Afghan government must give priority to the capacity building in all levels of government echelons. Unfortunately, as mentioned before, not enough has been done in this area and capacity building should be the government's number one priority. You cannot tackle the rebuilding of the country without the establishment of information technology. Computerization of government's routine activities without doubt plays a key role in the productivity of employees. The international community and Afghan professionals can be decisive in changing the workforce vision and the mentality of people in the country.

Bahaudin: How are businesses and entrepreneurs doing in Afghanistan at this time? Are they safe and can people earn a good living if they want to start their own businesses? Is it difficult for an entrepreneur to start his/her own business?

Samizay: There are many opportunities for entrepreneurs to do well in Afghanistan and some individuals have done well. I will say yes it can be difficult to start one's own business without large amounts of liquid cash. The government needs to ratify a fair tax law for business activities. The tax collection must be the main source of the state income. In Kabul, the number of large stores of merchandise, clothes, electronics, food, and construction materials is growing fast every day. The demand for the foreign goods is much lower than supply because of the low income for the local workforce. A large part of goods are imported from neighboring countries, particularly Pakistan and Iran, with very low quality. Investment Support Agency (ISA) is a new directorate established with assistance from the German government. This is a relatively non-bureaucratic agency, which supports the business activities in Afghanistan. The directorate issues the business license for Afghan and foreign private entrepreneurs. This agency also provides the land in designated industrial areas of Kabul for development of business with a reasonable low price in U.S. dollars. I think this is a very positive step toward development of business taken by the Afghan government. Keep in mind that there are challenges and problems in this matter as well. Some people get the business license in order to buy the land. There are individuals who get the license but show no business activities for several years.

Bahaudin: What advice do you offer for Afghan professionals living outside of the country who want to help? How can they assist their motherland without leaving their current jobs and families?

Samizay: Professionals who can go to Afghanistan at least for a few months would be very helpful to society there, as they can pass on their advice and expert suggestions to appropriate departments. Professionals and experts working in large companies can provide advice and instructions in their fields of expertise by contacting different ministries and agencies in Afghanistan. They could be good facilitators to establish contact between related Afghan agencies and their companies. They can encourage their companies for investment in Afghanistan and initiating of relevant projects that can produce good results for all parties.

Bahaudin: Is the war-torn country ready for international investors and why should people invest in Afghanistan? What does Afghanistan offer to global firms such as McDonalds, Wal-Mart and other large chains?

Samizay: The international community must understand that the security and stability of Afghanistan is necessary and beneficial to the whole region, as well as to the world's stability and security. The international community must not fail this time in Afghanistan. Some of the large international investors argue about the security in Afghanistan, and refuse to invest and participate in projects due to poor security conditions in some areas. They argue that they cannot invest in Afghanistan unless comprehensive security measures are established. I think you cannot provide stability and security, unless you improve the economic situation in the country through large investments in capacity building, and the welfare of every citizen. The stability and security of Afghanistan directly depends on how we can change the life of ordinary individuals and improve their economic situation locally. Then the migration of population toward large cities may be slower, which will be a relief for the congestion that currently exists in many large cities. Let's be optimistic. I believe Afghans have the courage and enthusiasm to successfully rebuild their country. The history frequently shows such traits of Afghan patriotism and traditions. I am certain that this tradition will continue. May all Afghans, and the world community, work jointly to successfully advance peace, fairness and stability in Afghanistan and around the globe!

REFLECTIVE QUESTIONS FOR CRITICAL THINKING

1. Discuss some of the current realities in today's Afghanistan. What are some of the challenges and concerns?
2. What are the current leaders doing to resolve today's dilemmas in Afghanistan? What can and should they be doing to bring peace and prosperity to the country? Discuss.
3. Can both women and men be, and hold, leadership positions in Afghanistan?
4. What is the role of leadership in leading Afghanistan toward peace and security? What is the role of leadership in leading Afghanistan toward prosperity and economic development?
5. What are some of the challenges that Afghans face when they return to their country after ten to twenty years of being away?
6. What are some of the challenges for recruiting, attracting and retaining Afghan expatriates to work in Afghanistan?
7. Discuss various ways that the international community can encourage and support professional Afghans to return to Afghanistan during the rebuilding process?
8. Is the "divide and conquer" strategy real? Are individuals and governments able and willing to use such tactics to achieve their goals? Provide examples.
9. What are some of the causes of ethnic conflicts and animosities that seem to exist among people of different cultures in third-world countries? Discuss examples and thoughts.
10. Why do some individuals feel that globalization for developing economies can be similar to "economic terrorism" by the developed countries? Discuss the advantages and disadvantages of globalization from the perspectives of developed and third world countries.
11. Read the United Nations Charter as well as what they say about wars and the launching of such acts on other nations and countries. Then discuss why some of the United States' political leaders are blamed for launching an illegal "*War of Aggression*" against Iraq.

CHAPTER 9

CAPACITY BUILDING AND A CONVERSATION WITH AMBASSADOR JAWAD

There are many talented and committed individuals who simply want to help the country of Afghanistan become better and continue to prosper. These individuals, as seen from the examples of Dr. Samizay and other expatriate Afghans, have gone out of their way to do their homework and get the "education" needed to become model citizens and effective contributors in the rebuilding process. Another one of these individuals, who has contributed much to the improvement process in Afghanistan by speaking with leaders of developing nations to provide financial and human resources support, speaking on behalf of the Afghan people to the international community, and by assisting Afghans in the drafting of appropriate strategies and policies in Afghanistan is Ambassador Sayed Tayeb Jawad. For years, like many others around the world, I read his commentaries and contributions about Afghanistan. In the later months of 2004, I had the pleasure of personally meeting Ambassador Jawad at the Afghan Embassy in Washington D.C. He is a very personable, passionate and talented human being whose vision for the country of Afghanistan seems unconditional. In the months of January and February, despite his busy schedule both in Afghanistan as well as at the Embassy in Washington, he was kind enough to grant this interview. His thoughts, vision and views are presented in the proceeding pages and this author thanks Ambassador Jawad and Ashraf Haidari for making this interview possible. May they both succeed with their vision of making Afghanistan peaceful, and the most prosperous it has ever been.

SAYED TAYEB JAWAD: A BRIEF BIOGRAPHY

In March 2002, Ambassador Jawad returned to Afghanistan from the United States to assist in the rebuilding of Afghanistan. He served as the President Press Secretary and Chief of Staff, as well as the Director of the Office of International Relations at the Presidential Palace. Ambassador Jawad has worked closely with President Karzai and his administration in formulating strategies, implementing policies, building national institutions and prioritizing reforms in Afghanistan. He worked with U.S. and Afghan military officials to reform the Ministry of Defense and rebuild the Afghan National Army. He was instrumental in drafting the foreign investment laws and served as President Karzai's principal liaison with the constitutional commission during the process of the drafting of the new constitution. Under his leadership, the Afghan Embassy in Washington is emerging as one of the most successful missions in Washington. He also serves as Afghanistan non resident Ambassador to Mexico and Brazil, and accompanies President Karzai on most foreign trips.

Born in Kandahar, Afghanistan, Ambassador Jawad was educated at the Afghan French Lycée Istiqlal and School of Law and Political Sciences at Kabul University. Shortly after the Soviet invasion in 1980, he left Afghanistan and went into exile in Germany, where he studied law at Westfaelische Wilhelms University in Muenster. In 1986 he migrated to USA, where he received his MBA from Golden Gate University in San Francisco and worked for a number of prominent law firms.

Ambassador Jawad is a writer and commentator. He has published hundreds of articles and conducted numerous interviews with the international media throughout the world. He is fluent in English, German and French. He is married to Shamim Jawad, a financial consultant, and they have a son who is now about sixteen years of age.

CONVERSATION WITH AMBASSADOR JAWAD

Bahaudin: You spent the last few years working with the interim government of Afghanistan and now with the new administration. Obviously, you have seen many improvements in the country. How would you describe your personal experiences and observations in Afghanistan? In other words, what is some factual information that people outside of Afghanistan may not be aware of but should know?

Ambassador Jawad: I greatly enjoyed working with President Karzai and the Afghan leadership. Afghanistan is taking great strides. For the 3 million refugees that have returned to their homeland, the Afghan Government is responding by building shelters and creating initiatives to reintegrate them back into society. The Afghan Diaspora is contributing significantly to this rebuilding effort. The Back to School Campaign has been very successful in reopening hundreds of schools resulting in some 5.6 million children now being educated, 35% of whom are girls. We also reached an economic growth rate of 30% and 20%, respectively, during the first two years. These efforts have been, and continue to be, enhanced through our sustained partnership with the international community and their crucial support in the rebuilding effort of Afghanistan.

Successes in Afghanistan have been hard-earned but imperative to a prosperous future, and I consider it an honor and pleasure to work toward these goals for my people and country.

Bahaudin: You mentioned that you have enjoyed your service to Afghanistan and working with the current officials. What has made your service to Afghanistan enjoyable and, in your roles during the past few years, how have you contributed to the welfare of the Afghan community?

Ambassador Jawad: Leaving a lasting imprint on society, and seeing positive results makes my service to my country most enjoyable. The people who have been in need of help for many years truly appreciate the assistance that is being offered to them. Fortunately, this sense of responsibility of mine has been coupled with opportunities. The opportunity to have the privilege to interact with Afghans from remote areas and to see how pragmatic and appreciative our people are –

opportunity to work with President Karzai in advancing reforms, policies and strategies for my people – opportunity to work with military experts to rebuild the Afghan National Army and the opportunity to partake in the drafting of foreign investment laws for Afghanistan.

Bahaudin: Who are some government officials that you met and thought they were both visionary and enthusiastic about the future of Afghanistan? Can you describe what made their vision relevant and realistic for the people of the country?

Ambassador Jawad: The true visionaries are the Afghan people themselves. As I indicated, they have demonstrated their desire to live in a stable and prosperous society. On the day of the election, 8 million out of the 10.5 million eligible voters turned out to cast their ballot. For the first time in our history, our people elected their own leader and chose their own political destiny. The people of Afghanistan are demanding a social revolution. One can see the hope in their eyes and smiles. It is the people who are leading while the government officials follow them. The visionary leadership of President Karzai is a beacon of our effort to rebuild Afghanistan.

Bahaudin: Afghanistan is going through an infrastructure development process at this time. What is the status of development and progress in terms of business and management in the country thus far? What are some business opportunities for and management or entrepreneurship development? What are some of the businesses or organizations that are now doing really well in Afghanistan? What are some of the reasons for their successes?

Ambassador Jawad: Afghanistan is in a very exciting period of time. There are tremendous opportunities for visionary businesspeople to take part in its rebuilding effort. As well, the country has opened its doors for business and investment opportunities. After years of conflict and isolation, Afghanistan has re-entered the global marketplace and is effectively reintegrating. First, the people of Afghanistan adopted principles of a free market economy in the new constitution, and the Afghan government has taken steps to implement that vision. Second, the Afghan government has identified the growth of the private sector as a high priority, and reform efforts are focusing on removing obstacles to private sector development. Third, our government has expressed its intent on becoming a policymaker, not an implementer of projects, which provides companies with contracting opportunities. Thus, the efforts of the Afghan government have helped lay the foundation for successful business development. Furthermore, many international institutions involved in the reconstruction process – the United States Agency for International Development, Asian Development Bank, World Bank, IMF, and United Nations - to name a few, have their own contracting and procurement process, which present additional business development opportunities.

Since the fall of the Taliban, Afghanistan has experienced and continues to experience high rates of growth. Of course, the baseline in Afghanistan is low given the 23 year period of conflict, but one needs to keep in mind that with the destruction of infrastructure and institutions, our achievements have been remarkable, and particularly in the following areas:

- Restoration of the highways has been an overriding priority of President Karzai. It is crucial to extending the influence of the new government.

Many sections of Afghanistan's highway and regional road system are undergoing reconstruction. The U.S. Agency for International Development, with assistance from Japan, completed building a highway linking Kabul to the southern regional capital, Kandahar. Plans are in place to extend the road into Herat and arching it back through Mazar-e-Sharif and Kabul. This route will be referred to as the Ring Road. With its completion, all central Asian capitals will be only 32 hours from the Persian Gulf. Our next priority is to increase power generation and build water dams.

- In terms of business infrastructure, there is increased access to capital. This has greatly improved in the last two years. Loans for projects in Afghanistan are available through the International Finance Corporation and the Overseas Private Investment Corporation (OPIC). Political risk insurance is available through OPIC and the Multilateral Guarantee Agency. Additionally, the first venture capital fund was announced this year, Afghanistan Capital Partners, and more venture capitalists are beginning to see the opportunities in Afghanistan.

- The industrial parks offer power, water, sewer and road connections that will allow investors to establish factories, plants and offices. Thus, while the government works with donors on improving physical infrastructure countrywide, the development of industrial parks can meet most investors' business infrastructure needs.

- The business environment has quickly improved in the area of banking and financial institutions. The Afghan government passed a new Banking Law in September 2003. Shortly afterward, licenses were issued. In April 2004, more than five international banks were operational in the country. This has greatly improved the country's business infrastructure since there is a mechanism to transfer and deposit funds inside Afghanistan.

- Since Afghanistan has always been characterized by a strong trading tradition, there are business organizations and chambers of commerce. In 2004, the Afghanistan International Chamber of Commerce was launched, with affiliates planned in different countries. Thus, there are mechanisms in place to identify local partners if needed, facilitating business and investment.

- There are also business opportunities through contracting and subcontracting with various institutions. Another major achievement for the Afghan government was the creation of the Afghanistan Reconstruction and Development Service, (ARDS), which handles procurement of Afghan government funded projects using internationally recognized procurement regulations. This open and transparent online system has made offering goods and services for Afghan government funded projects much easier.

Success stories include major companies such as DHL, Siemens, Alcatel, Hyatt and 11 foreign banks already invested in Afghanistan. Eleven private banks have received their licenses from the Central Bank in the past three years. The National Bank, Pashtani Tejarati, Standard Chartered, Pakistan National Bank and

Aryan Bank are among those private banks doing well in Afghanistan. Therefore, although there are many challenges, there are also many opportunities for business managers and entrepreneurs interested in Afghanistan.

Bahaudin: How would you describe the leadership in the new government and their vision for Afghanistan? How will such new leaders and their visions change the country of Afghanistan in the next few decades?

Ambassador Jawad: The new Afghan Cabinet consists of educated and qualified individuals, who are determined to establish a democratic state that will build on our rich traditions, and will make Afghanistan a long-term partner of the international community. All ministers have a higher education. It also reflects broadly the ethnic composition of the country, with Pashtuns, Tajiks, Hazaras, Uzbeks as well as Turkman and Baluch. Three women are in the cabinet including the former presidential candidate, Masuda Jalal.

Bahaudin: How would you describe the current government's entrepreneurship philosophy? What are they doing to attract more international businesses and organizations to invest in Afghanistan?

Ambassador Jawad: The private sector is to serve as the engine for growth in Afghanistan. Since a new currency was successfully introduced, a stable exchange rate against international currencies has been maintained. Businesses in Afghanistan are now experiencing an inflation free environment, ensuring the autonomy of the banking sector. After enacting a new banking law, several international banks have opened branches in Kabul and we expect more.

A new investment law has also been enacted and an open trade regime has been introduced. Traders and investors are faced with limited tariffs. Border formalities are being reduced to a minimum. In addition, we have set up, with the assistance of the German government, a one-stop-shop for investors known as the Afghan Investment Support Agency. To meet international standards, a National Bureau of Standards is now being established.

Bahaudin: Is the Afghan workforce ready for the progress envisioned by the government leaders? If not, what are your recommendations? How can the international community and other expatriate professional Afghans assist in the development?

Ambassador Jawad: In general, Afghanistan lacks human capital. Our workforce needs to be educated and trained. In this regard, we strongly favor plans, such as exchange programs, that will be aimed at training our citizens to serve as a more effective work force. We need increased training and education opportunities.

Bahaudin: Afghanistan created and instituted their new Constitution just about two years ago. Is the New Constitution able to keep a balance with the culture of Afghanistan and the expectations of the international community? What are some tasks and behavioral expectations needed from all adults in Afghanistan to make sure they live according to the intentions of the New Constitution?

Ambassador Jawad: Our new Constitution, which was signed by President Karzai on January 4, 2004, is a balanced national charter. It provides for equal rights and full participation of women. It seeks and finds equilibrium between building a strong central executive branch (to further strengthen national unity and rebuild the national institutions) and respecting the rights and volition of the provinces to exercise more authority in managing their own local affairs. It is also a careful combination of respect for moderate and traditional values of the Afghan society and adherence to the international norms of human rights and democracy. Our constitution further reveals that our Islamic and traditional values are fully compatible and mutually reinforcing with an open democracy. The Afghan people are satisfied with their constitution as it is serving as a guideline to achieve a civil society. The people of Afghanistan have illustrated their demand for a democracy. During the Constitutional Loya Jirga in December of 2004, 502 Afghans from all walks of life and every province and community of the country gathered together, put all intricate issues on the table, and after three weeks of intense debate and emotional deliberations adopted, with near unanimous acclamation, the most progressive constitution in the region. As we will be holding our Parliamentary elections in a few months time, we need to educate people about the culture of a Parliament and political parties.

Bahaudin: Many people in the United States may see Afghanistan as being controlled mostly by warlords and drug traffickers. Is this true to some extent or mostly misinformation? Please give us your thoughts and views. How can Afghans and the international community better deal with elimination of drug trafficking in Afghanistan and around the world?

Ambassador Jawad: This is an incorrect perception. The Elections proved who is in charge. Despite speculation that local warlords would be able to disrupt this process, the elections were successfully held with almost no serious security threats or intimidation. However, our government needs to increase its capacity to deliver services to all corners of the country. We have made progress in forming and strengthening our military institutions. With the assistance of our international partners, we now have an almost 17,000 strong Afghan National Army (ANA) and are aiming to increase this number to 40,000 by the end of this year. In addition, we have an almost 30,000 strong police force which are actively performing their duties or are in training. We are seeking to significantly increase this number as well. On the issue of narcotics, we realize that this is a problem that cannot be solved soon. The Afghan Government has enacted a "National Drug Strategy" to reduce drastically poppy cultivation and encourage alternative income streams. In our new Cabinet, we now have a Ministry of Counter-narcotics and are hopeful that it will improve coordination among the various initiatives being undertaken in the fields of eradication and interdiction. In addition, while the UK is the lead nation in the counter narcotics effort, the Afghan Government and the U.S. Administration have devised a more aggressive strategy. The new strategy, which will be launched this year, consists of five main components: Public Information, Law Enforcement, Alternative Livelihood, Aggressive Interdiction and Eradication. To fund this strategy, the United States will provide some $780 million.

Bahaudin: How do Afghans view the intentions of the United States of America with regards to business development in the country? Is the International Community doing what they can to assist in the speedy recovery of business infrastructure throughout Afghanistan?

Ambassador Jawad: Afghanistan's principal markets and trading partners include Pakistan, South Korea, China, Japan, India, UAE, Germany, UK, United

States, and Russia. In April, Afghanistan hosted a trade and investment conference for the Economic Cooperation Organization (ECO), and Afghanistan was selected as headquarters for a two-year period by its regional member countries. Thus, Afghans are very open to business and trade from any country in the world. Most Afghans view products from the United States as representing high quality and thus welcome investments from U.S. companies. Any companies that can create jobs, help substitute for imports, and generate opportunities, are wanted. Afghanistan has a long history of working with the U.S., especially USAID, to improve infrastructure in the country. Afghans continue to welcome the U.S.'s assistance in improving the country's business infrastructure and also working with the U.S. private sector through joint ventures, contracts and other business opportunities. In terms of international assistance for infrastructure improvements, many donors, including the United States, Japan, India and others have supported the improvement of the country's road network. The Asian Development Bank and World Bank are assisting in improvements in transportation, water, power and energy. Private investment in communications and logistics has also ameliorated the business infrastructure. However, given the lack of development during the period of conflict, Afghanistan needs greater assistance from the international community in order to rehabilitate and improve the country's basic infrastructure. Improvements in this area have many positive secondary benefits. By supporting a better environment for business and trade, Afghanistan will be less dependent in the long-term on foreign aid. We hope that donors and international financial institutions will increase commitments to infrastructure improvements. It is an investment not only in Afghanistan, but also in regional stability and economic development.

Bahaudin: Are there female entrepreneurs, managers, and leaders in Afghanistan? What are some of the typical business opportunities for female leaders in Kabul? Also, based on your views, what can the government officials do to increase management and leadership opportunities for Afghan females?

Ambassador Jawad: Yes, there are many female entrepreneurs, managers and leaders in Afghanistan. However, just like other entrepreneurs in Afghanistan, they need assistance to meet their full potential. Given the lack of opportunities and education during the period of conflict, especially during the time of the Taliban, typical business opportunities for women in Kabul are in handicrafts, carpet weaving, and small-scale industry. Recently, women have entered the service industry, including operating hair salons, dress shops and guesthouses. Women who have acquired the skills are also able to engage in other sectors. For example, Cisco has sponsored a learning academy in Kabul that is training women in computer, networking and IT skills. There are already many women who were educated abroad that have brought back information technology skills that they are applying in this sector. Women who receive such training in Afghanistan will then also be able to enter jobs in this market.

Women who were educated prior to the conflict in Afghanistan or who were educated in Pakistan, Iran or other countries are able to find opportunities in the workforce and in different business areas. Many women work for UN agencies, nonprofit organizations and private companies. These women are well equipped to start or operate their own businesses if they have access to capital and are therefore poised to become our country's future business leaders. Women outside of Kabul are engaged as well in handicrafts and carpet weaving, but are also involved in the country's agricultural sector. Many women own land, farms or small-scale agricultural businesses, including milk production, dried fruits and nuts, and canning and pickling of fruits and vegetables. Given access to capital, equipment and knowledge of marketing their products, these women will be able to expand upon their entrepreneurial talents. Women's entrepreneurship has been important to the Afghan government. In 2003, the Ministry of Commerce instituted the Entrepreneurship Development for Afghan Women office (EDAW) with the assistance of USAID's Economic Governance program. EDAW provides English, computer and business training for Afghan women. Women in this program have participated in regional trade shows, and met with foreign companies interested in employing or working with Afghan women. This year, they have launched the Afghan Women's Business Association and a journal dedicated to women's business issues. The Association plans to grow to cities outside of Kabul and to strengthen Afghan women's participation in business. The Afghan government encourages donors, nonprofit organizations and private companies to support projects that provide training and tools Afghan women need to become business owners. One of these areas is access to capital. Many organizations are supporting micro-credit programs, such as CARE, FINCA, and others. The UN also designated 2005 as the Year of Micro Credit and chose Afghanistan as one of eight focus countries. In November 2004, eight Afghan entrepreneurs, including many women, were given awards for their ability to use micro finance to start or expand their businesses. These programs have greatly assisted Afghan women entrepreneurs in the past two years. Ultimately, it will be the private sector that will be the key to providing opportunities for women that are sustainable. The Afghan government will continue to work on education and training programs to benefit Afghan women and will support initiatives that build their capacity to engage in business. In order to do this, the sustained assistance of the international community is vital.

Bahaudin: Will tourism be a good opportunity for business professionals in Kabul or other parts of Afghanistan? When do you think the country will be safe enough to where tourists can travel for sightseeing and vacationing?

Ambassador Jawad: Tourism is a growing sector and there are already many opportunities for business professionals. Due to many foreigners already traveling to Afghanistan for government, business and humanitarian projects, the demand for tourist related services is high. Afghan companies have already partnered with major companies and are building hotels such as the Hyatt Hotel and Intercontinental Hotel. There are numerous guesthouses that have opened in the city, as well as restaurants started by business entrepreneurs from China, Iran, the Philippines, Germany and the United States. Kabul now boasts a Chinese restaurant, Thai restaurant, and steakhouse as well as pizza parlors and cafes. Services such as transportation, communication and numerous others are also quickly being offered by the private sector to fulfill the demand from business and tourists. The issue in Afghanistan to promote tourism is one of infrastructure rather than security. Specialized tourism such as eco-tourism, historical tourism, and outdoor/adventure tourism have great potential in Afghanistan given its interesting topography and landscape. In 2002, a nonprofit organization based in the U.S. called Global Exchange, organized the first tours to Afghanistan. In August of 2004, a U.S. tour company called Distant Horizons, organized the first commercial based historical tour of Afghanistan since the fall of the Taliban. A group of 20 American tourists went on the two-week journey. As infrastructure improves and the remaining security issues are resolved in the border area between Afghanistan and Pakistan, tourism will once again draw travelers from around the globe. Given the hospitality of the Afghan people, this will be a sector of great potential for business and investment.

Bahaudin: What advice do you offer for Afghan professionals living outside of the country that want to help? How can they assist their motherland without leaving their current jobs?

Ambassador Jawad: Hundreds of prominent Afghan intellectuals, experts and entrepreneurs have returned to their country to assist in enhancing institutional capacity building or making major investments. Afghans who are living abroad can also play a positive role in the rebuilding effort of their country. They can organize and serve as effective advocacy groups, by actively speaking out or writing in favor of continued assistance for Afghanistan, and can also advise our government on how to implement projects.

Bahaudin: Is the war –torn country ready for international investors and why should people invest in Afghanistan? What does Afghanistan offer to global firms such as McDonalds, Wal-Mart, and other large chains?

Ambassador Jawad: Yes, Afghanistan is ready for international investors and has already welcomed many of them. A major achievement in 2003 was the creation of the Afghan Investment Support Agency (AISA), within the framework of the Ministry of Commerce to facilitate and promote investment in Afghanistan. AISA is the "One Stop Shop for Investors" and is responsible for the registration, licensing and promotion of all new investments in Afghanistan. AISA has been able to get rid of unnecessary bureaucracy and red tape and shorten the investment registration/licensing process from several months to just five days. Thus, the process to begin an investment in Afghanistan has been streamlined. Some of the major reasons to invest in Afghanistan include:

- One of the lowest custom tariffs in the region
- Low tax rates
- Low labor costs
- A growing domestic consumer market
- An opportunity to create employment for women
- An eager and committed work force
- Location and ability to reach neighboring markets
- Freely exchangeable currency, which has experienced remarkable stability
- Liberal investment law passed in 2002 that allows 100% foreign ownership, full transferability of profits outside the country, international dispute resolution mechanisms, and streamlined investment licensing procedures

Some of the key sectors for investment include:

- Agriculture
- Architectural, construction and engineering services
- Building and construction materials
- Power generation and transmission
- Oil and gas exploration
- Telecommunications
- Food processing
- Manufacturing
- Textiles and carpets
- Education services
- Consumer Electronics
- Transportation
- Equipment and machinery sales and leasing
- Irrigation technology
- Leather and leather processing
- Precious and semi-precious stones
- Marble and other industrial stones

These are just some of the sectors available for investment. Afghanistan's abundant mineral resources and agricultural raw materials, linked with considerable potential energy resources, provide a favorable scope for industrialization efforts. In addition, Afghan carpets, dried fruits and nuts enjoyed a reputation for quality and taste in the region, and large markets are available to absorb those products again. Afghanistan is not only an emerging market, but is a gateway to investment in Central Asia. A major part of the reconstruction plan has been connecting the nation to neighboring countries to make it a key transit point in the region. With increasing stability and increasing investments in roads, railways and air routes, entrepreneurs can trade not only with Afghanistan, but also with Central and South Asia. Already, goods are flowing from Central to South Asia, from India to Iran and back. Thus, by investing in Afghanistan, you are not only accessing a market of 25 million, but a market of 150 million just in the areas immediately surrounding Afghanistan.

Bahaudin: What are some things that the international community should know about the people of Afghanistan, their hopes and their desires? What are your best memories from the past few years as you toured Afghanistan?

Ambassador Jawad: Our people genuinely believe in engagement with the international community and have put their trust in the benefits of partnership. The only concern that Afghans have about our international friends is that they will leave too soon. Every time I visit Afghanistan, I am overwhelmed by the hospitality of our people and beauty of our country.

Bahaudin: I want to thank you for taking the time to share your thoughts with me and the readers. I wish you total success with the vision of rebuilding Afghanistan to make it a healthy, wealthy and prosperous country for each and every Afghan. Finally, what advice would you offer to an entrepreneur seeking to break into the business industry in Afghanistan?

Ambassador Jawad: The advice I can offer to an entrepreneur is to take advantage of the opportunities that are available from investment in a wide variety of sectors. Visionary investors have invested in Afghanistan and are making sizable profits. The markets are less competitive right now. This provides a great opportunity for "First Movers" to make large amounts of earnings. Afghanistan is the largest market in Central Asia and can serve as a trade hub for neighboring countries. Kabul is the largest city in Central Asia in terms of population, with high demands for consumer goods. Further stabilization and reconstruction of Afghanistan will re-establish the country's role as a land bridge between Central Asia, South Asia, and Southwest Asia – a historic and growing market with a total GDP of $ 4 trillion.

CAPACITY BUILDING LEADERSHIP

Afghanistan is moving forward on the highway of progress and development faster than speeding trains, a pace which can be difficult for some people or agencies to keep up with it; yet, by some people's standards, the progress is perceived to be moving at a pace slower than a turtle which can easily get "run over" or injured by oncoming traffic. While researchers can debate whose perspective is accurate and what the solutions are, this author focused on the constraints which must be looked at for the speedy progress of people's mindset and overall outlook. What Afghans, collectively, can mentally perceive and believe will be what they actually achieve in the years to come. The mindset constraints come from the fact that years of war and militaristic oppression has caused many individuals to rely upon their own independent powers or abilities, local leaders, freedom fighters, and/or governmental forces.

Independency can be problematic as one can only get so far without depending on others. Paternalistic mindsets, on the other side, can hold people back from risk-taking and innovation which are needed for a speedy progress and development. Furthermore, paternalistic mindsets can cause dependency on the public sector...which due to standardized rules and bureaucracy can at times appear to move at a snail's pace. So, the best paradigm is to live interdependently with local, national and international professionals and associations if Afghanistan is to realize maximum benefits from the highway of progress and development. Overall, with regard to foundational assessment, this book has discussed dependency, independency, interdependency, qualifications and prerequisites for leadership, and continuous learning.

To hope for any kind of a bright future in Afghanistan anytime soon, we need to have and appoint leaders who can avoid self-serving political strategies, and focus their efforts toward accomplishing what is best for the people of the country. Some leaders focus on promoting their own influence, while others focus on protecting the borders and soils of the country, which is not nearly as important as caring for the lives of those who live on that soil. As such, the right local individuals with the prerequisite skills should be nominated, selected, and appointed to management, development and official government positions. There must also be an ongoing training and development process to make sure these appointed leaders and professionals are continually "sharpening their saw." Through an interdependent paradigm and leadership, people must be given a voice and heard in matters that affect their livelihood. People must also be educated to see the future more clearly, not only in terms of their own well-being, but also in terms of everyone in the society. The secret to a truly empowered society, where people can make informed decisions, would be to share information with everyone so they can become better educated. When people are prepared to think for themselves, and are members of an autonomous society, they will be contributing more to themselves' and their people's wellbeing. Afghanistan needs leaders that would help everyone become educated, liberated, and leaders that would let them appoint government officials that are "people-driven" instead of self-centered and power motivated. These leaders should stick to the path and not give in to the pressures of the self-aggrandized warlords, outsiders and other rival forces. What is right must be done even if nobody is doing it, and what is wrong should not be done, even if all others are on this path.

In the mean time, Afghans should live and learn simultaneously as they enjoy a speedy transition to becoming independent and soon live in an interdependent or interrelated world. As leaders, Afghans managers, professionals and officials should have a clear vision of the future and must create safeguards to avoid any loopholes and short-comings. A leader's moral rectitude, creativity and charisma can affect all citizens in a positive way, if it is purposefully directed toward them or a general vision. A leader cannot survive or even become a great leader without the involvement of all relevant stakeholders. Political leaders can use innovative methods to involve people and challenge them to do the best they can for their country. The future is getting brighter for the people of Afghanistan, as can be seen from the building of relevant relationships with the international community. We must remember that healthy interdependent relationships with the international community and continuous learning within the country are not attained by chance. Such great initiative must be sought for with ardor, collectively by organized groups of individuals within the country and attended to with diligence, and fortunately, many Afghans are doing this passionately.

As can be seen from the visions of Dr. Samizay and Ambassador Jawad, it is apparent that many Afghan leaders are passionately focused on rebuilding Afghanistan, by providing an infrastructure that speeds up the process of enabling the population's capacity. This is good inspiration as they provide hope for millions of individuals throughout the world. Within the next twenty years, it is estimated that about 2 billion more individuals will be living and sharing this planet with us. It is also estimated that about 95% of the growth in population will be taking place in developing countries such as Afghanistan, Pakistan, India, and others. This growth will create unprecedented demands for additional and better infrastructure capacity in energy, food, land, water, transportation, materials, waste disposal, health care, environmental cleanup, and information technology. The role of effective leadership in education, manufacturing, engineering, information systems, and other such technical and non-technical fields will be critical in fulfilling the estimated demands on a proactive basis. The best vehicle for achieving this endeavor is to provide the infrastructure and resources for leaders to focus on capacity building so people can help themselves.

Creating a sustainable world that provides a safe, secure, healthy, productive, and sustainable life for everyone should become a priority for twenty-first century leaders. All professionals have a collective responsibility to work toward meeting the upcoming demands by creating appropriate and sustainable solutions for communication, water, sanitation, food, health, and energy while protecting the cultural and natural diversity that exist among various ethnicities. It is estimated that at least thirty to forty million people around the world are living in hunger, and improving the lives of these individuals, whose main concern is to stay alive, is an obligation for all leaders in Afghanistan and throughout the world. It is also estimated that about four to five million of the Afghan population are the "poorest of the poor," as they live without many of the basic necessities of life, while trying to survive on what mother-nature provides them through its natural resources.

Researchers and experts agree that "problems of the developing world cannot be solved by separate individuals, groups, disciplines, and institutions (big or small) or through short-term piecemeal actions." Researchers and experts recommend that "these problems must be addressed collectively by collaborations and partnerships that bridge across national and international boundaries, age groups, races, genders, cultures, and disciplines." As such, appropriate decisions must be made at various levels (global, regional, local, and individual) and over different time scales. It must be acknowledged that there is no such thing as one unique solution to all the issues facing the developing world.

Each profession's duty, along with the duties of all business and corporate leaders, is to work towards meeting the needs of the developing world by adopting a new paradigm or mindset that embraces the principles of effective leadership, sustainability, renewable resources, appropriate technology, and systems thinking. Today's technical and non-technical leaders, are encouraged to hone their traditional technical skills and people skills, as they develop the ability to work in collaboration with non-technical experts, and communicate effectively with people across different cultures and practices.

There is a need to educate a new generation of well-rounded globally responsible managers and leaders, to better meet the challenges and needs of the developing world, and offer sustainable and appropriate technology solutions to the endemic problems faced by developing communities worldwide. Both technical and non-technical leaders can become facilitators of sustainable development and social change, using effective leadership skills, if we are to meet the needs of the growing population in a timely manner while creating a peaceful world. Capacity building of individuals living in the developing countries should be addressed from diverse yet complimentary perspectives, by bringing together participants from industry, government, university, humanitarian organizations and, Non-Governmental Organizations of all disciplines.

If people, especially business leaders and managers, believe in, adhere to, and internalize ethical principles and moral standards and values, people and businesses will be afforded a considerably greater opportunity to continue, succeed, and flourish. Leaders must have good intentions and, at least attempt to, preach what they say they would do if they are to influence others. Chaney and Green (2002), in their article *"Actions speak louder than words,"* state that how leaders dress, their body language, vocal characteristics, and use of visuals when speaking to a group, largely determines whether they and their organizations are perceived as credible. The authors further mention that a speaker's credibility is linked to preparation and the effective use of his or her time. So, as leaders and managers present their vision to others, they need to know their audience because it is desirable to culturally fit into the audience (colleagues, employees, friends, vendors, community members, etc.) and make them feel comfortable.

The Indian writer, J. Krishnamurti, once said that "In oneself lies the whole world, and if you know how to look and learn, then the door is there and the key is in your hand. Nobody on earth can give you either that key or the door to open, except yourself." Living with honor and integrity may come at the price of learning, patience, and standing up for what is right, which are all virtuous endeavors for all Afghans. However, living with honor, by being honest and standing up for what is right, is the only way that one can remain truly happy in the long-term and become successful in the business of life. The Persian poet, Khushal Khan Khatak, once said, "Without honor and glory - What is the Afghan story," speaking about the integrity associated with his people and community. Another Indian poet is credited for saying, "I slept and dreamt that life was beauty - I woke and found that life was duty," emphasizing that honor and glory can be earned by truthfully performing one's duties. The proceeding poem emphasizes why learning about ethics and effective leadership are important for all human beings. The poem titled "*Life Is a Bother Life Is a Hurry*" is written by Charles Jarvis and it shows the importance of doing what is right while one has the opportunity to do so. Jarvis said:

> *Life is a bother, life is a hurry*
> *Life is a busy crowded way*
> *Good intentions go astray*
> *I had a friend the other day.*

> *I have not anymore, he passed away*
> *I meant to write, to phone, to call*
> *I did not do any of those at all.*

> *I only hope that he can now see*
> *How much his friendship meant to me*
> *Life is a busy crowded way*
> *Good intentions go astray.*

Yet life does not have to be "a busy crowded way," and good intentions would not go astray, if one is able to cherish and feed important relationships every day, and take appropriate actions in the present as opposed to waiting for someday. Having a clear conscience due to the successful performance of one's duties with honor and integrity can greatly assist in being victorious in the race of life. With a clear conscience and moral character, Afghan leaders will always be able to get up each time they fall and will eventually win their race with honor and integrity. As stated in "Law of the Harvest," one usually reaps what one has sown. Law of the

Harvest states: Sow a thought, reap an action; Sow an action, reap a habit; Sow a habit, reap a character; and sow a character, reap a destiny.

Mother Teresa created a destiny and the status of sainthood for herself because of her thoughts, actions, habits, and character. She is quoted as saying that "People are sometimes unreasonable, illogical, and self-centered; forgive them, anyway." She further stated:

- If you are kind, people may accuse you of selfish, ulterior motives. Be kind anyway.
- If you are successful, you will win some false friends and some true enemies. Succeed anyway.
- If you are honest and frank, people may cheat you. Be honest and frank anyway.
- What you spend years building, someone could destroy overnight. Build anyway.
- If you find serenity and happiness, they may be jealous. Be happy anyway.
- The good you do today, people will often forget tomorrow. Do good anyway.
- Give the world the best you have, and it may never be enough. Give the world the best you've got anyway.
- You see, in the final analysis, it is between you and your creator. It was never between you and them anyway.

The key is to stand for good causes, to do good deeds, and to encourage others who are harming themselves or innocent bystanders in the society to get on the right path. With regard to taking good actions, Albert Einstein said that "The world is a dangerous place, not because of those who do evil, but because of those who look on and do nothing." As stated previously, it is up to each individual to give his or her "best" to the world through worthwhile and calculated actions. We cannot change the past, but we can change our behaviors in terms of what we do now and in the future. Change is most effective when it starts from within, and each person should take personal responsibility for his or her own personal as well as professional growth and development. It is important to believe that "*I* must be a productive individual and a good leader in order to effectively contribute to the goal of creating a peaceful environment for *all*." The key is to start with "I" and end with "all." Of course, *being* productive individuals, and *becoming* effective leaders, is a good start for each person, since individuals have the most control over their own behaviors. The terms "being" and "becoming" are both verbs, which require action since intentions of doing something have really never resulted in much productivity. Afghan people and leaders know that good intentions are not sufficient for them to rebuild their country. So, they must be able to convert their intentions into deliverable actions effectively and synergistically, while working with national and international allies toward interdependent relationships. In the process, Afghan people and leaders must take the advice of Mother Teresa by being kind, honest, frank, happy, doing good, giving their best, and by leaving this world a little better than they found it regardless of what other say or do. May all Afghans be hopeful, faithful, and successful in achieving peace and prosperity!

BECOME THE "*LAULA*" FLOWER

In Afghanistan's several mountainous provinces, where people did not have electricity, it was customary to regularly gather wood and other "dried-crunchy" bushes that grow in the mountains before the winter season, so they can be used as firewood for cooking and keeping the house warm. During the winter, most of the mountains are covered with snow and it would be too cold to go out. As a result, most people worked on gathering enough of these bushes and firewood throughout the year so they could be comfortable in the winter season. During my teenage years, I was once gathering the thorny bushes for usage as "firewood" along the Khoshie mountains with my youngest uncle (Ghulam Farooq) and my grandfather (Ghulam Sawar, we referred to him as *Shah'aghah*). Typically, we would travel to the areas of the mountain where we could easily gather the most amounts of bushes or "firewood" in the least amount of time. Often it would take about an hour or two to get there, and then another four to eight hours to gather all that we could carry back on tops of two to three donkeys. The gathered bushes would be arranged, pushed down, and stacked in an organized manner so they could easily be loaded on the donkeys for the trip home. When we reached the bottom of one mountain about two hours away from home, there seemed to be miles and miles of weeds and thorny, dangerous bushes. Among the thousands of prickly and thorny bushes and millions of weeds covering the area, about one-hundred yards away, to my surprise, there was a beautiful red "laula" flower standing tall and distinctive, as well as implicitly making a statement that I "own" this area through my unique, bright colors and natural beauty. Laula flowers look like tulips, and are bright red, very slim and light, and they can grow anywhere in the mountains and deserts of Afghanistan where there is some rain and available sunlight. The fact that there were so many sharp, thorny, and dangerous bushes around it did not seem to bother its existence one bit. As soon as this beautiful laula flower captured my attention, as well as that of my uncle's, we immediately and simultaneously ran toward it, each trying to get the flower first. We both began holding each other and quarrelling in trying to stop the other from getting near it first. We were each arguing about who saw it first and why the person who saw it first should get it. Amid the struggle and wrestling, we each fell on the ground and got all kinds of thorns in our hands, legs, and "behinds." Parts of my fingers and arms began bleeding as I was pulling the "needle-looking" sharp and thorny bush-pieces out. Noticing the bickering and our struggle, my grandfather came, sat next to the flower, smelled the laula flower, and said "this is a beautiful flower and it would be a shame to pull it out of the ground and kill it." He further mentioned that "This is a brave laula flower which has grown and maintained its identity among so many dangerous and ugly thorny bushes. It makes the area look nice and pretty. If you pull it out for yourself, then its life will be over within the next ten or so minutes and you will no longer be able to enjoy its beauty. However, if you protect it from the ugly bushes, and feed it by pouring some of your drinking water at its root, then you can enjoy looking at this entire picturesque area all day long while we are here. So, the choice of what to do is yours." Then, as well-behaved teenagers we suppressed our selfish desires and poured some water at its root so that the beautiful laula flower could keep us company all day long.

During lunch, we sat next to it, ate our food, drank some tea, and did our afternoon prayers. When we left, the laula flower still looked beautiful, and we were certain that it was going to not only survive among the so many weeds and thorny bushes, but there would eventually be more of them as well.

Today, Afghanistan has many "laula" flowers that are helping the country attract attention, investments, and more colorful and diverse forms of tulips, roses, lilies, daisies, jasmine, marigolds, carnations, gardenias, magnolias, and orchids from around the globe. These different and beautiful flowers represent the kind-hearted, intelligent and well-intentioned people of Afghanistan. Among the violence and "thorny" obstacles facing the Afghan people, there will continue to be beautiful and strong individuals that will stand out like the "laula" flower among the bushes. They should be cherished, encouraged, developed, and joined by others. Each Afghan should be like the laula flower. Most importantly, each Afghan should also protect and feed all the "laula" flowers that surface and the others that they see and notice.

During the review process of this book, a dear colleague asked, how does one become a "laula" flower in a desert or wilderness where one is constantly surrounded by so many ugly "weeds" and "thorny bushes" that at times injure, hurt, and cause pain to people that come in contact with them? This is a fair question and one that requires individual reflection by each person; while the answer to this question is easy, the implementation of the answers can be difficult without a clear vision, strong values, patience, and persistency. Laula flowers make the environment bright, shiny and pleasant simply due to their existence and beauty. Similarly, each human being can make this world a little better through his/her existence and behaviors. One can make this world a little better by leaving it in a better shape than when he/she was born in it. Each person should reflect on how he or she is actually making the environment a little better due to his/her existence. The environment is often a reflection of our own "collective" thoughts, actions and behaviors; if we cause pain and injury to others, then this pain and suffering is going to continue to circle around and eventually trap us within it. So, in order to change the environment, we must change our own "collective" thoughts, values and beliefs regarding peace and its achievement. The laula flower has no intentions of ever taking anyone's space and it never hurts its neighbors; it simply grows where it can, and makes the world a little more colorful regardless of what else is growing in the environment. The laula flower lives peacefully and cheerfully with every neighbor regardless of the level of diversity. Are you making the environment better through your existence by being there and listening to others? Or, are you simply another weed or a prickly, sharp, or barbed bush that is occupying space or causing pain to others due to your existence? Simply put, are you a joy to be around or simply another thorn on people's "backside"? Reflect, think and see how you can make this world a little better than it actually is today. Then, continue to be a laula flower and live peacefully in whatever environment you have been given an opportunity to grow.

The laula flowers appear very weak, since even a mild wind can "push" them around; yet, amid chaos and mild winds, instead of resisting, they simply remain flexible and "bend" in the wind's direction without losing their identity. As the wind subsides, the laula flowers often immediately stand tall and continue to have a radiant appearance that is enjoyable and amusing to the eyes. In other words, the laula flowers are always beautiful in their own way, and they usually make the environment pleasant due to their existence without ever saying anything, forcing their opinions on other people, or talking to anyone about their likes or dislikes. Perhaps people can become like the laula flower by smiling often, clarifying their values and living according to universal principals, building trust with other people, listening to others intently instead of always trying to get their own points across first, and living with integrity by consistently delivering on their promises and doing what they said they would. As mentioned before, the terms "being" and "becoming" are both verbs, which require predetermined and worthwhile goals and actions. As laula flowers, Afghan people can effectively and synergistically live and co-exist with their neighbors, while working with national and international allies through interdependent relationships. As laula flowers, Afghan people and leaders can smile and remain kind, honest, frank, flexible, adaptable, pleasant, just, hopeful, faithful, and successful in achieving peace and prosperity. Consequently, a better world and eternal happiness will be the natural outcome.

POEMS FOR AFGHANS LEADING THE WAY TO PROGRESS!

As professionals, all Afghan leaders should "romanticize" for better days if they are to be visionaries and futuristic. Eva Gregory, coach and author, said "I see no point in looking back at what I did not get done. I choose, instead, to acknowledge where I am and where I want to be; then determine what steps it will take to get me there." Wisdom comes from experiencing an event, an idea, a concept, or an endeavor; therefore, all failures and negative events can be viewed as experiences which lead to knowledge. Professionals are good people, and they are good because they have come to wisdom often through learning, experimentation and failure. Ralph Waldo Emerson, philosopher and author, said that "Bad times have a scientific value. These are occasions a good learner would not miss." There is very little wisdom in success. So, success should be judged accordingly as Robert Louis Stevenson, author, said "Do not judge each day by the harvest you reap... but by the seeds you plant."

Effective leaders plan for learning and success through experimentation, structure, progress, and prioritization. Napoleon Hill, author, said "Reduce your plan to writing... The moment you complete this, you will have definitely given concrete form to the intangible desire." Professionals become leaders, because they are able to commit to these tangible desires and convert them into action. Anthony Robbins, motivational speaker, suggests that "Deciding to commit yourself to long-term results rather than short-term fixes is as important as any decision you'll make in your lifetime." Ben Stein, actor and author says, "The indispensable first step to getting the things you want out of life is this: decide what you want." This hard work of spending time to make the right decisions about a specific direction can be very worthwhile. Another author by the name of Ralph Marston said, "The creativity and positive energy you put forth come back to you many times over. So do the hurt and destruction. Which would you rather get back?" Once a decision has been made, then put your heart into its achievement. William James of Harvard University said, "Most people never run far enough on their first wind to find out if they've got a second. Give your dreams all you've got and you'll be amazed at the energy that comes out of you." According to Professor James, "It is our attitude at the beginning of a difficult task which, more than anything else, will affect its successful outcome."

Instead of focusing on being more determined, some people are way too concerned about their competitors and the actions of others. Grace Lichtenstein, author, wrote that "Your opponent, in the end, is never really the player on the other side of the net, or the swimmer in the next lane, or the team on the other side of the field, or even the bar you must high-jump. Your opponent is yourself, your negative internal voices, your level of determination."

Charles Kettering, inventor and businessman said the following about imagination: "Our imagination is the only limit to what we can hope to have in the future." Julian Simon, economist, put it nicely when he said "The main fuel to speed the world's progress is our stock of knowledge, and the brake is our lack of imagination." Besides determination and imagineering, one needs to envision the results and final outcomes. "Think and feel yourself there! To achieve any aim in life, you need to project the end-result. Think of the elation, the satisfaction, the joy! Carrying the ecstatic feeling will bring the desired goal into view" said author Grace Speare. Commitments must be aligned with one's actions and beliefs in order for progress and success to follow. Dorothea Brande, author, said, "All that is necessary to break the spell of inertia and frustration is this: act as if it were impossible to fail. That is the talisman, the formula, the command of right- about-face that turns us from failure toward success."

Ralph Waldo Emerson encouraged everyone to "Finish each day and be done with it. You have done what you could; some blunders and absurdities have crept in; forget them as soon as you can. Tomorrow is a new day; you shall begin it serenely and with too high a spirit to be encumbered with your old nonsense." Instead of being too focused on the past, all Afghans need to be forward-looking and anchored toward the future that we all desire for ourselves and our children. Productive individuals and effective leaders are forward-oriented and, at challenging times, use professionalism to create synergy with people of diverse backgrounds, ethnicities, religions, and languages. *Professionalism* can be operationalized at all localities at the individual level by putting the needs of others in the community, organization, industry, society, and country above one's own through accountability, compassion, integrity, and mutual respect for all human beings and living creations in the society. Professionals can use good judgment to develop their colleagues, peers, employees, students, friends, and children as per the requirement of each task or situation and their level of readiness. These professionals can use appropriate situational leadership styles (as recommended by Dr. Paul Hersey and Dr. Ken Blanchard, founders of the concept) to positively influence the development of everyone around them. My follow up book on rebuilding Afghanistan's workforce, includes a comprehensive coverage of effective management and situational leadership strategies for professional workforce development. In the mean time, all professionals are encouraged to review the poems presented in this chapter and share them with others for persistency and aspiration.

Rebuilding Afghanistan is a race without a clear finish line for the next decade or so, since the "finish line" may keep moving forward. However, restoring human rights and equality in Afghanistan and throughout the world is a race without a finish line for many decades to come, since so much need to be done. While the content of this book may have provided an awareness of many unfortunate effects of war, the book entitled: *The Ethics of Management and Leadership in Afghanistan,* offers the following skills as prescription for rebuilding and workforce development:

1. Ethical reasoning and moral decision making.
2. Delivering top value.
3. Managing and adjusting to the changing variables of people and customers.
4. Working synergistically as a team throughout the value chain.
5. Providing a fun work environment for all and having a sense of humor.
6. Coaching and mentoring associates to become the best that they can be.
7. Leading situationally to empower all managers toward a decentralized development process.
8. Providing inspirational and success stories toward a brighter vision for the future.

As professionals making a contribution to the rebuilding of Afghanistan and restoring human rights throughout the world, one can lead and manage situationally by using the relevant prescriptions provided. My support and prayers are with you and the workforce as you make contributions toward the betterment of this world. As a great global leader, may you always have the hindsight to know where you have been, the foresight to know where you are going, and the insight to know when you are about to go too far. Remember, if you can perceive and believe it, then you are very likely to achieve it as well. May we all achieve a peaceful world!

REFLECTIVE QUESTIONS

1. Discuss some of the improvements taking place in today's Afghanistan as presented by Ambassador Jawad?
2. What is Ambassador Jawad's vision for Afghanistan and how is he contributing to making this vision a reality?
3. Does Ambassador Jawad seem to be an optimist or a pessimist? Do his answers seem more focused on the future and development of Afghanistan or the violence of the past?
4. What makes Ambassador Jawad an extraordinary leader and what has enabled him to gather so much international support for the people and country of Afghanistan?
5. Think of three other individuals in the past three decades who have contributed enormously, through their talent and passion, to the rebuilding of Afghanistan. What makes their contributions exemplary and how have their efforts been converted to tangible results?
6. What are some of the challenges for recruiting, attracting and retaining Afghan expatriate women to work in Afghanistan?
7. How are women's opportunities increasing in Afghanistan?
8. Discuss various ways that the international community can encourage and support professional Afghans to return to Afghanistan, or at least assist in the rebuilding process?

DO NOT QUIT

When things go wrong as they sometimes will.
When the road you are trudging seems all up hill.
When funds are low and debts are high.
And you want to smile, but you have to sigh.

> When care is pressing you down a bit.
> Rest, if you must, but do not quit.
> Life is queer with its twists and turns.
> As everyone of us sometimes learns.

And many a failure turns about
When he might have won had he stuck it out:
Do not give up though the pace seems slow --
You may succeed with another blow.

> Success is failure turned inside out --
> The silver tint of the clouds of doubt.
> And you never can tell how close you are.
> It may be near when it seems so far:

So stick to the fight when you are hardest hit --
It's when things seem worst that you must not QUIT.

(Unknown)

BUILDER OR WRECKER?

I watched them tear a building down
A gang of men from a busy town
  With a Hi-he-hooh and a lusty yell
  They swung a beam and a side-wall fell

I asked the foremen, are these men skilled?
The kind you would hire if you wanted to build
  He laughed and said ohhh Noooh, indeed
  Unskilled labor is all I need

If I could easily wreck in a day or two
What it takes a builder a year to do
  I asked myself as I walked away
  Which of these roles have I tried to convey

Am I a builder who works with care
Measuring life by the rule and square
  And shaping my deeds to a well laid plan
  Carefully doing the best I can

OR am I a wrecker that walks the town
Content in the labor of tearing down.
       (Unknown)

IF I HAD MY CHILD TO RAISE OVER AGAIN

If I had my child to raise all over again; I'd finger paint more, and point the finger less.
I'd do less correcting and more connecting.
I'd take my eyes off my watch, and watch with my eyes.
I would care to know less, and know to care more.
I'd take more hikes and fly more kites.
I'd stop playing serious, and seriously play.
I would run through more fields and gaze at more stars.
I'd do more hugging and less tugging.
I would be firm less often, and affirm much more.
I'd build self-esteem first, and the house later.
I'd teach less about the love of power, and more about the power of love.
     Diane Loomans, *Full Esteem Ahead*

THE MAN IN THE GLASS

When you get what you want in your struggle for self
　　And the world makes you king for a day,
Just go to a mirror and look at yourself
　　And see what THAT man has to say.

　　For it is not your father or mother or wife
　　　　Whose judgment upon you must pass;
　　The fellow whose verdict counts most in your life
　　　　Is the one staring back from the glass.

Some people may think you a straight-shootin' chum
　　And call you a wonderful guy,
But the man in the glass says you're only a bum
　　If you cannot look him straight in the eye.

　　He's the fellow to please, never mind all the rest,
　　　　For he's with you clear up to the end.
　　And you've passed your most dangerous, difficult test
　　　　If the man in the glass is your friend.

You may fool the whole world down the pathway of life
　　And get pats on your back as you pass,
But your final reward will be heartaches and tears
　　If you've cheated the man in the glass.

　　　　　　　　Dr. Dale Wimbrow

THE RACE

"Quit! Give up! You're beaten!" They shout at me and plead. "There's just too much against you now. This time you cannot succeed."

And as I start to hang my head in front of failure's face, My downward fall is broken by the memory of a race.

And hope refills my weakened will as I recall that scene: For just the thought of that short race rejuvenates my being.

A children's race, young boys, young men. How I remember well. Excitement, sure! but also fear: It was not hard to tell.

They all lined up so full of hope. Each thought to win that race. Or tie for first, or if not that, at least take second place.

And fathers watched from off the side, each cheering for his son. And each boy hoped to show his dad that he would be the one.

The whistle blew and off they went young hearts and hopes afire. To win and be the hero there was each young boy's desire.

And one boy in particular whose dad was in the crowd was running in the lead and thought: "My dad will be so proud!"

But as they speeded down the field across a shallow dip, the little boy who thought to win lost his step and slipped.

Trying hard to catch himself his hands flew out to brace, and mid the laughter of the crowd he fell flat on his face. So down he fell and with him hope- He could not win it now - Embarrassed, sad, he only wished to disappear somehow.

But as he fell his dad stood up and showed his anxious face, which to the boy so clearly said: "Get up and win the race."

He quickly rose, no damage done, behind a bit, that's all and ran with all his mind and might to make up for his fall.

So anxious to restore himself, to catch up and to win. His mind went faster than his legs: He slipped and fell again!

He wished then he had quit before with only one disgrace. "I'm hopeless as a runner now; I should not try to race."

But in the laughing crowd he searched and found his father's face; that steady look which said again: "Get up and win the race!"

So up he jumped to try again - ten yards behind the last- "If I'm to gain those yards," he thought, "I've got to move real fast."

Exerting everything he had he regained eight or ten, but trying so hard to catch the lead he slipped and fell again!

Defeat! He lied there silently - a tear dropped from his eye- "There's no sense running anymore: Three strikes: I'm out! Why try!"

The will to rise had disappeared: All hope had fled away; so far behind, so error prone; a loser all the way.

"I've lost, so what's the use," he thought "I'll live with my disgrace." but then he thought about his dad who soon he'd have to face.

"Get up," an echo sounded low. "Get up and take your place; you were not meant for failure here. Get up and win the race."

"With borrowed will get up," it said, "You have not lost at all. For winning is no more than this: to rise each time you fall."

So up he rose to run once more, and with a new commit he resolved that win or lose at least he would not quit.

So far behind the others now, the most he'd ever been, still he gave it all he had and ran as though to win.

Three times he'd fallen, stumbling; Three times he rose again: Too far behind to hope to win. He still ran to the end.

They cheered the winning runner as he crossed the line first place. Head high and proud and happy; No falling, no disgrace.

But when the fallen youngster crossed the line last place, the crowd gave him the greater cheer, for finishing the race.

And even though he came in last with head bowed low, un-proud, you would have thought he'd won the race to listen to the crowd.

And to his dad he sadly said, "I did not do too well." "To me, you won," his father said. "You rose each time you fell."

And now when things seem dark and hard and difficult to face, the memory of that little boy helps me in my race.

For all of life is like that race, with ups and downs and all. And all you have to do to win is rise each time you fall.

"Quit! Give up! You're beaten!" They still shout in my face. But another voice within me says: "GET UP AND WIN THE RACE!"

D. H. Groberg

BIBLIOGRAPHY

ABC News, (January 2005). *Soldier Gets Six Months in Iraqi Drowning.* The case of Army Sgt. 1st Class Tracy Perkins. Retrieved on January 12th 2005 from: http://abcnews.go.com/US/wireStory?id=396680.

Abercrombie, T. J. (1968). Afghanistan: Crossroads of Conquerors. National Geographic. Volume 134, No. 3, September. Pages 297-345.

Adamec, Ludwig. (2003). *Historical Dictionary of Afghanistan.* Maryland: Rowman & Littlefield.

Adams, Brad, (December 2004). *Afghan Government: An Open Letter to President Hamid. Letter prepared by the Human Rights Watch-Asian Division.* Received on December 16th 2004 from: Karzai Fida Ghazi [fidaghazi@yahoo.com]

Afghan Constitution, 2004. *The Constitution of Afghanistan Year 1382 (2004)-Draft.* Retrieved on July 3rd from: http://www.afghangovernment.com/2004constitution.htm

Afghan-land, (2004). *Afghan Leaders Yearbook.* Retrieved on December 10th 2004 from: http://www.Afghan-Land.com/history/karzai.html

Afghan-land, (2004). *Who is Hamid Karzia?* Retrieved on December 10th 2004 from: http://www.Afghan-Land.com/history/karzai.html

Ali, M. Amir (1994). *JIHAD explained.* Published by The Institute of Islamic Information and Education. III & E Brochure Series No. 18. Amadei, Bernard (2004). *"Capacity Building and Enabling Poorest of the Poor."* Society for Afghan Engineers (SAE) 2004 Conference on "Infrastructure Rehabilitation and Development in Afghanistan." UC-Berkley, USA. July 30- August 1, 2004.

Annan, K. A. (December 2006). *As Secretary-General prepares to step down, five lessons learnt during difficult but exhilarating decade.* By the Secretary-General Kofo A. Annan, Truman Library. December 11, 2006. Retrieved from the United Nation's website on December 14, 2006 from: http://www.un.org/News/ossg/sg/stories/statments_full.asp?statID=40.

Azizi, Omar K. (2004). *"NEEPRA's Implementation Strategy in Afghanistan."* Society for Afghan Engineers (SAE) 2004 Conference on "Infrastructure Rehabilitation and Development in Afghanistan." UC-Berkley, USA. July 30- August 1, 2004.

Babukarkhail, Z. (2004). *Dowry debts force young men abroad.* Pajhwok Afghan News. December 13th 2004.

Bandura, A., & Schunk, D. (1989). "Cultivating Competence, Self-Efficacy, and Intrinsic Interest Through Proximal Self-Motivation." Journal of Personality and Social Psychology 41, 586-598.

Borovik, Artyom (1990). The hidden war: A Russian journalist's account of the Soviet war in Afghanistan. Atalantic Monthly Press. ISBN 0-87113-283-4.

Buckingham, M. & Coffman, C. (1999). *First, break all the rules.* New York: Simon & Schuster.

Buller, P.F.; Kohls, J.J.; and Anderson, S (2000, Spring). Managing conflicts across cultures. *Organizational Dynamics, 28(4),* 52.

Business Ethics (1996). Insider's report on responsible business. Vol. 10, No. 6.

Cavico, F. and Mujtaba, B. G., (April 2007). *Legal Challenges for the Global Manager and Entrepreneur.* Kendal Hunt Publishing Company. United States.

Cavico, F. & Mujtaba, B., (2005). *Business Ethics: Transcending Requirements through Moral Leadership.* Pearson Custom Publications. U.S.A. ISBN: 0-536-85783-0. Address:

75 Arlington Street. Suite 300. Boston Mass, 02116. Phone: (800) 374-1200. Or: (800) 922-0579.

Chaney, L. H. & Green, C. G. (2002, April). Presenter behaviors: Actions often speak louder than words. *The American Salesman, 47*(4), 22-27.

Coker, M. and Usher, A. (November 2005). U.S. Aid to Afghanistan Falls Short. Cox New Service; Nov. 19, 2005. Distributed by New York Times News Service via The Washington Times (USA).

Davis, J. H. & Ruhe, J. A. (2003). Perceptions of country corruption: Antecedents and outcomes. *Journal of Business Ethics, 43,* 275-288.

Dupree, Louis (1989). *Afghanistan: return, Repatriation, reconstruction.* Washington Report on Middle East Affairs. February issue. Retrieved on July 5th 2004 from WRMEA.com.

EA e-News, (March 2005). *Embassy of Afghanistan News.* Vol. 15, March 31. Address: 2341 Wyoming Ave. NW, Washington, DC 2008. (202) 483-6410.

EA e-News, (December 2004). New Cabinet Being Formed. *Embassy of Afghanistan News.* Vol. 9, December 15th. 2341 Wyoming Ave. NW, Washington, DC 2008. (202) 483-6410.

EA e-News, (December 2004). *Embassy of Afghanistan News.* Vol. 8, December 1st. 2341 Wyoming Ave. NW, Washington, DC 2008. (202) 483-6410.

Embassy of the Islamic State of Afghanistan. 2341 Wyoming Avenue, N.W.. Washington, D.C. 20008. Phone: (202) 234 - 3770. Fax: (202) 328 - 3516.

Embassy of Afghanistan, (August 2004). *Embassy of Afghanistan News.* Vol. 1, August 17th. 2341 Wyoming Ave. NW, Washington, DC 2008. (202) 483-6410.

Es'haq, M. (1987). *Situation in the North of Afghanistan.* Political Office of Jami'at Islami Afghanistan.

Evans, Gail, (September 2001). *Play Like a Man, Win Like a Woman: What Men Know About Success that Women Need to Learn.*

Goodwin, Jan (1987). *Caught in the crossfire.* E. P. Dutton, N. Y.. ISBN 0-525-24493-X

Graham. P. (Eds.). (1995). *Prophet of management.* Boston, MA: Harvard Business School Press

Graham, Stephen (2004). *Karzai Officially Leads Afghanistan.* Associated Press. Retrieved on December 8th 2004 from: http://www.ledger-enquirer.com/mld/ledgerenquirer/news

Haidari, M. Ashraf (2004). *"Rebuilding Afghanistan: The Diaspora Role."* Society for Afghan Engineers (SAE) 2004 Conference on "Infrastructure Rehabilitation and Development in Afghanistan." UC-Berkley, USA. July 30- August 1, 2004.

Hartman. (2003). Perspectives in business ethics: Ethical theories and approaches (2nd ed.). The McGraw-Hill Companies.

Hersey, Paul (July 2004). *Personal Communication on Situational Leadership.* One-week workshop by Dr. Hersey and facilitators of 'The Center for Leadership Studies." Escondido, CA. July 11-18. Phone: (760) 741-6595.

Hersey, P.; Blanchard, K.; and Johnson, D., (2001). *Management of Organizational Behavior.* Eight edition. Prentice Hall. ISBN: 013-032518X.

Hewad, 2004. *The ethnic composition of Afghanistan in different sources.* Retrieved on August 20th from: http://www.hewad.com/ethnic.htm

Holt, E., (1973). *The concept of consciousness.* New York: Arno Press.

Hosseini, Khaled. (2003). The Kite Runner. New York: Riverhead.

Jalil, Jannat (2003). *Afghans flout fur ban.* BBC Correspondent in Kabul. Monday July 21st 2003. Retrieved on July 2nd 2004 from: http://news.bbc.co.uk/2/hi/south_asia/3078559.stm

Jang Group, 2004. Jang Group of Newspapers web site can be accessed only by using http://www.jang.com.pk, http://www.jang-group.com, and http://jang.com.pk/thenews/may2004-daily/19-05-2004/world/w4.htm

Jawad, S. T., (April 2004). *Nation-Building: Beyond Afghanistan and Iraq.* Conference on April 13th at John Hopkins University: The Paul Nitze School of Advanced International Studies. Washington D.C.

Jawad, S. T., (May 2004). *Afghanistan: Promise & Fulfillment.* Conference by the Middle East Institute and the American Institute on Afghanistan Studies. Washington, DC - May 25th 2004.

Kacapyr, E. (2001). Business as usual: Corruption and business activity. *The Journal of Social, Political, and Economic Studies, 26*(4), 671-681.

Kaplan, Robert D. (1990). *Soldiers of God: with the Mujahidin in Afghanistan.* ISBN 0-395-52132-7.

Kazi, Laila (2003). Poem titled "Afghanistan: A War Torn Land." Recited at the 2003 SAE Conference in New Jersey. Stevens Institute of Technology. Retrieved on June 25th 2004 from: http://afghan-engineers.org/

Kelly, R. (2005). *I Believe I Can Fly.* Retrieved on 01/10/2005 from: http://www.geocities.com/rkellylyrics/r_lyrics/i_believe_i_can_fly.html

Kirby, Alex (2003). *War 'has ruined Afghan environment. BBC News –Science.* Wednesday, 29 January, 2003, 09:55 GMT. Retrieved on July 2nd 2004 from: http://news.bbc.co.uk/2/hi/science/nature/2704989.stm

Kidder, R.M. (1995). *How good people make tough choices.* New York: William Morrow & Co..

Khosti, Yasin (2004). *"Building a Professional Reserve for the future."* Society for Afghan Engineers (SAE) 2004 Conference on "Infrastructure Rehabilitation and Development in Afghanistan." UC-Berkley, USA. July 30- August 1, 2004.

Ibrahimi, Habib Rahman (2004). A thousand new recruits join the Afghan police. Pajhwok Afghan News. December 16th 2004.

Internet Center for Corruption Research. (2002, July 6). The 1999 Corruption Perceptions Index. www.gwdg.de/~uwvw/1999Data.html

Internet Center for Corruption Research. (2005, November 15) Transparency International (TI) 2003 Corruption Perceptions Index (CPI). Available from http://www.icgg.org/corruption.cpi_2003.html

Lamb, Christina (2006). *They'd rather die: brief lives of the Afghan slave wives.* The Sunday Times, UK; November 9, 2006.

Lohbeck, Kurt (1993). *Holy war, unholy victory.* ISBN 0-89526-499-4. Regnery Gateway, Inc.

Lovins, Hunter (2004). *Afghanistan as a Country of the Future.* Society for Afghan Engineers (SAE) 2004 Conference on "Infrastructure Rehabilitation and Development in Afghanistan." UC-Berkley, USA. July 30- August 1, 2004.

Madsen, P. & Shafritz, J. (1990). *Essentials of business ethics.* New York: Penguin Books.

Maxwell, J. (1993). *Developing the leader within you.* Nashville, TN: Thomas Nelson, Inc.

Mitchell, C. (2003). *A short course in International Business Ethics: Combining Ethics and Profits in Global Business.* World Trade Press: Professional Books for International Trade. Pages 110 –122.

Mohammadi, Zainab (2004). *France pledges cotton for poppy incentive.* Pajhwok Afghan News, December 20th 2004.

Mojaddidy, Zabihullah (2003). *Empowerment of the Afghan Professionals.* Society for Afghan Engineers (SAE) 2003 Conference Summary." New Jersey, USA. Steven Institute of Technology. October 2003.

Moritz, S. (2004, March 2). *The Feds charge Ebbers with fraud and conspiracy.* Retrieved July 4th, 2004, from: http://www.thestreet.com/tech/scottmoritz/10146447.html

Munir, Makia (2004). *Drunk driving is the main cause of traffic accidents in Kabul city.* Pajhwok Afghan News, December 21st 2004.

Mujtaba, B. G. (April 2007). *Cross Cultural Management and Negotiation Practices.* ILEAD Academy Publications; Florida, United States. ISBN: 978-0-9774211-2-1. Website: Ileadacademy.com.

Mujtaba, Bahaudin G. (2007). *The ethics of management and leadership in Afghanistan (2nd edition).* ILEAD Academy. ISBN: 978-0-9774211-0-7. Davie, Florida USA. ISBN: 978-0-9774211-0-7. Website: Ileadacademy.com.

Mujtaba, B. G. (2007). *Workpalce Diversity Management: Challenges, Competencies and Strategies.* ISBN: 1-59526-548-1. Llumina Press; Phone: 866-229-9244 or: 954-726-0902).

Mujtaba, B. G. and McCartney, T. (2007). *Managing Workplace Stress and Conflict amid Change.* Llumina Press, Coral Springs, Florida, USA. ISBN: 1-59526-414-0.

Mujtaba, B. G. (2007). *Mentoring Diverse Professionals (2nd edition).* Llumina Press. ISBN: 1-59526-444-2.

Mujtaba, B. G. and Preziosi, R. C. (2006). *Adult Education in Academia: Recruiting and Retaining Extraordinary Facilitators of learning.* 2nd Edition. ISBN: 1593114753. Information Age Publishing. Greenwich, Connecticut. Phone: (203) 661-7602.

Mujtaba, B. G. (2006). *Cross Cultural Change Management.* ISBN: 1-59526-568-6. Llumina Press, Tamarac, Florida. Toll free phone: (866) 229-9244 or Reg. (954) 726-0902.

Mujtaba, B., (April 2005). Entrepreneurship and Development in Afghanistan: A Conversation with Mahmoud Samizay, Advisor to the Ministry of Urban Development and Housing. *Journal of Applied Management and Entrepreneurship.* Volume 10, Number 2.

Munir, Makia (2004). Afghans Deprived of Basic Human Rights. Pajhwok Afghan News. December 16th 2004.

Munsef, A. Q. (December 2004). *International Move to Increase Drug Prosecutions.* Pajhwok Afghan News. December 13th 2004.

Nelson, C.A. (1999). *International Business: A Manager's Guide to Strategy in the Age of Globalism.* International Thomson Business Press. Pages: 72-74.

Nikpai, Qadam Ali (February 2005). *Higher education in Afghanistan is expected to be revamped.* Pajhwok Afghan News, Kabul, Feb. 01.

Olmeda, A. Rafael (2004). *Afghan teens find nothing to fear in South Florida stay.* South Florida Sun-Sentinel, Sunday September 19th; Section B.

Patrick, J. & Quinn, J. (1997). *Management ethics: integrity at work.* Newbury Park, Ca: SAGE Publications Ltd.

Pajhwok Afghan News, (2004). Received on November 30th through December 2nd 2004 from pajhwak@hahoo.com

Popal, Rona (2004). *"Women's Challenges and Needs in Afghanistan."* Society for Afghan Engineers (SAE) 2004 Conference on "Infrastructure Rehabilitation and Development in Afghanistan." UC-Berkley, USA. July 30- August 1, 2004.

Rakin, Hadi (2004). *"Reconstruction Issues and a Recommended Approach for Establishing Priorities."* Society for Afghan Engineers (SAE) 2004 Conference on "Infrastructure Rehabilitation and Development in Afghanistan.." UC-Berkley, USA. July 30- August 1, 2004.

Ralph, M. (2000). Effects of transformational leadership on subordinate motivation, empowering norms and organizational productivity. *Journal of Organizational Analysis,* 8(1), 16-48.

Rameen, (2004). *Salaaam from Kabul.* www.afghancommunicator.com. Received on December 10th 2004 from: ACMojala@aol.com

Roberts, Michelle (2005). *Program helps women entrepreneurs.* The Herald. Sunday January 23rd.

Roashan, G. Rauf, (2005). *Karzai and Triple Ms.* Article distributed to all subscribers on January 7th 2005 via AfghanServer@yahoogroups.com

Ryan, M., (1995). *"Personal Ethics and the Future of the World." Varied Directions International.* (800) 888-5236. Narrated by Meg Ryan.

Saba, D. S. & Zakhilwal, O. (2004). *Afghanistan National Human Development Report 2004: Security with a Human Face: Challenges and Responsibilities.* United National Development Programme 2004. Available from:
http://hdr.undp.org/docs/reports/national/AFG_Afghanistan/afghanistan_2004_en.pdf

Sadat, Mir Hekmatullah, (2004). *Afghan History: kite flying, kite running and kite banning.* June. Retrieved on June 2, 2004 from:
http://www.afghanmagazine.com/2004_06/articles/hsadat.shtml

Samsor, A. M., (2004). *Many girls still being prevented from getting an education.* Pajhwok Afghan News. December 13th 2004.

Sandholtz, W. & Gray, M. M. (2003). International integration and national corruption. *International Organization, 57,* 761-800.

Senge, P. M. (1990). *The Fifth Discipline: The Art and Practice of the Learning Organization.* New York, NY: Currency/DoubleDay.

Seyoum, B. (2001). *The State of the Global Economy 2001/2002: Trends, Data, Ranking, Charts.* New York: Encyclopedia Society.

Siddiqi, Nadir (2004). *"Integrated Agricultural Production in Afghanistan."* Society for Afghan Engineers (SAE) 2004 Conference on "Infrastructure Rehabilitation and Development in Afghanistan." UC-Berkley, USA. July 30- August 1, 2004.

Sims, R. L. (March 2006). The influence of human development on national corruption. *Society of Afghan Engineers Journal, Vol. 3,* Num. 1; Pages 47-56.

Sims, R. L. (November 2005). Culture and Human Development as Predictors of National Corruption. Paper presented at the Southern Management Association's Annual Conference, Charleston, South Carolina.

Sirat, Abdul Sattar (2004). *The Long Way for Peace in Afghanistan.* Emailed by Muhammad Kabir to the afghaniyat@yahoogroups.com on Friday, January 16th 2004.

Soler, Eileen (January 2005). *Answering the Call.* The Herald. Sunday January 23rd.

Spaeth, Anthony (1996). *A peace that terrifies.* TIME. Page 62.

Stasek, Rosemary (2004). *"The Women of Afghanistan."* Society for Afghan Engineers (SAE) 2004 Conference on "Infrastructure Rehabilitation and Development in Afghanistan." UC-Berkley, USA. July 30- August 1, 2004.

Stephens, Joe and Ottaway, David B. (November, 2005). *A Rebuilding Plan Full of Cracks.* Washington Post, A01.

Suranovic, Steven (2004). *The Theory of Comparative Advantage: An Overview.* ©1997-2003. Retrieved on 2/17/04 from: http://internationalecon.com/v1.0/ch40/40c000.html.

TIME Inc., 2006. *The Middle East: The history, the cultures, the conflicts, the faiths.* Introduction by Jimmy Carter. Time Inc. Home Entertainment.

Vogl, F. (1998). The supply side of global bribery. *Finance & Development, 35*(2), 30-32.

Wilhelm, P. G. (2002). International validation of the corruption perception index: Implications for business ethics and entrepreneurship education. *Journal of Business Ethics, 35,* 177-189.

Tamarov, Vladislav (1992). *Afghanistan: Soviet * Vietnam.* Translated by Naomi Marcus, Marianne Clarke Trangen, and Vladislav Tamarov. Mercury House, San Francisco.

The Washington Post Company, 2004. *Sergeant Says Intelligence Directed Abuse. By Josh White and Scott Higham.* Thursday, May 20; Page A01. Retrieved on June 08, 2004

from: Soldier Says Intelligence Directed Abuse or
http://www.washingtonpost.com/wp-dyn/articles/A41035-2004May19.html

The Boston Globe, 2004. *Bad timing in Afghanistan*. Tuesday, June 8.

Thompson, D. (1996). *Death of a city*. Time Magazine, June 24. Pages 40-43.

Zawab, Ezatullah (2004). *Heroin producing equipment smuggled in from neighboring Pakistan has to be stopped, say officials*. Pajhwok Afghan News, December 22nd.

Zawab, E. (December 2004). *Poppy Framers Destroy their own Crops*. Pajhwok Afghan News. December 13th 2004.

Zikria, G. (2004). *"Health Infrastructure in Afghanistan."* Society for Afghan Engineers (SAE) 2004 Conference on "Infrastructure Rehabilitation and Development in Afghanistan." UC-Berkley, USA. July 30- August 1, 2004.

Index Table

Other Books by the Author

1. Mujtaba, B. G. (April 2007). *Cross Cultural Management and Negotiation Practices.* ILEAD Academy Publications; Florida, United States. ISBN: 978-0-9774211-2-1. Website: Ileadacademy.com.

2. Cavico, F. & Mujtaba, B. G., (April 2007). *Legal Challenges for the Global Manager and Entrepreneur.* Kendal Hunt Publishing Company. United States. ISBN: 978-0-7575-4037-0.

3. Mujtaba, Bahaudin G. (2007). *The ethics of management and leadership in Afghanistan (2nd edition).* ILEAD Academy. ISBN: 978-0-9774211-0-7. Davie, Florida USA. ISBN: 978-0-9774211-0-7. Website: Ileadacademy.com.

4. Mujtaba, B. G. (2007). *Workpalce Diversity Management: Challenges, Competencies and Strategies.* ISBN: 1-59526-548-1. Llumina Press; website: http://www.llumina.com/store/workforcediversitymanagement.htm.

5. Mujtaba, B. G. and McCartney, T. (2007). *Managing Workplace Stress and Conflict amid Change.* Llumina Press, Coral Springs, Florida, USA. ISBN: 1-59526-414-0. Website: Website: http://www.llumina.com/store/managingstress.htm

6. Mujtaba, B. G. (2007). *Mentoring Diverse Professionals (2nd edition).* Llumina Press. ISBN: 1-59526-444-2. Available at: http://www.llumina.com/store/mentoringdiverseprofessionals1.htm

7. Mujtaba, B. G. and Preziosi, R. C. (2006). *Adult Education in Academia: Recruiting and Retaining Extraordinary Facilitators of learning.* 2nd Edition. ISBN: 1593114753. Information Age Publishing. Greenwich, Connecticut. Phone: (203) 661-7602.

8. Mujtaba, B. G. (2006). *Cross Cultural Change Management.* ISBN: 1-59526-568-6. Llumina Press, Tamarac, Florida. Website: http://www.llumina.com/store/cccm.htm or www.Llumina.com. Toll free phone: (866) 229-9244 or Reg. (954) 726-0902.

9. Mujtaba, G. B. (2006). *Privatization and Market-Based Leadership in Developing Economies: Capacity Building in Afghanistan.* Llumina Press and Publications, Tamarac, Florida. ISBN: 1-59526-551-1. Website: http://www.llumina.com/store/privatization.htm.

10. Mujtaba, B. G. and Cavico, F. J., (2006). *Age Discrimination in Employment: Cross Cultural Comparison and Management Strategies.* BookSurge. ISBN: 1-4196-1587-4.

11. Cavico, F. & Mujtaba, B. G., (2005). *Business Ethics: Transcending Requirements through Moral Leadership.* Pearson Custom Publications. U.S.A. ISBN: 0-536-85783-0.

Author Biography

The name "Bahaudin" means the "magnificence of faith" and it is a popular name in Persia or countries such as Afghanistan, Iran, Pakistan, and others surrounding them. There are many religious leaders, cities, and schools named Bahaudin. So, this "Bahaudin" has to live up to great expectations but will be happy to fulfill his own vision of seeing, and contributing to, a peaceful Afghanistan.

Dr. Bahaudin G. Mujtaba is currently an Associate Professor and Management Department Chair. Previously, he was the Director of Institutional Relations, Planning, and Accreditation for Nova Southeastern University at the H. Wayne Huizenga School of Business and Entrepreneurship in Fort Lauderdale, Florida with Nova Southeastern University. Bahaudin has worked as an internal consultant, trainer, and teacher in the corporate arena. He also worked in retail management for 16 years. Bahaudin is the founder of ILEAD Academy, LLC, which is a serviced-oriented consultancy firm for management and employee development programs. As a consultant, he coaches, trains, educates, and develops managers. In his capacity as a consultant and trainer, Bahaudin has worked with various firms in the areas of management, cross-cultural communication, customer value/service, and cultural diversity training.

His doctorate degree (from NSU) is in Management, and he completed his dissertation research on the topic of business ethics in management. He has two post-doctorate specialties: one in Human Resource Management and another in International Management. He has been listed in the publications of *Who's Who in America, Who's Who in Management,* and *Who's Who in the World.* Bahaudin is co-author of the book entitled *"Business Ethics: Transcending Requirements through Moral Leadership"* with Professor Frank Cavico and the co-author of *"Adult Education in Academia"* textbook with Professor Robert Preziosi. Bahaudin's first book about Afghanistan is titled: *"The Ethics of Management and Leadership in Afghanistan."* Overall, he is the author of about fifteen different academic and professional books. Bahaudin has been the author, co-author, and presenter of nearly one-hundred professional journal articles and papers in the areas of management, leadership, culture, diversity, ethics, higher education, and personal development.

During the past 25 years he has had the pleasure of working in the United States, Afghanistan, Pakistan, Brazil, Bahamas, St. Lucia, and Jamaica. He was born in Khoshie of Logar province and raised in Kabul, Afghanistan. Bahaudin and his family moved to Pakistan for one year during the Soviet invasion of Afghanistan and then moved to the United States when he was a teenager. This has provided him many insights in culture, leadership, and management from the perspectives of different firms, people, and countries. He is grateful for such opportunities in the past years and looks forward to learning each and everyday.